The President as Policymaker

Laurence E. Lynn, Jr.
and
David deF. Whitman

TEMPLE UNIVERSITY PRESS/PHILADELPHIA

THE
PRESIDENT
AS
POLICYMAKER

Jimmy Carter and Welfare Reform

Temple University Press, Philadelphia 19122
© 1981 by Temple University. All rights reserved
Published 1981
Printed in the United States of America

Case material was developed by the John F. Kennedy School of Government, Harvard University, © by the President and Fellows of Harvard College, and is used with their permission.

Library of Congress Cataloging in Publication Data

Lynn, Laurence E., 1937–
The President as policymaker.

Bibliography: p.
Includes index.
1. United States—Social policy. 2. Public
welfare—United States. 3. Carter, Jimmy, 1924–
4. Whitman, David deF., 1955–   . II. Title.
HV95.L915   361.6'0973   81-2527
ISBN 0-87722-223-1   AACR2
ISBN 0-87722-238-X (pbk.)

To Stephanie

The following is an excerpt from W. H. Auden, "Alonso to Ferdinand,"
in *Selected Poetry of W. H. Auden* (2nd ed.; New York: Vintage, 1971),
p. 85:

. . . the king's advice given on the occasion of Ferdinand's succession
to the throne:

> But should you fail to keep your kingdom
> And, like your father before you, come
> Where thought accuses and feeling mocks,
> Believe your pain, praise the scorching rocks
> For their desiccation of your lust,
> Thank the bitter treatment of the tide
> For its dissolution of your pride,
> That the whirlwind may arrange your will
> And the deluge release it to find
> The spring in the desert, the fruitful
> Island in the sea, where flesh and mind
> Are delivered from mistrust.

CONTENTS

PREFACE

THIS STUDY OF THE CARTER ADMINISTRATION'S DEVELOPMENT OF A WEL-
fare reform proposal originated as a teaching case for use in the educational programs of the John F. Kennedy School of Government at
Harvard University. It was undertaken for three reasons. First, several
participants in the process suggested to us that President Carter's handling of welfare reform provided an excellent opportunity to help
students in public policy and public management understand how
policymaking occurs in practice. Second, an outstanding piece of inves-
tigative reporting by Nick Kotz in the *New Republic* (May 14, 1977) on the
first four months of the Carter welfare reform process reinforced our
impression that this particular case was rich in instructive lessons for
students of American government. Finally, an account of the Carter
administration's handling of welfare reform would bring up to date the
history of welfare reform policy development since Nixon's Family
Assistance Plan, which had been documented in teaching cases as well as
in numerous other publications. (A bibliography of the most useful
sources is included at the end of this book.)

We want to caution the reader at the outset that it is not the primary
purpose of this book to explain why Carter's welfare reform plan failed
to be approved by the Congress. Nor is it our intent to argue that, if
Carter administration officials had come up with a different proposal or
had handled their proposal differently, they would have been successful
in achieving welfare reform. Rather, our intent is to describe Carter's
leadership of the policy development process within his own administration, then evaluate this experience by comparing it with the experiences
of other presidents who have handled large issues of a similar kind. Our
objective is to develop insights into how presidents can perform their
policymaking role in such a way as to create the greatest chance of
success for their initiatives.

The research, interviews, and writing of the teaching case that have
been incorporated into Chapters three through ten was begun by Cynthia L. Horan and carried out chiefly by David Whitman under the
general supervision of Laurence E. Lynn, Jr. Chapters one, two, and
eleven are the joint responsibility of Lynn and Whitman, assisted by
Christopher Allen.

A number of people provided us with invaluable help during the
course of this study. We are particularly grateful to those participants
and observers who granted us interviews. (A complete list of interviews

xi

with dates can be found in the Bibliography.) We would like, therefore, to thank the following individuals (their affiliations are those at the time of the case): From the Department of Health, Education, and Welfare—Joseph A. Califano, Jr., Ben Heineman, Jr., Henry Aaron, Michael Barth, John Todd, Dan Marcus, James Cardwell, Hale Champion, and Wray Smith. From HEW's Income Security Policy Office—William Barnes, Tom Gustaffson, David Lindeman, Richard Michel, Charles Seagrave, Douglas Wolf, and Mark Worthington. From the Department of Labor—Ray Marshall, Arnold Packer, Jodie T. Allen, Gary Reed, and Robert Lerman.

From the Council of Economic Advisers—Charles Schultze, William Nordhaus, and William Springer.

From the Office of Management and Budget—Suzanne Woolsey, David Kleinberg, and Barry White.

From the president's Domestic Policy Staff—Bert Carp, Frank Raines, and William Spring; and James Parham, an aide in the office of the president's Coordinator for Intergovernmental Affairs.

From the legislative branch—Senator Daniel P. Moynihan (D–N.Y.), former Representative James C. Corman (D–Calif.), M. Kenneth Bowler, and Michael Stern; and Robert Reischauer, William Hoagland, John Korbell, and David Mundel of the Congressional Budget Office.

From outside the federal government—Barry Van Lare and Scott Bunton from the National Governors' Conference; Bert Seidman, director of the Department of Social Security of the AFL-CIO; Tom Joe, a private consultant; Henry Freedman, director of the Center on Social Welfare Policy and Law, a welfare advocacy organization; and Robert Harris of the Urban Institute.

Helpful and often detailed critiques of early drafts of the case were offered by Henry Aaron, Jodie Allen, Michael Barth, Ben Heineman, Jr., and Arnold Packer. While acknowledging their generous assistance, we, of course, absolve them of responsibility for any errors or shortcomings that remain or for the views presented herein, which are at variance with those of many participants. Alicia McFall did her usual thorough job of copy-editing and patiently correcting the case studies as they underwent numerous revisions, then overseeing the manuscript through the production process. Anna Trask calmly typed the final manuscript under considerable time pressure.

Our chief thanks go to Stephanie Gould, editor of the Kennedy School's Case and Curriculum Development Program. Stephanie supervised the day-to-day development of the original teaching case, provided thoughtful guidance on ideas and topics to pursue, and, through her considerable interest in the subject, greatly improved the depth of our research and of the writing. She also helped to write and organize some early portions of the teaching case and added whatever dash of eloquence chapters three through ten manage to contain. Our debt to her is great indeed.

To our knowledge, this book constitutes one of the few sustained examinations of Carter policymaking based on both the benefit of fresh recollections and access to confidential documents. Due to the unusual richness of detail on Jimmy Carter's involvement in welfare reform, we have directed most of our analysis of the case to the role of the president in policymaking. The case, however, certainly raises other issues—including the ethical foundations of policy development; the proper role of the president's staff, cabinet officers, and outside advisers; the president's role vis-à-vis Congress; and so on—and we encourage readers to use the material in this book for a variety of purposes.

Our greatest hope is that the book will be of at least modest assistance to future policymakers, perhaps especially those who will deal with welfare reform, so that they may avoid the pitfalls of the past. Although, as we noted, we do not judge the quality of policymaking by whether or not a bill passes Congress, we believe that presidential leadership of policy development has an important influence on the ultimate fate of social policy initiatives. We all have a stake in the effectiveness of that leadership.

The President as Policymaker

CHAPTER ONE

The Perils of Policymaking

EVERY PRESIDENT WANTS TO MAKE POLICY. EACH TAKES OFFICE HAVING promised to establish new directions for government and to leave a legacy of programmatic achievement and administrative reform. The president has abundant opportunities to be a policymaker. In state of the union messages, in budget submissions to Congress, in legislative proposals, in appearances before virtually any group he chooses, as well as in the countless opportunities created by the need to respond to events outside his control, the president is in a position to articulate public purposes, to mobilize support for policies he favors, to influence the content and timing of public debate, and, through use of the powers of his office, to move others to act. How he takes advantage of these opportunities will have a major bearing on his success as a policymaker.

Achieving success has always been problematic, however, the more so in recent decades as government has grown more complex. Success virtually always requires the president to obtain the support and cooperation of others: the leadership and committees of the Congress, governors and mayors, the media, interest groups, and executives in the departments. To make policy, he must enlist them in his cause, meld their interests with his, temper his actions in the light of their needs. The more of these "others" there are—the greater the number of separate administrative units of government, congressional committees and subcommittees, and organized interest groups, for example—and the more their interests diverge, the more complicated the task of assembling support for a policy initiative and the greater the amount of give and take that will be necessary to achieve success.

The problem of obtaining support for a policy initiative often begins in the president's own family—in the executive branch, with the officials he has chosen to run federal commissions, agencies, and departments, and with their subordinates. These officials usually have ideas and con-

3

stituencies of their own and a power base independent of his. Moreover, as supervisors of the "permanent government," that is, as career officials whose knowledge and cooperation are usually essential in designing policies that will survive partisan scrutiny, cabinet and agency executives can give the president important help. Even before he tackles the Congress, the president's most difficult task is often to obtain the wholehearted and active support of his own administration.

Managing policy development within his own administration is especially difficult when the issues cut across agency and departmental jurisdictions and when such issues are regarded by subordinates as of great importance to their own interests. In these instances the president must not only persuade; he must coordinate, resolve conflicts, and orchestrate the actions of individuals and agencies to achieve a coherent result. Because the time he can devote to such activities is limited, he needs help from his immediate staff and from the agencies within the Executive Office of the President that can help him in his policymaking role: the Office of Management and Budget, the Domestic Policy Staff, and the Council of Economic Advisers. But obtaining their help adds to the president's management burden; in addition to dealing with departmental officials, he must decide how to use his own staff and support them in their efforts to help him. In his memoirs, Richard M. Nixon commented that the Family Assistance Plan, his ill-fated welfare reform proposal (see below), "had a rocky passage through my own staff and Cabinet."[1] Most recent presidents have had similar experiences.

How should the president go about the complicated business of being a policymaker within his own administration? What must he do to be effective in this role, especially when delegating the task of policy development to a single cabinet officer is inappropriate? This question is the concern of the book.

The question is exceedingly broad, however. In a fundamental sense, the president is continuously involved in policymaking of some kind. Most things he does have "policy significance," that is, have some bearing on the ends and means of governmental activity. When he meets with congressional or interest group leaders, approves budgets, legislation, and executive orders, asks for studies, information, or advice, guides his staff in their relationships with the departments, and works with members of his cabinet, he is engaged in policymaking, that is, in shaping the directions of governmental activity.

Most studies of presidential decision-making have been concerned with understanding general patterns of presidential activity and influence and with how the organization of the Executive Office of the President and the administration as a whole can support the president in his policymaking role. In contrast, this book examines in considerable detail a single episode of presidential policymaking: President Jimmy Carter's experience during the first year of his administration in developing a proposal to reform the nation's public welfare programs. The specific question addressed in this examination is, How can a president be effective as a policymaker in specific circumstances? What should he do himself and what should he leave to others? How much time should he spend, and how (and with whom) should he spend it? What must he know and how must he act?

The reason for this sharper focus is that, though the president is involved almost daily in policymaking of some kind, this involvement is usually ad hoc, piecemeal, and reactive. More general analyses of presidential policymaking, which are concerned with organizing this ad hoc activity into coherent patterns, often leave out of account the subtle influence of presidential style, personality, and motivation, techniques of presidential leadership, persuasion, and communication, and presidential sensitivity to the nuances of bureaucratic and political processes, all of which are apt to be decisive in sustained episodes of policymaking. While instances of a president's sustained involvement in major policy initiatives, especially in the realm of domestic policy (as distinguished from foreign policy), are relatively few, they are usually of overriding importance in creating a sense of direction for his administration as well as in shaping his programmatic legacy (not to mention his reelection prospects). For this reason, they warrant separate examination.

The choice of Jimmy Carter's development of a comprehensive welfare reform proposal as a focus for this study is based on several considerations. First, the episode cast participants in roles that are broadly representative of major presidential policymaking; several offices and agencies were involved, disagreements were sharp, and the president's personal role was decisive in governing the process. Thus, it is a case that will permit generalizations to other issues and circumstances. Second, most participants, including Carter, had had previous experience with the issue of welfare reform; they were not confronted with an unfamiliar problem for which they were unprepared. Moreover, presidential involvement with the issue had a precedent: Richard M. Nixon's initiation of a major welfare reform proposal, christened the Family Assistance Plan (FAP). There is a putative basis, therefore, for assessing how this particular episode of policymaking was handled by the president. Third, virtually all participants were accessible to interviewers, their recollections were fresh and detailed, and their records were intact. A relatively accurate picture of what happened could be assembled.

The question remains as to whether much of use can be learned from a single case study. The answer is that, when the Carter experience with welfare reform policymaking is compared not only to Nixon's experience with the same issue but to episodes of successful presidential policymaking from other administrations, a variety of instructive insights emerge. Though few if any of these episodes have been documented in anything approaching the same detail as that characterizing Chapters three through ten, what is known is sufficiently precise to permit useful comparisons.

In the remainder of this chapter we summarize several previous episodes of presidential policymaking that we regard as relatively successful and distill from them those aspects of presidential performance that will be used as the basis for analyzing Jimmy Carter's experience with welfare reform. Chapter two presents background on the welfare reform issue, including a brief account of Richard M. Nixon's effort to formulate a comprehensive policy for welfare reform. These first two chapters, then, set the stage for the examination of the Carter administration's development of welfare reform policy, contained in Chapters three through ten. An assessment of Carter's leadership of the welfare reform policy process follows in Chapter eleven, which compares Carter as a policymaker to other presidents and offers conclusions as to how presidents can be effective in this role.

PRESIDENTS AND POLICY

Franklin D. Roosevelt has become known for a distinctive style of administrative leadership. "Roosevelt liked the competitive approach to administration," said Arthur M. Schlesinger, Jr., "not just because it reserved the big decisions for the President, but perhaps even more because it enabled him to test and develop the abilities of his subordinates. How to tell which man, which approach was better? One answer was to let them fight it out. This solution might cause waste but would guarantee against stagnation. . . . One consequence . . . was a darkling plain of administrative confusion, where bureaucrats clashed by night. Another was a constant infusion of vitality and ideas."[2] He operated with no White House chief of staff and few fixed assignments. He sought advice from a wide variety of sources inside and outside of government, often assigning the same task to several advisers and using the inevitable conflicts among them to educate himself.

Though he had campaigned on the promise of balancing the budget and reducing the cost of government by 25 percent, Roosevelt also knew he had to achieve economic recovery, and he had several of his advisers working toward that end during the first one hundred days of his administration. One question associated with the recovery issue was the administration's position on a public works program. Although Secretary of Labor Frances Perkins favored a large public works program, Director of the Budget Lewis M. Douglas opposed it, and Roosevelt himself was skeptical. Undecided on an approach to economic recovery, periodically pressed by Perkins, and in daily communications with Douglas, Roosevelt procrastinated.

Roosevelt's hand was forced in April 1933 by the introduction in the United States Senate of a bill to restrict the hours of work on articles entering into interstate commerce to thirty per week per worker, which, according to Senator Hugo Black (D–Ala.), its sponsor, would increase the number of available jobs. With support from organized labor, Black's bill, christened the Thirty-Hour Bill, had passed the Senate by a wide margin and hearings were being held in the House. Anxious to avoid being put in the position of vetoing a measure supported by Democrats and aimed at curing the Depression, yet wishing to avoid endorsing a measure that, because it was not closely identified with his administration, threatened his political leadership, Roosevelt sought to slow the measure's momentum in the House while at the same time developing his own proposal. He asked Perkins to take the lead in devising a substitute. Her approach, offered in testimony before the House committees reviewing the Thirty-Hour Bill, was to modify that bill by authorizing the secretary of labor to oversee the establishment of fair wages for workers whose hours of work were reduced, thus providing a measure of protection for their incomes. This unprecedented intrusion of the federal government into business decision-making caused a storm of protest, especially in the business community, and the administration backed off.

The president then encouraged several groups who were working more or less independently to develop a program of industrial recovery that could gain congressional approval. One such program was put together by Perkins and her solicitor, Charles E. Wyzanski, Jr., and emphasized federal expenditures for public works. Another came about as a result of Roosevelt's having asked Raymond Moley, the political science professor who had become his close adviser, to devise a recovery plan. Because of business opposition to the Black bill, Roosevelt told Moley to be sure to obtain the thinking of business concerning industrial recovery. The president saw an opportunity to move toward his general goal of working out a system of business-government cooperation. Pressed for time, Moley, on the advice of financier Bernard Baruch, turned to Hugh S. Johnson, a retired cavalry general working for Baruch, and Johnson in turn enlisted Donald R. Richberg, an attorney

for several railroad unions and former partner of Secretary of the In-
terior Harold Ickes, for his knowledge of labor issues[3] and his "clear and
concise habit of thought."[4] Their plan was to suspend for several years
some provisions of the anti-trust laws, so industry representatives could
coordinate their decisions on hours and wages. A small public works
program was included.[5] Yet another plan, differing from the Johnson-
Richberg approach in its enforcement scheme, was put together by a
group led by Assistant Secretary of Commerce John Dickenson and
presidential adviser Rexford G. Tugwell. A fourth effort, led by U.S.
Senator Robert F. Wagner (D–N.Y.), like Perkins' proposal emphasized
public works and the right of unions to organize and bargain collectively.

In order to reach a decision, Roosevelt convened a meeting in the
White House on a Saturday afternoon late in April. A feature of the
meeting was Roosevelt's biting criticism—Ickes attributed it to "nervous
strain"[6]—of Perkins' presentation of her public works program. Yet, at
the conclusion of the meeting, Roosevelt had agreed to submit to Congress an industrial recovery act with both an industrial cooperation provision and a scaled-down public works program, and Perkins left feeling
triumphant. Much work concerning industrial cooperation remained to
be done, however, in drafting the provision. Since key advisers were still
unable to reach agreement on the issue, Moley encouraged an impatient
Roosevelt to call another meeting on May 10. After listening to compet-
ing arguments, Roosevelt ordered that an advisory group be formed and
"locked in a room" until it could come out with a single proposal.
According to Richberg, the group consisted of Douglas, Wagner, Johnson, and himself, who "worked almost continuously for several days in
the office of the director of the budget who kept in close touch with the
President."[7]

At one point in May, at the behest of Budget Director Douglas,
Roosevelt apparently changed his mind about including the public
works provision in the industrial recovery bill. Perkins arranged to see
Roosevelt at the White House on a Saturday after his scheduled meeting
with Douglas. Supported in principle by Wagner, whom she had notified
of the problem, and accompanied by Wyzanski, she persuaded the president to reconsider. While still in his office, she phoned Wagner to inform him of Roosevelt's new decision, and Roosevelt took the phone and
confirmed it. Of this episode, Wyzanski remarked to Perkins as they
drove away, "This is really a most revealing thing. I've studied law, I've
studied political science. I never could have conceived that important
matters were settled like this, but this is the way government operates
apparently."[8] To Douglas, the episode illustrated how Roosevelt, anxious
to be liked and not always remembering what he had promised this or

that person, tended to agree or at least not disagree with whomever he was talking to. Decisions were made because of today's problems for today's reasons.[9]

Within days a bill was ready for Congress.[10] It was submitted on May 13, and the National Industrial Recovery Act was signed into law by Roosevelt on June 16, 1933, near the end of the "one hundred days."*

Roosevelt had clearly "managed" the development of his administration's policy for industrial recovery. He hardly did so, however, by mastering the substance of the issue and making the key decisions concerning the content of the proposal himself. He did not play the role of problem-solver. Rather, he was at once political strategist, watching and waiting for (or reacting to) opportunities to further a general goal,† and catalytic agent for experienced individuals inside and outside of government who could provide ideas and energy for the policy development effort. His oversight of and involvement in their work was casual, though his directive to Moley to get the viewpoint of business was decisive to the policy development effort because it measurably improved the prospect that the resulting plan would enjoy business support. Roosevelt relied on and supported trusted lieutenants who knew his style to maintain the pace of staff work and see that the disorganized activity he loved to foster somehow got pulled together in the end. He was, in James P. Warburg's phrase, "a tireless, serene and often amused referee."[11]

Dwight D. Eisenhower's relatively passive reliance on orderly bureaucratic process provides a sharp contrast in presidential styles. The contrast is illustrated by Eisenhower's role in securing passage of the National Defense Education Act of 1958. In the mid-1950s some authorities began to advocate increased federal assistance for education, especially for classroom construction and college scholarships. As early as 1954, Eisenhower himself spoke favorably of the possibility of federal scholarships for the training of scientists.[12] But conservative Republicans and southern Democrats in Congress repeatedly turned back legislation creating programs of aid for education, and Eisenhower, too, questioned the wisdom of federal intervention in something traditionally left

---

*The act would be declared unconstitutional by the U.S. Supreme Court in 1935.

†Did Roosevelt's political caution reflect a clever strategic sense or opportunism? In 1945, Roosevelt aide Samuel Rosenman was to tell Harold Ickes that in certain things, such as tackling the problem of helping poor people pay for medical expenses, Harry Truman proved much braver than Roosevelt. Whereas Roosevelt never could bring himself to propose national health insurance, Truman, who cared deeply about the issue, did so without much ado (Robert J. Donovan, *Conflict and Crisis* [W.W. Norton, 1977], pp. 125–126).

to state and local control. With the October 4, 1957, announcement of the launching of Sputnik by the Soviet Union, however, the mood in Congress changed and the prospects for some kind of federal program dramatically improved. Though skeptical of "crash programs," Eisenhower, like Roosevelt in the case of industrial recovery, was under pressure to act.

In his speeches, Eisenhower began advocating federal assistance for training scientific and engineering manpower. With Eisenhower's approval, his secretary of Health, Education, and Welfare, Marion Folsom, had already been preparing a modest legislative proposal for federal aid to education, and now Folsom accelerated his effort to ready an educational development proposal for submission to Congress. Following an hour-long meeting with Eisenhower at his Gettysburg farm on December 30, 1957, Folsom announced to the press the administration's plan. In his state of the union message the following January, the president recommended that one billion dollars be spent on the program, and he sent a special message on education to Congress on January 27, 1958, giving further details of his proposal. Though he occasionally met with his advisers or wrote a letter to a legislator as the proposal moved through Congress, so long as congressional action stayed within the broad limits he thought appropriate, Eisenhower left the policymaking on an issue of historic significance to others, notably congressional Democrats. Concludes James L. Sundquist of Eisenhower's policy leadership, "As the domestic issues of the 1950s developed, the President for the most part stood aside and permitted them to become Democratic issues."[13]

When aroused, however, Eisenhower was able to play a more active role in policymaking. He was determined, for example, to strengthen the role of the secretary of defense and the joint chiefs of staff in order to eliminate the enfeebling effects of interservice rivalries within the Department of Defense. Late in 1957, his new secretary of defense, Neil H. McElroy, created an advisory group to study the need for organizational reform within the department. Though McElroy had wanted to wait a year to tackle the issue, Eisenhower insisted on moving more quickly.[14] Evidently dissatisfied with the group's reluctance to alter the status quo, Eisenhower, according to his memoirs, was "determined not to gloss over the problem," and he lectured the group on the need for change.* Then, three days later, he told Republican legislative leaders, "I

---

*Charles A. Coolidge, who assisted McElroy in drafting the reorganization proposal, remembers that Eisenhower "seemed to have difficulty expressing himself clearly" but that his assistants, General Andrew Goodpaster and Bryce Harlow, could clear up any points in what the president said then and later (interview with Charles Coolidge, Columbia Uni-

want the Pentagon people to develop an effective plan. . . . But if something good doesn't come out of the Pentagon study, I will just have to take the bull by the horns—call in the leaders of the Senate and the House, including Democrats, in an effort to try to get their support directly."[15] McElroy and others began drafting the plan he wanted.* When Carl Vinson (D–Ga.), chairman of the House Armed Services Committee, jumped the gun on the administration and, in February, introduced a reorganization plan unsatisfactory to Eisenhower, the president had three of the committee's leaders to breakfast to discuss his own ideas, which were evolving during hours of discussion with his reorganization advisers. The meeting led Eisenhower to realize that Vinson would continue to oppose his plan, and he designed his legislative strategy accordingly.

Shortly before the administration proposal was sent to Congress on April 3, 1958, Eisenhower met one evening with the secretary of the navy and the chief of naval operations. He correctly anticipated that the navy would be emotionally opposed to his plan, and he wanted to secure the support of navy leaders so that Vinson and others would not exploit divisions within the administration. A briefing was also held for Republican leaders and then for a larger group of leaders from both parties. In the middle of April, in an effort to mobilize public backing, Eisenhower declared his strong support for the plan in a speech before the American Society of Newspaper Editors. He began to write directly to hundreds of influential citizens all across the nation "to explain the issues at stake and to ask them to make their own conclusions known to the members of Congress, especially to its military committees."[16] According to former Eisenhower aide Emmet J. Hughes, "A vast amount of presidential energy was expended, throughout the spring of 1958, in fighting for this cause so close to the President's personal desires and experience."† Congressional sentiment began to change, but the House Armed Services Committee reported out a bill that, while largely satisfactory to the Pentagon, still contained features objectionable to Eisenhower. He issued a

versity Oral History Project, pp. 6–7). It was in November 1957 that Eisenhower suffered the stroke that left his speech temporarily impaired.

*Emmet J. Hughes wrote that Eisenhower "drafted most of the wording of the proposal legislation himself," a version that is contradicted by Coolidge (see Emmet J. Hughes, *The Ordeal of Power* [New York: Atheneum, 1975], p. 260).

†Transcripts of the oral history project of Columbia University indicate that officials working on the reorganization plan recalled the president as somewhat less of a force for change than Eisenhower's memoirs suggest and that Eisenhower's White House advisers, principally General Andrew Goodpaster and Bryce Harlow, clarified the president's wishes and intentions.

statement emphasizing his objections, then, on the evening of May 27, met with Speaker of the House John McCormack (D–Mass.) at the White House to go over them one by one. The House remained adamant, but the president's efforts with the Senate had better results. The Senate amended the bill to Eisenhower's satisfaction, the House accepted these changes, and the Defense Reorganization Act was signed into law on August 6, 1958.[17]

Eisenhower emerges in this episode as less the politician and serene referee than Roosevelt and more the executive acting out of a personal interest in solving what he saw as a problem of administration. Yet he did not master the details of all the statutes involved, and he did not become more expert than those whom he was trying to persuade. Like Roosevelt, he depended on trusted assistants to see to it that his ideas got across, though, unlike FDR, he more readily delegated policy development and implementation to departmental officials. Eisenhower took the time to meet personally with those whose support he would need to move his proposal into policy. He effectively used the various instruments of presidential leadership at his disposal to generate and sustain momentum for his reorganization plan. Capitalizing on his credibility in such matters, he did what he had to in order to gain a favorable outcome.

Lyndon B. Johnson furnishes yet another example of presidential style in policymaking. On November 24, 1963, his first full day in office following the assassination of John F. Kennedy, he was informed by Council of Economic Advisers Chairman Walter Heller that Kennedy had approved Heller's proposal to devise a comprehensive plan to deal with the problem of poverty in America. The idea resonated with Johnson personally and politically, and he told Heller, "I'm interested. I'm sympathetic. Go ahead. Give it highest priority. Push ahead full tilt."[18] In his memoirs, Johnson wrote of his reaction to Heller's idea: "I believed that I could—for a while at least—really get things done."[19] Observes political scientist James L. Sundquist, "The issue itself was peculiarly suited to the personality of Lyndon Johnson, who could talk feelingly of his firsthand knowledge of poverty in the Texas hills and recall his experience as the director of Franklin Roosevelt's National Youth Administration. It gave him the excuse to stand on the same southern courthouse steps where Roosevelt stood and pledge himself to carry on the war on want that FDR had started."*[20]

---

*The same sense of history was evident when, upon the enactment of Medicare in 1965, Johnson journeyed to Independence, Missouri, to sign the bill in the presence of Harry S Truman, who was the first president to propose national health insurance. "We have come back here to his home," said Johnson, "to complete what he began."

The staff work for devising what became Johnson's War on Poverty was supervised by Heller and Kermit Gordon, director of the Bureau of the Budget. However, Johnson spent many long hours with them at the LBJ ranch during Christmas week 1963, "discussing, planning, and evolving the outlines of a poverty program."[21] Staff members occasionally sat in on these discussions, as did associates from earlier days and a group of Texas cattlemen, invited so that Heller and his colleagues could get a taste of the opposition their plan would later encounter. Johnson recalled how "one evening during those Christmas holidays in 1963, I walked from the main ranch house to a little green frame house we call the 'guest house,' a distance of about two hundred yards. Inside, seated around a small kitchen table, were Walter Heller, Budget Director Kermit Gordon, Bill Moyers, and Jack Valenti [both of Johnson's White House staff]. The table was littered with papers, coffee cups, and one ash tray brimming over with cigarettes and torn strips of paper. . . . I sat down at the table to talk about the program they were preparing."[22] Johnson urged them away from considering a demonstration program toward a big and bold program. At his instruction, $500 million, obtained largely through defense department economies, and another $500 million already in the budget for programs that would strike at poverty were incorporated into the new poverty program. Two budget bureau staff members contributed the notion that the funds would be channeled directly to and through local organizations, bypassing the mayors. In this way the Community Action Program was born.*

Following his announcement of the War on Poverty in his January 8, 1964, state of the union message, Johnson decided, against the advice of Secretary of Labor Willard Wirtz and Attorney General Robert F. Kennedy, to assign the program to a new agency, as advocated by Heller, Gordon, and economist and Kennedy adviser John Kenneth Galbraith (and much as Franklin D. Roosevelt would have done), rather than to the existing cabinet departments. Johnson chose Sargent Shriver, director of the Peace Corps, to direct the new agency, then closely monitored Shriver and his associates, who would have to run the new program, as they designed the authorizing legislation that would be submitted to Congress. Six weeks later, on March 16, a bill was submitted. In what Johnson himself regarded as a crucial step, he convinced Phil M. Landrum, a conservative Georgia Democrat who had successfully sponsored

---

*Professor Richard E. Neustadt recalls Bill Moyers telling him that Johnson would never have allowed that feature to be written into the legislation had he known the controversies it was to produce. However, preoccupied with getting as much progressive legislation enacted as he could in the limited time during which he could have his way with Congress, Johnson supported any provision he thought would facilitate enactment.

"right-to-work" legislation, to sponsor the bill in the House, then persuaded George Meany, the powerful head of the AFL-CIO, to cooperate with Landrum.

As the bill was being debated in Congress, according to Johnson's memoirs, "Lady Bird and I made a special trip to the Middle West and through the scarred mountains of Appalachia to focus the nation's attention on the problem of poverty." He repeatedly lobbied delegations of visitors, appealing, for example, to labor editors to help mold public opinion, and ask people to write their congressmen and senators. In making his appeals, however, Johnson "built the rhetoric far beyond that which had been planned by his advisers,"[23] a habit that contributed to the disillusionment that would set in when it was realized that the high expectations Johnson helped create could not be met. On August 20, 1965, the Economic Opportunity Act was signed into law.

In this episode Johnson combined a Rooseveltian instinct for using people and situations to accomplish his political objectives with his own personal and intense passion in mounting the War on Poverty. Roosevelt ordered his advisers locked into rooms until they could agree; Johnson brought them to his ranch, encabined them, and subjected them to the force of his personality. Then he, like Roosevelt and Eisenhower, employed the instruments of presidential leadership to mobilize support for his cause.

THE PRESIDENTIAL CONTRIBUTION

Why was it that Roosevelt, Eisenhower, and Johnson were successful in putting their policies into practice? Certainly, different historical circumstances confronted each president, and one could attribute their successes to these circumstances. Roosevelt, confronting an economy in severe depression, capitalized on economic distress and on the momentum of his first one hundred days in office to pass industrial recovery legislation. Eisenhower used his credibility as a military man and his freedom from the need to seek reelection to strengthen civilian authority over the defense establishment. Johnson, newly in office and confronting a nation in shock, an expanding economy, a vigorous civil rights movement, and the need for a theme and a program, capitalized on public willingness to respond to strong leadership on a moral issue to pass his War on Poverty.

Yet these successes were not achieved independently of the presidents' actions as policymakers. Each episode illustrates how a president influences policy: by the quality and ideas of the people whom he appoints to high office, by the nature of his relationships with those who advise him, including the signals and guidance he gives, and by the specific actions he takes on behalf of the policies he favors. Each president had opportunities, but each had to make the most of those opportunities. Each had to spend time getting his own administration to move. The three episodes suggest that, despite wide variations in intellectual and personal style, presidents are successful at policymaking when they demonstrate a tenacity of purpose, a vision that transcends the details of programs and legislation, a sense of personal involvement in the issue, as shown by the visible willingness to spend time mobilizing support and overcoming opposition, and, perhaps, some emotion. Some combination of personal interest, talented subordinates, political acumen, a strategic sense, and general knowledge of the issues is necessary if the president is to move the government in new directions of his choosing.

Even with the right combination of factors, however, a president's policy initiative may fail, at least in the form he proposed it. This is clear from the history of presidential involvement in welfare reform, to which we now turn.

CHAPTER TWO

Welfare: The Solution Becomes the Problem

THE FEDERAL WELFARE SYSTEM WAS BORN IN A PERIOD OF SEVERE ECO-nomic and social distress. The Depression had wiped out the jobs and savings of millions of people and had strained the ability of the states to help the needy. Though many early New Deal programs provided federal relief and emergency assistance, there was growing pressure on the federal government to provide more permanent forms of income security.

In response, at President Roosevelt's initiative, Congress established in the 1935 Social Security Act two federally assisted systems of income support. One was a contributory social insurance system consisting of old age insurance and unemployment insurance. The other was a public assistance or welfare system, financed by general revenues, comprising programs to provide public assistance to special classes of the needy—the indigent aged, the blind, and dependent children; the latter category, it was assumed, would include largely those children who had lost one parent before he or she had become eligible for social insurance benefits. It was generally expected that the welfare system would dwindle to insignificance as social insurance programs reached their maturity.

Instead of withering, the welfare system grew luxuriant as the population of needy children and adults grew following World War II.[1] As it became clear that many of America's mobile, increasingly urbanized population would remain needy even in a healthy economy, the original programs were incrementally expanded and new programs were added: a public assistance program for the disabled, a program to assist the poor to get medical care, job training programs, food stamps, social services (including day care), housing assistance, school lunch and school break-fast programs, and many others with similar intent. By the late 1960s, total social welfare outlays by the federal government alone had reached nearly $70 billion and further explosive growth was feared.

Whereas program growth and proliferation up until the election of Richard M. Nixon had been motivated by the desire to meet specific social needs, the patchwork of programs that had been created piecemeal over a thirty-year period itself was becoming an issue. Policy analysts in the Office of Economic Opportunity (OEO), the agency created to administer Lyndon Johnson's War on Poverty, and in the Department of Health, Education, and Welfare (HEW) had begun to criticize the welfare system as undermining work incentives: welfare recipients who went to work and thus lost their welfare benefits were often worse off than if they had remained on welfare. In the meantime welfare rolls and costs were increasing rapidly and contained more blacks, thus arousing political opposition, especially from conservatives and southern legislators. The other major complaint was that there was too much variation among benefit levels in the states. With the support of both conservative and liberal academic economists, poverty analysts in government began advocating replacement of welfare programs with a negative income tax to ensure an adequate income, with appropriate work incentives, for poor Americans. Under such an arrangement, families whose earned income fell below a certain level would receive a cash supplement; as their income rose, the cash supplement would be phased out gradually, so that working more would always be more rewarding than staying on welfare. OEO Director Sargent Shriver campaigned annually to enlist White House interest in the idea, but neither President Johnson nor his assistant for domestic policy, Joseph A. Califano, Jr., showed any interest in it. Their preference was to fight poverty by expanding social security benefits and increasing compensatory services for the poor. As Califano explained, "He [Johnson] thought of the War on Poverty as an extension of the New Deal as helping people get in positions where they could be on their own and where they could pull off their own share of the economic pie. That was the reason for all the vocational education, health, but especially the manpower training. It was a 'hand up' rather than a 'handout.'"[2]

Complaints about the existing welfare system grew more insistent, however. In 1967, Congress amended the public assistance statutes to permit a more gradual phasing out of benefits as earnings rose and also to force able-bodied welfare recipients to register for and accept training for paying jobs. Finally, bowing to pressure to examine reform ideas such as the negative income tax and a government-guaranteed jobs program, Johnson reluctantly created the President's Commission on Income Maintenance Programs in January 1968, and its chairman, Ben

W. Heineman, chairman of the C.&N.W. Railway Co., began soliciting ideas for reform. To the end of his administration, however, the president refused to entertain any such thoughts,* and the problem of the welfare system was passed to Richard M. Nixon.

THE FAMILY ASSISTANCE PLAN

Nixon had developed a conservative's distaste for the welfare system, and he campaigned in 1968 on the promise to change it. While he indicated a determination to cut welfare costs and reduce the welfare rolls—standard conservative goals—late in his campaign he also criticized the wide differences among state benefit levels and promised to recommend a national benefit standard, widely regarded as a "liberal" reform,[3] and, in the view of his domestic adviser, Daniel P. Moynihan, "extraordinarily in advance of any proposal ever made by an incumbent president."[4]

Within days of his election, Nixon created a task force on welfare and poverty (along with several other task forces on major policy issues). Of his interest, he said:

> From the first days of my administration I wanted to get rid of the costly failures of the Great Society—and I wanted to do it immediately. I wanted the people who had elected me to see that I was going to follow through on my campaign promises. The worst offender was the welfare system, and welfare reform was my highest domestic priority.[5]

Headed by Richard P. Nathan of the Brookings Institution, who would later become one of Nixon's assistant directors of the Office of Management and Budget (OMB), the task force recommended shortly after Christmas 1968 that Nixon propose a nationwide minimum floor for welfare benefits financed by the federal government through the existing Aid to Families with Dependent Children (AFDC) program at an additional cost of $1.4 billion. Though academically staffed task forces such as that headed by Nathan were regarded by Nixon's political aides as little more than window dressing, the Nathan proposal was to become the fulcrum for moving the Nixon administration toward a radical welfare reform proposal incorporating a negative income tax.[6]

On his third day in office, Nixon created and convened a cabinet-level Council for Urban Affairs, and he appointed his urban affairs adviser, Daniel P. Moynihan, formerly a professor at Harvard and an assistant

---

*He was encouraged in this course by Wilbur J. Cohen, a senior HEW official who had been present at the founding of the Social Security System and whom Johnson named as secretary for the last eight months of his term.

secretary of labor in the Johnson administration, to be its executive secretary. Among the subcommittees of the Urban Affairs Council was one on welfare, headed by Secretary of Health, Education, and Welfare Robert H. Finch, a long-time political associate of Nixon's from California. (Other members included Secretary of Labor George P. Shultz, Secretary of Agriculture Clifford M. Hardin, Attorney General John N. Mitchell, and Secretary of Commerce Maurice H. Stans.) The president had already asked Moynihan to take a hard-nosed look at fraud and abuse in welfare administration in New York City and to head off a punitive Nixon attack on the welfare system. Moynihan decided to respond to Nixon's request by urging him to accept the Nathan plan for welfare reform, and he enlisted Finch's sympathetic cooperation in using his Urban Affairs Council subcommittee as the vehicle to move Nixon to a decision.

Opposition to the Nathan plan surfaced in Finch's subcommittee at its first meeting on February 6, 1969. It would, critics argued, continue to treat poor families headed by males inequitably and increase the pressures on their families to break up. Nathan then suggested the creation of a sub-cabinet working group to "perfect" his plan. On February 12, in a meeting with Moynihan and Finch, Arthur Burns (counselor to the president on domestic affairs), Nixon said that he wanted to establish national payments standards. However, the sub-cabinet working group was staffed largely by HEW policy analysts who had been part of the anti-poverty effort in the Johnson administration and who were critical of Nathan's plan. Thinking it had received a signal to do so, the group promptly moved in the opposite direction from that taken by Nathan and instead devised a plan, christened the Family Security System, built around a negative income tax. All families with no income would receive a basic cash benefit. That benefit would be reduced a certain amount with each dollar of earned income the family might receive until the family earned enough to be fully self-supporting. Finch and Moynihan liked the group's idea and were willing to abandon the Nathan plan and take the new plan to Nixon. But when the new plan surfaced in Finch's subcommittee, the opposition was immediate. Martin Anderson, an assistant to Burns, argued that a negative income tax would, by providing benefits to poor families with a working member, swell the welfare rolls and increase welfare budgets, and that a guaranteed annual income, which the plan would create, was bad public policy.[7] An epic struggle began over the nature of reform, pitting traditional conservatives like Stans and Burns against liberals like Moynihan and Finch and the Johnson administration holdovers in the working group.

While this debate was going on in February, March, and April of 1969, the Nixon administration was without a domestic legislative program.

An impatient president finally asked Burns, Finch, and Moynihan to submit their proposals to him at Key Biscayne during the Easter weekend.[8] Bypassing the Urban Affairs Council machinery in which their favorite plan had stalled, Finch and Moynihan pressed the Family Security System on the president. Despite Burns' protests that seven million people would be added to the welfare rolls, Nixon surprised his conservative advisers by replying, in effect, "I understand, Arthur, that you don't like it; and I understand your reasons. But I have a problem. If you don't like it, give me another solution."[9] Nixon was clearly attracted to the negative income tax idea. It appeared to offer the simplicity and efficiency he sought. (He had asked Moynihan whether the plan would get rid of social workers and had received assurances that it would.)[10]

With one side excited and the other alarmed by the president's cautious interest in the negative income tax scheme, the debate within the administration intensified. Any semblance of due process was now gone as cabinet officers fought for the president's heart and mind. In character, intensity, and quality, this particular social policy debate equalled any held in Franklin Roosevelt's administration. The Burkes summed up the diversity of the debate as follows:

> Cabinet officers and other advisors poured arguments of morality, philosophy, politics, and economics into secret memos to the president, each choosing what he hoped would be decisive with him. Moynihan shunned analytic debate and played to Nixon's ego, enticing him with the promise of historic greatness and the chance to "all but eliminate" poverty. Burns warned that FSS [i.e., FAP] would undermine the nation's work ethic. Finch argued that FSS made good sense and good politics. Budget Director Mayo complained that it would deepen the budget deficit. Agnew said it would convert self-reliant workers into welfare "addicts," calling to mind Franklin Roosevelt's complaint that "to dole out relief . . . is to administer a narcotic." Commerce Secretary Stans opposed even the modest Burns plan and asked why welfare recipients couldn't grow gardens, fish, and hunt [in Central Park?].[11]

Increasingly the debate before Nixon focused chiefly between White House protagonists Daniel Moynihan and Arthur Burns. By late April, Burns had developed an alternative to FAP, similar to the more modest approach advocated by the original Nathan task force. Burns had only a small staff working for him, but he was a close friend of the president and his judgment was highly regarded. Moynihan, on the other hand, had the resources of HEW and the support of Finch, and Moynihan's grandiloquence appealed to Nixon. As Nixon acknowledged, "Even when I found Pat Moynihan was wrong about a particular issue or problem, I found his intellect scintillating and challenging. As I said after he had left the administration and returned to Harvard, 'I disagreed with a lot of what he said—but he certainly did light up the place!'"*[12] The conflict between Moynihan and Burns was not entirely unanticipated or unlooked for by Nixon. He had reasoned that Burns' "conservatism would be a useful and creative counterweight to Moynihan's liberalism"[13] in setting up his White House staff.

As the disagreement intensified between the Finch-Moynihan faction and Burns, it came often to bear on philosophical and historical issues. In late April, for example, Nixon was treated to a memo debate between Anderson and Moynihan over the effect of the poor relief system in eighteenth-century Speenhamland, England. Moreover, Nixon, on his own, solicited comments on the two plans from friends and academics outside the administration, who often reflected on considerations other than political and economic ones.[14]

The split between the protagonists was so wide that they were unable to agree on a plan to recommend to the president. Consequently, in mid-May Nixon turned to his advisers for advice. Secretary of Defense Melvin R. Laird, who had been chairman of the House Republican Conference while in Congress and a proponent of the negative income tax, temporized by arguing for a six-month delay of action until a study could produce a "thoroughly thought-out welfare package."[15] Unsatisfied with this recommendation, Nixon asked Secretary of Labor Shultz for counsel. Shultz, with his assistant Jerry Rosow, devised a work expense disregard that would improve the work incentives in the Family Security System at an additional cost of one billion dollars. But here the adversary system began to sputter. Shultz did not know that the public assistance amendments of 1967 already called for improved work incentives. HEW analysts, who knew, did not volunteer the information because they feared it would jeopardize their plan. (To incorporate an equally generous work incentive into the Family Assistance Plan would raise its cost, further reducing the chance that Nixon would support it.)[16] Commented the Burkes on this situation: "Ignorance probably was constructive, for if the President at the outset had been fully informed, welfare's dilemmas and facts might have deterred him from action."[17]

---

*As Martin Anderson recalled: "In the sea of dark gray and blue that surrounded Nixon, Moynihan, in his cream-colored suit and red bow tie, gleamed like a playful porpoise. He was a charming Irish rogue, a delightful dinner companion, a fascinating teller of tales. His presence lighted the gloom of national policy deliberations, and even his opponents liked to have him around. The President liked to read his memoranda, sometimes even searching through the pile on his desk to find them" (Martin Anderson, *Welfare* [Stanford, Calif.: Hoover Press, Stanford University, 1979], p. 6).

Nixon, however, remained intent on reform, and a June 10 memo from Shultz which included a work expense disregard that essentially endorsed the Moynihan-Finch approach, gave him a bolster. Also, several days earlier, Moynihan had sent Nixon a memo that, according to some participants, "persuaded Nixon to go with the Finch-Moynihan proposal."[18] Moynihan first appealed to Nixon's sense of history:

> *It is open to you to dominate and direct this social transformation. . . .*
> In September, *President Johnson's* Commission on Income Maintenance will be coming in with a $1.5 million report that will propose a system very much like Family Security, but somewhat broader.[19]

Moynihan went on to place welfare reform in a budgetary context, describing the FAP initiative in rather glowing terms:

> I am really pretty discouraged about the budget situation in the coming three to five years. I fear you will have nothing like the options I am sure you hoped for. Even more, I fear that the pressure from Congress will be nigh irresistible to use up what extra resources you have on a sort of ten percent across-the-board increase in all the Great Society programs each year. This is the natural instinct of the Congress, and it is hard for the President to resist.
> If your extra money goes down that drain, I fear that in four years' time you really won't have a single distinctive Nixon program to show for it all.
> Therefore I am doubly interested in seeing you go up now with a genuinely new, unmistakably Nixon, unmistakably needed program, which would attract the attention of the world, far less the United States. We can afford the Family Security System. Once you have asked for it, you can resist the pressures endlessly to add marginal funds to already doubtful programs.
> This way, in 1972 we will have a record of solid, unprecedented accomplishment in a vital area of social policy, *and not just an explanation as to how complicated it all was.*[20]

Whether due to the appeals of Moynihan and Shultz or for other reasons, Nixon was apparently making up his mind. On a Sunday afternoon in late June, the president told John Ehrlichman, who by then was emerging as Nixon's chief domestic policy coordinator, "I've decided we should try to advance a welfare reform proposal along the lines we've been studying. It will be expensive, but in the long run the present system will be more expensive if we don't change."[21] Nixon, however, wanted the legislation drafted in secret—that is, without Burns knowing about it—by a small White House team. The secrecy did not last long. Under fire from Republican liberals for several early decisions, including that on the anti-ballistic missile program, Nixon had Ehrlichman inform Burns of his intention and step up the pace. Ehrlichman in turn provided the draftees with the following guidelines:

1. The system should eliminate social workers' snooping which is essentially berating [*sic*].
2. A work package is necessary.
3. The factor of cost is not as material as the foregoing since the message should make clear that the cost involved is not this year's cost.
4. You should attempt to develop a descriptive name for the program which connotes a strong work element.
5. The program should include a federal floor of income, much work incentive, provisions that if there is an opportunity to work the recipients must work and the scheme must lead the recipient to be better off if in training than if he were idle and better off working than if he were training.
6. The system should provide day care for women with children except in the instance of extremely large families. The message should make clear that day care is a constructive program which contributes in the long run to cure the basic recurring encyclical [*sic*] problem. Children should not just sit around the house since this leads to their becoming non-workers.

We are committed to a long-run effort to get the amount of welfare down. The younger generation must be kept off welfare.

7. The "first five years of life" program can be shown to have some relationship to this day care operation.
8. We oppose a pure negative tax because it includes no work incentive.
9. The program with work incentive, job training, etc. is counter-inflationary since it includes the productivity of the population. Putting more people in the work force is anti-inflationary.
10. The system should be explained to the [congressional] leadership Monday morning [July 14]. It should be announced Monday afternoon and should go to the Hill on Tuesday Noon. Shultz, Finch, Rumsfeld and Moynihan will appear at the television briefing.[22]

Aware that he was losing, Burns continued his efforts to change the president's mind, and the president, reluctant to overrule him and concerned about the impact of FAP on an income tax surcharge then before the Senate, agreed to delay the plan's announcement until August 8, thus giving Ehrlichman further time to pull things together. At this point, the contending parties began to bargain over the design of the program, with Ehrlichman as the mediator. A plan neared completion.

Finally, a decisive meeting was held at Camp David. The president, now determined to make his historic proposal, took charge of the strategy for the meeting, his objective being to prevent his badly divided cabinet from disintegrating. He ordered Finch and Shultz to stay out of the main debate. Finch later told an interviewer, "The president asked me, 'You really think this will work?' He said he was going to come on real strong for [the Family Security System] and that we should stay out of it."[23] Present were the "secretaries of eleven departments and the undersecretary of the twelfth, plus Agnew, Burns, Mayo, Moynihan, Rumsfeld, Ehrlichman, Haldeman, the welfare working group, Representative Rogers C. B. Morton (R–Md.), Republican National Committee chairman, and White House staffers."[24] The president encouraged the briefers to explain how the current welfare system worked, as well as the new proposal. Then he asked cabinet members what they thought.[25] Few openly favored it. As critics stated their case, Nixon became the proposal's defender. Finally he said, "We don't know whether this will work, but we can't go on with the present system."[26]

These words communicated both his determination to push ahead with reform and his ambivalent feelings about this particular plan. "At times," said one researcher who spoke to many participants in welfare reform policymaking,

> after talking to Moynihan or Finch, he believed it was the right thing to do politically and because it would reduce poverty. Other times he worried about the effect of a guaranteed income on the work efforts of the poor and how he would defend a proposal that doubled federal welfare costs and recipients. . . . When pressed in private by senators, congressmen, governors, or members of his staff, his consistent response, according to interviews, was that he was "not absolutely sure FAP would work" or "that it would take us down the right road." But he felt "something had to be done about welfare" and he was convinced the present system "was taking us down the wrong road."[27]

Nixon himself seconded some of these observations:

> The Great Society programs had poured billions of dollars into supplying a formidable range of social services for the poor; if you could prove that your income was below a certain level you could qualify for any number of free or subsidized goods and services. I felt that this kind of approach encouraged a feeling of dependence and discouraged the kind of self-

reliance that is needed to get people on their feet. I thought that people should have the responsibility for spending carefully and taking care of themselves. I abhorred snoopy, patronizing surveillance by social workers which made children and adults on welfare feel stigmatized and separate. The basic premise of the Family Assistance Plan was simple: what the poor need to help them rise out of poverty is money. . . .

FAP was a risk. I knew that. We would be making thirteen million more people eligible for federal help than were currently eligible in an effort to reward work and not punish the poor for holding jobs. We would be incurring a first-year cost increase of $4 billion on the speculation that once people were not penalized for work—once they were certain they could earn more in jobs than solely on welfare—they would prefer to work. We hoped that the stability that the increased money would provide would be an incentive to get better and better paying jobs, ultimately taking people off the welfare rolls. It was a speculation that no one was certain would work.[28]

On August 8, 1969, Nixon announced his Family Assistance Plan on national television, declaring that the welfare system had to be reformed because it was fueling an "urban crisis, a social crisis—and, at the same time, a crisis of confidence in the capacity of government to do its job." And, for nearly three years thereafter, he and his advisers consistently advocated FAP's adoption in a wide variety of forums. Nixon was often personally involved in pushing for FAP, as Kenneth Bowler points out:

In regard to FAP and other welfare issues he met several times with Wilbur Mills and John Byrnes and held special breakfasts in the White House for Republican congressmen in 1970 and early 1971. He addressed the National Governors Conference in Washington in February 1970, spoke to the 50th annual convention of the Junior Chamber of Commerce in St. Louis in June, met with key Finance Committee members at San Clemente in August, met with other congressional leaders and visited the Washington headquarters of the Retail Clerks International Association in November—all in behalf of welfare reform.[29]

Presidential involvement in welfare reform was necessary in part because welfare reform turned out to be an extraordinarily divisive issue. Staunch conservatives claimed that FAP was a "megadole," while many liberals contended FAP was inadequate and regressive. The lines of debate over FAP, moreover, were not drawn simply along traditional lines. As Moynihan observed:

Organized labor achieved a measure of tolerant ambivalence that could pass for unity, although, as noted, even there a number of union leaders took independent positions. Elsewhere all was conflict. Civil-rights groups divided; social-welfare groups divided; liberals divided; conservatives divided—later both political parties divided . . . [and] representatives of business.[30]

Moynihan's victory in the internal debate did not presage Nixon's victory in the external debate, however. FAP was essentially a new idea, and, as such, there was no predictable line-up of interests for and against it. Sometimes the staunchest opponents of FAP were leaders whose constituencies had the most to gain from the proposal. FAP, for example, would have increased the amount of income available to the poor, especially in the South. Conservative southern Democrats were concerned, however, by the possibility that generous welfare payments would undercut the low wage structure that prevailed in the region and worried that FAP would lead to a massive increase in black political power. Most liberal black organizations, fueled by the rhetoric of the National Welfare Rights Organization (NWRO), opposed FAP as well, despite the demonstrable fact that FAP would significantly increase the income poor blacks received and simplify the welfare system. Many of these liberal leaders had come to power in urban areas in the North, where FAP would not have much effect and might, in some cases, lower recipient benefits. They held out for something more generous, often arguing that the government should fund a guaranteed minimum income equivalent to the poverty line, a proposal that would cost fifteen to twenty times as much as the $4 billion FAP proposal.

Despite the polarization that FAP engendered, it was reported out of the House Ways and Means Committee with relatively few changes, and, with the sponsorship of Nixon and Wilbur Mills (D–Ark.), the committee's powerful chairman, FAP passed the House in April 1970. During the summer and fall of 1970, however, the bill was held up in the Senate Finance Committee. Liberal and conservative members of the committee both opposed FAP, and Senator John J. Williams of Delaware, a senior conservative Republican on the committee, subjected FAP to a devastating critique with the aid of charts HEW reluctantly supplied for him. Williams pointed·out that FAP did not remove all of the so-called "notches" of the welfare system—that is, points at which a very small increase in earned income caused a large reduction in benefits (larger, even, than the income increase)—and thus maintained the confiscatory tax rates and weak work incentives that characterized the existing welfare system.[31] Caught in a wave of antipathy to the welfare system, FAP was also slowed by the uncertain support of Russell Long

(D–La.), chairman of the Senate Finance Committee, and was overtaken by other events, such as the invasion of Cambodia, which diverted the energies of administration officials and strengthened liberal opposition to Nixon.

By late July 1970, the administration had made a number of changes in FAP to remove the "notches" Senator Williams had highlighted, but, in so doing, it created higher tax rates on low earnings. As both conservatives and liberals on the committee became more implacable, they seized upon the new problems the administration had created. In an effort to find a compromise, Senator Abraham Ribicoff (D–Conn.) offered an amendment that would require that FAP be pilot-tested for a year before becoming a national program. In August, Nixon began to lobby for Republican votes by meeting with minority members of the Finance Committee and at the end of the month announced he would accept the Ribicoff amendment. On September 3, a bipartisan committee of six senators from the Finance Committee were flown to San Clemente to meet with the president. Nixon pleaded that the Senate Finance Committee "must write this bill," but added that "if what comes out of the Committee is an uncertain trumpet . . . I might have to veto the result." He closed with an impassioned appeal to the senators:

> We might be at one of those historic points in history where a great step forward is going to happen because a few men have had the boldness and the stamina to do so. If we go on as we have been there will be a general national revulsion [to welfare]. I am for Family Assistance because while, (a) it is a possible disaster, (b) AFDC is a certain disaster. . . . The future . . . lies with the men in this room.

Turning to Long, Nixon inquired, "Russell, is there a chance?"[32]

Long acknowledged there was and offered the observation that cost was not a problem; rather the "objection is to paying people not to work." He allowed there was a "rising objection to people who lay about all day making love and producing illegitimate babies."[33] But Senators Ribicoff and Wallace F. Bennett of Utah, the ranking Republican on the committee, seconded Long's feeling that a bill could be reported out of committee.

Despite the upbeat tone of the meeting, the controversial legislation remained stalled during September; by October, the 1970 elections dominated White House attention, and Vice-President Spiro Agnew was campaigning nationwide denouncing the "radical liberals" in the Democratic party. When the election had passed with a resounding Democratic victory, a White House team was reassembled on November 11 to conduct one last intensive campaign to pass FAP before Congress adjourned in January. The *National Journal* reported, "The Administration has devoted more manpower and manhours to the Family Assistance Plan . . . than to any other single piece of domestic legislation it has proposed."[34] Moynihan described the effort as follows:

> Cabinet Officers and their aides now roamed the corridors of the Senate Office Building during the first full "lame duck" session of Congress in twenty years. Veneman [HEW under-secretary], Patricelli [HEW deputy assistant secretary] and Rosow manned a continuous watch. Legislative liaison officers, notably Howard A. Cohen of HEW, came into their own. In-telligence reports came hourly to the White House. The Presi-dent talked to congressional leaders, and was available for other chores. Once again morale rose. What no one realized, or wanted to acknowledge, was that all was different in the after-math of the campaign. . . . There was some bitterness, much vindictiveness, and a minimal disposition [among Democrats] to enable [Nixon] to recoup his position by an epic legislative achievement.[35]

The vote on FAP was scheduled for November 20. Three days before the vote, Common Cause cancelled a coordinated lobbying effort of organizations supporting FAP when George Wiley, head of the NWRO, threatened to show up with one to two hundred welfare mothers. However, Senator Eugene McCarthy (D–Minn.), who had sponsored an NWRO bill guaranteeing a minimum income at the poverty level, agreed to hold "people's hearings" on November 18 and 19 in the Senate Office Building. The sensational hearings were described by columnist Mary McGrory as a scene "where scores of militant welfare mothers bellowed their opposition to being driven out of the house to do underpaid work."[36] The meeting enraged Senate conservatives and, according to some accounts,[37] eliminated any chance that undecided liberal Demo-crats on the committee might vote for FAP. On November 20, in a 10 to 6 vote, the Senate Finance Committee turned down FAP, with three Democratic liberals joining the conservative majority. Attempts by Sena-tors Ribicoff and Bennett in December to get a liberalized version of FAP into a conglomerate bill on the Senate floor were defeated, and the 91st Congress ended without action on FAP.

As 1971 and the 92nd Congress began, Nixon again declared his commitment to FAP in January by announcing welfare reform as "White House priority number one." Working with the Ways and Means Com-mittee, the Nixon administration reported out yet another version of FAP, which passed the House in June 1971. H.R. 1, as it was labeled, continued, however, to provoke both conservative and liberal opposition. The bill's federal cost had risen to $7.0 billion (chiefly because of the provision giving added fiscal relief to state and local governments), the basic benefit had been raised by incorporating food stamps into it, and the work incentives in the bill had been weakened. Such changes fueled the arguments of conservatives, who were unappeased by the addition of a Work Opportunities Program that would create 200,000 jobs for welfare recipients. Liberals, on the other hand, were concerned that the removal of requirements that states continue providing benefits above the federal floor would hurt recipients, especially in the high-benefit northern states.

In July 1971 the Senate Finance Committee held hearings on H.R. 1. An ominous sign at the hearing was that Long, who had reluctantly voted for FAP in 1970, now refused to support a guaranteed income and was going to push for a guaranteed job program (at sub-minimum wages) to replace AFDC. Long was reluctant to deal with welfare reform at all; he reasoned that H.R. 1, which had a provision for increasing Social Security benefits, would be an attractive bill, but that the guaranteed income aspects would be unappealing in 1972, an election year.[38] Long's plan to stall on H.R. 1 got a tremendous boost on August 15, 1971, when Nixon announced his new economic program, which delayed the implementation of welfare reform by a year and preoccupied the Finance Committee for the remainder of 1971.

On October 29, 1971, Senator Ribicoff announced a liberal alternative to FAP that contained most of the basic features of H.R. 1. At the same time, Ribicoff, Senate Majority Leader Mike Mansfield (D–Mont.), and Elliot Richardson (who had replaced Finch as HEW secretary) met with Long and got from him what "they thought was a commitment . . . to get welfare reform to the Senate floor by March 1972."[39] The Finance Committee held more hearings on H.R. 1 in February 1972 but took no action on the bill by March. On March 27, 1972, Nixon sent a "strongly worded" message to Congress urging the committee to act. Long responded, "I suggest that the Administration folks keep their britches on long enough for us to act. . . . We're moving along as fast as we know how."[40] From March until June, the conservatives on the committee worked on a guaranteed jobs alternative to FAP.

Nixon at this point was given three options by his advisers. Members of Nixon's White House congressional relations team (a group that no longer included Moynihan) were not sympathetic to FAP and urged Nixon to find a center-right compromise with Senators Long and Bennett. Ehrlichman contended that the middle ground struck by H.R. 1 between the Long and Ribicoff proposals was the only ground worth cultivating. Finally, members of the president's cabinet, including

Richardson and Secretary of Labor James Hodgson (Shultz had moved to the Treasury), pushed the president to look for a compromise with Ribicoff. Lively debate between the parties occurred in a White House welfare reform working group that, according to Ehrlichman, was "a forum for deciding how to get done that which the President wants done— He's calling the shots."[41] The president and Ehrlichman approved negotiations between Richardson and Ribicoff and ordered the congressional relations team to attempt to move the Senate Finance Committee closer to H.R. 1.[42]

By May both Richardson and Ribicoff were sure that neither H.R. 1 nor the Ribicoff measure could pass the Senate, and Richardson, who had ruled out a compromise with the Senate Finance Committee, stepped up efforts to gain Nixon's support of a Ribicoff-administration accommodation. In mid-May, Richardson sent Nixon a memo outlining a compromise that he and Ribicoff supported and requested a meeting to discuss the matter with the president.[43] Nixon, who was preparing to leave for Moscow, sent word back to Richardson that he would meet with him on June 16. In the interim, Richardson and Moynihan unsuccessfully tried to get through to the president, and Richardson was "compelled to make his arguments to the President through Ehrlichman."[44]

The month delay, as Ribicoff put it, "was critical."[45] In May, Democratic presidential candidates George McGovern and Hubert Humphrey met in a nationally televised debate in which Humphrey successfully lambasted McGovern's "demogrant" welfare reform proposal for its exorbitant price (upward of $210 billion). Although both Nixon and McGovern were sponsoring forms of a guaranteed income, Nixon did not want to move toward the more expensive improvements advocated by Ribicoff for fear of becoming associated with McGovern's extravagance. At the June 16 meeting Nixon refused to budge from H.R. 1 even though he was warned by Richardson, Hodgson, and nineteen Republican senators (via a June 15 letter) that H.R. 1 would not pass the Senate. According to one report, Ehrlichman made a number of crucial points in the meeting about accommodation with Ribicoff:

> A hasty move [Ehrlichman explained] would only offend the Republican members of the Finance Committee whose support the President needed on such key votes as general revenue sharing and ratification of the SALT agreement. . . .
> Ehrlichman questioned the wisdom of President Nixon's closing ranks with many of Ribicoff's Democratic cosponsors, some of whom had been abusive of the President in the past three

years and whose commitment to the President was suspect in an election year. He also noted that Ribicoff himself was a key adviser in McGovern's campaign and could not be counted on to support the President if such support might embarrass McGovern.[46]

Nixon himself stressed the political liabilities of reform in accounting for his decision:

> By 1971 the momentum for FAP had passed and I knew it. I still believed in the validity of the idea, but I no longer believed in the political timing. In 1969 the American people had been ready for change; in 1971 they were thinking of other things—of Vietnam and the economy. By 1971 there was also the prospect of the 1972 election; I did not want to be in a losing fight with the conservatives over FAP in an election year. Therefore, in the summer of 1972 when I was given a choice either to endorse a more costly version of the bill proposed by Senator Ribicoff or to stay with our original FAP even though it would surely fail, I decided on the latter.[47]

In October, Ribicoff's bill was defeated on the Senate floor and a House-Senate conference committee deleted both FAP and the Senate Finance Committee's "workfare" provisions. Ultimately, the only section of FAP that passed was an income guarantee for the aged and disabled to be administered through a federalized system known as Supplemental Security Income, or SSI.

Although Nixon abandoned the welfare reform legislation in 1972, he never abandoned the goal of welfare reform. Over the next year, work was done internally at HEW on welfare reform proposals,[48] and as late as 1974, Nixon said in his state of the union address that he would reopen the welfare reform debate; he had Secretary of Health, Education, and Welfare Caspar Weinberger working the problem through once again when he resigned.

NIXON'S LEGACIES

Nixon does not appear to have been more intimately involved in the details of welfare reform than was Roosevelt in the case of industrial recovery. Yet the development of welfare reform policy in his administration was very much his process; the Family Assistance Plan was his plan. It reflected his sense of both historical and political opportunity. He had picked the people, given them their theme, and, working with his advisers, intervened where necessary. Finally, when fundamental disagreement remained, Nixon took charge and made final decisions. Though he abandoned FAP and it failed to gain full congressional approval, the eight-year period from 1968 to 1976 brought changes in the states of welfare policies and programs that had an important influence on the opportunities Jimmy Carter would face.

In the broadest terms, these changes reflected the receding crisis in American politics. A divisive war had ended, a significant proportion of the black population was making economic progress, and the ghettoes were quiet. Radical social protest had diminished and the 1973 death of George Wiley, the charismatic leader of the National Welfare Rights Organization, had helped send welfare advocacy into decline. Within the area of welfare itself, changes had also occurred that lowered the passionate pitch of debate that had characterized FAP. Much more, for example, had been learned about the nature of poverty and the poor and about the likely consequences of welfare reform. The large-scale experiments with negative income tax schemes seemed to show that relatively high-benefit levels would not provoke large-scale reductions in work effort by male heads of families, as conservative critics of welfare reform feared. Other studies showed that, for the most part, poverty was a temporary phenomenon; for a majority of recipients, welfare "dependency" was not a way of life but a cushion against temporary adversity. Moreover, changes within the welfare system—including the passage of the Supplemental Security Income Program, the expansion of Medicaid, the enactment of an earned income tax credit, and a general increase in benefit levels—made the plight of the poor seem less urgent than before. The AFDC rolls, which had doubled between 1967 and 1971, had not expanded since 1972. As a result of such changes, Richard Nathan argued that the combination of AFDC and a reformed food stamps program operated much like a negative income tax, so structural reform had already been achieved. Indeed, by the time of Carter's election, some policy analysts were going so far as to conclude that poverty in the United States had been virtually eliminated. Although such statements were exaggerations, considerable progress in providing income supports for the poor had been made.

The backlash against welfare system "generosity," however, and anger at fraud and abuse were becoming emotional issues with many legislators just as the existence of grinding poverty and hunger had provided emotional fuel for the welfare reform debate in the 1960s and early 1970s. At the same time, dissatisfaction with the cost and structure of the existing system continued to mount, especially among state and local officials who had to contend with both the fiscal pressures of administering their share of the welfare programs and the difficulties of coping with the tangled regulations. Perverse incentives, inequities, inefficiency, program administration high in cost and low in quality, unaccountability, and stigmatization of those forced to deal with the system continued, and in some ways worsened.

Most observers of the welfare debate contended that such changes favored the passage of a comprehensive welfare reform bill. Indeed, J. Glen Beall, Jr., a senator and former congressman (D–Md.), waxed so euphoric over them that he declared in the spring of 1977 that "the political climate for achieving comprehensive welfare reform would seem to be almost perfect."[49] Beall concluded that "the degree to which the welfare system is reformed will depend on the extent of the Carter proposal and the effectiveness with which the Administration can bring the presently unaligned forces [that is, congressional moderates] together in support of the President's plan"[50]—a point that Senator Ribicoff seconded. As Ribicoff explained in May 1976, "I don't believe that we are ever going to have welfare reform until we have a courageous, farsighted President who is willing to go to the American people to explain it, and go to the Congress to fight for it."[51]

Other policy analysts (including one of the authors) who were favorably disposed to comprehensive reform stressed other aspects of the altered welfare debate. In a paper prepared in 1975, Laurence E. Lynn, Jr., suggested that "the sum total of experience with the existing system and the results of research on poverty have irrevocably altered the context of the welfare reform debate in a manner that should be favorable to welfare reform. Perhaps the most difficult obstacle to welfare reform in the future will be budgetary. Welfare reform can win broad support only if most existing recipients, as well as states that administer welfare programs, are not made worse off under the reformed system."[52] Observing that the resulting costs could well be in excess of $11 billion, Lynn concluded, "Though cost is not an insurmountable obstacle to significant reform, the momentum to overcome it is likely to be more easily generated during a change of Administrations by a new President personally concerned about the issue."[53]

Advocates for incremental reform, however, assessed changes in the welfare debate in a different light. Richard Nathan and Martin Anderson, for example, contended that the case for comprehensive reform had weakened because the system had become more generous and the political polarization surrounding welfare reform continued. Anderson delineated the continued, acute political dilemmas confronting Carter's reform effort by observing:

> In the next election, [the President] is the one who will have
> to answer his opponent's charge that he voted for welfare "re-
> form" that lowered welfare benefits for hundreds of thousands,

or even millions, of poor people, or that subjected welfare recipients to higher tax rates approaching confiscatory levels, or that added billions of dollars to the welfare budget. He is the one who will have to explain why so many more Americans went on welfare, why so many of them stopped working, and, perhaps, why so many of their marriages broke up.

Politically, it's all very risky.[54]

Jimmy Carter was soon to find that out for himself.

CHAPTER THREE

The
Welfare "Mess":
The Cast
and Chorus

"The reason Congress has found it difficult to find a plan that provides universal benefits at a level regarded as reasonable, that preserves work incentives, and that is not vastly more expensive than President Nixon's proposals is that no such plan exists or can be devised: These objectives are mutually inconsistent."
—Henry Aaron, *Why Is Welfare So Hard to Reform?* (1973)

ON JANUARY 25, 1977, AT ONE OF HIS FIRST PRESIDENTIAL PRESS CONferences, a beaming Jimmy Carter announced that Joseph A. Califano, Jr., the man he had selected to run the Department of Health, Education, and Welfare, would produce a comprehensive plan to reform the welfare system by May 1. Despite the issue's political volatility, Carter had made welfare reform a key component of his domestic program in his campaign against Gerald Ford the previous year. Carter's interest in welfare reform dated back to his days as governor of Georgia, when he had become concerned about the inadequacy of welfare benefits, the disparity in payment levels between different states, and many of the anti-work, anti-family provisions built into the welfare system. In the early 1970s, this concern prompted him to support the Family Assistance Plan (FAP), the Nixon administration's welfare reform plan, even though not a single other southern governor supported it.

Just as Carter had a longstanding interest in welfare reform, Califano seemed an appropriate choice to organize the attempt to restructure and simplify the patchwork of programs that constituted the welfare system. After a meteoric rise in the Defense Department (where, in the space of three years, he went from special assistant to the general counsel to Secretary McNamara's special assistant in 1964), Califano was appointed President Johnson's special assistant for domestic affairs in 1965 at the age of thirty-four. Soon known as LBJ's "alter ego" in domestic affairs

35

and the "deputy president for domestic affairs," Califano was assigned primary responsibility for organizing the Great Society programs into one coherent strategy. His former boss, Robert McNamara, claimed that Califano was "the man who, next to the President, has contributed more than any other individual to the conception, formulation, and implementation of the program for the Great Society."[1] Although Califano had only dealt with welfare reform through the short-lived Johnson Income Maintenance Task Force in 1968, his experience in organizing complex domestic programs seemed a good preparation for Carter's attempt to reform the welfare system. Well versed in congressional politics, and with a reputation for political acumen, Califano seemed an especially suitable choice to lead the hazardous trek through the welfare reform minefield.

Finally, Califano did not believe that liberal sentiments were incompatible with managerial efficiency. Early in his tenure at HEW he would remark:

> I'd like to demonstrate to the American people that HEW can be managed. . . . The importance of that is to show that we can make investments in social services and social programs for the most vulnerable in society in an efficient way, as well as a compassionate way, that it is worthwhile, that government can indeed do a lot of these things and that government should indeed do a lot of these things because if you don't do it through the commonweal, it won't get done by an isolated charity. Some of these problems are too big. That I'd like to demonstrate.[2]

Califano seemed to have lost none of the zeal of the sixties. As he remarked at one of his first staff meetings, "We've got to pick up where we were in 1968. We've lost a lot of time."

BACKGROUND: THE WELFARE SYSTEM IN 1977

In January 1977, the welfare system was composed of a plethora of programs that had sprung up at different moments over the previous four decades, more typically as a result of political or economic exigencies than from any clear consensus about federal welfare goals. Aid to Dependent Children, for example, the forerunner of Aid to Families with Dependent Children (AFDC), was established by Congress in 1935 in the midst of the Depression. The Food Stamp Program, on the other hand, was not enacted at the federal level until 1964, when America "rediscovered" poverty. The piecemeal manner in which these programs had been established permitted fundamental inconsistencies and inefficiencies, commonly lumped together under the label "the welfare mess."

(A glossary of key welfare terms appears in Appendix 1.) Although the 1970s witnessed several significant efforts at improving the system, there was widespread agreement that serious problems remained, including inadequacies and inequities in benefit levels, weak work incentives and strong incentives for family breakups, administrative cumbersomeness, increasing caseloads and costs, and the need for local and state fiscal relief.

THE CRITICS

Critics of the system were united in their distaste for the "mess," but they were by no means united in their views of "reform," which meant quite different things to different people. The political spectrum of welfare reform included powerful congressional conservatives, welfare rights organizations, labor unions, academicians, administrators of welfare programs, and financially hard-pressed state and local governments.

Within the Democrat-controlled Congress, conservatives headed the two key committees through which welfare reform would have to pass. Senator Russell Long, chairman of the Senate Finance Committee, and Congressman Al Ullman (D–Ore.), chairman of the House Ways and Means Committee, agreed that the current welfare system contained few incentives to move people from welfare to work,[3] and they were adamantly opposed to cash assistance being "doled" out to welfare recipients who were capable of working (other than on a temporary, emergency basis). Despite his flirtation with the first version of FAP, Long was skeptical of grand welfare reform schemes, preferring to proceed with pilot demonstration projects, and was insistent that any reform effort include strong work incentives and a heavy emphasis on job creation, if necessary by direct intercession of the federal government. During Califano's confirmation hearings (January 13, 1977), Long opened the session by informing the incoming secretary, "I believe that we have worked enough in this vineyard of trying to help disadvantaged people so that by now we should know that we do something useful for society in return for adequate compensation, or even in some cases compensation that may overpay that person for his contribution, rather than the demoralizing alternative of simply paying a person to sit idly doing nothing."[4]

In company with some congressional representatives and a large segment of the American public, Long believed welfare reform meant cutting the welfare rolls rather than expanding them. Disillusionment over the increased costs and caseloads of the welfare programs had intensified during the early 1970s, primarily because of the expansion of Aid to

Families with Dependent Children. Originally envisioned as a program that would serve dependent children whose parents were disabled, ill, widowed, or between jobs, AFDC was increasingly perceived as a repository for women who had illegitimate children or whose husbands had deserted or divorced them. The rapid growth of female-headed families on the welfare rolls led Long and others to question whether the welfare system was encouraging the breakup of families and helping to create a "welfare class" that continued from one generation to the next.

Like Long, Congressman Ullman was attracted to large public service employment programs as an alternative to this cash "dole" for able-bodied adults. Shortly after Califano took office, Ullman wrote him:

> Income support programs should clearly differentiate those who are expected to work outside the home from those who are not. . . . The dual track, Manpower / Public Assistance approach embodied in the REACH proposal [which Ullman developed in the early seventies] emphasizes employment opportunities rather than cash assistance for those expected to work. . . . [As of] yet, however, [we have not] fully committed ourselves through enactment of the necessary legislation or the provision of adequate funds to the goal of getting low income Americans into adequate employment. The next attempt at welfare reform must make this commitment.[5]

In contrast to the concerns of Long and Ullman, state and local representatives (such as the National Governors' Association, the National Conference of State Legislators, the National Conference of Mayors, and the National Association of Counties) were preoccupied with a very pragmatic issue—fiscal relief. Even before Carter's arrival in office, the National Governors' Conference had pressured him for greater federal financing of welfare. In June 1976 the governors had declared:

> Cash assistance to the poor is not bankrupting the Nation, but it is creating severe inequitable pressures on many States, counties, and cities. In fiscal 1977 combined federal, state, and local costs of public assistance are projected to be about $25 billion. Medical assistance expenditures and food stamps raise this figure to $47 billion, or 12 to 13 percent of total public sector expenditures. As a result of existing federal law and policies, particularly the lack of a uniform minimum benefit, this burden is not equally distributed. At the present time total per capita welfare costs range in the States from $44 to $267. The variation in state and local shares is even greater, as the federal government pays a higher percentage of costs in those States with the lowest per capita expenditures.

It is already clear in some States which are coming closest to meeting minimum needs that the costs of the attempt are too large a burden on state and local resources. In some counties more than 50 percent of county revenue is devoted to welfare purposes. This burden must be assumed by the federal tax base if we are to reduce inequitable pressures on narrow state and local tax bases.[6]

The governors, however, were not a lone voice crying in the wilderness: they had an articulate spokesman in freshman Senator Daniel Moynihan (D–N.Y.), one of the chief sponsors of FAP while an aide in Nixon's White House, who was now chairman of the Senate Finance Subcommittee on Public Assistance, in which hearings on any welfare reform legislation would occur before reaching the full committee.

State and local governments were also sympathetic to the needs of their administrators. The ad hoc development of the welfare system had created an administrative tangle that was exceedingly complex, duplicative, and burdensome for both welfare workers and recipients alike. Each of the ten or so major welfare programs, for example, had its own rules and regulations even though they often served the same recipients. Not surprisingly this administrative cumbersomeness created high error and fraud rates, especially in the AFDC program, which was widely decried as being loaded with "welfare cheaters" who were underreporting their incomes. Welfare administrators wanted a redrawn, consolidated system with uniform eligibility criteria, which would greatly simplify the evaluation of recipient needs for case workers and lessen the stigma associated with applying for welfare. As the American Public Welfare Association editorialized about the reform effort during the spring of 1977:

> Extensive federal regulation within each program has curtailed the ability of states and localities to respond to special circumstances existing in their respective areas. The unnecessarily complicated procedures by which eligibility and payment level are determined have contributed to relatively high error rates in program administration. This, in turn, has led to strained federal-state relations. . . . The rise in [program] participation also tends to reinforce the popular misconception that ineligibles and "cheaters" comprise a significant segment of welfare participants. . . . These concerns should in some way be addressed in any systematic reform that may be adopted. Administrative simplicity and efficiency should be emphasized. Programmatic costs should be equitably distributed across the nation. Perhaps, above all, the income maintenance system should be *accountable* to both the public-at-large and the population to

be served. The public should be confident that dollars are well spent. . . . Those who receive benefits should be assured that the system is responsive to their needs.[7]

Finally, the labor unions and welfare rights groups also had notions of how welfare should be reformed. The AFL-CIO felt that welfare reform should include "a full employment policy, including a permanent public service jobs program," but they maintained that the welfare portion of the program "should be entirely federally financed and provide a payment raised as quickly as possible to not less than the poverty level, with living cost adjustments."[8] Welfare rights groups had traditionally been critical of work requirements as well as of large, low-wage public service job programs, feeling that such programs were "makework" and punitive. On raising benefits and indexing them to inflation, however, the welfare groups were in full agreement with the unions. Welfare rights representatives felt that the single most important objective of welfare reform should be the raising of benefit levels. The National Welfare Rights Organization, for example, had argued for years for a basic benefit pegged to the Bureau of Labor Statistics' lower-income family budget. These groups also complained of unjustifiable variations in benefit levels,* noting, for example, that in only fifteen to twenty states could a female-headed family of four with no other income receive enough from AFDC and food stamps to be lifted out of poverty.[9] Finally, welfare recipients and unions alike condemned the gaps in existing coverage, which excluded huge segments of the poor population from receiving benefits other than food stamps. (In 1975, 46 percent of the poor population lived in households that were ineligible for cash assistance under the two major cash assistance programs, AFDC and SSI. The ineligible poor fell primarily into three groups: single individuals, childless couples, and families headed by able-bodied males. The unemployed father [UF] provisions of AFDC extended only to roughly half the states.)[10]

The mutually contradictory demands of these various groups constituted a policymaking dilemma of major proportions: Lowering the cost of welfare and cutting the welfare rolls was not compatible with expanding coverage to the working poor and raising benefit levels. Complaints about demeaning "means tests" collided with complaints about inefficient targeting of welfare payments to the middle class. The demand for state and local fiscal relief ran afoul of efforts to reduce federal expenditures. Computerized systems to combat fraud similarly did not square

---

*In Mississippi, for example, the benefits for a family of four amounted to only 13 percent of the poverty threshold, while in Wisconsin they were as high as 90 percent.

with the demand for more personal, individualized administrative procedures.

Finally, the prospects for welfare reform were complicated by an inherent structural dilemma with welfare programs in general. Often described as the "tough triangle," this dilemma can be illustrated by a diagram of a simple negative income tax scheme (NIT), one of the most widely advocated solutions to the welfare problem, originally championed by conservative economist Milton Friedman in the early 1960s. Negative income tax proposals would use the reverse side of the tax system to replace the existing cash assistance and in-kind transfer programs, with benefits ideally phasing out at the tax entry point.* All recipients would receive an annual guaranteed income; a portion of benefits would be reduced for each dollar earned.

A negative income tax scheme with a 50 percent benefit reduction rate, for example, might have the parameters shown in Figure 1. In this diagram, a family with no earnings would receive an annual income of $4,000. If a member of the family began working, benefits would decline at 50 cents for every extra dollar earned until benefits were phased out at the welfare "breakeven" point—in this case $8,000.

Now suppose one finds these parameters objectionable. Suppose, for example, that one reasonably wishes to raise the $4,000 annual benefit the family is receiving to the poverty line (roughly $6,500). As point A moves up, the slope of AB becomes much steeper, resulting in high

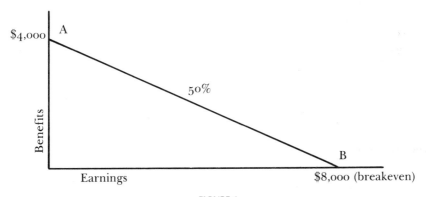

FIGURE 1
Sample Benefit Structure for an NIT for a Two-Parent Family with Children

*The point at which an individual or family would begin to pay federal taxes.

benefit reduction rates, which create strong work disincentives. On the other hand, if B is moved out to lessen the slope of AB and the benefit reduction rate, then welfare benefits end up being doled out to the middle class. Furthermore, moving line AB up even a small amount greatly increases the cost of welfare reform, which would seem politically suicidal, particularly at a time when states were vociferously demanding fiscal relief. Lowering line AB, of course, reduces the payments to what most people would consider an inhumane level for the millions of recipients. As of 1977, no welfare reform alternative had emerged that addressed these fundamental conflicts to everyone's satisfaction.

ALTERNATIVES FOR REFORM IN 1977

In 1976, there were few attempts to reform the welfare system, but much discussion about the most appropriate means of doing so. After the demise of FAP in 1972, no major welfare reform proposals were given serious legislative consideration, although a host of proposals were put forward over the next five years. The bulk of these proposals envisioned folding in a number of existing programs under the auspices of a negative income tax and a guaranteed minimum income. The most fully developed were two proposals put forth in late 1974—one by the Subcommittee on Fiscal Policy of the Joint Economic Committee, under the direction of Congresswoman Martha Griffiths (D–Mich.), and a second by Caspar Weinberger, secretary of HEW, at President Gerald Ford's request. The Griffiths plan received some brief congressional consideration in both the House and the Senate in 1976 but ultimately died, while the Weinberger program, the Income Supplement Program, was rejected by Ford in favor of working toward some short-term incremental improvements.

The concept of the negative income tax, however, still held tremendous sway among academic economists and within HEW. Proponents of this approach pointed to the results of a series of massive government-sponsored experiments conducted in the late sixties and early seventies, testing the impact of an NIT on recipients' work efforts.[11] These experiments seemed to suggest that a guaranteed annual income did not create intolerable work disincentives. One HEW report, for example, described the results of the New Jersey Graduated Work Incentive Experiment as "clearly indicating that a negative income tax plan with a basic benefit as high as the official poverty line will not trigger large scale reductions in work effort among male heads of families."[12] Advocates of the negative income tax also cited the recently released results of the Michigan longitudinal study of five thousand families, which indicated that the poor were a transitory group, with different families and individuals falling below the poverty level from one year to the next. Thus NIT proponents claimed that the relatively generous cash assistance benefits that an NIT provided would simply relieve those temporarily in need and not create a large and permanent welfare underclass, as was often feared.

In spite of such optimistic claims, the concept of a negative income tax remained difficult to sell to Congress and the public, who associated "cash assistance" with the "dole." Consequently, would-be welfare reformers began to look at alternative reform strategies.[13] These strategies for the most part coalesced around "job creation efforts." As the departing HEW assistant secretary for planning and evaluation, Bill Morrill, stated in an April 1976 survey of the income security system, eight months prior to the arrival of the Carter administration, "We are witnessing a revived interest in so-called 'job creation' strategies, i.e., programs that would have the government create jobs in the private and public sectors through tax forgiveness and new positive expenditures. These programs are often advanced as alternatives to existing welfare and unemployment insurance (UI) programs."[14]

Whereas income and need were the sole factors distinguishing recipients under NIT proposals, job creation strategies called for the grouping of recipients into tracks based on their abilities to work—with the number of tracks varying from proposal to proposal. The most prominent multiple-track proposal, developed by Tom Joe* and termed "triple track," divided welfare eligibles into three groups: families not expected to work (that is, families with disabled or aged heads or single-parent families with preschool children), families where the head was expected to work, and the working poor (persons who worked full time but still earned less than the poverty level). Families not expected to work would receive a basic income guarantee with a benefit reduction dollar for dollar on all earned income (that is, a 100 percent marginal tax rate). Unemployed family heads capable of working would receive regular unemployment insurance benefits roughly equivalent to the basic guarantee level for twenty-six to thirty-nine weeks while they sought a job; any earned income during this period would be taxed at approximately 60 percent. If the would-be worker had not found a job after twenty-six or thirty-nine weeks, he or she would then register for special unemployment benefits, which would be income tested to assure they were directed to needy workers; workers would have to accept a job offer in public or private employment or risk termination of benefits. To help ensure that there would be jobs available, the Community Employ-

---

*Joe was a private consultant in Washington who had directed the University of Chicago's Center for the Study of Welfare Policy and worked during the development of FAP as a special assistant to the HEW undersecretary. Joe had close ties with organized labor.

ment and Training Act (CETA) program would be expanded and re-targeted on low-income workers. The third track for the working poor would essentially consist of a tax credit—like, for example, the existing earned income tax credit (EITC)—to help supplement low incomes.

In spite of the widespread interest in the kind of comprehensive reform implied by NIT and job creation strategies, critics of the existing welfare system by no means agreed upon the desirability of making any kind of sweeping changes to the system. In fact, a sizeable group argued that the most serious problems could be cleared up by incremental reforms of one sort or another. Conservative "incrementalists" advocated a "curtailment" strategy that would reduce eligibility and benefit levels; others advocated "minor incrementalism" that would emphasize improved management; still others emphasized substantive structural reforms, such as the creation of housing allowances, expansion of the earned income tax credit, and mandating AFDC-UF nationally. Disagreeing over the particulars of reform, incrementalists were united in the belief that most existing programs should be maintained and that any comprehensive reform would prove politically impossible.

THE GENESIS OF A REFORM POLICY

Carter's statements during his presidential campaign left considerable leeway for his administration's approach to welfare reform. In a speech to the National Governors' Conference on July 6, 1976, Carter outlined a rough vision of what a restructured welfare system might look like:

> Throughout my campaign, I have stressed the urgent need for a complete overhaul of our nation's welfare system. . . .
> We should have a simpler national welfare program, with one fairly uniform standard of payment, adjusted to the extent feasible for cost of living differences by areas and with strong work incentives built in. In no case should the level of benefit make not working more attractive than working. And we should have welfare rules that strengthen families rather than divide families. Local governments should not be burdened with the cost of welfare, and my goal would also include the phased reduction of the states' share as soon as that is financially feasible.[15]

On several other occasions Carter had outlined a view of welfare reform that went beyond these elements and resembled the triple-track approach advocated privately to him by Tom Joe. Joe's approach was also warmly endorsed by Carter's close friend and adviser Jim Parham, who had served under Carter as director of welfare for Georgia. In a major address on urban policy in April 1976, Carter stated flatly that "the system lumps together dissimilar categories of poor people. . . . We must recognize that there are three distinct categories of poor people—the unemployable poor, the employable but jobless poor, and the working poor."[16] In a policy briefing several months later, on August 16, Carter outlined a three-tiered structure for targeting federal assistance to the needy. Carter seemed particularly attracted to triple track as a way of keeping the number of payments from a "welfare" agency to a minimum:

> [First, we need] to remove those people who are able to work from the system altogether and to provide them with employment assistance rather than the dole. These persons need to be given manpower opportunities, matched with a job, offered a job, and be treated outside the so-called welfare system itself.
>
> Second, we need to deal with the working poor—those who presently work full-time but whose incomes fall far below the poverty level should also be outside the welfare system itself, and helped perhaps through the tax structure.
>
> Third, those who cannot work full-time ought to be treated with respect, with compassion, with understanding, given encouragement to work part-time if they are able. Any program to help these people should always insure that it is never more attractive for someone who can work to stay on the welfare rolls instead of working either part-time or full-time.[17]

These broadly stated views set the stage for meetings of Carter's transition teams during November and December 1976. The two transition teams concerned with welfare reform (for HEW and OMB) quickly narrowed the options under consideration to a negative income tax (similar to the Griffiths plan) and Tom Joe's triple-track proposal. On December 9 a synopsis of the options and a presentation on incremental versus comprehensive reforms was shown to the president-elect.[18] Carter refrained, however, from selecting an option at the briefing. Bert Carp, who was the incoming deputy director of Carter's Domestic Policy Staff and was heading up the HEW transition effort, recalls:

> We had a very short and not very satisfactory meeting with the president; we only had an hour to go over the whole HEW transition effort. He very clearly wanted something comprehensive and that motivated our subsequent work. We all knew that an incremental bill would be much easier to pass and we told the president that. He felt that he had campaigned on this issue, he had made speeches to the governors, the mayors, the

poor people and everyone else, and if the Congress wasn't going to pass a comprehensive bill, that was their responsibility, but he had a responsibility to propose it. It was a campaign promise.

According to a second source present at the briefing, Carter did "blanch at some of the cost estimates of comprehensive reform;* his feeling seemed to be that we should be able to do it for less. We never really seriously considered the options, though, because it was uncertain who would be managing HEW. Carter basically said to go back to the drawing board."

THE ACTORS ASSEMBLE†

In mid-November, President-elect Carter called Joe Califano and asked him how much time it would take to put together a plan to reform the welfare system. Califano, who was unaware that he was to be the next secretary of HEW, suggested that a plan could be prepared by May 1. On December 24, Carter announced Califano's appointment as secretary of HEW, and a few days later, at a meeting of the president-elect's future cabinet at the Smith Bagley plantation on St. Simon's Island, Georgia, the welfare reform policymaking process began to take shape. The atmosphere and attire of the meeting seemed informal and so, when Carter asked Califano for the second time when a welfare reform plan might be ready, Califano again responded with his off-the-cuff estimate of May 1. Califano did express some concern about going after welfare reform immediately. As he recalled, "I said welfare reform might have to await some level of economic recovery because we needed money for it, and Jody Powell [Carter's press secretary] promptly said, 'No, the President wants to go with welfare reform regardless of the economy.'" On January 12, Stuart Eizenstat, director of the Domestic Policy Staff and Carter's chief domestic adviser, announced that the administration's internal target for a welfare reform package was May 1, although "comprehensive welfare legislation might not be proposed until fiscal year 1979."[19] On January 25, Carter upped the commitment to have a welfare reform plan ready by May 1 by publicly announcing that date as his own deadline. Califano, who never imagined that his offhand private estimate might become part of an official administration timetable, began to scramble to organize a welfare reform process.[20] Califano had mixed feelings about the deadline. As he recalled:

*Very rough estimates of the cost of the Griffiths plan were between $15 and $19 billion. The Joe plan was thought to be even more expensive.

†A list of key participants and a chronology of events appear in Appendices 2 and 3.

> I was bothered by the time deadline. . . . It's a very complicated subject . . . but my fundamental feeling was that a President has at most the first two sessions of Congress in which to get his legislation passed. No significant legislation is going to pass in the last half of his term. I felt we had to get it done to get it passed and that's why I wanted to do it so fast.

Califano was pressed, however, for more than time. Since occasional public statements from Carter indicated that he expected a plan from both Califano and Ray Marshall, the incoming secretary of labor, it was unclear to what extent Califano had been given control of the impending process.* In the rush of activity that occurred during the first days of the administration, the issue of how the welfare debate should be handled was very much an open one. On January 21, for example, after reading a paper by Tom Joe on the triple-track approach to welfare reform, Carter nebulously responded by directing Eizenstat to "get Califano, Marshall, Kreps [Juanita Kreps, secretary of commerce], you, and Tom Joe together and begin working on the welfare proposal. Keep me informed, include Congress."[21]

Before Califano could begin to interact with other departments, however, he had to get his own department in order, which he started to do in mid-January by appointing Henry Aaron as assistant secretary for planning and evaluation—a key position in welfare policymaking. Aaron, a senior fellow at the Brookings Institution who had little previous experience in government,† was chosen over other candidates with more administrative experience and familiarity with HEW—reportedly because Califano wanted a top-notch economist to establish a shop on the order of McNamara's "whiz kids."

Aaron was known to be unenthusiastic about comprehensive cash assistance proposals and to favor incremental reforms of existing programs. In Aaron's view, the American public exhibited a deeply rooted preference for programs with specific aims—like food stamps or unemployment insurance—over any kind of general-purpose income transfer program. He concluded, therefore, that the political climate engendered by this preference would permit a larger overall income transfer through a range of limited-purpose programs than through any single cash program.

---

*In his first White House address to the nation, on February 1, Carter explained, for example, that "the Secretary of Labor and the Secretary of HEW and others have already begun a review of the entire welfare system. They will, of course, work with Congress to develop proposals."

†Aaron had worked as a staff economist for the Council of Economic Advisers during 1966 and 1967.

Aaron chose Dr. Michael Barth to be deputy assistant secretary for income security policy analysis, with responsibility for coordinating the welfare reform effort. Aaron saw his own role as "bringing a certain perspective to the subject and also acting as a translator between the technical staff and the political people who are non-technically trained—people on the sixth floor like the secretary, the undersecretary, and the secretary's personal assistants." Barth, on the other hand, was responsible for dealing with the public and with other governmental agencies, and for overseeing—rather than directing—work of the Income Security Policy (ISP) staff. Barth had come to HEW from OEO in 1973 and soon became the director of the Office of ISP, with responsibility for organizing and directing the staff work. Of his new position as deputy assistant secretary, Barth commented: "I did not perceive my role as only 100 percent analytic because I was in a different kind of situation than I was in before; it was a lot more judgmental. . . . I would spend an enormous amount of time outside of the office giving talks, briefings, and briefing the secretary so it was just impossible to be that close to the analysis." Barth was also aware that he brought to his new job a certain liability from his old job:

> I was very sensitive about my role in the Income Supplement Program [the NIT-type plan Barth had played a key role in developing under Caspar Weinberger] because I knew I was suspect with Aaron. I had been associated with a specific proposal, and Aaron and I had a very candid discussion about that when he was considering whether to appoint me. I understood that was a problem, and we agreed that one of the things I would have to do was to be very careful to be objective and not let my prior biases, or whatever you want to call them, guide the process.

Barth was not the only person at HEW, however, who was associated with a specific welfare reform proposal; virtually the entire ISP staff (consisting of six or so senior members, including Director John Todd)* had worked on the Income Supplement Program. The staff was quick to admit that they did lean toward a negative income tax solution. As one staff member explained:

> When we came into the welfare game none of us had any predisposition, anything to gain by it. But when you're an analyst and you look at the same issues for four years, you come to a point of view. And I think that if I had people working for me

*Todd had worked under Barth during 1973 and 1974 and taken over for him as director in 1975, when Barth left to spend a year at the University of Wisconsin.

who had worked on something for four years and didn't have
any idea what they thought was good, I'd want to get a new set.

In spite of the staff's admitted predispositions, their analytic capability
was widely respected. As Frank Raines, a member of the Domestic Policy
Staff who would be helping guide the reform effort, commented: "The
ISP staff is very good. They're old veterans. Mike Barth had been
around a long time; Todd had been around a long time. They were
known as the 'wizards' around Washington. . . . There was no question
about their substantive capabilities."

Following the completion of the Income Supplement Program in late
1974 and its subsequent rejection by Gerald Ford, the ISP office had
fallen into a state of comparative inactivity, relegated for the most part to
examining broad conceptual questions divorced from political reality.
(During the spring of 1976, for example, as part of a review of the
department's activities, ISP staff had performed such a broad examination of the income security system that it came to be labelled facetiously
as "state of the world" among staff members.) Thus, the staff looked
forward to working on welfare reform in 1977 with considerable enthusiasm. As one staff member remarked, "It was a period of real excitement. I mean, we'd sat in this office for a couple of years and had
literally done nothing except answer letters from the American people."

The enthusiasm of the ISP staff for the work ahead was echoed at the
Department of Labor (DOL),* where a new staff was arriving that pos-
sessed considerably more expertise in welfare reform than the Department had traditionally held. In particular, the new outspoken assistant
secretary for policy evaluation and research, Arnold Packer, had strong
views on welfare reform and was an old veteran of welfare debates.† In
1973, Packer had written one of the first proposals laying out a job
creation alternative (for the Griffiths subcommittee).[22] Packer's paper,
"Categorical Public Employment Guarantees: A Proposed Solution to
the Poverty Problem," essentially spelled out a two-tier income support
system that would combine most in-kind aid programs. In a March-April
1974 article in *Challenge* magazine, Packer elaborated on this paper:

> The solution to the problems of welfare and the working
> poor is to provide jobs for those who can work, support for

---

*Secretary of Labor Marshall gave the welfare reform effort a high priority and, in a
February 8 memo, he assigned Assistant Secretary Arnold Packer responsibility for interagency coordination, congressional and interest group liaison, and interaction with
Domestic Council staff; Packer was also given primary responsibility for data collection,
model-building, and estimates of the gross and net budget costs of various alternatives.

†Packer served as chief economist at the Senate Budget Committee before coming to DOL.

those who can't work, and some combination of work and support for those who can work only some of the time.

The proposal's keystone is the guarantee of a full-time job for
one person in every family. Every family that contains one or
more children would be entitled to one job paying one-half the
median family income. . . . No other options would be guaranteed to families that contain two able-bodied adults of working
age.

The same guarantee of a full-time job would also apply to
single-parent (primarily female-headed) families. . . . The single head of a family with children could also choose, if he or she
preferred, a guaranteed half-time job paying three-eighths the
median income. . . . Both half-time and full-time jobs would be
considered fulfilled under the same conditions: when the earnings of one family member or the total unearned income received by the family exceeded one-half the median income.

These two options—full-time or half-time employment—
would be the only alternatives open to single-parent families
unless there were preschool children. Single-parent families
with preschool children could choose to forego both work options and elect, instead, to receive a welfare payment.[23]

Packer's proposal was similar to triple track in that it categorized the
welfare population into those who should work and those who should
not, but this design did not include a tax credit and so, in effect, the
"working poor" track was eliminated. (He subsequently endorsed the
use of the EITC.) Also unlike triple track, Packer's proposal did not have
an elaborate extended unemployment insurance system, nor would it
provide training stipends to recipients for whom a job could not be
found in private or public employment. In place of these assurances,
Packer flatly declared that we should guarantee a job to at least one
person in every family. Of a lesser order of importance, Packer's proposal also let the aged, blind, and disabled keep some additional earnings
rather than taxing them at 100 percent, as in triple track.

Packer and triple-track advocates were united, however, in their
opposition to the universal treatment that an NIT extended to the poor
population. As Packer saw it, the NIT rested on unrealistic economics:

There was a certain amount of bloodless analysis by economists
who had been in this debate for many years and come to the
negative income tax view. By bloodless, I mean not trying to
answer the question, the moral question, which in my mind is
predominant here. That is, is this a society that can take a man
or a woman who has family responsibilities and say, you're not
worth more than five or six thousand dollars a year and still

expect that family to be stable or that a family member would work at that level? That is, in my judgment, the minimum wage is satisfactory for a kid who is trying to make some money on the side but there is a moral issue as to whether the economy is appropriate if it can't give people who want to work, who have family responsibilities, an opportunity to make some sort of decent living. There was a tendency among economists not to deal with those issues, to get lost in a lot of economics, numbers, efficiency, and, well, a lot of bullshit as far as I'm concerned.

Packer's determination to keep working-age adults away from the welfare system was not simply a moral one. He felt too that the jobs program would make an essential political difference in the way the new program was perceived. As he explained:

With an economist cash is cash—you don't care where you get it. But *people* do care where they get it. In fact, it's another mathematical model compared to empirical reality. If recipients are assisted by taking a job or money from an earned income tax credit, they feel different about the income than if it comes in the form of a check from the government.

A third agency that was expected to play a role in the welfare deliberations was the president's Domestic Policy Staff (DPS). The role of Bert Carp* and his staff would be to help clarify to the agencies the president's intentions in the welfare debate and to help mediate and move the welfare debate in directions that were politically feasible. After Califano assumed office, however, a stand-off attitude developed between HEW and DPS. Califano's own experiences in the White House had left him deeply suspicious of overzealous White House aides, and he let it be known that the White House staff would not be allowed to dilute his control of HEW. As Califano explained:

Nixon did severe damage with his concept of such a large White House staff. It's a disaster for government. The programs are too complicated to operate from the White House and all the president does is create another bureaucracy for himself. . . .
By and large the people in HEW were much brighter than the people on the White House staff. They were much brighter and maybe more arrogant. . . . I wouldn't let the White House

---

*Carp was deputy director under Stuart Eizenstat. Carp had worked as legislative counsel for Mondale while he was in the Senate, and had some exposure to welfare issues during the two years he worked in the Office of General Counsel at HEW (1968–1970). Carp favored an incremental reform strategy that utilized tax credits to create incentives for employers to hire welfare recipients.

staff come in except through a couple of people. We ran that ship in the early days and when they did come in I raised hell about it.

Frank Raines, a member of the Domestic Policy Staff, argued that Califano's protective attitude was unlikely to facilitate a quick settlement of the welfare reform debate:

> The Secretary of HEW established a rule that nobody from his department should deal with anybody from the White House without Ben Heineman's knowledge [Califano's executive assistant]. That was Califano's notion of cabinet government. And he was quoted as saying that he wasn't going to let the White House do to him what he did to cabinet members when he was in the White House. As time moved on our role became more clear, but they didn't make it easy for us early on, especially since Ben didn't know much about welfare initially. Califano, I feel, underestimated the view that the president had in favor of cabinet government—even if we wanted to run HEW, the president wouldn't have let us.

Carter apparently felt that welfare reform should be managed in the agencies. As Bert Carp recalled, "The president didn't give us any specific guidance as to how he wanted the process handled. He viewed Califano and Marshall as the key people in putting this together."

ENTER THE CHORUS

On January 13, during his confirmation hearings, Califano announced that welfare reform legislation would be introduced in 1977 and that HEW would conduct a broad study of welfare reform with "help" from other federal agencies, Congress, and recipients and would ultimately make recommendations on reforming the system. In a draft of a memorandum to Califano on the 21st, Aaron agreed that a "benefit of [that] proposal is that it would give the department the lead in determining the course of the consulting process."[24] In a press release on January 26, Califano announced the formation of a "consulting group" on welfare reform:

> We are beginning a comprehensive study of welfare reform in a very special way. While this study will be led by the Department of Health, Education and Welfare, we intend from the beginning to involve in the preparation of our program not only other executive departments but, even more importantly, key Senate and House Committee staffs, the governors, the cities, and the counties and the state legislatures that are so intimately concerned with the problems of our welfare systems.

The Welfare "Mess"   53

... [W]e will also solicit the views of numerous private organizations and individuals who are vitally interested in welfare reform, especially including the beneficiaries of income security programs.

The work of this study group will form the basis for the recommendations that I will submit to President Carter. Those recommendations will be my responsibility and I am not asking the members to support them.[25]

The Welfare Reform Consulting Group, which was to be chaired by Assistant Secretary Aaron, had thirty members. The following institutions were originally represented: HEW, Social Security Administration, Social and Rehabilitation Service, Office of Management and Budget, Domestic Council, Senate Finance Committee, House Ways and Means Committee, National Governors' Conference, National Conference of State Legislators, National League of Cities, National Conference of Mayors, National Association of Counties, the New Coalition, the Department of Labor, the Department of the Treasury, the Department of Agriculture, the Department of Commerce, the Department of Housing and Urban Development (HUD), the Council of Economic Advisers, and a White House aide for intergovernmental affairs.

Califano had a number of reasons for establishing the consulting group besides soliciting ideas on welfare reform and seizing the lead in the reform process. Several days after his confirmation, Califano had met individually with Senator Long and Congressman Ullman, since he would be dealing with them on a wide range of issues in their capacities as chairmen of the Senate Finance Committee and House Ways and Means Committee respectively. Briefly touching upon welfare reform with both men, Califano was quickly apprised of how difficult substantive reform would prove. Ullman had staunchly opposed FAP, and his views had not changed much since that time. As he told Califano, "I'm deadset against any kind of negative income tax or guaranteed annual income. It's unworkable and a political disaster." Long was no less critical of comprehensive reform and advocated instead several experimental pilot projects. He told Califano quite frankly, "You've got to get those welfare mothers to work. . . . You test my plan and I'll give you the money to test any two of yours."[26] The consulting group was intended to defuse this kind of opposition. As Califano recalled, "There was a congressional history of ten years on this and if we didn't bring the Hill in from the first day we wouldn't have a chance." In a memorandum to President Carter, Califano similarly pointed out that "[we] expect that these deliberations will make a Cabinet consensus and congressional action easier to obtain. At the very least, these deliberations will illuminate the major points of disagreement and the critical choices you and the Congress will have to make."[27]

One major point of disagreement surfaced almost immediately: a disagreement over the composition of the consulting group. Welfare rights organizations, which emerged in the late 1960s as the voice of welfare recipients, were not content with merely having their views "solicited" and soon were demanding membership in the group. Reinforcing the beneficiaries' rage was the fact that the thirty-member panel had no low-income individuals on it, only one member of a minority, and no blacks.

Although Califano had written Carter that he was "sensitive to the importance you place on your pledge to reform the welfare system and to operate the government openly,"[28] he was firmly opposed to adding welfare rights advocates to the consulting group, as numerous HEW sources privately attested. Hale Champion, undersecretary of HEW, also objected to the inclusion of the welfare constituency and when first informed of Henry Freedman's interest* in joining the group is alleged to have protested, "No, by God, we're not having any of those people in the door!"[29] Califano frankly admitted that he felt that "the typical welfare mother who beats and screams across the table (typical is unfair—but those organizational types) lose more votes than they get." He went on to observe:

> I opposed adding recipients to the group because I thought there were so damn many other groups that would want in. I tried to draw the line at "government" for fear that once I put the welfare mothers on, then another welfare group would want on, and then [Governor] Reagan's people would want on, and the whole thing would become absolutely unwieldy. There would be public meetings in which the recipient groups could sit in, participate, and give their views. . . . This is a very difficult problem, this public versus private decision-making.

At the time of the formation of the consulting group, however, apparently no one at HEW realized that the Federal Advisory Committee Act, under which the consulting group had been constituted, mandated that "representatives of nonprofit private organizations concerned with social welfare programs, other persons with special knowledge, experience or qualifications with respect to such programs, and members of the public"[30] had to be included among the group's mem-

---

*Freedman was the director of the Center on Social Welfare Policy and Law, a research organization that performed legal advocacy for low-income people.

bership. As one high-ranking HEW official remarked, "Califano was unaware that things had changed since 1968. He didn't know that in 1977 he was required to add welfare advocates to the group." One of Aaron's assistants subsequently alerted Aaron to the problem, and Aaron advised Califano of the representation requirement. The director of Legal Services, a welfare advocacy organization, had written to Califano, offering to designate welfare representatives for the group. But as of the group's meeting, HEW had not officially conceded the right of welfare groups to representation.

At the first meeting, on February 11, the conflict came to a head. Califano opened the meeting himself with a brief welcome to the participants. He announced that he would chair an all-day public hearing on March 10 to provide a forum for a public exchange of views and that HEW would conduct a major "outreach" effort to solicit the views of the concerned public on welfare reform. Aaron then took over and described the agenda the group would pursue, flatly stating that "the group would serve as a conduit for all issues, and would not prepare recommendations or a final report."[31] The purpose of the group was, in short, to be a consulting body that would serve as a discussion group, rather than a decision-making body. Barth then briefly discussed the timetable for the issuance of discussion papers on welfare reform, and the meeting was opened for public discussion.

Welfare rights representatives present in the audience immediately bombarded the consulting group with criticism. One such representative argued, for example: "At least 50 percent of the committee [should] be current welfare recipients and their advocates. You cannot come up with a program. Only we can do that. We are professionals at being poor, at starving and suffering . . . we live like dogs."[32] Aaron acknowledged that the lack of representation by blacks was unfortunate, but nevertheless defended the makeup of the group, responding, "This is a governmental body, but we welcome and invite your participation in these meetings."[33] In response to the welfare advocates' criticism, several members of the committee (who mostly represented congressional committees and state and local lobbies on welfare reform) disavowed any intention of keeping the welfare advocates out of the debate and urged the inclusion of a few welfare recipients in the consulting group. Several HEW minority employees also attacked the composition of the group, and the only minority member of the consulting group, Arabella Martinez, who was the HEW assistant secretary designate for human development, suggested that welfare rights representatives should be added. Shortly thereafter, the one-hour meeting was adjourned.

Later that afternoon, following this embarrassing display, HEW announced that representatives of welfare recipients would be added to the group. Califano phoned the director of Legal Services to inform him that his letter had been "found" and to ask that he designate one welfare advocate for the group. The director rejected this offer and successfully negotiated for the addition of three welfare rights representatives to the consulting body: Nezzie Willis, a black welfare mother; Catherine Day-Jermany, a former welfare recipient and currently manager of paralegal training at Washington Legal Services Corporation; and Henry Freedman.

Despite the eventual addition of the welfare advocates, HEW did manage to maintain some of the original character of the consulting group as a governmental body. As John Todd recalled:

> At the beginning it was intended that there would be a group of people, all of whom were government people, from the executive and congressional branches, who would meet just to talk out the thing and find out where everybody was. Those meetings were perceived to be very important to the outside world, until it became clear that one couldn't restrict attendance in the way it was originally intended. Nor could you expect to have frank and personal discussions. So two sets of meetings were set up. One [the Friday meetings], a public set of meetings that had good attendance; press and public were encouraged to attend. The meetings were held in an auditorium and questions from the audience would always be a staple at the end—they had that kind of character and flavor to them. Then we also set up a set of meetings which we called the Monday meetings. They were a much smaller group, not opened to the public, and there were no nongovernmental people involved in the meetings.

By setting up the Monday/Friday schedule Califano managed to keep representatives of the welfare constituency out of the Monday meetings, but he was also forced to exclude the state and local lobbies,* whom he was anxious to bring into the consulting process as full partners. Aaron felt the separation of the two groups was a "necessary evil which nobody wanted," but opening the Monday meetings to representatives of state and local groups and welfare advocates would have made these meetings a matter of public record. Coming as a reluctant afterthought, the inclusion of welfare advocates in the consulting group and their exclusion from the private Monday meetings is said to have created a feeling of a

---

*State and local representation was authorized by the same clause of the U.S. Code as was welfare rights representation (42 U.S.C. 1314b).

"federal 'them' versus a nonfederal 'us.'"[34] The welfare rights representatives discovered the existence of the separate Monday group at the second public meeting of the consulting group, when they overheard members of the private group hotly discussing Monday's meeting.

CHAPTER FOUR

Cross-Signals:
HEW
and DOL

AT THE FIRST MEETING OF THE WELFARE REFORM CONSULTING GROUP ON February 11, 1977, Michael Barth described how HEW intended the policymaking process to unfold. He announced that the ISP staff would prepare five analytic papers, moving from a description of the current system and the purposes of welfare reform to a critical review of the welfare system and, finally, to a discussion of approaches for reform. The Five Papers, as they came to be known, were initially titled: "Overview of the Income Security System" (no. 1), "Purposes and Goals of the Income Security System" (no. 2), "The Low-Income Population: What We Know About It" (no. 3), "Critical Analysis of the Welfare System" (no. 4), and "General Approaches to Welfare Reform" (no. 5).

While the Five Papers were intended to be used as a basis for discussion among the consulting group, they would serve the dual purpose of helping to inform Secretary Califano, with perhaps one briefing devoted to each paper. Aaron felt that the analytic papers could also provide a means for eliciting Califano's preferences. As he observed, "The initial stage was an education stage. We felt that on this subject there was a lot of basic instruction that had to be provided to the Secretary because he didn't know much about the system . . . [and] on the five papers we also wanted to get signals from Califano and ultimately the President."

There were several aspects about the reform process, however, that troubled Aaron as well as Barth and Califano. Aaron felt that President Carter's May 1 deadline was simply unrealistic and wrote Califano that "the deadline would be extremely tight, particularly in view of the added time and staff demands of the open process now being developed."[1] As Califano began the complicated task of organizing his department, he also became concerned by the deadline and, in the month following Carter's January 20 announcement, tried to delay the May 1 date on five separate occasions. Carter flatly told him, "You just do the best you can with the time you've got."[2] (As Bert Carp recalled, "Those of us who were managing the process always thought the deadlines were too tight and consistently told the president so. . . . I think he figured that was self-serving.") Barth was concerned enough over the May 1 deadline to prepare two different schedules: a "one-option" schedule with a May 1 presentation of the secretary's preferred option and a July 1 legislation target date, and a second, multi-option schedule with a May 26 presentation of options and a September 5 legislation target date. Barth felt the May 1 schedule "allows for no slippage . . . , allows little or no time for consultation with interested parties and requires a very early narrowing of options."[3]

If there was concern over the amount of time available for formulating a welfare reform plan, there was also considerable confusion over how HEW was to interact with other agencies and with White House staff. Even what HEW was ultimately supposed to produce on May 1 was unclear. As Aaron wrote Califano about the May 1 schedule, "The process presumes naively that the department will be operating more or less on its own until, say, our initial presentation to the White House on one or a few specific options. . . . We do not yet know the intended full extent of likely interaction."[4]

When Aaron met with Califano on January 27, he sought further guidance on these issues, asking how and when the president and White House staff were to be involved in welfare reform, and whether HEW was expected to develop one proposal or a set of options. Califano was unsure and offered to check with Eizenstat. Eizenstat fended off detailing a commitment for the White House staff, however, and indicated that President Carter would make his mind up at a later date on whether he wanted one plan or a set of options.

THE EDUCATION STAGE

BRIEFING CALIFANO

In spite of the vagueness of their mandate, the ISP staff approached the first briefing with some excitement and considerable curiosity, since no one on the staff or their superiors (Aaron, Barth, and Todd) knew Califano well or had worked with him in matters of policymaking. Califano had requested the briefings to help him update his understanding of the welfare reform problem—a subject to which he had had some exposure during the Johnson years.

Califano's previous involvement in the welfare area had apparently left him with a high regard for the capacity of systems analysis to contribute to the resolution of complex social problems. In an April 1967 speech unveiling an HEW study of the number of "employables" (healthy adult males) on the welfare rolls, Califano had extolled the "startling" findings to be gotten from "systems analysis"* and had confidently predicted that such findings could lead to "abandon[ing] many old slogans and conduct[ing] our national dialogue on the basis of facts and through the prism of a total approach."[5] Fourteen months later, Califano had set up an internal Task Force on Income Maintenance to develop a "strong and imaginative [welfare reform] program,"[6] but the effort was scuttled in late 1968 once it appeared that Richard Nixon would defeat Hubert Humphrey in the upcoming presidential election. In the intervening years, Califano had developed a lucrative private practice as an attorney and, by his own admission, did not "follow [welfare issues]. . . . A hell of a lot happened and I needed a reeducation." The briefings then, Califano felt, "would be a course in welfare" that would update his understanding of welfare reform issues.

While Califano did not have a detailed understanding of the welfare system, he did approach the briefings with several notions of what a reformed system should look like. As he explained:

> I had a strong sense that we had to have a system simple enough to get the fraud and leakage out. The people of this country would not continue to pay for a system with that kind of leakage in it and that's where we came upon this national computer system. . . . I wanted a national system in effect, not just a national minimum benefit, but a whole host of standards that would make it easy to administer. . . . I thought that if we got a spanking new vision of welfare out there, we'd get better people to work on the program. . . . I thought a jobs component might help with that.
>
> Second, I had the sense that we had to give more money to poor people. Third, in terms of public education, I came to feel that it would be necessary to explode some of the myths about welfare.

The first briefing for Califano, given on February 10, one day before the first meeting of the consulting group, was introduced by Mike Barth and given by John Todd in Aaron's absence. Todd prepared the briefing on the basis of an outline of Paper 1 ("Overview of the Income Security System"), prefacing his remarks with a survey of the major areas for reform decisions. Todd then moved on to explain the history of the income security system and a taxonomy of welfare programs.

*In this case, the particular finding—really, a preliminary estimate—was that only 50,000 males, or 1 percent of those on the welfare rolls, were employable.

Todd's carefully outlined briefing, however, was not a smash success. An ISP staff member vividly recalls Califano's reaction:

> The first briefing was a disaster. It was supposed to be two hours long but it turned out that Califano only had about half an hour. He was completely, totally, absolutely bored. That's the only way to put it. He was not interested in anything that he was briefed on. Our presentation, *the* presentation, fell flat, the material fell flat.
>
> The marginal tax rate diagram [similar to Figure 1 on page 41] was the absolute, ultimate end of the meeting. I mean that's when we had to leave the room quickly.

John Todd describes what he felt went wrong in the first briefing:

> Given Califano's focus on policy issues, we were trudging through some dreary background material. For us it seems absolutely essential to understand all this before you can really have a full appreciation of the policy issues. I think people like the secretary pick up the background as they are motivated to pick it up, i.e., once they seize upon an issue of public policy where they see a genuinely difficult choice to be made which requires their attention. They're not students and they're not schooled to sit there and believe you that all this is essential and important information because eventually there is going to come a question where you're going to need it. They go backwards from the question to the information, and until you really grab their interest with a question where they understand their choice is going to make a difference, you haven't seized their attention. . . . We organized the briefings in a traditional and academic way and that's probably not the way to organize briefings for a very busy secretary.

The reaction in ISP to Califano's disinterest was that "we failed to communicate and how the devil could we do things differently so next time around we could communicate." The briefings were modestly altered in several ways. First, Aaron, who had been mostly preoccupied with matters involving Social Security, made sure to attend the briefings. Second, Aaron, Barth, and Todd began to divide up the briefings. As Todd recalls:

> I remember sitting around Hank [Aaron's] table and we would say, "if you would take the first part I can take the second," because we had this notion that he would fall asleep if one of the three of us did all the talking. Even if we weren't necessarily the expert we would usually try and share equally between the

three of us. Hank usually gave an introduction, laying out, to a certain extent, what's going on. Most of the technical information was mine although technical information was not a large fraction of the briefings.

While these stylistic changes were made in the briefings, the formal content was not greatly altered; the analysts essentially stuck to their plan of having the briefings precede circulation of the papers to the consulting group. Aaron considered revamping the briefings, which he viewed as a "short course in the welfare system," but decided against it, feeling the secretary simply did not know enough about the welfare system to make informed decisions. Aaron did not consult the secretary on whether he wanted the briefings altered, nor did Califano indicate what he wanted done differently.

THE FRIDAY MEETINGS

While preparing the briefings for Califano, ISP staff worked on two other tasks. First, three members of the staff began to labor furiously on completing a complex, microsimulation model for costing out welfare alternatives.[7] (HEW began work on the model before the arrival of the Carter administration, and hoped to have the model ready for early April, when the president would select options.) The other half of the staff began preparing the Five Papers for the consulting group.

During the group's first meetings in February, however, it quickly became apparent that the members had little interest in the background materials that HEW was so laboriously developing. The Friday consulting group, for example, on which the welfare advocates and state and local lobbies sat, had largely turned into a public relations display. The two-hour meetings were held in a large auditorium and usually had a good-sized audience (one or two hundred attendees). After about an hour and a half of discussions among the consulting group, the final half-hour would be allotted to questions from the audience. A Congressional Budget Office analyst, William Hoagland, who was familiar with welfare reform, commented that "the consulting group was a place where people whose philosophy had existed for the last ten years came to give it again." Henry Freedman recalls, "The meetings weren't a real knocking of heads. . . . We felt ourselves a part of a show rather than a consulting process." An ISP staff member similarly remarked, "When we talk about the consulting group, we don't even talk about the Friday group. We're talking about the Monday group." Bill Springer, a senior staff economist with the Council of Economic Advisers, observed that "the meetings were pretty much a waste of time. I had the feeling that Califano was off doing his own thing somewhere and this was just somehow to provide a facade of bombing everybody."

One important point that became apparent as a result of the meetings was that welfare rights groups were beginning to change their tune in the 1970s. As Arnie Packer explained:

> The welfare groups had changed their views substantially from what they were a decade [before]. Senator Moynihan later summed it up when he said that, a decade ago, an emphasis on jobs would have looked like slave labor and had all kinds of negative connotations. In 1977, the women's movement and welfare groups had changed their whole attitude toward welfare. Their complaint was that the jobs might not pay enough or there might not be sufficient training and so forth, but there was a clear indication from the welfare groups themselves that providing work was an important objective. The welfare rights groups said "we want regular CETA jobs."

Beyond this educational point, however, there seemed to be little substantive value to the Friday meetings. By early March, attendance at the meetings had dropped off noticeably, and many members began sending their assistants.

THE OUTREACH EFFORT

ISP staff and participants in the consulting group were similarly dismayed by the outreach effort that Califano had announced at the first meeting of the group and that the staff regarded as a "massive time waster." This effort was in high gear by March. As he had promised, Califano did chair an all-day hearing on March 10, at which some fifty-eight witnesses presented a wide range of views on welfare reform. HEW also solicited opinions from each congressman and senator, the fifty-four governors, and two hundred local officials, and Califano instructed the ten HEW regional officers to cast an even wider "opinion net." The scope of, and response to, the outreach effort was impressive. Over 169,000 persons were directly solicited by HEW for their views on the welfare system through either handouts or direct mailings; 10,635 media contacts were made, including 535 newspapers that printed letters from regional directors on their "letters to the editor" pages; 145 meetings were held, including seventy open "town meetings" with 2,109 speakers and a total attendance of nearly 7,000 people; and 760 people were personally interviewed by regional office staff. In a space of less than two months, over 15,000 individuals and organizations responded to the outreach, sending 4,038 letters and making 1,179 phone calls to regional offices.

Barth once euphorically characterized this process as "policy analysis in the sunshine,"[8] and Califano seemed to share his enthusiasm. In a retrospective article (summer 1978) entitled "Putting the Public into Public Policy Development," Califano outlined what was learned from the public consultations:

> One of my highest priorities when I became Secretary of HEW was to enable the people most affected by a decision, a program or regulation to have a real say in the process by which we made our decisions. . . . We have made great strides in opening up our decision-making processes to the most affected and interested members of the public. . . . The public has been deeply involved in the development of the Administration's welfare proposal. . . .
>
> Across the country there was wide agreement that welfare needs reform, but little agreement on how it should be reformed.
>
> Several recommendations received strong, widespread and recurring support, including the following . . . a national minimum payment as a base for an adequate assistance level; coverage based solely on need with clear and uniform eligibility rules; the provisions of ample and meaningful jobs; and mechanisms to implement the work segments of the program. . . .
>
> Again and again, the testimony and letters we received emphasized the need to provide, not just work *requirements*, but opportunities for those people on welfare who can work.[9]

Many of the elements that Califano noted would eventually work their way into the Program for Better Jobs and Income, although they probably would have done so even without the outreach effort; except for the question of how many work opportunities should be provided, there was little disagreement about the other issues Califano cited. In response to allegations that Califano was using the broad consulting process simply as a media event, Deputy Secretary Barth responded:

> A lot of people said that the public input was a fraud and a farce. That's baloney. Sure, the welfare consulting group has been criticized in various ways and perhaps fairly, but no one has come up with a better way. This is a first attempt to really bring people into the process which in itself is controversial. This was something rather extraordinary; I don't think it's ever been done before.

> When we met with the states in June we specifically changed several elements in the proposal but before May there were also some benefits to the consulting process, especially for someone in my position. The consulting group speeded up my introduction to the whole state and local interest group, recipient group, social welfare group, and public welfare association networks. These groups would be in a position to make an enormous impact on the proposal once it came down and it was vital that I establish some contact with them, especially given our tight schedule. I don't think I can overemphasize the importance of personal knowledge here. . . . Just being able to look someone in the eye and being able to talk to them helps enormously the next time you have a phone conversation with them.

Barry Van Lare, then chief lobbyist for the New Coalition, was also wont to emphasize that the consulting group would set up a political network that could expedite welfare reform discussions. As far as Van Lare was concerned, "Even if the mechanism was flawed, it provided for early and active state participation. Our concerns have been presented more clearly and faster than they would have been without it."[10]

THE MONDAY MEETINGS

The private Monday meetings of the consulting group also had their problems. Although the discussions were considerably franker outside the public eye, many of the participants had been involved in welfare reform for years and felt that the educational background materials were a waste of time. Most members on the panel had already developed their own views about welfare reform and were not likely fundamentally to reconsider them. As Bob Reischauer, associate director for human resources of the Congressional Budget Office (CBO), observed of the meetings, "The great majority of the people who were in the room whenever I went knew each other, had known each other beforehand, will know each other afterwards, knew each other's views beforehand, and had a great desire to have their own views expressed once again. I don't think many of them even read the briefing papers." As one ISP staff member recalls, "The members of the consulting group were all sure they knew what was wrong even though they didn't necessarily share the same idea of what was wrong. But instead of wanting to talk about criteria that might have illuminated those differences, they wanted to talk about those differences in the context of concrete proposals."

The Five Papers were in roughly the same order and covered the same topics as the papers prepared three years earlier during the Weinberger era. Although not much additional information had been learned in the interim, the analysts did not want merely to duplicate portions of the Weinberger papers. As one analyst recalls, "We were a suspect group since we had been around during the Weinberger years and we didn't want to appear as if we were consciously borrowing from the ancient regime." The papers, nevertheless, inevitably covered much of the same ground that had been plowed in previous administrations. It appears that the impetus to write the papers grew as much from partisanship as from an effort to educate the public and members of the consulting group. As Sue Woolsey, associate director for human resources at OMB, recalled:

> My impression is that they were laundering the analytic work which had been done under the Republicans—which was very good work—but somehow this time-consuming process was necessary to make it politically palatable to the administration. At the first meeting I thought, rather than generating these papers, why not give us a reading list? What they were doing was trying to attempt to change some already very good work, and I'm not sure that reading that work would not have been just as useful.

The impatience of consulting group participants with the gradual, thorough process HEW established prompted them to push to move more quickly to considering options for welfare reform. Pressed at the first public meeting of the group, Aaron agreed to have a broad outline of Paper 5 ("General Approaches to Welfare Reform") prepared for discussion at the group's second meeting. One of the people leading the charge to consider options was Arnold Packer. As Packer flatly stated, "There were two approaches in the consulting group. One was to set up objectives and criteria, which I thought was a bit late for a problem that had been worked on for a decade. The other approach, which I preferred, was to lay out two or three alternatives and fight over them."

HEW staff were aware that Packer had some experience in welfare reform, although few members at the staff level (or their superiors, including Barth and Aaron) had had much previous interaction with him. Consequently, they were a little unprepared for Packer. Nevertheless, as one staff member commented:

> We knew that Arnie had been pushing jobs in his *Challenge* article and the piece for the Joint Economic Committee. And we knew that as soon as Arnie and the Labor Department were invited to play, we better find out what Arnie thought about these things. So when the consulting group jumped the gun on

us and forced us to look at generic approaches to welfare reform at the second meeting, I included Arnie's option in the
paper prepared for that meeting as one of the six approaches to
be considered.

Discussion during the second week of meetings tended either to
bypass unpopular options quickly, to get bogged down in discussing the
details of a specific option, or simply to wander to the idiosyncratic
preferences of various speakers. For example, at the second public meeting the comprehensive cash coverage approach (NIT) received relatively
little critical discussion, as did the "mutually exclusive jobs and cash
assistance" approach (Packer's approach). Bill Springer, representing
the Council of Economic Advisers (CEA) did, however, express opposition to Packer's approach. Springer was worried that Packer would use
the welfare reform initiative as a substitute for a Humphrey-Hawkins
bill,* which the council was strongly opposed to for macroeconomic
reasons, feeling it was technically unfeasible as well as inflationary. As
Springer noted:

> CEA was very instrumental in reworking Humphrey-Hawkins
> and so we didn't want the welfare reform program to be a
> backdoor way of getting it. Arnie's agenda was to try first to get
> a Humphrey-Hawkins, but if he couldn't get it, and it soon
> became clear that he couldn't in its original form, he was going
> to try and get it through welfare. Both Charlie Schultze [chair-
> man of the CEA] and Bill Nordhaus [one of the council's three
> members] were concerned about the inflationary impact of a
> large program with relatively generous wages.†

Despite the opposition of the CEA, Packer continued to argue his case
vociferously during February at both the Monday and Friday meetings.
(As one HEW senior staff member described him, "He has no compunc-
tion about saying the most outrageous things, but he pulls it off, much
like a charming rogue.") After the first meeting, with the help of others,
he had managed to persuade the group to abandon HEW's "education-

---

*The Humphrey-Hawkins Act would require the federal government to ensure that low
national unemployment rates were not exceeded (if necessary through the creation of
massive public service employment programs). A greatly watered-down version of the bill
passed in late 1978.

†The council's concerns were not totally unfounded. As Frank Raines of the Domestic
Policy Staff pointed out: "You have to remember that the administration was moving on
the economic stimulus package at the same time and that included a large dose of public
jobs. Once you had gotten the government interested in providing the 600,000 or 700,000
jobs in that package, the prospect of public employment as an income transfer scheme was
very real."

al" agenda and to devote the third week of meetings to a review of the combination jobs–cash assistance approach, with three successive weeks each then being devoted to one prominent welfare alternative. The Department of Labor was designated to make the presentation for the last of these alternatives, the triple track, to which Packer was favorably disposed.

The fact that Packer was receiving nearly equal time in the presentation of welfare reform options did not make for more coherent debate in the consulting group. For example, at the group's third Friday meeting (February 25), HEW laid out a long checklist to help evaluate alternative approaches to welfare reform. The checklist included fifteen criteria to evaluate proposals, three different cost considerations, eleven impact considerations (tax system, wage rates, income distribution, for example), four intergovernmental issues, nineteen target populations, ten income conditioning parameters, twelve public service employment parameters, four emergency and special needs issues, eight administrative and managerial considerations, and five transition problems. This exhaustive list might have ultimately proved helpful if the consulting group had been able to organize it successfully, but no one was able to generate a consensus about which criteria were most important. As Bob Lerman, a consultant working on Packer's staff at DOL commented, "There was too much emphasis on the fact that welfare reform meant a variety of goals. Sure, it meant twenty goals, but they all didn't have the same weight." A memorandum from the welfare rights advocates to Califano similarly argued:

> The staff papers do not identify the provision of an adequate income as a goal for welfare reform, nor are any other principles specified which have guided your staff to select those "options" which they have presented to you. Attempts by the consulting group and the public attending its meetings to discuss guiding principles were rebuffed on the ground that we were not there to engage in an "academic exercise." The result is a value-free option paper which truly puts the cart before the horse—options are conjured up, and then compared in light of a range of conflicting criteria for welfare reform, without any decision as to which are the relevant criteria, and which of those take precedence. It is as if the delivery systems are more important than what is being delivered. This makes it impossible for the public to enter into a dialogue.[11]

In the absence of an evaluative framework, consulting group meetings generally turned into a random airing of people's views about the specific reform approach that happened to be on the table for discussion that week. Besides often being aimless, the discussions apparently were not even particularly helpful in illuminating institutional preferences and concerns. For example, on March 1, Aaron notified Califano that the consulting process was not defusing congressional opposition in quite the manner he had intended:

> Alair Townsend [welfare analyst, House Budget Committee] reports that Congressman Corman is feeling left out of the welfare reform process. Conversely, Congressman Ullman is under the impression that the process is moving in the direction of ideas he supports. Both developments are dangerous: the first because we may inadvertently alienate a powerful potential supporter, the second because the "let-down" should we go another way (as is quite likely) may be severe.
>
> We should cultivate Congressman Corman by calls from the Secretary, ASL [assistant secretary for legislation], ASPE [assistant secretary for policy evaluation], or in some other way. We should solicit his views expressly.
>
> We should also make clear to Congressman Ullman that his views represent only one of several approaches to reform that we are considering and that we may well support one of the others. The key here is to show that his approach is getting careful and sympathetic consideration.[12]

While the consulting process sent out confused signals and was apparently misleading some participants, it did serve to highlight a heated debate that emerged between HEW and DOL over the viability of a large-scale, full-time jobs program. HEW did not oppose the creation of several hundred thousand part-time, minimum-wage jobs—since the cost was not exorbitant and adding jobs to the welfare package would make it politically more palatable—but they staunchly opposed having a massive employment program become a key component of welfare reform. Aaron, Barth, and HEW staff felt it would be an extremely difficult administrative task to filter those who were expected to work from those who were not expected to work, and were also worried that any sort of job guarantee would be unrealistic and too costly—the government would not be able to create enough jobs and the ones it did create would be largely meaningless "makework" jobs. As Barth recalled, "[We] feared setting up a system that depended on job programs which would never appear. . . . There was good reason to believe that the political will—both within and outside the administration—to create jobs simply did not exist."

At the very heart of the HEW opposition lay a question of equity. HEW favored the negative income tax because it extended universal treatment to the welfare population, with assistance based solely on family size and need. The categorical approach that Packer and his staff were pushing would treat families with similar needs differently, ferreting those eligible to work out of the welfare system. As Frank Raines observed, DOL was emphasizing equity in a fundamentally different manner:

> In the multiple-track approach you worry about equity within those two groups but don't spend too much time worrying about equity between them. HEW worried a lot about equity between them and so a negative income tax made sense to them because everyone in similar circumstances is treated equally. . . . The Labor Department, Tom Joe, and the labor unions felt that you needn't sit and worry about somebody in one category receiving ten dollars more a month than someone in a different category. The kind of question which greatly concerned HEW did not concern the labor people because they were very anxious to make it clear that what people were getting was a job, and that they had to go to work to get it. The multiple-track approach, in short, really represented a conceptual break with the negative income tax.
>
> By the end of FAP everybody who dealt with welfare reform had changed from being social workers, as was the case up through Wilbur Cohen, to being economists. The multiple-track approach represented the emergence of the labor economists; labor economists who were now fighting the income maintenance economists who took over after FAP.

Packer and some of his staff were convinced that a large jobs program could work. They admitted that past programs had had mixed success but argued that nothing on the scale of the one to two million jobs program they were proposing had ever been attempted. Acknowledging that there might be some administrative problems, they still contended that their plan was feasible and at a reasonable cost. DOL stressed repeatedly that the negative income tax had no political appeal and that the categorization DOL was proposing only reflected the popular notion that those who can work should work.

Packer was not averse to using the Friday meetings as well as the Monday meetings to ensure that his points were driven home. For example, as one ISP staff member recalled:

> At one of the public meetings he made an impassioned speech about bureaucrats. "Carter and Marshall are going to guarantee a job for every individual. The bureaucrats who can't deliver them can go to the end of the unemployment line and queue

up for them." There was applause and cheering. Packer would then cite some promise Carter had made in his campaign and so on; he definitely did his homework.

Packer felt that HEW had a misleading view of welfare recipients and took great pains to emphasize this in the consulting group. According to Packer:

> We rejected what I would call the reservation theory. That is, that there is a large group of people, mostly black and poor, who are too goddamn ignorant to be of any use, so we simply pay them a humane amount of money to keep them out of our hair. The idea is that it's too expensive to do something with these people; just put them on a reservation.
>
> The people at HEW do have a strong feeling for the poor, their hearts are in the right place, but they felt that it was government's responsibility to provide an adequate income via cash. We continued to emphasize what we thought was a dual responsibility—a responsibility on the part of society to provide an opportunity to work, but then an equal responsibility on the part of families that could work to send somebody out to do the jobs. In some ways our viewpoint was more rigorous, more conservative, in that we were asking people to go out and earn it.

In this fundamental conceptual debate with HEW, Packer was abetted by several factors. First, Packer had a very small staff working for him, consisting of an assistant (Alan Gustman, a labor economist from Dartmouth), the director of Income Maintenance (Gary Reed), and Bob Lerman, a part-time consultant from the University of Wisconsin. Packer also contracted with Jodie Allen, vice president of Mathematica, Inc., to provide independent cost estimates of the jobs portion of the program. The small staff and generally informal atmosphere at DOL allowed Packer to move quickly on issues. As Allen, who formally joined the staff in early June, observed:

> We had a huge advantage over HEW. We never could have stayed in this game. We were only four people; we could see Ray anytime we wanted. We knew exactly what his parameters were so we were very efficient. We were the strike force, we came back and did all the cost estimates, wrote the memos, and we didn't have any clearance process, and it was really very hard on Barth and Aaron because they didn't know what to do , whereas we could shoot from the hip.

Marshall added that his personal affinity with Packer made him comfortable with delegating responsibility:

Once we agreed on the general principles for the jobs program, Arnie represented me in negotiations. He produced several briefings for me and after sitting down and thinking the matter out, we found our views on welfare did not differ at all. I occasionally discussed welfare reform with Joe [Califano] before or after Cabinet meetings, chiefly to express my concern to him that we didn't create disincentives for people to work or a jobs program that wouldn't work. We were pretty much in agreement though about the broad outlines of the program and the need to keep the process moving . . . essentially I didn't pay a lot of attention to supervising or to details . . . I felt comfortable delegating to Arnie.

Commenting on Packer's free hand, Aaron rather wistfully observed, "I had the feeling that if Packer came down a certain way that was the way the Department of Labor would come down. You couldn't say that about any issue here unless you were Califano."

HEW: A PAINTED SHIP UPON A PAINTED OCEAN

Reacting to Packer's public and private salvos, ISP staff and their superiors sought further direction from Califano in their briefings as to what he wanted out of the welfare reform process. The staff felt that "the briefings were most important and the consulting group came second. The briefings were regarded as the way decisions would be made." Califano was not forthcoming, however, during the two additional briefings he reviewed in February. As ISP staff commented:

Califano was bored during the briefings. We often had to cut them short, he would sometimes pick up and answer the phone, and in one meeting he turned to the executive secretary and complained that there were too many people at the briefings. He just didn't seem to focus on what we were saying.

Ben Heineman, Califano's executive assistant, who was also learning about welfare reform, points out why the analysts may have failed to get through to Califano:

The analysts were very ineffective in the early briefings. . . . The briefings were too formless, giving a broad view of the universe without structuring it to where the policy conflicts had been in the past and were likely to be in the future.

In welfare you're making tradeoffs. . . . Given a certain amount of money you can spend there is a tradeoff between jobs, basic benefit levels, benefit reduction rates, breakeven points—there are only three or four critical variables.

The analysts ultimately didn't give a real sense of the dynamics and systems dimension of welfare. All your problems revolve around where you come out with respect to those three or four key variables, and you can't just talk about one variable and fix it, since, as Joe [Califano] said, welfare reform is the Middle East of domestic politics because the tradeoffs are so very difficult. It took us a while to get to the point where we really understood that.

Heineman's views were echoed by others who were familiar with the briefings. Like Heineman, Barth felt that the briefings could have been structured more toward dealing with future policy conflicts:

The briefing process was similar to what we did for Secretary Weinberger, but in retrospect I think we should have done these briefings differently. We should have gone to the secretary with a specific policy question, an issue which would be a tough call for him and say, "This is how Long will probably go on this issue, this is how Ullman will go, this is how Corman will go. . . ." I'm convinced that it would have been better to go to the heart of the issue and give him the background information as he needed it and requested it.

Aaron felt the problems in the briefings stemmed primarily from time constraints and related analytic limitations:

The May 1 deadline led Califano to insist on briefings and that meant we had to give them. But we were not able to give the kind of briefing that would have grabbed Califano's attention because we lacked the necessary information. Until May we lacked the capacity to prepare estimates of costs or caseloads because the model we were going to use was still in preparation. We did not want to use older models that would produce estimates we would shortly have to disavow when the new model was finished. One did not have to be a junior analyst attending those briefings to understand that Califano wanted something else, but we did not know what to give him. I felt he should have wanted the information we were giving him. . . . But until May we could not enter a concrete discussion of alternatives because we could not report on estimates of costs and caseloads. We could, and did, assert that triple track was inefficient and costly, for example; but until we could tell him *how* inefficient and costly, we were loathe to get into specifics. We understood that Califano would not make decisions until he had such information. What we did not understand was that he would not, and perhaps could not, have made the decisions even if he did have the information. . . .

The basic problem was that we were disabled in discussing specific programs by a realization of our own ignorance on matters crucial to addressing the cutting political questions in which both Califano *and* his subordinates, including me, were interested. The key point is that we were hemmed in by two dates: the May 1 deadline which made briefings seem mandatory and precluded orderly development of a plan; and the earliest time at which the KGB [Kasten-Greenberg-Betson] model would be operational and, hence, at which cost and caseload estimates that we would be willing to live with would become available. In short, we became slaves of our analytical technology and a ridiculous deadline.[13]

An HEW official present at the briefings, however, stressed Califano's personal style in assessing the failure of the early briefings. As he recalled, Califano "would get a theme, a set of questions he would want to pursue, and just go off on a tangent. It was very difficult to proceed sequentially." Aaron similarly observed:

Califano did no reading—virtually none—and it was almost impossible to have a linear presentation. It's his style. He did it on everything. He just didn't read very much because he was too busy and I think he didn't really like to read long—even moderately long—or complicated papers. But he really did absorb a lot orally over the table. It was standard for him to prepare himself for testimony or briefings at the last minute. He's a very quick study.

For all his inattentiveness during the briefings, Califano maintained at least a formal commitment to them: at one briefing, for example, he noticed the absence of several assistant secretaries and promptly sent them a note informing them that, barring pressing matters, their attendance was required. John Todd observed that the note alone indicated "the briefings were not an exercise for him." Nevertheless, Califano's interests remained obscure. As Aaron observed:

Califano has a talent for remaining aloof from things he doesn't want a cut on. He can be very closed-mouthed for a very long time. I suspect in this case that either of two things happened. Either there was some private communication with the president of which I was not aware, but more likely than that, I think that he just chose to remain aloof until he felt more comfortable with the question and until he felt he knew how the president thought about the issue. Only when both of those things happened was he ready to speak publicly.

Now we could have used some clearer instructions than we

got, not as to substance, but as to procedure for reaching decisions on substance. We could have used a clearer reading like,
"Look I don't want to cut on these issues right now. I don't
understand them well enough—you take a tentative position
and give me the options but I want you to make a tentative
decision." We never got that kind of reading so we had to feel
our way along the wall of a dark closet so to speak. That would
have helped a lot.

The lack of signals from above resulted in considerable confusion for
the ISP staff. As one member recalled:

We didn't know what the hell was going on. First of all, every
once in a while, Carter would say, "I expect Califano and Marshall to come up with a plan," so even though Califano made an
attempt to pre-empt the process right at the beginning by setting up the consulting group, our control of the process was
somewhat suspect. Beyond that, we received almost no substantive direction from above. For example, sometime in early
February, Heineman or Califano told Barth that memos should
use lots of bullets and underlining along with white space to
accentuate important points. So we were at this staff meeting
and Barth actually took some papers and said things like "not
enough white space, Califano won't read this page full of print"
and so on. In the future, when we wrote memos where we
thought everything was important, we underlined everything.
It was a giggle and a half.

It turns out that in spite of all that, if you sent Califano a
six-page, single-spaced memorandum and he wanted to read it
because he was concerned about that particular subject, he'd
read it. You sent him a two-pager with lots of bullets and lots of
underlining, and it's about a subject he didn't care about, he
wouldn't read it. In retrospect it indicated that he didn't really
want to read the stuff we were sending. But we weren't being
told what he needed, what he wanted. What information did he
want?

In the view of some of the staff, the situation was exacerbated by the
fact that neither of their superiors—Aaron and Barth—knew Califano to
begin with:

The shocking difference between this time and when we did
the ISP proposal was that Morrill [former assistant secretary of
HEW] knew Weinberger [secretary of HEW] so well that he
could say this is the sort of thing we've got to give to Weinberger. There was absolutely none of that this time around because
nobody in the process knew Califano. Aaron had to worry ab-

out pleasing Califano whereas Morrill came over with Carlucci [former HEW undersecretary] and Weinberger. He already had that relationship, didn't have to worry about it, and they trusted him. So we were guessing as to what he wanted, as well as trying to make ourselves look good, communicate our analytic capabilities.

Although most of the staff did favor the NIT over other alternatives, they made an effort to maintain visible neutrality during this period. As Barth observed:

It was a new administration, a new secretary, and they felt these people deserved good hard analysis, felt that they could provide it in an objective way, but also felt it important to appear objective. It was partially a matter of pride in their own abilities as good analysts and partially a sense that the appropriate policy levels ought to be making the policy calls and that they should be presented with the right information on which to base those decisions.

In an effort to maintain visible neutrality, at least, the analysts felt they were successful. As one of them commented: "We didn't hide evidence, or manufacture evidence, and as far as we could tell [Califano] didn't see us as a group which had pre-cooked the issues. It seemed that he was not aware that his staff had a viewpoint until mid-March."

Virtually unbeknownst to Aaron, Barth, Todd, and ISP, however, Califano had deliberately refrained from indicating any preferences in the briefings, viewing himself more as the representative of the president than as the champion of a department. Unsure of Carter's wishes and aware of the institutional conflict between HEW and DOL, Califano had elected to (in Barth's words) "let the process run." As Ben Heineman explained:

I didn't, and nor did Joe, have a particularly pro-HEW analyst position. We were trying to figure out the best thing for the president and Joe was not necessarily concerned that it be all cash. I think he was aware that the jobs were going to be very important. He was much more willing than HEW staff was at the beginning to accept a big jobs program. . . .

In a process as complicated as welfare reform, Joe may spend only two days over a course of six months. So he has to structure a process where people with different points of view have an opportunity to argue with each other so that the argumentative process will hopefully flesh out—it doesn't always work— basic disagreements.

Califano's recollections of the briefings subsequently confirmed some of the speculations sounded by Aaron, Barth, Todd, and others:

> The briefings were too academic. They did not have a lawyer's sense of relevance. They weren't hard enough on the politics of some of these issues or hard enough on the economics of some of these issues. Part of it wasn't their fault. . . . Also, in the early stages, I don't see any point of imposing specific notions. A lot of percolation was necessary.

Califano went on to explain why he did not direct Aaron to alter the briefings:

> I let the early lectures ramble some because I wanted to get to know Aaron and Barth and John Todd and their prejudices, so I'd have a sense of where they were coming from when we ultimately had to make decisions. . . . You have to remember, I knew Aaron was brilliant, but I didn't know him. It's different when you hire a personal aide, a special assistant, or some guy out of the Kennedy School or Harvard Law School, than when you're dealing with a guy like Aaron or Barth. They are professionals immersed in a subject and have strong views about the subject. People, however, rarely articulate their views early on, and it was important to get a sense of what those views were and why they held them. You can talk to somebody for two hours and they won't tell you what's really on their mind.

LOOKING TOWARD THE WHITE HOUSE

The private debate between HEW and DOL as well as the public one over generic approaches in the consulting group had stalled by mid-March. None of the various alternatives that were being considered could be ultimately evaluated until it was known how much federal money would be available for welfare reform. As the New Coalition commented on the consulting group's efforts:

> While we have appreciated the opportunity to contribute to the work of the consulting group, we have also been concerned by the limits imposed on process. Since it was made clear in the initial meeting that the group was not expected to prepare a recommendation, the discussions have lacked a clear focus and have tended to avoid the identification of the real compromises among and between program objectives which must be made in the development of a workable reform plan. In addition, the lack of cost estimates and of any guidance as to the size of the

potential federal financial commitment have made it difficult to evaluate the relative feasibility of the plans presented.[14]

The size of the federal financial commitment, however, was a political decision and one that Aaron told his aides to stay away from, warning them that "it would be suicidal to take an advocacy position." Bert Carp, deputy director of the Domestic Policy staff, continued to fend off White House involvement in early March, saying, "the ball is in Joe Califano's court."[15] Seeking to draw out Carter's views, Califano decided it was time to brief the president and directly request further guidance.

Early in March, the analysts began preparations for sending Califano and senior staff to the White House to get further guidance. As they envisioned the internal process, there would be a briefing with Califano on a key welfare issue on March 9, and on March 15 a descriptive briefing on viable reform options based on an early version of Paper 5, with successive briefings devoted to criticizing and evaluating the various options as well as preparing Califano for his March 25 meeting with the president. Initially, three or four briefings were planned for Carter, each to be given by either Aaron or Barth, but subsequently Califano announced that he, rather than one of his senior staff (as was traditionally the case), would be giving the briefings himself. (Carter indicated to HEW that if Califano was going to send him recommendations on reforming the welfare system, he should also be prepared to explain the nature of the existing system and the problems in it.) Califano also decided to accelerate the planned schedule slightly by inviting several key cabinet members or their representatives to the March 15 briefing on Paper 5.

On March 9, Aaron, Barth, and Todd briefed Califano during the evening on "how the issues of work and basic income support are related in the context of welfare reform alternatives." The discussion focused on four different options: cash support with financial work incentives (NIT); meager cash support ("a bone") plus work registration requirements; increased work opportunities through more money in CETA; and work-conditioned benefits engineered either through tax supplements (EITC, wage subsidy) or income support in work form (that is, public service employment as the only support alternative or work relief in the context of current income assistance programs). Apropos of the first alternative, the analysts reported the (qualifiedly) positive results of the income maintenance experiments performed by HEW during the 1970s:

> For our purposes, we shall present the results of the latest and largest experiment, Seattle-Denver. . . . The results for

intact families are summarized [elsewhere]. For husbands, the hours reduction is under 10%. Except for the Gary experiment, this has come mostly in the form of reduced hours rather than not working. The results for wives are larger (and children).

There are various reasons why we are concerned over reduced labor supply. Some of this concern relates to who does the reducing. For example, even if the social security system plus SSI reduces the hours worked of the aged, we are generally less concerned. Even for employables, if the reduction is less moonlighting or training or more effective job search, the reaction is much different than if it is complete withdrawal for leisure.

One important effect of labor supply withdrawal is its effect on program costs. This depends critically on who is covered, the guarantee level, the tax rate, the integration with the tax system, and other characteristics. One plan on which attention has focused is the [Seattle-Denver] plan referred to earlier. Under this plan, the induced labor supply response would increase outlays by about \$2 billion (or less depending on the concept of cost employed). This is not a large fraction of total outlays, but it would be about one quarter of total net costs.[16]

In evaluating the effect of various NITs on work effort, the analysts had stressed the modest declines that had occurred among male heads of families in the experiments, but apparently did not place much emphasis on the substantial work decline that occurred in Seattle-Denver among single female heads (11 percent) and secondary earners (spouses, 22 percent). As the above excerpt indicates, they were also careful to point out various factors that might mitigate the seriousness of any decline in work effort.*

The analysts were less sanguine about the second option: mandating work registration provisions. They cited problems of defining who was employable, what a suitable job was, what constituted a job refusal, the extent of voluntary unemployment, the number of available jobs, and so forth. And they concluded: "Cost benefit analysis indicates that increases in service costs, especially day care, and administrative costs are greater than savings in program costs. Of course, for ethical reasons to prevent

---

*The analysts also did not inform Califano of the high marital dissolution rates that occurred in the Seattle-Denver experiment. Although the Stanford Research Institute, which was running the experiment, had sent a report to HEW in June 1976 outlining the results, the absence of any formal procedure through which HEW project officers communicated "research" findings to Barth and Aaron meant that the two did not learn of the findings until the summer of 1977. This data subsequently caused a furor in hearings before Senator Moynihan in November 1978.

the worse offenses to public morals, society may still be willing to pay the price."[17] On the subject of benefits for the working poor, the analysts indicated their preference for an EITC over a wage rate subsidy, but were still strongly opposed to the inclusion of either option in the welfare reform plan.

Moving on to a consideration of work-conditioned benefits that might replace income support in its entirety, the analysts outlined four possibilities for a public service employment program (PSE):

1. Exclusive form of support—open-ended funded, i.e., guaranteed job.
2. Cash support underneath but enough closed-end funded jobs provided to make the work test a *de facto* guaranteed job.
3. Cash support underneath—some closed-end funded jobs provided with a clear set of priorities established so that all of some groups would be guaranteed a job (and required to take it as a precondition of assistance).
4. Cash support plus modest CETA type effort but primary reliance on private sector, macro policy, and individual incentives to achieve full employment.[18]

Summarizing the pros of a PSE as they saw them, the analysts cited: "(1) value to recipients (self image and future employability), (2) taxpayers prefer it, (3) matter of equity and justice, (4) value of output produced." After this rather abbreviated list, they cited a number of cons:

> Though there are a lot and we will be spending a lot of time on them, it is not to be argumentative or because we are set against any such option but to be sure you are acquainted with the full range of problems before decisions need to be made and private discussions take place.
> 1. Low skill level of target population may mean little value to output. (Ability of training to alter this limited.)
> 2. Administrative, supervisory and capital costs may exceed value of additional output.
> 3. Disruption of the private labor market. If we're interested in the impact on people working for pay (i.e., instead of for a transfer unrelated to productivity), large-scale PSE may cause more work withdrawal than a cash transfer program.
> 4. Given inflationary and budgetary constraints (and displacement if operated by state and local governments), can we really create net new jobs? This macroeconomic debate is essential and we are trying to get the CEA directly involved.*

*One reason ISP was so eager "to get the CEA [Council of Economic Advisers] directly involved" was the fact that they perceived CEA and its chairman, Charles Schultze, as

This issue is intimately connected to the issue of whether and for what purposes we wish to distinguish among the target populations on the basis of employability or related characteristics. We shall return to that issue.[19]

Such was the view at HEW of reform possibilities just before the March 15 briefing.* At the same time, at DOL, a very different picture of welfare reform alternatives was emerging. In a memo to Marshall on March 14, Packer wrote:

> *Tomorrow's meeting would be very useful if you could get Califano to agree to the importance of two words: work and family.* One can think of the traditional American family structure with two parents and children in which the family head goes out to work and makes enough of a living to keep the family together. The major thrust of any program ought to be to support this as the predominant situation for Americans. Secondly, for families in which there are small children and only one parent, there should be enough support for those families to live a dignified life. The incentives should be arranged so that individuals prefer the two-parent arrangement. The earnings at work should be sufficiently greater than the dole on welfare to encourage families to stay together or to encourage women who are single parents to remarry. *Meeting these objectives means providing jobs and/or training to family heads who are unemployed and earning subsidies to working poor families.*[20]

Packer proceeded to tick off four conventional economic assumptions that he considered fallacious. First, he attacked the CEA's macroeconomic concerns that a large jobs program would have a calamitous and

representing "anti-public employment, anti-guaranteed jobs. . . . Schultze was the guy who was going to undercut, to beat the Labor Department's proposal for us." Aaron, who by now was firmly convinced on analytic grounds that a large-scale, full-time PSE was unworkable, made sure that Schultze was invited to the March 15 meeting, where options, including Packer's guaranteed employment scheme, would be discussed. In a note to Califano on the 23rd, Aaron also suggested that separate pre-presidential briefings be given to Bert Lance (OMB) and Secretary Michael Blumenthal (Treasury). Aaron felt that "these agencies are important actors and perhaps allies" (Henry Aaron, "Cabinet Briefings on Welfare Reform," Memorandum to the Secretary, March 23, 1977, p. 1).

*Whether this was, in fact, Califano's view remains a moot question, although he already appeared disposed to a comprehensive solution. When Califano held his public hearing on March 10, he had refrained from commenting on the fledgling debate between HEW and DOL. He did, however, confidently "guarantee" to one witness that AFDC would be expanded to cover two-parent families, told another that he wanted to move away from a pilot approach, and told yet a third witness that "welfare may need very radical surgery." See *Report on the 1977 Welfare Reform Study: The Secretary's Report to the President*, Supp. 3, vol. 1 (Washington, D.C.: HEW, 1977), pp. 146, 259.

inflationary effect on labor markets by sucking people out of the private sector into better-paying public service jobs (a phenomenon commonly known as the "vacuum cleaner" effect):

1. *Labor Market "Rationalization"*

Most economists believe that labor markets in this country are "O.K." right now. If anything, they believe that the minimum wage laws and union pressure to maintain higher wage rates are the major problems with the labor market. I believe, and I think you agree, that any labor market that denies someone with family responsibilities a "decent" living at a "decent" job is not doing well.

A guaranteed job at a reasonable wage *may* disrupt labor markets. While those who think the labor markets are "O.K." find the disruption a calamity, others look forward to that sort of disruption. Moreover, I am not convinced that the disruption would be as great as it might seem at first blush. *Although many persons do work for very low wages, the greater portion of these workers do not have family responsibilities.* Moreover, secondary workers are coming into the labor force at a rapid rate and these could take the poorer paid jobs that are left open as family heads move on to better positions. We are looking at the data now and hope to be able to support that statement with some facts.[21]

Packer then returned to his primary concern, the need to support the family as an institution:

2. *Family Structure*

Economists are not accustomed to differentiating among people on the basis of family responsibilities. According to the theory, individual wages should equal their marginal product and should not be based upon need. The significance of the family itself has no place in the traditional theory. But the family may be the most important institution in the country. *While policy should not strive to keep bad marriages together, it should strive to provide an economic foundation families can depend on.* Therefore, it seems especially important that family heads be given the opportunity to have a decent job.

The policy conclusion is to target the public service jobs on families and not on individuals. None of this is anti-feminist. It could be the woman in the family who takes the job. Moreover, job availability provides enough financial independence for a woman to leave a bad marriage situation and know that she can make a living on her own. But for most cases, it is important to provide the male head of the family with the opportunity to work.[22]

Having laid out a defense of his own preferences, he then lobbed a few criticisms at the negative income tax:

3. *Full Employment*

Work incentives and work tests clearly make more sense in a situation of full employment. But work incentives and work tests in less than full employment just create cruel and unnecessary harassment. Job creation is unnecessary if there is full employment, but it becomes crucial if not. *While most economic theories are based on the assumption of full employment, the assumption is more usually correct* [*sic*].

4. *Economics is Everything*

In the ideal economic case where information is available, discrimination does not exist and all people have equal capabilities—the only thing that the poor need is more money. Therefore, a negative income tax and accessibility to building human capital and the reduction of discrimination will, in fact, do all that is necessary. Thereafter, everyone's financial condition will depend primarily on their own tradeoff between work and leisure and their own desire for human capital, etc. This economic model does not describe reality. Many more things than economics impinge on most people's lives. The clearest case is perhaps sheltered workshops for those who are physically or mentally unable to make a living in our industrialized world. There are others who, for many reasons, could not fit into traditional jobs either and for whom less demanding or just different types of work is appropriate. *Some persons do need a measure of extra social services and manpower training if these services can be delivered in a humane and dignified fashion.*[23]

Packer's plan, calling for a guaranteed job for family heads at a wage range of $3.50 to $4.00 an hour, was one of the seven options presented at the pre-presidential meeting on March 15. Present at the meeting were Califano, Champion, Aaron, Barth, Todd, several HEW assistant secretaries, Charlie Schultze, Marshall, and Packer. In spite of the fact that the draft of Paper 5, which served as a basis for the discussion, was primarily descriptive and only broadly evaluative,* a number of people had the impression that the meeting might help to eliminate some options and narrow differences between the two departments before they went to President Carter. Merwyn Hans, for example, director of the Work Incentive Program (WIN) in the Department of Labor, remarked

---

*Cost, caseloads, and administrative complications were not included since HEW had not completed its computer model and since many of the specific parameters of different plans were still undecided.

to one ISP staff member that "the dice will roll today." John Todd noted, however, that he and his staff were not looking for a consensus from the meeting. The purpose of inviting Schultze, Marshall, and Packer to the briefing was rather that

> the secretary didn't want to look like he was springing things on people and thought this was the time to bring everybody else in so they could see what we were looking at. If they wanted to jump on us—tell us that options 4 and 5 were absolutely out of the question—better to do it then than later. We didn't want a consensus out of that meeting; before going to the president that would have been premature. We did want the secretary of HEW to tell us what he needed to know in order to choose.

The meeting did not produce a consensus. Neither did it produce a narrowing of options or a clearer indication of the information Califano was seeking. Although only four of the seven options (at most) were being given serious consideration by HEW or DOL (major incremental revision, comprehensive cash coverage, jobs–cash assistance, and triple track), each of the seven options was patiently reviewed and none were dismissed. Apart from an occasional outburst from Packer, the meeting tended to wax philosophical, as Charlie Schultze, Califano, and Marshall engaged in a gentlemanly discussion over whether people would take any old job or just a "good" job at reasonable wages. The meeting most clearly revealed the ambiguous position Califano had worked himself into. As one ISP staff member commented:

> Califano had tried to pre-empt the White House and the Labor Department by setting up the consulting group. But by trying to take hold of the process he had put himself in the position of being the presidential surrogate for the process and at the same time superintending a department that had a point of view. The conflict between the two was very clear at that meeting. On the one hand, he would press Marshall about the jobs program, pointing out the same problems which we had pointed out the week before, yet, on the other hand, he would try and win Marshall's assent and engineer agreement between HEW senior staff, DOL, and Schultze. Califano had got himself in this impossible situation; he could not be an advocate or a combatant vis-à-vis Marshall.

ENTER THE PRESIDENT

On March 16, in a nationally televised meeting from the Town Hall of Clinton, Massachusetts, President Carter outlined his plans on a number of priority matters. The president left no doubt about his intention to stick to his welfare reform deadline, informing his listeners that, "on May 1, Joe Califano, a tough, knowledgeable administrator, . . . will come forward . . . , and propose to the Congress a comprehensive revision of the entire welfare system." The next day, Califano's preparation for the March 25 meeting with the president began in earnest. An ISP staff member described the process:

> We started going over the material with Califano on the 17th and he did not focus at all. We met for one, two, three days in a row; we met with him almost daily to go over the charts. At that time we were working with an outline and a chart but it became apparent that he wasn't going to use an outline.
>
> He'd sit in his office, take phone calls, and so on, and just did not zero-in on what the briefing was to do or what he was supposed to learn in order to give it. When he started focusing was on Thursday the 24th, when we had a full set of charts made. We were trying to get his reaction the entire time whether the charts were okay, and finally had to get them made because of the time deadline. We started going over them with him on Thursday at 11:00 A.M. and quit at 8:00 P.M. And during that time you could see him at first not knowing the stuff and then learning the material. He was a good lawyer. The next morning he indicated the changes he wanted made, so we rushed back and fixed the charts. That morning he also gave his first full-dress briefing and went through it a couple of times. He could definitely give a good briefing.

Barth and Aaron were both relieved that the secretary had acquired some mastery of the topic and were astonished at how rapidly Califano could pick up material when he wanted to. As Aaron remarked:

> He is a good advocate, [plus] on short notice he could learn enough about a subject to make a very credible and effective presentation as a witness or a briefer. It was a little short of miraculous, in fact, how fast he could pick that stuff up. Literally two run-throughs and he was very, very good. With one practice he might be a little fuzzy, misconstrue a question, or miss a key fact, but give him a couple of briefings and he was very, very strong.

In advance of the meeting with Carter, Califano had forwarded to the president the full text of the Five Papers and a staff memorandum summarizing basic information on welfare reform issues and income maintenance programs. In a cover memorandum he spelled out the purpose of the briefing and identified five issues on which he felt the need for further guidance:

> From my point of view, the main purpose of Friday's meeting is to report briefly to you on the work done to date, to provide a general profile of the poverty population, to describe the cash transfer and in-kind programs presently in place, and to discuss the process for formulating a reform proposal. In addition, while it is premature for any decisions, I would like to get your tentative views on some of the initial issues we will confront in developing specific alternatives:
> - *Which government programs should be included in "welfare reform?"* AFDC, the Supplemental Security Income program, and food stamps are likely candidates. Other possibilities include some unemployment insurance extensions (beyond 26 weeks? beyond 39 weeks?), housing assistance, the means-tested veterans compensation program.
> - *What is the level of income that should be set as the national standard?* Should there be variations for different regions and/or metropolitan areas? Who should pick up the cost of those variations—the federal government or the states?
> - *Should we cover intact families, as well as single parent families?*
> - Since more than 90% of the people on AFDC are mothers and single parent families and their children, to what extent do we want to *encourage* them to work or *require* them to work?
> - To the extent we can identify the "employables" by law, *are we prepared to guarantee them public service jobs if there are inadequate opportunities in the private sector?* This may involve expensive training programs and public service jobs—as many as three million if we guarantee everyone a public service job at salaries between $6,000 and $8,000 per person per year.
> These are difficult questions with serious economic, political and human implications. We do not need decisions on them, but we do need any thoughts you may have.[24]

A memo from Eizenstat to President Carter on the 24th warned against giving a specific commitment on the issues Califano raised. Eizenstat counseled Carter:

> The design of a reform proposal is still in the preliminary stages. The discussion by HEW to date has centered on the relative roles of cash assistance, jobs and training, and income tax reform directed toward low income workers. Three crucial items have not been dealt with as of yet: *costs, caseload estimates,* and *administration. . . .*
> The questions raised in Secretary Califano's memo are very

difficult ones. We suggest that you not commit yourself on these issues, or on any specific reform alternative, until data on costs, distribution among income groups, caseload impact and impact on state and local government is available.[25]

Eizenstat did, however, offer several positive suggestions:

In addition we recommend:
- That you ask the Secretary to develop and provide basic cost estimates for *several* reform options, representing a range of approaches and cost levels for your review with his recommendation.
- That you stress the need for interagency consultation, particularly in developing employment aspects of the plan. (Although the Secretary has established a Consulting Group with representation from Labor, Commerce, Treasury, Agriculture, CEA and OMB, the Group is functioning as a "sounding board" for general discussion rather than a working group. As options become more specific interagency discussion will be easier and more fruitful.)
- That you compliment the Secretary for his outreach efforts.[26]

Eizenstat was not the only presidential adviser who felt it necessary for the president to indicate what he wanted produced on May 1. Jack Watson, one of Carter's chief political advisers at the time, also emphasized in a cover memo to the Eizenstat memo the importance of Carter's clarifying his intentions.* While Eizenstat had been concerned that Carter urge Califano to consult broadly with other federal agencies, Watson was concerned not only that Califano work out a compromise plan, but also that Califano make an effort to deal more extensively with the Hill and various interest groups:

A primary objective of the meeting tomorrow should be to establish a clear understanding of what you expect to receive on May 1—e.g., a set of options costed out for your review?—a specific recommendation for comprehensive reform with fall-back alternatives as to cost?—both?—a *preliminary* report of findings and tentative proposals, but not a final reform proposal? If you want a specific comprehensive recommendation, how much freedom should Joe have to discuss with key congressional leaders, state and local officials, public interest groups, and

---

*Jim Parham, Carter's director of welfare in Georgia and a man influential in shaping Carter's views on welfare, was an assistant to Watson. As friends of Carter's, Watson and Parham were on an "independent track" in the White House and the extent of their influence was not clear. Parham sat on the consulting group and represented Watson at most presidential briefings on welfare reform.

others, what he is "leaning toward" on recommendations? Some groups are expressing a feeling of being "left out" of the substantive decision-making process thus far. They have presented their ideas but have received no feedback as to whether those ideas coincide with HEW inclinations. It is crucially important for as many groups as possible to have some sense of "parenthood" for what we propose—especially key congressional people.

I recommend that you reiterate to Joe and to Ray Marshall your interest in dealing differently with the "employables" and your desire to receive on May 1st a recommendation on that subject that both can endorse.[27]

The briefing took place at 2:30, Friday, March 25. Present at the meeting, besides President Carter, were Vice President Walter Mondale, Califano, Aaron, Barth, Marshall, Packer, Schultze, Parham, Eizenstat, Carp, and several others. The briefing lasted for about an hour and a half, most of it taken up by Califano's chart show. Califano took roughly twenty charts to the meeting, each chart adorned in different colors, easy to read, and with simple and often dramatic messages attached. The first four charts showed what the income maintenance system looked like and how it had expanded in recent years; eight more charts showed what the analysts called "the horrors" of the welfare system (inequities in payments, wide variation in eligibility standards, byzantine administrative mechanisms); three charts described dynamics of the low-income population, refuting the stereotype of the "welfare cheater"; three charts outlined the work disincentives in the existing system; the final charts showed the potential demand for jobs and the number and cost of public service jobs currently being funded. Califano's critical run-through of "the system" and Carter's reaction to it were brought into focus by the discussion of the work disincentives facing welfare recipients. Califano noted that a family head earning the minimum wage would be able to keep only five dollars out of a one-hundred-dollar increase in earnings because the combined marginal tax rates from AFDC, EITC, food stamps, and housing assistance would reach 95 percent. In Wisconsin, he added, if a woman earning $2,500 in a half-time job switched to a full-time job, her total income would actually decline by $1,249, and being disqualified from receiving Medicaid could potentially add another $1,688 to the penalty. Carter shook his head in dismay at this point, saying, "When people really understand this, I'm sure they will do something about it."[28]

After a presentation such as this, it was not surprising that Carter reiterated his interest in comprehensive reform. He added, however, a new twist to the reform effort: "Joe," he began, "if you had to start over from scratch, is this the kind of system you would create?" When Califano shook his head, Carter continued: "In that case, I want you to take all the money that is now being spent on welfare programs and redesign the whole system using the same amount of money. Then show what you can do, adding new money in $1 billion increments. You give me the perfect plan and I'll worry about the politics. Give me a report in two weeks."[29] With that, the meeting adjourned.

CHAPTER FIVE

The Cost Crunch

WHEN, AT THE PRESIDENTIAL BRIEFING OF MARCH 25, JIMMY CARTER ordered Joe Califano to redesign the welfare system without spending more money, he was pursuing something called "zero-cost planning," of which he had long been an enthusiastic advocate and (as governor of Georgia) practitioner. Zero-cost planning is predicated on the belief that one can redesign a problematic system in a beneficial and comprehensive manner without spending additional money. In addition to these substantive benefits, Carter credited the technique with integrating the budgetary and planning functions, promoting both better analysis and a more austere budget.[1]

Two theories were subsequently advanced for why Carter had imposed the zero-cost constraint. One was that the president wanted to redirect funds completely and come in with a genuine zero-cost program for which he would be willing to take the political heat from those who had been made worse off by redesigning the system. The second theory, and generally the more popular one, held that Carter was using the zero-cost planning as a managerial technique to keep down the cost of welfare reform. As Frank Raines put it, "The President was going to force his liberal secretary of HEW to come in with a tight program, so that he could see the value of each increment, rather than having this big blob in which he couldn't understand where the money went." Califano also subscribed to the latter theory. As he explained:

> The same thing was going on in the president's mind that went on in my mind when Julius Richmond [the surgeon general] would come in and say, "I've got a great new health program, this is what I want you to do," and I'd say, "Fine, where are you going to take the 10 million dollars?" It was that simple; it was a good management tool. That's how I read it. . . .
> I think the technique was fine. If I had been president, I

would have done the same thing or something similar. I would have made my secretary of HEW justify all the additional dollars in a program that's inherently unpopular.

Despite its implication of fiscal austerity, the order to use zero-costing was received with some enthusiasm in ISP. Carter was, as John Todd observed,

taking an approach which only policy analysts can identify very closely with. He wanted to analyze the problem. He was not coming at this from the point of view such as "well, what can I sell, bring in Gerald Rafshoon" [assistant to the president for communications] or "what's going to make political hay here, I don't care if it works." He was really trying to find out the biggest things that can be done, was removing the political wraps, and was saying let's propose the absolute best thing that we think we can do.

And Frank Raines observed:

The president understood there was no real political gain in proposing welfare reform. He didn't see this as a centerpiece of how it was going to help him out politically. Welfare was just one of those problems—one of those nasty problems—that ought to be solved, and he was a problem-solver president.

He thought the system was corrupting people but it didn't come through as being mainly a moral issue. It was more of a sense that this was a lousy program and that we ought to fix it.

IN SEARCH OF THE ZERO-COST PLAN

Immediately following the March 25 meeting, HEW began work on the presentation of zero-cost options for a second briefing with the president, scheduled for April 11. Aaron eliminated the four incremental options,[2] which had been indifferently reviewed at the March 15 meeting, narrowing the focus to three remaining options: comprehensive cash coverage (favored by HEW), Tom Joe's triple-track proposal (favored by the AFL-CIO and AFSCME), and Packer's guaranteed jobs proposal. The first order of business for HEW was to iron out as many kinks as possible in the multivariate microsimulation model that HEW had been developing to estimate the costs of the various alternatives.

The zero-cost restraint had given the importance of cost estimates a new dimension. If the idea had been prevalent that costing would be a key factor prior to the first meeting with President Carter, it is perhaps fair to say that after the meeting cost had become the primary determinant for selecting among options. Califano had for a long time been an enthusiastic supporter of information technology (computers)[3] and pushed HEW staff to get details of the model programmed into the computer as soon as possible. As he recalled:

> I thought we had a better welfare data base than it turned out we had, particularly vis-à-vis the states. They hadn't really called in the states and got them plugged into the computer [for state-by-state estimates of fiscal relief and recipient worseoff/betteroffness] so that took longer. As we got into it, it was clear to me that it would take more time. We didn't have that data, it took time to make those decisions, and it's a very complicated subject.

PREPARING COST ESTIMATES

The pressure to get the immensely complicated model operational precluded ironing out serious shortcomings, chief among which was that all cost estimates were being done in 1974 dollars. Since the program would not go into effect until at least 1981, the cost figures at best were good rough estimates; an inflation factor, for example, could not accurately measure changes in the size of the eligible population, or variances between the rates at which the costs of the program, and the offsets to the costs of the program, would expand. Nevertheless, the designers did refine enough details to ready the model for some very preliminary estimates of costs and caseloads. As one ISP staff member recalls, an almost mystical faith in the costing process prevailed in the agency:

> Aaron and Barth, I'm convinced, thought there would be a resolution of a lot of issues through the costing process and Califano really believed that truth comes out of computers. References kept being made to "wait until the numbers come down." Califano felt that people who worked with computers were wizards; in fact, he gave a magic wand and T-shirts that say "Wizard" to Aaron, Barth, and Todd. This damn computer thing was the functional equivalent of the twelfth century scholastics talking about the nature of the Trinity!
>
> We couldn't find out what Califano wanted out of welfare reform. Did he want more income for poor people, and if so, for two-parent families? How much fiscal relief did he want? What was his conception of federal versus state roles in income maintenance? He just sort of superintended the decision-making process, which seemed to be one of somehow throwing all these issues in with costs [and having] an answer appear. If you put consultation together with a computer and get them to mate, welfare reform will be reproduced as a by-product.

In developing the cost model, considerable emphasis was initially placed on developing the costing procedures in an open manner. In late February, HEW brought together a group of analysts from the Congressional Budget Office, DOL, OMB, the Treasury, the Council of Economic Advisers, the Urban Institute, and Mathematica, Inc., to generate ideas about data bases and models that could be used to estimate the costs of welfare proposals. In a memo to a staff member of the Senate Budget Committee on March 30, Aaron stated:

> We feel strongly that it is undesirable for one group or one model to monopolize the estimation procedures. . . . We hope to involve most of those groups [which met in February] either directly or indirectly, in the estimation process. . . .
> As a particular plan emerges as the leading welfare reform candidate, we hope to ask independent analysts to examine carefully the cost estimates. We have done this in the past, and it has increased our confidence in the estimates. For example, estimates of the costs of the Income Supplementation Program, developed for Secretary Weinberger in the fall of 1974, were reviewed by independent analysts. . . .
> We hope that these processes will result in cost and caseload estimates that are as accurate as current data and methodology permit. These open processes are also essential if the assumption behind these estimates and the margins of error necessarily attendant to each are to be made as clear as possible.[4]

Welfare rights advocates in the consulting group, however, were not so pleased with the "open" procedures HEW was developing. When the consulting group met on Friday, April 1, Aaron cautioned that communication with the public might suffer as the May 1 deadline approached, and suggested that it would be "fair"[5] to present cost estimates of various proposals in the version of Paper 5, to be released at the final meeting on April 8. (Subsequently, an April 15 meeting was added.) Henry Freedman immediately asserted that this would be unfair; by only providing the public with a one-shot estimate of various welfare reform approaches, sponsors of plans outside the government would be unable to evaluate the variations of a plan that HEW might experiment with in response to cost limitations.[6] Aaron attempted to quiet the disgruntled Freedman by assuring him that his views would be solicited even after the final meeting, throughout April.

The following day, Barth and ISP staff met with Packer and his staff to clarify the specific parameters of the Labor Department plan so as to expedite the costing-out and analysis of the DOL approach. Between the March 15 and April 2 meetings, Packer had changed several aspects of his plan significantly. More specifically, Packer was planning on creating a good-sized EITC (rather than merely expressing interest in utilizing the tax supplement) and, with the advent of the zero-cost restriction, had retreated to lobbying for minimum-wage jobs instead of jobs at a "meaningful" wage. The analysts, however, were stunned to see what Packer was presenting as a zero-cost, "comprehensive" restructuring of the welfare system:

> At first Packer didn't want to produce a no-cost plan, but then he decided he'd better. The first crazy plan was on April 2. As a welfare reform plan it did nothing for welfare. They must have cooked it up on April Fools' Day. It left AFDC where it was except for abolishing AFDC-UF (which is for employable people), redirected the CETA money for jobs to low-income people, and folded extended unemployment benefits into an expanded earned income tax credit. Because of the wage in the jobs program they also lowered the cost of food stamps about a billion dollars, which they placed in the jobs program to create more job spots. The entire scope of income assistance programs was virtually unchanged by their proposal; only on the employment and training side were any significant modifications made.
>
> The Labor Department's game was "we'll take all the money that's in CETA, redirect it to jobs, take the savings and reduction in welfare and add that to the jobs—what's left over in terms of the existing transfer system monies, you guys can do whatever you want to," and that's a direct quote from Arnie Packer. Analytically he was very shrewd because he simply said, "take whatever's left."

HEW nevertheless accepted Packer's plan and began work on charting it and distilling important advantages and disadvantages of the plan. As with all three plans, the programs that were eliminated were crucial to estimating the costs of the proposed new program, since they would help to "offset" the cost of a new program. Beyond these self-evident offsets, the analysts needed to know any other offsets that might be available to lower the cost of the program. Following the March 25 meeting with President Carter, representatives of various agencies had stayed around for a "post-meeting meeting" to discuss which offsets might be available in calculating the cost of a zero-cost plan. Aaron, Barth, Packer, Eizenstat, Schultze, Sue Woolsey (associate director for human resources, OMB), and others drew up a tentative list for interim use, which would eventually require presidential approval. On the list of potential "official" offsets given to ISP staff on April 5 were the following:[7]

AFDC & other Maintenance Assistance	$6.6 billion
SSI	5.7
Food Stamps (except Puerto Rico)	5.0
EITC	1.3
Section 8 New Starts (would amount to 0.4 billion over a period of years)	—
Unemployment Insurance (over 26 weeks)	1.3
CETA	5.1
Veterans Provisions	3.2

Several legitimate questions could be raised about those offsets which did not directly result from the imposition of a new program. The notion behind the section 8 starts and extended unemployment insurance (UI) offsets was that, if in a new, improved income maintenance system, people are given more money, outlays from regular UI benefits and new housing starts will diminish. This was perfectly legitimate reasoning assuming that the Labor Department would be able to prepare and pass legislation for phasing out the UI benefits. Far more problematic (and much more central to keeping down the cost of the plan) was the CETA Title VI offset, which Packer had pushed hard to get on the list. CETA was set to end in 1979, and, as of April, the administration had not proposed any extension or reauthorization of Title VI. Since the welfare program was not to be in place until at least 1981, the fact that CETA might not exist brought into question its validity as an offset. Even if CETA were reauthorized, however, questions could still be raised about its use as an offset. First, Title VI, which was added to CETA in 1975 as a countercyclical measure to ease the impact of high unemployment, was not specifically targetted on low-income people (only roughly half of the beneficiaries of the program had been subject to an income test)[8] and would have to be redirected in any new legislation. Second, there was no guarantee that the amount of money available in a new program would in fact amount to $5.1 billion. And third, the administration was assuming that the unemployment rate would be low enough in 1981 to "capture" some of the countercyclical aid (partly because of the jobs program) for a PSE program. Considering the number of questionable assumptions, it would clearly be a contestable matter of political judgment if Carter decided to use CETA as a standard offset. As Sue Woolsey observed:

> I don't think anybody presumed it would be standard accounting, but it is also a very standard political act. When they proposed the SSI portion of FAP, for example, it was supposed to be offset by cashing out food stamps but two weeks after SSI was passed they decided not to cash out food stamps after all.

Without the use of the CETA offset, it would have been virtually impossible to present Carter with a zero-cost plan that any of the planners would have considered humane.

As it was, the HEW plan under preparation was a spartan one, and, consequently, Barth and Aaron had directed ISP staff to make sure the benefits for the aged were politically palatable in the event that Carter seriously wished to opt for a no-cost plan. The ISP staff were not altogether happy with this directive. As one staff member commented:

> I think we made a serious mistake by not taking Carter at his word. Had we come back and said, "let's take this pot of money and design a system that we think is the best," and then tell him what he can get with increments, we'd have been in a lot better shape than designing the system we did (and almost got stuck with). If I were going to design a normative system without regard to what presently exists or political considerations, I would not decide that aged people need more to live on than non-aged people. What we did, however, was essentially replicate the SSI benefit structure to make sure that SSI recipients or aged people got more than non-aged people. We were concerned that he was not going to give us any more money, so we wanted to make sure we proposed something the department could live with politically.
>
> I think he might well have been more disposed to give additional money if we had taken the analytically literal route. What we did instead was say, "Here's our proposal, it's not all that bad . . . 25% of current recipients will be worse under the proposal, but if we have an extra billion dollars, we can increase benefit levels across the board and only 22% will be made worse off." Well, if I'm the president, that doesn't buy me much. On the other hand, if you tell me that raising the benefit levels for a particular portion of the population would buy me a lot of people not being made worse off, and a very important group of people at that, then I can see spending the billion. . . . At least then it's his judgment about how to spend additional money.

Califano's role in this particular decision is not clear, but apparently he was at least aware of it, if not at the source of it.* As Mike Barth recalled, Califano was generally emphasizing the need to produce a politically saleable proposal:

---

*According to Barth's calendar, a one-hour "information-decision" meeting was planned for the secretary during the week of April 4 on issues involved in categorizing the welfare population and benefit levels. The issue paper to be provided for the meeting was to discuss specifically differentiating the aged from the non-aged and the "benefit level differences implicit in [those] distinctions."

When we did the ISP proposal for Weinberger it was totally in-house and very antiseptic and vacuum-like. There were no real issues such as "will organized labor buy this?" With Califano, you were always dealing with those kinds of issues: "We've got to come up with something good that we can enact." That's the policy game. Come up with something that makes sense from the point of view of public policy, that you can enact.

THE SECOND PRESIDENTIAL BRIEFING

On April 6, Califano met with ISP staff to go over the briefing charts for the meeting with the president on the 11th. The analysts had drawn preliminary diagrams of the three proposals and presented them to Califano for his reaction. As one staff member recalled:

> We charted the plan the Labor Department had given us on April 2. We charted the current system on top and the new system on the bottom and dramatized the differences between the two by using a color code. The current system we put in blue and we had six or seven boxes under income assistance for programs like AFDC, SSI, veterans' pensions, food stamps, and so forth, and then we had a couple of boxes under employment and training like CETA and WIN. Anything which was new was done in red, in the new system. Well, in our plan, we had consolidated AFDC, SSI, and food stamps and redirected CETA; so for our plan there was a big new, red box that said "Consolidated Cash Assistance." The Labor Department's plan showed the same boxes on the top and bottom, so the chart was a beautiful physical representation of one plan doing nothing and another plan restructuring the system.
>
> I pulled this out and said, "I haven't made this into a formal chart yet but we think it shows what is being proposed here. Do you want me to get this reproduced so that we can give it to the people who are coming to the meeting tonight?" Califano responded, "Oh, no, we'll spring this one on them at the White House." He had an instinct for the jugular. He liked having something visible, too. He liked the symbolism. [See Appendix 4 for copies of the two charts.]

Later that day, Califano, Aaron, Barth, Marshall, Packer, Frank Raines, and Woolsey met for dinner to discuss the three proposals. Most of the discussion focused on the relative merits of the HEW and DOL plans. Califano subsequently recalled that by this time he was coming around to the HEW viewpoint. As he stated, "The jobs program troubled me; as somebody once said to Marshall, there are terrific jobs in the woods of Yosemite National Park, but how the hell are they going to get a welfare mother out there?" Califano was not overly troubled, however, about the HEW-Labor disputes. As he recalled, "I thought Labor thought there was a turf problem and I think the two staffs fought about turf . . . but I wasn't surprised at that." Califano's prime concern appeared to be the zero-cost constraint. As he commented that evening, "The real problem is that $22 billion [the amount spent on AFDC, SSI, food stamps, and CETA] just doesn't stretch far enough. Everybody's ideal is a decent income supplement and a good job. But when you try to squash that down to $22 billion, you just don't get much."[9]

None of the differences between HEW and DOL were resolved at the meeting, but in one area at least a consensus had emerged: neither Califano nor any of the other officials would recommend any of the three options at zero cost. In a memo to President Carter on April 8, Eizenstat and Raines stated:

> Each of the plans increases the number of persons aided and also raises the benefits for some current recipients. In order to achieve these improvements at zero-cost, the benefits for many others had to be significantly reduced. The secretary would not recommend any of these plans without an amelioration of these adverse impacts. We would agree.[10]

Sue Woolsey was passing similar advice to the director of OMB, Bert Lance.* She argued in an April 9 memo that, "At zero-cost, none of [the plans] is worth pursuing; too many present recipients would be made worse off, and a number of positive features of the present system—such as the work incentive under AFDC—would have to be sacrificed to keep costs down."[11] She was especially critical of the Labor Department's plan and Tom Joe's plan. She advised Lance that "the Multiple-Track System and guaranteed jobs proposals, as presented, also have serious structural defects, which would be difficult to remedy at any price."[12] Woolsey felt, as did the Council of Economic Advisers, that guaranteed jobs would make it unprofitable for people to seek and stay in low-wage and mostly seasonal private-sector jobs. Regarding the triple-track proposal, Woolsey felt that, in the track for unemployed but employable family members, the relation between regular UI benefits (which were not

---

*OMB views apparently rarely reached the president, at least in written form. Lance preferred to express his concerns to Carter informally, rather than relying on prepared analytic materials. Sue Woolsey observed that Lance "had two major characteristics in this process. One is that he didn't want to be bothered with the program details, and he had staff which felt that program details are the program, so I found it very difficult to get my whale to fight with the other whales. On the other hand he had fantastic access to the president, so he was an unpredictable actor. If I got him upset about something he'd immediately get word to the president, but I could not predictably get him upset."

income tested and lasted for the first twenty-six weeks of unemployment) and subsequent income-tested benefits was unclear and could create work disincentives. (A description of the plans as of April 9 and Woolsey's criticisms of them is in Appendix 5).

On April 8, Califano himself met with the consulting group and sought their advice as to how the deficient zero-cost plans could be best improved, by requesting them, as Carter had of him, to select where expenditures above the $22 billion then being spent on welfare should be directed. Concerned that a zero-cost plan would have either inhumane benefit levels or inadequate fiscal relief, Califano pressed the group for a "prioritization" of these two issues. Although Barry Van Lare objected to the "choices inherent in the question,"[13] he nonetheless indicated the governors' preference for fiscal relief and the welfare advocates similarly indicated their own preference for higher benefit levels. Apparently frustrated by the difficulty of forgoing fundamental compromises in the welfare debate, Califano commented on the "immense political problems" of attempting to consolidate the welfare system, and soon thereafter left the meeting.[14]

Califano had good reason to be pessimistic. During the week preceding the consulting group meeting, Califano had received letters from Congressmen Ullman and Corman that gave little cause for optimism about the course his department was pursuing. Ullman remained unrelentingly opposed to the negative income tax and wanted to present welfare reform in an incremental package rather than an omnibus bill. Corman, who was also a key figure in the House in determining the course of welfare legislation (and was perceived to be more sympathetic to HEW aims), similarly expressed his preference for a dual-track approach, feeling it was likely to generate more political support.

In light of the limitations of the zero-cost plans, uncertain congressional support for the HEW plan, and the rapidly nearing May 1 deadline, HEW hoped that at the April 11 meeting the president would either select from the three options the one he preferred (in which case it could be more extensively developed) or at least lift the zero-cost limit and indicate how much additional money he would be willing to spend and for what purposes. At the White House, however, Carter was being counseled to be cautious in the upcoming briefing. Eizenstat and Raines advised Carter to "explore" the three options but suggested that he refrain from making any decisions regarding them. Their "Talking Points" for the meeting were as follows:

A. The three plans represent different concepts of how an income support system might be structured. You may want to explore with the Secretary the comparative merits of each concept from a social policy standpoint.

B. The Secretary has not had time to obtain complete information on who gains and who loses in each of the plans. We recommend that you ask him to provide you with that information, broken down by recipient characteristic and region, at his next briefing.

C. The Secretary and his staff have done an admirable job in responding to your request for zero-cost reform alternatives. Their analytical work has been consistently outstanding.

D. There is no need for you to make any decisions at this briefing.[15]

In a memo of April 9, Watson and Parham offered similar counsel, advising Carter not to pick a specific option but push instead for a compromise plan. After listing twelve criteria by which a welfare plan could be evaluated, Watson closed the memo by saying:

> I suggest that you mention again to Joe and Ray that you want HEW and Labor to *strive* for concurrence on their recommendations on the jobs component of the package. . . . I want to stress again how important it is to have the signals clear between you and Joe as to exactly what he is to submit on May 1.[16]

On April 11, at a few minutes before 1:00 P.M., Califano arrived at the White House carrying roughly twenty charts. Besides Carter, approximately fifteen people attended the second briefing, including Califano, Aaron, and Barth from HEW, Marshall and Packer from DOL, Lance, Bo Cutter (executive director), and Sue Woolsey from OMB, Charlie Schultze from CEA, Watson, Parham, Eizenstat, Carp, and Raines from the White House staff, and Vice President Mondale. With the aid of his charts, Califano began the briefing by quickly pointing out the current expenditures which would be available for welfare reform, including the CETA offset. He then proceeded to show diagrammatically that an improved zero-cost restructuring of the system would necessarily leave many current recipients worse off. (See Appendix 4 for a copy of the chart.) As Aaron observed, "We were pointing out that if you are going to raise anybody's benefits in the zero-cost system, you've got to lower somebody's benefits. When you talk about lowering people's benefits, that's politically very difficult to do, so it is much easier to carry out reform if you are willing to spend some additional money. Simple. Basic."

Califano then proceeded to the bulk of the briefing: the review of the three zero-cost options. He outlined the workings of each option, compared each to the existing system (see Appendix 4), roughly noted "gainers" and "losers" by demographic groups (aged, blind, disabled, single-parent families, two-parent families, childless couples, and singles), reviewed major achievements, shortcomings, and unresolved issues, and finally supplied what one HEW official called a "menu" of increments.*

Beginning with the HEW plan, Califano pointed out that, at zero cost, work incentives would appear inadequate and many recipients made worse off. He noted that without state supplements to the federal minimum, the plan would provide $7 billion of fiscal relief, but 60 percent of the current recipients would be worse off. With state supplements, perhaps 10 percent to 20 percent would be worse off, but fiscal relief would be less. He noted that the DOL proposal reduced all CETA jobs to minimum wage, left AFDC benefit disparities unchanged, did not help single persons or childless couples, was administratively complex, and might place the development of a large PSE program in the hands of the Employment Service, which was widely acknowledged to have a bad track record with the poor and uneducated. He pointed out many of the same shortcomings for the triple-track approach, also noting that many recipients would be worse off, that there were insufficient work incentives, and that it provided no fiscal relief, since it froze state supplements at the existing level.

Carter clearly appeared to be uncomfortable with Califano's presentation of the difficulties of large-scale jobs programs. As Charlie Schultze recalled:

> We were discussing the jobs programs, and I thought I was making some headway in squaring this circle; that is, I was pointing out, first, the inflationary impact of a jobs program with attractive wages, and, second, alternately that at low wages the jobs might be dead-end and hence lead to creating a kind of public service ghetto. All of a sudden, the president took the 1.4 million figure we were using, divided it by the ratio of the national population to the Plains, Georgia, population, and figured out that we would roughly need to create three jobs in Plains. "Well," he said, "I can figure out how we can use three jobs in Plains or ten in my county," and started ticking them off.

*For example, under the consolidated cash assistance proposal the following increments were listed (with rough estimates): "Reimburse states for supplements exceeding current expenditures" ($0.5–5.0 billion); "Standard work expense deduction" ($0–1.5 billion); "Enlarged emergency assistance" ($1.0 billion); "Retain extended UI" ($1.3 billion); "Eliminate income taxes for recipients" ($0.5 billion); "Tax relief to lower income taxpayers" ($2.5–15.0 billion); "Higher benefits and more tax relief" ("?"). These increments appeared in a chart entitled "Consolidated Cash Assistance (Zero Cost)," presented at the April 11, 1977, briefing for the president.

Then Mondale, who is from some little town in Minnesota, did the same division, and chimed in all happy; his town would need eight jobs and he could see how they could be used.

I came charging in with "what do you do with 150,000 jobs in New York City?" But I'm quite certain that the concreteness with which Carter envisioned the jobs rendered absolutely null and void my attempt to raise difficulties, and changed, at a critical point, the president's attitude toward a big jobs program from modest skepticism to fervent support. That change occurred the minute he made that calculation; as a peanut warehouseman from Plains he understandably could picture concrete low-wage jobs that were needed. Had his background been different—had he been Hugh Carey [governor of New York] or Abe Beame [mayor of New York City]—I don't know what he would have done, but it would have been different.

Having seemingly been rebuffed on the jobs issue, Schultze went on to question the use of the CETA offset in the zero-cost base, noting that the $8 billion proposed for CETA as part of the economic stimulus package was planned to diminish as the economy improved. According to the notes of someone who was present at the meeting, the conclusion of the discussion went roughly as follows:

> *Califano*: It might be that at zero-cost no one would recommend changes other than tinkering with the administrative apparatus and perhaps creating 100,000 CETA jobs for the poor.
>
> If we want this plan to be politically viable we need to at least moderate the cost structure to get structural reforms. There are problems, too, in creating jobs for this kind of population. Mr. President, I don't think that any of these plans is really adequate unless we increase present spending, and I am asking your approval on that.
>
> We also need to be careful with making sure we know the details of the plan in order to avoid the problems which besieged FAP. I can't give you a program on May 1 with every *t* crossed and every *i* dotted. I would like to do a state-by-state analysis of the program and am not confident that details can be provided on May 1.
>
> *President*: At zero-cost, is the present system the best one? As far as I'm concerned what you've just told me is that our welfare system can't get any better.
>
> *Aaron*: If there were no prior history then maybe one of the new systems would be better, but people become accustomed to the current benefit levels.

Eizenstat: Don't forget your promise to [Mayor] Beame about reducing the local share of costs.

President: Joe, as you've explained it, we should just leave it as it is. We don't have five to ten billion dollars to put into a new system. Why not say to hell with it!

Califano: Changes would take time to implement so we could take a Russell Long approach and do demonstration projects.

President: I was pleased with the first presentation because you showed inequities and abuses of the welfare system. But if you are going to keep inviolate the privilege of making eight- to ten-thousand dollars a year in welfare payments, then I agree nothing can be done. It's a travesty on the taxpayer. I think we are wasting our time.

Califano: Only $1.7 billion can be gotten by stopping welfare cheating.

President: What about administrative graft? Are there zero savings from that? The American people will be delighted that we have the best system possible at the present level.

Marshall: I don't agree. I think we can make some changes to meet problems.

Califano: At zero-cost we are retaining so many inequities that we would be shot out of the water. I haven't expected these alternatives.

President: Simply to say take the highest benefit level and pay everybody the same— . . . Well, I don't buy the assumption that once you set a benefit level you have to bring everybody up to it. I don't think the federal government should be responsible for an income higher than a husband working at the minimum wage.

We must present this to the American people very soon. I would like to change the state supplement structure as you outlined and perhaps freeze the existing state supplements. Also, in two families of the same size, I want it so the family in which a member works always makes more than a family in which they don't work. I'm not committed to reaching the seven billion dollar mark in fiscal relief and am perfectly willing to shift CETA to minimum wage jobs . . . but stop protecting those receiving benefits.

Packer: If the programs work, then you will also have more resources.

Califano: Only after several years.

President: Why would it take several years? Sixty percent of the people who work full-time in Plains are high school dropouts. We can present the jobs portion of it. It has some logical basis. The biggest problem is between those who have pride and those next door who are really not bad people.

Aaron: It will be very difficult to create jobs for this population. Most welfare recipients are illiterate and unskilled.

President: People on my farm work complicated machinery, drive fork lifts, and put herbicide on peanut plants—which has to be done in just the right proportions so as to kill the bugs and not kill the plants—and when it comes time to cash their paychecks, they sign with an X. If you give people a chance, they will work.

Packer: Of course, across the long span of history, and even now in many countries, most workers are not literate.

Watson: We could include Title XX and some revenue sharing money in the zero-cost base, too.

President: It is the government's responsibility to keep the family together and not effect vast movements of population from one place to another. People move from Chicago to New York to get higher welfare benefits. New York benefits are too high due to political influences and poor administration. . . .

I would like to consider including other programs. In the next day, list things we would like to accomplish. If we do relieve the states of some welfare costs I might be able to give you some money by reducing federal aid to the states under LEAA [Law Enforcement Assistance Administration]. I can also get you some of the revenue sharing money. Over a period of time I would be willing to put some more money into the welfare system, but you must continue to look at zero-cost options to keep the variables down.

Schultze: We could lower the basic benefit by $1,000 and add a new housing allowance.

President: It's not fair to have the same benefit in rural areas and New York City. It doesn't cost as much to live at home as it does up here.

Meeting adjourns.

DEVELOPING THE PRINCIPLES

Carter's interest in a zero-cost plan and his momentary willingness to junk the entire welfare reform effort had stunned the HEW contingent: it was later reported in the *Washington Post* that Carter's outburst had "caused in Califano a rare moment of speechlessness."[17] Stu Eizenstat explained that the HEW officials "were frankly in a state of shock because it's virtually impossible to talk about a new design without spending more money. You've got to talk about something like $15 billion, even if you don't spend it all the first year."[18] Sue Woolsey had a similar recollection of the meeting:

Everybody at HEW had been working their tails off to get this thing together, to design it fully, and they got this comeback which was "that's not what I'm looking for." I recall sitting in the meeting and just watching their faces and realizing that they didn't know that's the way he thinks—it was a terrible shock to them. They didn't function very well for a while after that. Their reaction was "my God, what are we going to do, what are we going to do?" which is not unpredictable. Had I been in their shoes I probably would have had the same reaction.

Frank Raines observed about Califano's reaction:

I don't think Joe understood what the president was saying. You couldn't achieve the reforms, all of the significant reforms which Joe was talking about, without spending any more money. You could improve welfare over time. Later in that meeting Joe began to explain that, yes, you could make some reforms, and that we would present a package to him of what you could do for no cost and what it would cost to do more on top of that. So the president left the meeting still positive about welfare reform but there was that moment when he thought the agency was simply saying "we need more money, there is nothing that can be done without more money." That just got his back up. He thought they were trying to sandbag him.

Although Califano was not opposed to "the technique" of zero-cost planning, he was distraught over the thought of an actual zero-cost plan. As he recalled:

The zero-cost limit was unrealistic. Even Ullman and Russell Long realized that. You basically had too many losers [at zero cost] to use our parlance. You couldn't pass anything with that many losers.

I understood the macro judgment, "I want to balance the budget, I don't want to be a spender. I want to change that image." I appreciate that, but the reality was that there were a lot of poor people out there getting nothing, so you've got to spend some extra money. . . . I expressed those concerns in memos, some tough memos, and expressed it privately [to the president].

THE GUIDELINES MULTIPLY

When Califano returned to HEW on April 11, he quickly drew up a memorandum of "guiding principles" in response to Carter's closing request that he list goals of the welfare reform effort. Califano argued for a consolidated cash approach with universal coverage, requested approval on the offsets, and asked once again for additional funds. Roughly two weeks prior to the May 1 deadline, Califano's principles for welfare reform were as follows:

1. Simplify administration and introduce efficient systems management by consolidating in one cash assistance program: SSI, AFDC, Food Stamps, "Section 8" housing, earned income tax credit, extended unemployment benefits (26 to 39 weeks). Amount $20.7 billion.
2. Redirect CETA public service employment and training to jobs for the poorest people who can work. Amount: $8 billion.
3. Freeze the state supplement to AFDC and SSI at current level. Amount $8 billion.
4. Provide a universal minimum federal benefit, with some variation to reflect different community costs of living. Try to use housing allowance as a way to reflect cost variations.
5. No non-working family will have higher income than a comparable working family.
6. Provide special health, education, and training programs to those who need them to be prepared for redirected CETA jobs.
7. Set up priorities for CETA jobs: e.g., first, two-parent families with minor children; second, single-parent families with children in secondary school, etc.
8. Provide maximum incentive to work: if necessary, in the redirected CETA program; and provide incentive to move from redirected CETA jobs to the private sector jobs.
9. Place as many incentives as possible for keeping the family together and eliminate all incentives for breaking up the family.
10. Use funding increments above zero-cost to increase equity and make package more politically attractive.[19]

Califano's memo was given to President Carter on April 15, along with an addendum from Ray Marshall, a memorandum from Jim Parham summarizing comments on Califano's proposed principles, a brief comment from Eizenstat and Raines, and a memorandum from Watson and Parham incorporating a separate list of principles to help guide the welfare effort. Marshall agreed with most of the principles that Califano stated, although he felt it was "too early in the program design to set specific details in concrete."[20] Marshall's real concern was that he did not want Carter to adopt the consolidated cash approach Califano outlined in his first principle. He went on to add:

Under Item 1, I agree that we should aim to simplify administration and introduce efficient systems management by consolidating cash assistance programs as much as possible. It is too
early, however, to be sure that the consolidation should include
the earned income tax credit or extended unemployment benefits. Clearly, we are not going to have a consolidated cash
assistance program that includes all unemployment insurance
benefits. And we will have different systems that pay out black
lung benefits and disability payments. The objective is correct,
but how far we can go will depend upon the specific design that
you choose.[21]

Eizenstat and Raines supported Marshall's claim that the first principle was too specific. They advised the president that "we also agree with
Secretary Marshall's observation that the details of item 1 . . . should be
worked out in the design of a specific proposal."[22] They went on to
counsel Carter once again to be cautious and suggested that the relatively noncontroversial principles that Califano had sent to the White House
would help establish criteria for evaluating the welfare effort. They
wrote, "These memos do not require any action on your part. HEW and
Labor are in the process of developing detailed options based on these
principles. When they present those options the list of principles can be
used as a basis to test the various options."[23] Parham's memo expressed
several additional concerns. Under the second principle he reminded
Carter of Schultze's warning about the use of the CETA offset and
expressed the fear that CETA not be associated with the welfare system
so as to make sure recipients' stigma was minimized. Carter noted on the
side of the memo that the "concepts may be for them to 'graduate' from
welfare to work program (DOL)" and checked off Parham's warning
about CETA. (In the Carter White House, checks appeared to be the
equivalent of "good point.")

If the complaint, however, was that Califano's principles were actually
too specific, no such complaints could be lodged against the additional
list that Watson and Parham forwarded to the president. Despite the
dire view of the fiscal constraint prevailing elsewhere, Watson and
Parham described the potential welfare reform program in glowing
rhetoric:*

We sense some genuine frustration on your part at the difficulty of putting together a welfare reform package. It is an area

---

*Parham, who was an old friend of the president's, was convinced that the zero-cost
stricture was simply a temporary managerial ploy.

of public policy that arouses deep passions, and much of the controversy reflects historical legacies of slavery, segregation, poor schools, job discrimination, and economic exploitation.

We know you will not permit such frustration to impel you to a premature or forced judgment about a reform plan. *We believe you have an historic opportunity to establish new ideals for social and economic justice that will set the pattern in this country for the next several decades.* Judgment on such a vital issue should not be rushed. Unrealistic deadlines should be tempered until you have a proposal with which you are comfortable philosophically, intellectually and pragmatically.[24]

They went on to lay out twelve goals that made Califano's principles appear as marvels of specificity; the first two principles, for example, read:

1. The purpose of welfare reform should be to encourage self-support; strengthen families; provide adequate subsistence resources; reduce the stigma associated with receipt of benefits; simplify and make more efficient the administration of the system; promote social and economic justice; and build national pride.
2. Effective opportunity for productive, contributive employment, self-support and self-esteem is the first responsibility of an organized society.[25]

Carter indicated his agreement by writing "O.K." along with his initials on the upper right-hand corner of the memo. He similarly placed little checks next to the principles Califano laid out.

While the White House was preoccupied with such broad conceptual matters, ISP and DOL staff were scrambling to prepare specific new zero-cost options for the May 1 deadline. Perhaps in response to the president's dismay that little could be done at zero-cost, or perhaps in reaction to the HEW diagrammatic displays of the Department of Labor's plan, Packer began to send a constant flow of alternative plans over to HEW to be costed out. Over the next few weeks, the burden of analyzing these plans created considerable tension between HEW and DOL staff and some bitterness. An ISP staff member described what began to happen shortly after the April 11 meeting:

We met with Labor on the 13th, 16th, 21st, 23rd, and 25th and I would literally be on the phone hour after hour getting a new plan. Barth's idea of fair play was to do a formal analytic piece on every proposal that they would come up with. So we would analyze the plan, and then they would come up with a new one.* "Change the filing units, vary the parameters of the EITC," and so on. Suddenly, for example, he was pushing for a very large EITC. Conceptually the changes were rather trivial, but there was a lot of staff time spent treating them as if they were very important. Three analysts at the Labor Department were creating all this Sturm und Drang and Barth with his army was bogged down and tied up in knots. We couldn't be advocates because we were the analysts who were supposed to be fair and cost out all of these plans.

As we visualized it, they were on the other side of the wall and lobbing bombs over to us every day—"here, have another one, you guys." It was a rational bureaucratic move for an advocate. In fact, it was a brilliant one, but it was very frustrating because there was nobody from top to bottom who was willing to say, "enough, we analyzed seventeen plans."

Packer, for his part, denied any intention of tying up the HEW staff and argued that their emphasis on finalizing a plan was inappropriate. Packer saw the issue primarily on larger, conceptual grounds:

It wasn't anything as sophisticated as that. We would send them a proposal, which, incidentally, we would first have costed out in a rough model at Mathematica, before sending it over to HEW. People at HEW would then find criticisms with the proposal.

We had these three or four principles which were our keystone. They were, that for those expected to work there should be a job, that the benefit reduction rates would be less than 50% in order to encourage people to work, and that we would keep people away from the welfare system as much as possible through the use of the earned income tax credit. When people found that this detail was a problem or that detail was a problem, we would just modify the program design to accommodate that. There was criticism that, "gee, where is your proposal?" but we didn't think that was appropriate. We thought that you ought to know your basic principles and build around them. We never did change our fundamental principles, but within those principles we would accommodate whatever problems people brought to our attention.

---

*Analysis of the plans typically entailed a couple members of the staff drawing up a summary of the advantages and disadvantages of a proposal: was it target efficient? how would it affect current recipients? what rhetorical and political advantages did the proposal contain? what current inequities did the proposal redress or fail to address? and so forth. Major alterations in the program would be put into the computer for costing; more minor cost adjustments were usually calculated manually by John Todd.

Packer's rapid adjustments inevitably fostered confusion in HEW. As Aaron observed:

> Labor had a very different approach to the issue, which may have flowed from their institutional arrangement. They just didn't stick on any particular plan. They would press on something and if you objected to that they would jump a long way off and try something completely different. So it was very difficult to have a sequential development of a proposal. It was inevitably disorderly, sometimes productive, and very hard to deal with.

With regard to the directives they were receiving from Aaron and Barth, ISP staff commented:

> Barth was giving us some direction. It wasn't particularly what we wanted and Packer was sort of running circles around him, but he was ordering us to be analytically responsive. . . .
>
> Aaron was playing the in-house Brookings analyst. A fine analyst, the best analyst in the tribe, but largely functioning as a one-man analyst. He was not planning tactics or strategy, he was not saying, "Look, here's how we handle this particular situation." He was not functioning as a staff director.

Aaron and Barth, however, seemed themselves to be placed in a difficult position by Califano's aloofness and unwillingness to commit himself to a particular strategy or course of action. As one ISP staff member recalled:

> There was a Saturday meeting with Califano (I think it related to charts) and Packer had not been told about it. He came storming across the mall, came storming into this meeting, and started screaming at Califano that he had not been treated appropriately, that this meeting was going on and that he should have been invited.
>
> At this point, Califano said, "Wait a minute, Arnie, I'm doing everything I can to be fair. Aaron's troops, you know, have developed this plan and I've been looking at that plan and simultaneously listening to you, too."
>
> Califano dealt with him really well and Mike may have been reading those signals; he had a boss who did not really know where he wanted to come out. . . . It's not clear that from his point of view being responsive every time wasn't the best strategy for Mike Barth.

On April 16, Barth, Todd, ISP staff, and Packer and his staff met for two hours to go over their respective plans, disagreements, and the structure of the next Carter briefing, set for April 26. They agreed that the briefing would present the areas where HEW and DOL were in agreement, the areas where they were in disagreement (along with some pros and cons), a description of the two proposals in complete form, and a request for further guidance in areas of disagreement or the selection of a preferred approach. In a memo from Todd to Aaron that summarized the meeting Todd claimed:

> They [DOL] seemed particularly anxious to achieve as much agreement as possible and to minimize the disagreements. To that end, they seemed to make several important changes in the proposal they are putting forward:
> • Closed-end funding of the CETA jobs.
> • Back-up cash assistance for those employables for whom we are unable to find a job.
> Their proposal continues to change by the moment on many points. They seem willing to let us make their decisions—in fact, in some instances they seemed to be insisting on it.[26]

Todd went on to discuss the DOL proposal and then outlined the areas of agreement and disagreement:

> As we understand it, the areas of agreement are:
> 1. Jobs not guaranteed, i.e., closed-end funding of CETA.
> 2. Back-up cash assistance for those family heads for whom we cannot provide a job.
> 3. Elimination of food stamps.
> 4. Putting AFDC, SSI and cash assistance for individuals and childless couples into a single administrative agency.
> 5. Provision of some kind of income supplementation for family heads with earnings below $8,333.
> 6. Some redirection of CETA in the form of minimum wage jobs targetted on the low income population.
> 7. Federalization of AFDC with a national minimum and standardization of benefit computation.
> This is more agreement than we have had before, but the list above may make it appear that we are closer than we actually are.
> In addition, there may be some disagreement over how to phrase the agreement on not offering guaranteed jobs. Packer seemed to resist our characterizations of the agreement. He

wants to keep as much of the rhetoric of guaranteed jobs as he can. This could be troublesome.

The major areas of disagreement are:

1. Whether individuals and childless couples should be given less generous support levels than families with children.
2. The size of the CETA program.
3. The extent of CETA redirection.
4. The total wage offered in PSE:
   - we offer $3,900 (30 hours)
   - they offer $5,200 (40 hours)
5. The number of agencies providing income tested cash support:
   - we have one,
   - they have three:
   - Welfare (which really has three separate sub-programs).
   - The stand-by cash assistance under DOL.
   - The Earned Income Tax Credit.
6. The financial parameters of support offered to employable family heads:
   - How [is the] guarantee family-size conditioned?
   - Tax rate on earnings.
   - Account taken of other income.

Note that, in our opinion, the different administrative agencies and benefit levels and tax rates for different groups in their program will make it very difficult to sustain an extended filing unit or a relatively long accountable period. If so, this will make their approach inherently more expensive in those respects.[27]

While HEW and DOL struggled to reach a compromise plan, the consulting group held its final meeting (April 15), at which the zero-cost plans were unveiled. No one was very enthusiastic about either plan. Alair Townsend, a welfare analyst for the House Budget Committee, observed about the HEW plan, "You're making people vastly worse off. In what sense is this welfare reform?"[28] Henry Freedman criticized HEW's plan for part-time, minimum-wage public jobs, contending that it was "in every way the opposite of meaningful work."[29] Distressed by Packer's proposal for guaranteed jobs at the minimum wage, Catherine Day-Jermany exclaimed, "We're creating the new plantation! People are being put into a second-class work situation with no rights and no opportunities."[30] Packer, who was himself very disappointed that the wage had to be lowered, admitted, "We can't tell you it's a living wage. It's a way to scrape by for a year."[31]

On the Monday following the final meeting of the consulting group, Aaron outlined in a memo to Califano his concerns about the political viability of the direction the welfare reform debate was taking. Aaron stated:

The objective of our work on welfare reform is to develop a proposal that will
- secure the *support of the President,* and
- win *approval from Congress*
  Unfortunately these objectives may be incompatible.
  The President seems attracted to proposals that satisfy *the ten principles of welfare reform* you set forth in your memorandum. The Plan that best satisfied these principles would consist of
- a *uniform negative income tax* applicable uniformly to all households, combined with
- a program of *public service jobs* directed to the maximum feasible extent to the poor.[32]

After going on to outline the opposition of Ullman and Long to a negative income tax, Aaron summarized:

In short, *the plan to which the President is likely to be most attracted seems unlikely to pass Congress.* Therefore we must design
- one plan that incorporates the most desirable structure (i.e., comprehensive cash), and
- another plan that retains most desirable structural reforms but sacrifices some for political acceptability.
  The second plan should
- satisfy your ten principles of welfare reform
- fulfill the President's desire for bold and imaginative reform, and
- have some chance of appealing to Congressman Ullman.[33]

Aaron went on to suggest his own version of what was nominally a dual-track system but was actually a thinly disguised version of the comprehensive cash plan HEW was promoting.* Aaron felt that:

This system
- *in structure,* differs negligibly from the program of comprehensive cash with jobs we presented to the President and which he found appealing.
- *in form* it is a two track plan that, based on three conversations with Congressman Ullman, I think he could be convinced to accept.[34]

---

*Aaron's proposal would have created one track for those households in which no member was expected to work: this track would have a basic benefit of $4,300 for a family of four and a disregard up to $100 a month of earnings and would reduce benefits by 100 percent of earnings over $100 per month. Essentially this track was the same as the "not expected to work" tier in triple track (with slightly stronger work incentives). Track 2, for households where a member was expected to work, also offered a guarantee of $4,300, taxed earnings at 50 percent, and would offer part-time or full-time public service jobs at the minimum wage. Track 2 was a negative income tax with a jobs component attached—that is, essentially HEW's original proposal.

While Aaron struggled to find a politically viable reform option,* Packer continued to fan the flames of philosophical debate between the two agencies. Returning from an April 18 meeting with HEW, Packer ordered a memo to be drafted from Marshall to Califano that would rebut HEW assertions that a large-scale, full-time jobs program was not feasible. The memo, which was sent on the 21st, flatly asserted that "the answers" to "the questions" raised about "our ability to offer jobs rather than cash to over a million adult members of low income families . . . must rest on our judgment and interpretation of the available information."[35] Marshall admitted that "we have not yet mounted an effort precisely analogous in terms of scale and specifications to what we now propose," but nonetheless went on to argue that "federally funded employment and training programs have involved 9–10 million poor over the past 15 years. It is my judgment that there are lessons in this experience that indicate that we can do the job."[36]

Marshall outlined four factors that would present a challenge to a successful DOL proposal: the scale of the program, the low wage offered by the program, the targetting of the program on low-skilled workers, and the nature of the program, that is, whether meaningful and productive jobs could be created. Reviewing the history of past programs along these four dimensions (see Appendix 6), Marshall concluded that "[in] our past record I have found that we have succeeded in separate programs at different times in meeting the conditions posed on our proposal. What is needed now, and has not yet been done, is to put these elements together in a single effort."[37]

Competition between the two agencies intensified as the debate over the feasibility of job creation heated up even further. Pointing to the inadequacies of the U.S. Employment Service, Barth claimed that unless a better mechanism could be found, "Labor shouldn't make its proposal."[38] "That's saying to hell with it," Packer retorted. "That's saying the employment service is no good and people are no good, so just give welfare recipients a minimum amount of money and say to hell with it."[39] Barth sent a note to Califano on April 23 in an effort to counter Marshall's memo of the 21st:

> The purpose of Secretary Marshall's memo is to convince you that recent experience with Public Service Employment suggests that it will be feasible for them to create a large number of suitable jobs in the appropriate time. This note puts Marshall's memo into some more neutral perspective.
>
> The issue is accurately posed: does whatever success the Labor Department has had in its separate, relatively small pro-

---

*Califano did not take Aaron's suggestion that his proposal be given equal billing with the HEW proposal in the upcoming briefing.

grams suggest that job opportunities can be developed (1) in much larger numbers, (2) while paying the minimum wage, (3) which are suitable for low-skilled workers, and (4) which provide meaningful and productive work experience. The answer is highly uncertain.[40]

Barth proceeded to consider briefly the four issues that Secretary Marshall had raised, giving them an alternative interpretation (see Appendix 7), and concluded:

> Secretary Marshall's memo has not changed the statement that *we have had very little experience in rapidly creating large numbers of minimum wage jobs for prime-age workers.*
> One final caution. We should not be put in the pure naysayer position. We should support a re-targetting of CETA as fast as is possible. But we should point out that raising false expectations has costs, as does developing a job program mess to parallel the welfare mess.[41]

HEW's adamant opposition to Packer's guaranteed jobs program, and the manner in which the DOL program had been presented in the April 11 meeting, made Packer wary about any HEW presentation of the DOL plan to President Carter. An early draft of the charts for the president that were to outline areas of agreement and disagreement, along with some pros and cons, confirmed Packer's suspicions. As a consultant to the Labor Department recalled:

> I've never seen anything like the junk that was going to go to the president. The most extreme case was when HEW came forward with draft charts with a set of pros and cons which went "HEW Pros, DOL Cons," then it had "HEW Cons, DOL Pros." I've never seen a memo where you put the pros of your argument and the cons of the other guy's argument! They took one of the arguments in our favor and just turned it into a simple declarative sentence. It was an outrage. We were arguing that the public favors a reduction of welfare caseloads and this is something which our program would do. FAP, or an NIT for that matter, would not reduce the caseload burden. So we had for one of our pros something like "improves incomes while minimizing welfare caseload burden." HEW turned it into some nullity like "caseload burden in offices would be reduced"; all we were going to do was close the local welfare offices between one and two! We were just livid.

When Packer and Gustman (Packer's assistant) met with Aaron and Barth on Saturday, April 23, there was little agreement on how the pros and cons of each approach should be presented. By this time it was becoming increasingly clear that the differences between HEW and

DOL would not be resolved before the April 26 meeting, and since the differences were so fundamental, it was agreed that the charts would present principles upon which there was agreement and disagreement, with pros and cons supplied on principles on which the two departments differed. Unable to reach agreement on the pros and cons, Barth finally suggested that DOL write two of its own pros and two HEW cons on each problematic principle, with HEW conversely writing two of its own pros and two DOL cons. Packer agreed and the meeting was concluded shortly thereafter.

Analysts on both sides of the fence expressed apprehension about this method of handling interdepartmental differences. As one ISP staff member commented, "The charts were serving as memos in the process and it was on this sound basis—two HEW-DOL advantages and disadvantages—that the President was to make his decisions." Gary Reed of the Labor Department expressed similar doubts that the HEW-DOL competition served Carter's interests:

> HEW was deathly afraid that if they went to Carter and said "to guarantee jobs to this category of people and to stay within your cost limitations, you're going to have to reduce the guarantees for everyone in the income maintenance program." They never presented him with that kind of trade-off because they were afraid he'd buy it.
>
> In a sense, the entire process was never really put into what you can buy with additional increments of money. It was always they presented one proposal, we presented another, and it was always a little ambiguous as to what you were gaining.
>
> Also, because of the questionable offsets, Carter was not really seeing a zero-cost option but a more expensive one. In effect, he was looking at a five to ten billion dollar option although he never had a chance to decide in a rational way what he would like to buy with that extra money. Did he want more jobs? Higher guarantees? Lower tax rates? It was all muddled up in this process.

At least one observer concluded that the HEW-DOL stalemate was not simply attributable to analytic differences or Packer's outspoken advocacy:

> A lot of those people have rough edges on their personalities, from Henry on down. If you take Henry, Barth, and Todd as a group, their reaction is not to roll with the punch and come back in a different form; it's bristle and try to put the other guy down. Arnie doesn't roll because he doesn't let anybody punch him.

CHAPTER SIX

The Principles Go Public

AS THE MAY 1 DEADLINE APPROACHED, THE ADMINISTRATION ACCELER-
ated the consultation process on the Hill. Members of the Domestic
Policy Staff held several meetings with Senators Moynihan and Long,
and HEW assumed primary responsibility for the House side. Senate
Majority Leader Robert Byrd (D–W.Va.) was concerned about the scope
and number of the comprehensive reform programs the administration
was developing and was relieved to learn that Carter was considering
delaying welfare reform. As Byrd remarked at a press conference on
April 23:

> We can't deal with all the hodgepodge of massive problems that
> confront our system in one session. To the extent that I can,
> I am not going to allow a lot of other areas of legislation to be-
> come roadblocks to this energy legislation [the National Ener-
> gy Plan had been released on April 20]. . . . I would seriously
> doubt that comprehensive tax reform could be effectuated in
> this session . . . [and] the President knows we're not going
> to do welfare reform this year. I told him so. He understands
> that we can't do everything at once.[1]

Carter's decision to announce principles on May 1 in place of a concrete
plan, however, did stir consternation in some quarters of the Senate.
Senator Moynihan was especially indignant over the delay. As Moynihan
snapped on April 25, "This is HEW at it again. They produce wonderful
books on how you cannot do it. . . . [Someone] with a first-rate mind and
three months' experience could draft legislation in a morning."[2] Noting
that welfare reform was part of the Democratic platform, Moynihan
added: "We have a commitment, damn it, we made a commitment. I
don't want us to weasle out of it on the grounds that we now have a more
glamorous crisis."[3]

Consultation in the House also raised some problems. Barth and

Aaron had already met separately with Ullman and Corman several times and met one more time with Ullman on April 22. Aaron recalled what happened:

> We had three meetings with Ullman, the first two of which were relatively uneventful. We talked about issues and I thought we were making some progress. In light of where Ullman ultimately came out, nothing that he ended up agreeing to, or being close to agreeing to, would have come as a surprise after those two meetings. The third meeting [April 22] was a disaster personally, from my own standpoint, and, in general, just a bad show. An article had leaked in the *L.A. Times* just before the meeting saying that the administration, notwithstanding its listing of options, was really going to come out for a guaranteed income. Ullman, I think, without having any clear picture of what is a guaranteed income and what isn't—food stamps isn't but FAP was—feels that a guaranteed income is a disaster and put it to Califano during the hearings that he thought it was a disaster for the nation and the Democratic party. So that article had just appeared when we walked in there, and he was very much on the warpath. And I didn't just roll over, so he ended up getting very upset and that was the last time I saw him.

The Domestic Policy Staff was very aware of the limited political appeal of the consolidated cash approach HEW was proposing. In fact, in a memo to President Carter on April 26, the DPS listed the primary disadvantage of the NIT approach as "the strong and announced opposition of Russell Long, Al Ullman, —and the coalition they can muster. . . . They can be expected to fight bitterly and to base their opposition on the large number of persons added to the welfare rolls." They concluded by observing:

> As we see it the choice is between a negative income tax which is administratable but faces a very difficult road, at best, in the Congress and a multiple track approach like Tom's or the Labor Department's, which faces costly administrative problems but is a more saleable program and would be equally effective.
> You should not approve any plan with announced benefit levels and cost figures until you have seen statistical breakouts of the impact by region, family size, income level, urban-rural, age and other relevant factors.[4]

Eizenstat, Carp, and their associates were apparently unaware until the last moment that, several days before the briefing, HEW and DOL had jointly agreed to drop Tom Joe's plan from the list of options, feeling it was too expensive and administratively intricate. Joe prepared a paper, however, which he delivered to Eizenstat the morning of the 26th, and Eizenstat was determined not to let the triple-track option slip by so easily. In a note to Carter on the 26th, following his earlier memorandum, Eizenstat wrote:

> Tom Joe prepared this paper and had it delivered to our office this morning.
> We have not had a chance to summarize it, but we thought you might want to look at this before the welfare reform meeting with Secretary Califano. This plan details the conceptual outline of the three-track policy which Tom has talked to you about since at least 1974. While I do not believe Secretary Califano is headed down this road, Tom's plan certainly is worth serious consideration.[5]

Several other last-minute maneuverings occurred during the day preceding the briefing. OMB drafted a memo to the president, strongly siding with HEW that the guaranteed jobs program was unworkable. Whether the director of OMB, Bert Lance, signed off or actually sent the memo is uncertain. The memo stated:

> I do not believe you have been adequately briefed on the budget costs or the unresolved conceptual and practical problems these proposals raise. . . .
> The costs—up to 6 to 9 billion per year for the one to one and a half million recipients even at minimum wage—are *not* included in our current projection. They are add-ons to the budget. Our budget estimates do not include the employment and training resources from the stimulus package beyond what is necessary for phase out after 1978.[6]

After reviewing past job creation programs and citing the same difficulties and uncertainties that HEW had pointed out, OMB recommended:

> The key elements of the welfare reform effort—achieving benefit system restructure and equity—are not dependent on massive job creation. Those elements can and must proceed. . . .
> Notwithstanding the obvious attractiveness of the concept of jobs vs. the dole, a massive public jobs program is not justified on the merits. . . .
> There is an alternative. Begin now a several year developmental process which builds on the WIN resource base and uses large-scale demonstrations with rigorous research and evaluation methods aimed at discovering how to develop private as well as public sector jobs and employment services for the welfare

population. . . . Our recommended approach can lead to the design of a workable employment and training program—a design which we do not have now.[7]

At the Department of Labor, DOL staff were giving Marshall some last-minute instructions before the briefing. Gustman, Packer's chief assistant, wrote Marshall:

> The agenda on p. 1 [of the briefing charts] has a third item added—review implications of agreed upon principles. Secretary Califano will try to use these to imply agreement for comprehensive cash coverage. Uniform administration does not necessarily imply folding everything into one Negative Income Tax program. However, that appears to be implied by the first agreed upon principle. [Consolidation meant replacing AFDC, SSI, and food stamps with a new federal cash system.]
>
> Don't let them keep the focus on one central computer—keep bringing up IRS, black lung, etc.[8]

THE THIRD PRESIDENTIAL BRIEFING

Califano arrived at the White House for the April 26 briefing with roughly twenty charts, considerably more intricate than those presented at the earlier briefings. Present at the briefing, besides the president, were Califano, Aaron, and Barth from HEW, Marshall and Packer from DOL, Watson, Parham, Jody Powell, Eizenstat, Carp, and Raines from the White House, Lance, Bo Cutter, and Sue Woolsey from OMB, Treasury Secretary Blumenthal, Schultze from the CEA, and Jim Fallows, Carter's chief speech writer. The agenda for the briefing was to seek to achieve agreement on three unresolved principles, to use two proposals to illustrate alternatives, and to review implications of agreed-upon principles. The pros and cons of each principle upon which there was disagreement were delineated in several charts:

1. *Reliance on Jobs and Training*
   DOL—Expand and redirect CETA to assure jobs or training
   Pros:
   - Family heads expected to work must work—assured a job or training
   - Improves chances of achieving unemployment and inflation goals
   Cons:
   - Questionable ability to create enough jobs and training slots (would be sole program to assist family heads expected to work)

HEW—Redirect some CETA gradually
Pros:
- Less incentive to switch from private to public sector
- Less risk of overpromising

Cons:
- Provides fewer public services
- Does not guarantee job or training to family heads expected to work

2. *Benefit Standards for Different Groups*

DOL—Benefits vary by characteristics of recipients
Pros:
- Assistance to family heads expected to work related to wages or training stipend
- Earned Income Tax Credit expands existing program without requiring an assets test

Cons:
- Negligible assistance to families with low earnings—incentive to shift to assured job
- Program costs increased by need to retain "narrower filing unit"

HEW—Benefits vary only by income and family size
Pros:
- Assistance more closely related to need
- Encourages private sector employment relative to assured job program

Cons:
- Perceived as expanding the "welfare rolls"
- Long and Ullman object to any program resembling negative income tax

3. *Administrative Options*

DOL—Two or more federal or state agencies
Pros:
- No "welfare" stigma for those in manpower track
- Separate agencies for family heads expected and not expected to work

Cons:
- Households whose circumstances change must switch programs
- More expensive and complex to administer

HEW—Single agency for federal cash assistance with state-administered work test
Pros:
- Unified system assures consistent treatment of recipients
- Cheaper to administer and more understandable to recipients

Cons:
- Requires assets test and monthly payments for over 10 million filing units
- Employment and training programs more difficult to administer[9]

As the briefing proceeded to a discussion of the DOL plan, Barth and Aaron fired out a barrage of criticisms similar to the ones they had presented internally in the HEW-DOL debate: the jobs program would be inflationary and difficult to administer;* history gave no cause for optimism that such a program would work; and the plan was unfair since it offered jobs to family heads but not to singles and childless couples.[10] Marshall and Packer defended the plan, contending that past job programs had failed because of inadequate funds and commitment, that the jobs approach was politically saleable, and that the cost of the program would be held down by using CETA funds. Carter expressed dislike for the administrative intricacy of the DOL plan but conceded: "I unwillingly agree to a multiple administration if it has to be."[11]

The meeting then turned to a consideration of the HEW plan, covering what was by then very familiar ground to HEW and DOL. Aaron noted the simplicity and equity of the HEW approach, stressing that families and individuals with similar needs would be treated equally; Packer countered by observing that, because of the "tough triangle," it was impossible to have generous benefit levels and strong work incentives at the same time. He also reminded the president that a similar welfare plan (FAP) had already been rejected by Congress.[12] As the meeting came to its conclusion, after nearly two and a half hours, Carter took over and directed several questions to the HEW and DOL contingents. According to the notes of a source present at the briefing, the rest of the meeting went something like this:

> *President*: If we overestimate our ability to create jobs, it doesn't increase the cost of the program?
> ?: That's right.
> *Schultze*: A program which counts on jobs creates problems if the system does not have a fall back point.
> *Marshall*: The fall back point would be the wife and family going on welfare.

---

*Although HEW continually cited administrative problems with the DOL plan, the only analysis of administrative issues that had been done to date in fact suggested that HEW's plan was as administratively problematic as DOL's. (A preliminary analysis of administrative issues was forwarded to Aaron by John Trout, an aide to Social Security Commissioner James Cardwell, on April 22).

Aaron: The Labor plan would violate the principle of workers making more than those who don't work. Under the Labor plan other private jobs pay less than public service employment.

[Packer and Aaron argue about differences in the two plans in terms of earnings supplements and work incentives.]

Blumenthal: These cost estimates assume a 5.0% unemployment rate in 1981. We might well need to create 2 million or more jobs.

Packer: Actually it is based on 5.6% unemployment rate.

President: Let me ask this: What is the consequence of the failure to create all the jobs? Suppose we fall short by 400,000?

Califano: Well, you need a net for those who don't have a job.

President: Is that a catastrophe?

Califano: No.

Packer: You could also give them a training stipend until a job becomes available.

Eizenstat: That's Tom Joe's suggestion.

Aaron: The failure to produce jobs as promised would just increase the sense of hopelessness among the poor.

President: Will the cost of the jobs program move? . . . There are lots of people who are underemployed. Underemployment is in the eye of the beholder. I felt underemployed when I was governor of Georgia; I thought I should be president. [Laughter.]

Califano: If there is adequate cash assistance and you are not overpromising in the jobs program then you wouldn't have to worry.

President: We don't need to worry about overpromising if going on to cash assistance is not a catastrophe. Look, suppose we promised a million jobs and only created 600,000. Six hundred thousand would have been a tremendous achievement, but it would have looked like we failed. Let's not promise a particular number, let's just try our best to create jobs. . . .

Schultze: If Congress were to mandate prevailing wages rather than minimum wages there might be a shift from private employment into the public sector jobs.

Packer: You could reduce the attractiveness of the PSE jobs by making a smaller EITC for those in PSE employment.

Califano: Let me review the congressional picture for a moment. Long wants to put AFDC mothers to work and give the AFDC money to states in block grants. Ullman opposes the negative income tax. [Wilbur] Mills [chairman of the Ways and Means Committee before Ullman and during the FAP debate] burned on it. Ullman hasn't thought about the nuances the way Long has. The committee is actually closer to Corman. In Senate Finance, they're closer to Long. Pat Moynihan is also on Senate Finance and we need to get his vote to push the program on the states. We'd be sending our proposal to reluctant recipients except for Moynihan. The New York delegation is also very interested in fiscal relief.

Packer: The jobs component doesn't have to move through the Senate Finance Committee. I could start on this.

Califano: I feel strongly that you go all together on one proposal.

President: At present, we have the public's attention at our command. Damn if the public doesn't want something done on this issue. I'm willing to have a session with the governors, Long, Corman, and others and go to blows if necessary.

Eizenstat: The closer we come to calling our plan a guaranteed income the harder it will be for people to accept it.

President: I'm not that sure about that; if the NIT is only one element of a comprehensive plan I think I can sell it. [Pat] Caddell's poll shows that.

Powell: It's a wash.

Califano: Let's get rid of catch words. It should be the Carter plan.

President: Joe, when you want to call it the Califano plan, then I'll know we have a good one!

Blumenthal: We would need to work on any possible IRS administration to make sure the tax levels match the work incentives.

President: I would like you to put the information in orderly written fashion.

Califano: We have scores of written reports to submit.

President: The first presentation to the public should show the advantages of what we want to do. Joe, I want you to consult with the states and Congress after our May 2nd announcement and we will produce legislation in early September. On May 2nd I want a list of principles, an amalgamation of the two approaches, and an announcement that we plan to produce legislation in September. August 1st will be the end of the internal process and we will produce the bill for September 1st. This would leave us a point to withdraw in secret and put the plan together.

Califano: Ullman said he could get something reported by the end of the year.

President: It helps me if I have a time framework.

Blumenthal: How does this affect the timing of tax reform?

President: I'd like to do the most we can on both.

Blumenthal: Events, like with every program, will force the tax issue. We may have to go with tax reform more quickly than we thought.

President: Well, changing priorities may force changes in our time schedule. You can tell the American people we will have tax proposals to Congress first.

Califano: You may want to put welfare off until next year.

President: That illustrates the problem of organization in the Congress. Everything we want to do goes through two committees. . . . Congress may want to put it off until next year.

Eizenstat: The problem with being too specific about the options is that Moynihan may grab one and hold hearings on it.

President: Have another meeting and try to resolve some of your differences. I have no preference; my preference is to move ahead on everything at once. We will need to tell [Senator] Byrd and the Speaker before talking to the committee chairmen. But I am determined to meet my commitment of making an announcement on May 2nd.

Powell: We're already getting static on backing off.

Lance: Will one of the assumptions be that the plan will be at zero-cost?

Schultze: There is some inconsistency in the benefit numbers and the supplement numbers in 1981 assuming no more inflation.

President: You will need to begin putting together the statement I will make.

(President leaves.)

CHOOSING THE PRINCIPLES

In a memo to the president the next day, Watson informed Carter that, in post-briefing discussions, most of his advisers and cabinet members had agreed on accelerating delivery of tax reform legislation to early July and announcing on May 2 basic principles and general directions for a comprehensive welfare plan, the continuation of the consulting process, and an early September target date for welfare legislation. He went on to add:

Everyone agrees that it is important for us *not* to give the indication that we are subordinating, or even deferring, our commitment to comprehensive welfare reform. . . .

Frank Moore says that it is *essential* for us to consult with, and even to bring into the *decision-making process*, not only Senator Byrd and the Speaker, but also Senators Long, Jackson, Muskie, and Al Ullman. Mike Blumenthal has already spoken to you about his suggestion that he speak directly with Russell Long and Al Ullman, prior to your conversation with Byrd and O'Neill.*[13]

Within the administration, substantial disagreements remained. At Carter's request, Charles Schultze, who was known as an excellent mediator and clarifier, assumed the role of an "honest broker" between HEW and Labor. Schultze met for four hours with Packer and Aaron on the night of April 28 and again on April 29 but was unable to resolve outstanding differences between the two departments. Schultze informed Carter in a memo on the 29th that "I [was] trying to find an approach which would merge the best points of the HEW and Labor positions. I do not want to rule out the possibility that such an approach could be found. But at the moment the chances are less than 50–50."[14] Schultze went on to outline the three major issues as he saw them:

I. *The future as it would look under the two plans*:
1. Under the *Labor* plan, the incentives are so structured that family heads would no longer be likely to take part-time, sporadic private jobs at low wages. The supplemental income benefits for part-time or part-year workers under the Labor plan are small. It would almost always pay for such workers to move over to year-round, minimum wage (plus), public service jobs. The U.S. labor market would, in effect, be changed so that youngsters and second-earners (mainly women) would be the sole source of labor for such private jobs.

There would be incentives under the Labor plan for workers to leave public service jobs for *full-time* private jobs. But the incentive isn't very large—about $420 a year—and might be affected by the security of a public job compared to the uncertain job tenure of a low-wage private job.
2. The *HEW* plan provides for somewhat less attractive public service jobs (30 hours a week maximum) and somewhat greater income supplements for people working part-time or part-year in private industry. Thus it would still pay many family heads to offer their labor services in part-time or part-year jobs.
3. For the "unemployable"—single parent families with children under 12, for single people, and for childless couples, the two plans are basically the same.

*It was not actually until April 29, three days before his announcement, that Carter began to call congressional leaders to get their thoughts on the May 2 announcement (Nick Kotz, "The Politics of Welfare Reform," *New Republic*, May 14, 1977, pp. 20, 21).

II. *What happens if the 1½ million productive public service jobs cannot be provided:*
   1. In the *Labor* plan, those for whom no PSE jobs are available would be given a "training stipend," of $83 a week, $4,300 a year (for a family of four), and have to show up for eight hours a day at a training program. Except for "moonlighting," they would not be able to take part-time private jobs.
   2. In the *HEW* plan, if no PSE job were available, a family of four would get $4,300 (with no "training" requirement), and could keep 50 percent of any earnings from a private job.
   3. I believe *everybody* agrees that if we fall far short of the 1½ million public service jobs, the Labor plan is inferior.
   4. The Labor plan "requirement" for 1½ million PSE jobs assumes a 5 to 5½ percent unemployment rate. If unemployment rises in a future recession, a much larger number will be needed. What is the answer?
      A. Under the *Labor* plan, if new PSE jobs couldn't be created, the newly employed family heads (or those exhausting unemployment insurance) would be placed in a "training position" and given $32 a week to show up 8 hours a day. Again except for moonlighting they couldn't take part-time private work.
      B. At the present time, in a recession, what often happens is that full-time earners, when fired, take part-time jobs usually held by youth or secondary workers. Labor's plan in effect, would pull such full-time workers out of the labor force into a "holding pattern" until prosperity returned.

III. *Assume that we can get 1½ million public service jobs. Do we like the "future" as envisaged by the two plans?*
   1. There is some attractiveness in an objective which aims at a *full-time* job for every employable family head. The American economy would then have to depend upon youngsters and secondary workers to fulfill its need for part-time and sporadic work.
   2. But would we create a permanent class of public service workers, engaged in "make work" projects, not much better than welfare? Would abuses here begin to equal abuses under the current welfare system?
   3. The answer hinges on whether or not we can create 1½ million *productive* jobs for the very least advantaged, lowest skilled segment of the labor market? Nobody knows the answer.[15]

Schultze went on to describe why it was so very difficult to merge the plans and from his comments it is clear that neither DOL nor HEW had fundamentally altered its position over the entire course of the debate:

IV. *Why not go with the HEW plan, but simply try very hard to provide 1½ million full-time PSE jobs for employable family heads?* If we make it, great. If we fall short, the HEW plan provides income support plus incentives to find private part-time or full-time work.

    1. *Labor* believes it is essential that all the income received in a public service job be either a *wage* or a tax credit and not a wage plus an income-supplement check from the "welfare agency." The very essence of the HEW plan is that income supplements are based on *family size* and *family income,* including the earnings of all members of the family. Thus, under the HEW plan, the *total* income a person on a PSE job received would vary from time to time, as earnings of other members of the family increased or decreased.

       Thus, argues *Labor,* the HEW plan is fundamentally inconsistent with their objective of providing income in the form which is as close to a pure *wage* payment as possible. (As a consequence of this desire, a PSE worker earning, say $6000 a year under the Labor plan, would *not* have his income reduced when his wife took a $5000-a-year job.)

    2. I spent hours with Aaron (HEW) and Packer (Labor) trying to merge the two plans, but kept being hung up on this difficulty.

    3. The chances are perhaps 1 in 4 that with more time we could work it out.[16]

With fundamental differences like this still remaining and with details of the plan still not settled, Schultze advised the president to limit his May 2 announcement to some general principles. He concluded:

V. *What should you do?*

    1. The details of the plans, particularly the Labor plan, have been changed frequently in the past two weeks. I doubt if anyone is aware of the full implications of each plan. I know that I haven't had a chance to understand them.

       A. Each side claims there are major *administrative* difficulties with the other's plan that may be critical to success or failure.

       B. There may be intricate problems which occur in

both plans, particularly Labor's, when family status changes; and in the welfare population this happens frequently.

C. I am very uncertain whether the cost estimates will hold up.

2. *Therefore,* I suggest:

A. On Monday you announce the *principles,* i.e., the consolidation of AFDC, SSI, and food stamps, and that the plan will have a major job component.

B. That you set an *internal* deadline, say two weeks after you come back from the Summit, when you will decide which of the two ways to go. (In the meantime, we can do more work on the implications of the plans and try, once more, to merge the two approaches.)

C. *After* that decision, Califano should start working with the Hill and with the governors. I do *not* think that he should begin negotiating without such a decision.[17]

Although Schultze evidenced considerable skepticism about the potential for agreement, White House Staff remained sanguine. A memo from Eizenstat, Watson, Carp, and Parham to President Carter on Friday, April 29, stated that "we believe that agreement can be reached on most of the key welfare principles over this weekend. As Secretary Califano's memo indicates, there is broad agreement among all parties on a wide range of issues."[18]

Secretary Califano's memo, also sent on the 29th, in some ways bore a striking resemblance to the charts that had been presented to the president on April 26. The thirty-seven-page memo listed and described areas of agreement, "three basic issues on which disagreement persists that require your decision," a detailed discussion of the three issues, and descriptions of the HEW and DOL programs. The six principles upon which Carter's advisers agreed were also contained in the memo and watered down further from the lists of principles supplied two weeks earlier. (Califano's original list, for example, had caused consternation at DOL and the White House because one principle called for widespread program consolidation; the reworded goal now simply was to "simplify administration and introduce efficient systems management.")[19]

The three areas of disagreement were exactly the same as those that had been presented to Carter on the 26th without successful resolution: whether the program should rely heavily on jobs and training, whether cash assistance should be provided through a single program, and whether cash assistance should be provided through a single administrative agency. Once again the pros and cons of each principle on which the two departments differed were methodically laid out in considerable detail. Califano also pointed out that the three issues were inextricably linked:

> The three issues are closely related, but the guaranteed jobs issue is a key. This decision changes considerably the nature of the debate over the other two issues. For example, if a job is *guaranteed* for some groups, it becomes easier to defend the fairness of *separate* cash assistance schedules for those groups. For another example, the decision on benefit standards largely determines the decision on administrative structures. If all those in need are to be offered some supplementation based only on income and family size (*presuming, of course, that they fulfill the conditions of a work requirement*), then the arguments for a single administrative structure for cash assistance are much stronger.[20]

There were, in fact, a wide range of unresolved issues on program design that were conspicuously absent from the main body of the memo. Appended to the memo was a list of some of the basic issues that the welfare effort had not yet dealt with. They included the role of state supplements to welfare payments, the fiscal relief that would appear in the program, the administrative feasibility of the programs, the agencies that would bear responsibility for administering the programs, how and whether benefits in the programs would be indexed, and the relationship of social services, including day care, to the welfare reform effort. Even the areas of consensus described in the main body of the memo were very limited; the basic benefit structure, for example, had not been agreed upon and, as Califano noted,

> there is not agreement within the administration as to whether we should treat the $6–9 billion currently budgeted for the CETA program—but scheduled to be phased out in 1979—as available for zero cost welfare reform. Marshall and I support retention of these funds. Lance does not. Without this $6–9 billion, neither proposal discussed below would be zero cost.[21]

In discussing the zero-cost estimates Califano warned Carter of the need for a larger filing unit and longer accountable period. After briefly explaining why these changes could be argued for on grounds of equity, Califano continued:

> *These two administrative changes in the filing unit and the accountable period are the key to welfare reform when resources are limited.*

Changes in the filing unit and accountable period have two important implications:

1. They are a principal reason why these proposals make some current recipients worse off. In particular, most SSI recipients who live in larger households would receive reduced benefits.
2. These changes will increase the importance of providing an emergency needs program.[22]

Califano, in short, was indicating that the "improvements" that could be bought at zero cost were not unmixed blessings and that, in any case, they resulted more from tinkering with technicalities than from any grand reform design.

Califano and the White House staff agreed to advise President Carter not to select a specific option for the announcement on May 2. Accordingly, in a memo sent to the president before the April 30 meeting (at which it was hoped disagreements over the principles would be resolved), Eizenstat, Watson, Carp, and Parham wrote:

We would . . . strongly urge you not to make a final decision, in the welfare statement next week, between the specific negative income tax proposed by HEW—under which those who work in public service employment, those in private employment, and those not expected to work would be served by a single cash-grant system—and the specific multiple-track approach proposed by the Labor Department and Tom Joe.
- We believe that the basis for your ultimate decision will be improved by additional work on both plans. It is quite likely that a single compromise could be reached which would be stronger than either plan is presently.
- A final commitment to either approach at this time would permit opponents to attack our plan before we can complete the detail work necessary to defend our position. We can expect that Administration representatives would be asked by Senator Moynihan and others to testify on our approach long before we are prepared to do so.
- It will be much easier to sell either approach to Congressional leaders and other key constituents if they are involved before the final decision is made.

Secretary Califano agrees with this approach.[23]

Although the Labor Department had also agreed that it would be appropriate to announce some general principles on May 2, and had collaborated with HEW in arriving at the conclusions and drafting of Califano's memo to the president, Packer persuaded Marshall to send an additional memo to Carter in what ISP staff members described as an

"Arnie Packer sneak attack." The April 29 memo had an eleven-page attachment stating Packer's case once again. The body of the memo stated:

> You have received a long, detailed, and competent HEW paper. Therefore, it would not be useful for me to send in a separate DOL analysis of the competing welfare reform proposals. However, I do wish to convey my personal views on welfare reform. The memo is not meant to provide a balanced list of pros and cons, but to let you know why I favor a welfare reform program that assures jobs to those who can work and cannot find employment, supplements the income of the working poor, and provides a decent minimum standard of living for those who cannot work.
>
> We and HEW agree that there are three issues. When you boil down all the complexity, it comes down to this:
>
> a. *Reliance on Jobs and Training*
>   Is it possible to change the American economic system so that by 1980 or 1981 we can assure every head of a family with children a full-time job paying at least the minimum wage? There is no way to avoid the question: either we can or cannot. Clearly, the Department of Labor believes we can, even though it agrees to create a backup safety net of training stipends in case we fail.
>
> b. *Benefits Structure*
>   Either we create three benefit systems that maximize the incentives to work and minimize the incentives for fraud or we create one more complicated program that reduces the work incentives for two-parent families and requires cross filing and asset tests for millions of additional persons. DOL believes that it needs to be able to pay a full wage and earning stipend through the employment and training system to make the job program workable.
>
> c. *Administrative Structures*
>   There is no way that we can eliminate the IRS for those who work, the employment and training system for those who need work, or the HEW apparatus for those who cannot work. The only question is whether individuals have to come to one organization or to two or more at any point in time. DOL believes that dividing the responsibility among Labor, HEW, and IRS and letting an individual work with one organization at a time is the best administrative arrangement.[24]

Despite ISP anger at Marshall's memo, HEW was not immune to getting in its own last-minute licks. In a cover memo attached to the joint memo sent to the president, Califano wrote:

This is the guts of what I think you should say to the American people on May 2nd.

Announce your intention to scrap the entire welfare system. . . . As a result of your study and ours over the past 3½ months, the surgery to be performed is far more radical than you had previously imagined. . . .

State that AFDC, SSI, and food stamps have lots of leakage, complicated administrative structures, are often degrading to recipients and wasteful to taxpayers, and provide an unacceptable administrative burden. You intend to consolidate them into a single cash assistance program.

State candidly that the employment service has never done well in providing jobs or training for the poor population of our country. You intend to establish a special new employment program with targetted health, education and training, and (to the maximum extent possible) public jobs at the end of the road for those that can't find private employment.

State candidly that you want to stay away from the code words that have plagued prior attempts to deal with the welfare system.[25]

Califano apparently still believed that the two approaches could be merged with additional time. He was more concerned about the zero-cost constraint and the public perception of the plan. As he stressed again in the body of the joint memo, "I believe elements of each [plan] should *fold into an* ultimate plan, and I believe you must avoid being drawn into such sharp alternatives of using traditional code words in your public statements."[26]

SATURDAY, APRIL 30, AND MAYDAY

On the morning of Saturday, April 30, Califano and Marshall rose early in order to meet with Charlie Schultze to see if their differences could be resolved.[27] Apparently unable to narrow the gap between them, the two returned to the White House for a three-hour afternoon meeting, where they discussed different versions of the principles. HEW staff, including Barth, were under the impression that whatever principles the president eventually announced would be very broad ones and that, as agreed at the meeting of the 26th, thorny problems would be worked out after the May 2 announcement, in consultation with Congress and the states. As one ISP staff member characterized the principles agreed upon to date:

Everybody agreed that people who are not able to work should have adequate income. Everybody agreed that people who are able to work but are not working should get some assistance.

Everybody agreed that people who are working but don't make enough money should get supplements to their incomes. These three goals in the plans were subsumed under one principle: cash assistance to the needy. The Labor Department also had cash assistance for the same three groups although they would have, for example, provided the cash to the working poor through an EITC rather than an NIT. The important point is that we were told the principle would just go down as extending assistance to these groups, rather than selecting the specific means of assistance.

HEW was convinced, in short, "that we had a nebulous set of principles [those outlined in the joint April 29 memo] that was neither going to help us nor hurt us, and that they would probably by and large be helpful."

The meeting opened up with several surprises. On Friday night, before the meeting, DOL had delivered a slightly different set of eligibility requirements that made a difference in the demand for jobs. HEW worked feverishly throughout the night to compute the new figures and, as it turned out, the 1.4 million jobs that DOL had been estimating would be needed now, apparently, came to 2.2 million. Partly because of the time deadline and partly because of their desire to spring a telling surprise on DOL, HEW neglected to inform DOL of the higher estimates. Shortly after the meeting commenced, HEW announced that Labor was underestimating the demand for jobs by roughly 800,000 and thus had significantly underestimated the cost of their proposal. A DOL official present at the meeting recalls, "This was unethical and unprofessional. There was, of course, a logical explanation for the differences in the two estimates but you can't get into that kind of technical detail in front of Califano, Marshall, Charlie Schultze, and the president." A White House aide present at the meeting recalled that Packer "looked like he'd been hit in the groin when they announced the figures." Carter was unfazed, however. He commented, "Well, maybe we need 2.2 million jobs." Later in the meeting Califano began to talk about the difficulties of creating so many jobs, citing the high illiteracy rate among high school graduates in Los Angeles, and once again Carter halted him, saying, "I thought I made that clear to Henry at our second meeting. Walter and I agree that in a small town, where people know what work needs to be done and who the unemployed individuals are, it's no trick to find useful work for the less qualified. We can do it. One to two million jobs is what we need out there to clean up the cities and the small towns." The jobs question was one issue that apparently would be decided on the basis of presidential preferences, without regard to expense.

The rest of the meeting focused for the most part on the May 2 announcement, the arrangements that would be carried out beforehand, and further thrashing out of the principles. Carter would wander in and out but most of the discussion over the principles was at the assistant secretary level—Packer debating with Aaron, with Bert Carp mediating and Sue Woolsey chipping in occasionally. The meeting was inconclusive, and Aaron left with the impression that the principles would be very broad ones.

One issue that was resolved, however, before the briefing closed was the use of the CETA offset. Although the risks of the CETA offset had been discussed in the two previous briefings and had formed the basis of the zero-cost offsets for a full month, Carter had not explicitly given his approval to the use of the offset. As Jim Parham recalls:

> There was a question of whether the CETA money would be available in 1981, so we had a little bit of collusion and I was selected to ask the president about it. I was planning to raise the question with the president anyway.
>
> Bert Lance, who is a good friend of mine from Georgia, just happened to be out of the room or not there. Anyway, I said, "Before we close the meeting, Mr. President, we need to know, can we count on that $5.6 billion as a part of your no-cost program?" He said "yes" sort of reluctantly and cautiously, and that closed down the meeting.
>
> When Lance heard about it he apparently fell out of his seat and told the president that you couldn't spend $5.6 billion on a casual question. I believe he sent a note to the president on the matter. Of course, it really wasn't a casual question since we had been talking about it a good bit.

As the meeting adjourned, DPS took the draft of the principles from the HEW-DOL April 29 memo and that evening began reworking them for the May 2 message. On Saturday night, Domestic Policy Staff members decided to put an explicit commitment to the EITC in the message although HEW had been told that the form an earnings supplement would take would not be specified. As one DPS member commented, "There was always the occasion where we got into something from HEW which didn't represent everybody. It was always clear to us that something like the EITC would be in the principles. . . . The reasons we insisted that the EITC be there was because it was [Russell] Long's thing."

When the Domestic Policy Staff met with Carter on Sunday to go over the draft, the president immediately put back the zero-cost limitation as his number one principle. Jim Fallows, Carter's chief speech writer, had also drawn up a version of the principles along with a statement the night before, and as a result of the feedback he received, several other changes were made in the principles. On Sunday, he had circulated the version to, among others, Califano, Marshall, Schultze, Carp, Aaron, Packer, Barth, and Parham. Schultze complained that the draft was too lyrical in its praise of public jobs and not strict enough in emphasizing incentives for private work, so one principle was restructured to emphasize private sector employment. During the Saturday meeting Carter had suggested that the message could lay out "levels of achievement" whereby if a million jobs were created there would be a certain amount of cash supplement created, if 1.5 million were created there would be this much less supplement, and so forth. Califano and Aaron, wary of too large and explicit a commitment to the jobs program, successfully recommended to Fallows that the message should simply state that the more jobs created, the less cash there would be, and to stay away from any numerical estimates. Califano did make several other suggestions for the text of the speech. He suggested that Carter use a quote from a Sister Corita poster that read "to do a common thing uncommonly well will bring success" and felt that Carter might properly employ his religious background in the message. Our varied religions, Califano argued, taught us that different types of people deserve each other's respect. He pointed out facetiously to Fallows, "After all, Joseph and Mary would have been on welfare."[28]

On Sunday night, Carter met with Califano, Eizenstat, and Marshall to discuss the principles that were to be released the next day. Carter had dictated a set of principles of his own (modeled after the DPS draft) and handed them out to the participants of the meeting as they arrived. As Califano recalled, "There was discussion for a couple of hours and there was rewording of the principles, but it was optical rewording. The biggest fight occurred over 'initial cost,' getting the word 'initial' in there." The "initial cost" phrase, suggested by Eizenstat, loosened the president's zero-cost limit; the no-added-cost edict would now apply to the reformed system only in its first year of operation.

On May 2 the president held his long-awaited press conference. He made a brief statement, announced the principles, and then let Califano and Marshall field questions for him. In reading the statement, Carter stated that, in his welfare program, every family with children and a member of the family able to work "will have a job" (which, in remarks following the president's, Marshall hastily amended to "should have access to a job").*

Carter went on to state that "the most important unanimous conclu-

---

*Marshall indicated that he and Carter felt two million PSE jobs would be adequate for the purpose.

sion is that the present welfare system should be scrapped and a totally new system implemented."[29] The principles under which this comprehensive restructuring would be accomplished were:

1. No higher initial cost than the present system's;
2. Under this system every family with children and a member able to work should have access to a job;
3. Incentives should always encourage full-time and part-time private sector employment;
4. Public training and employment programs should be provided when private employment is unavailable;
5. A family should have more income if it works than if it does not;
6. Incentives should be designed to keep families together;
7. Earned income tax credits should be continued to help the working poor;
8. A decent income should be provided also for those who cannot work or earn adequate income, with federal benefits consolidated into a simple cash payment, varying in amount only to accommodate differences in costs of living from one area to another;
9. The programs should be simpler and easier to administer;
10. There should be incentives to be honest and to eliminate fraud;
11. The unpredictable and growing financial burden on local governments should be reduced as rapidly as federal resources permit; and
12. Local administration of public job programs should be emphasized.

We believe these principles and goals can be met.

There will be a heavy emphasis on jobs, simplicity of administration, financial incentive to work, adequate assistance for those who cannot work, equitable benefits for all needy American families, and close cooperation between private groups and officials at all levels of government.

The more jobs that are available, the less cash supplement we will need.

We will work closely with Congress and with state, local and community leaders, and will have legislative proposals completed by the first week in August. Consultations with each of the fifty states are necessary.[30]

The *Washington Post* editorialized that "only a churl could find anything to complain about in the goals for welfare reform President Carter announced,"[31] which were described in the *Los Angeles Times* as being altogether "about as controversial as the Boy Scout oath."[32] Barth and

Todd, however, who attended the press conference and were hearing the principles themselves for the first time, were stunned. Barth commented, "The principles as I had understood them were not going to make such a strong public commitment towards the jobs or insurance of a guarantee. They certainly went a long way towards that and that was a surprise." As Todd saw it:

> There were discussions over the weekend that I still don't know what transpired. The president's commitment to the EITC was more explicit than we had been led to believe. Another surprise was that there were some subtle changes in the job language which clearly entailed a larger commitment to jobs than we thought we were going to see. Also, the three groups we were going to help through consolidated cash each now had a separate principle [nos. 2, 7, and 8], so it had some images that struck people as looking very triple track and brought up specters that all kinds of deals had been struck that we didn't know about.

ISP staff were even more disheartened:

> We were shocked when we read the principles on Monday morning. The term "earned income tax credit" was there and instead of trying to assure everyone a job Carter had read it as a guarantee. We never found whether that was exuberance or whether somebody slipped something in on us. Who was covered became three separate points—a lot of people said triple track really had won out! We all went out and got drunk.

Commenting on the inability to reach a compromise, one government official laid the blame at Califano's feet. Recalling the presidential briefings, this individual observed:

> I don't like processes in which the papers are handed to you at the beginning of the meeting and you're supposed to sit there and watch somebody do a chart show and make a decision. I think that is a bad way of doing business. That is Califano's way of doing business. I'm sure it comes out of his background—that's the way they do it in the Defense Department—but I found it exceedingly irritating. It required a phenomenal amount of wasted effort, especially on the part of the analysts at HEW—do all the work, write all the papers, get all the charts ready, pump the secretary full of enough information to last him for two hours—which he will then forget. We could have gotten much further with a less exciting kind of process—here are the main clusters of decisions, and here are the pros and cons for the various ways to go.

It was my feeling that Joe would not go before the President and say anything other than "I've got the answer and here it is. You gave me the job; I did the job; and here is the answer." I find that not very good because then the President is put in the position of either saying yes or no, and things weren't so clear because Ray disagreed with Joe.

Packer, however, thought the process was a good one:

I think the competition was good. It would help sharpen the thing. It made the debate very clear. It was a good analytic procedure. For all the problems that we had with welfare reform, the process I thought was quite good. It was good because there were two strong views—well thought through and well articulated views—and you could lay out the differences.

Aaron also felt that the interaction between HEW and Labor would eventually create a plan that was better than if either department had been left to its own devices. Nevertheless, he still had serious reservations about the process:

This was a classic example, in my opinion, of how to not set up the development of a major proposal. That is, there was parallel responsibility, joint responsibility, with nobody having the lead cut on it. The result was any issue on which there was significant disagreement had to be resolved at the White House, or at the very last minute. The same dynamics that lead unions and businesses into always settling the contract at twelve midnight, just before it expires, drove us into resolving our disagreements in one way or the other at the last minute. It made it very difficult to proceed because there were sequential decisions, which ultimately meant that events became very hectic at the end.

CHAPTER SEVEN

From
Principles
to
Plans

THE PRINCIPLES FOR WELFARE REFORM THAT JIMMY CARTER HAD AN-
nounced on May 2 were scarcely controversial, calling (as they did) for
strong work incentives and minimal incentives for family breakup. But
neither did the principles provide a clear indication of what reform
would actually involve.

Shortly after the president's May 2 announcement, Califano and Marshall were called upon to explain to the House and Senate just what
Carter's principles might mean. The president had expressed some un-
certainty himself about welfare reform, admitting to a Democratic party
group on May 2, "I've been surprised at the difficulty of it."[1] Columnist
George Will observed that Carter's confession about the complexity of
reform "was the most enchanting understatement since Admiral John
Rushworth Jellicoe, watching his battleships blown to smithereens at
Jutland, observed, 'There seems to be something the matter with our
bloody ships today.'"[2] However, congressmen on the liberal Corman
subcommittee, before whom Califano testified on May 4, read somewhat
more ominous signs into Carter's irresolution. As Congressman Charles
Rangel (D–N.Y.) observed to Califano, "What I don't understand is how
the President was able to get a handle on the complex defense budget
and make legislative recommendations on the energy program, but on
welfare reform he's merely restating what Gerald Ford said." Rangel
contended that Carter's indecision clearly revealed "that the poor are
not a priority in this administration."[3]

Also of considerable concern to the congressmen was Carter's "no
higher initial cost" constraint. In comments on the "CBS Morning News"
on May 3, Califano had indicated that "no higher initial cost" was not
exactly synonymous with "zero-cost," but had also revealed some confusion over just what the former terminology did mean:

Barry Serafin [CBS reporter]: The president talked about holding the cost of welfare down at the current level. [Congressman Corman and Senator Moynihan] say they don't know if that's possible, in view of the changes you want to make, and they aren't crazy about the timetable you've set up, four years away before this is implemented.

Califano: Well, let me say the president very carefully used the term, "initial cost"—that he would like to hold the initial cost to what it is. And that cost includes five-point-four billion dollars that was scheduled to phase out of counter-cyclical public-service employment jobs under the tax-stimulus package. That cost may also include some of the money from the wellhead tax in the energy program, because Mr. Schlesinger [then White House energy adviser], and President Carter indicated that when that money was returned to taxpayers, it would also be returned to the non-taxpaying, poor citizens.

Serafin: Does that mean Bill Brock, the GOP chairman, was right—that you're going to use the energy tax to finance social programs? [Brock and the Republican minority leaders, Senator Howard Baker and Congressman John Rhodes, issued that charge at an April 25 news conference.]

Califano: No, we're—we're using—we're—we—we said that the energy tax should be rebated to those who—who, in effect, can—rebate it to those who would—would be paying it in another way; so that we make the price of energy expensive, but we don't have a depressing and adverse effect on the economy.[4]

When Califano appeared before the Moynihan Senate subcommittee on May 5, the issue of adequate financing for welfare reform was brought up anew. Moynihan himself told Califano: "I would like you to take a message back to the director of Management and Budget when you next see him. He has sent you up here to make bricks without straw, and it is not easy to do." Califano responded, "Mr. Chairman, if you would like to directly deliver the message to the director of the Office of Management and Budget, I would be delighted."[5]

Elsewhere in his testimony Califano made no bones about his opposition to the cost constraint and evidenced his preoccupation with the fiscal rather than philosophical aspects of welfare reform. He indicated again, for example, his intention to use an anticipated $1.3 billion in tax rebates from the wellhead tax to help offset the costs of the welfare program. These rebates, which were part of Carter's energy program, had been scheduled to go to taxpayers, as well as to poor people who did not pay taxes, on a per capita share (roughly forty-five dollars), with payments for those who did not pay taxes administered through an income maintenance program. The energy legislation had not in fact passed, however, and appeared headed for trouble in Congress. Senator John Danforth (R–Mo.) expressed some skepticism about this method of underwriting reform:

> It is a little bit of concern to me, when you talk about no initial increased costs other than the countercyclical jobs money [CETA]. I do not think it is doable, I think it is pie in the sky unless you have some other source of income that you are talking about. That is what I am trying to smoke out.

Califano candidly responded:

> I do not have any other source of income. I would like to have all the money that I could get my hands on to put together a welfare reform proposal. . . . I do not have any other source of income other than those [offsets]. Whether the no initial cost goal can be met is something we will find out in the next two months when we run these computations. . . . We will hopefully start and set as a goal—not an unwavering objective, you will notice—what would you do, to begin a program to revamp this system without increasing the costs over and above it: with the caveat I mentioned that we have always included in the initial costs,* the $5.4 billion [CETA], and whatever we get out of the wellhead tax.[6]

Despite the committee's concern over the cost limitation and the delay, the reaction to Carter's principles was generally positive. Moynihan was concerned about the hesitant support Carter had lent to fiscal relief,† but liked the emphasis on jobs, as did Russell Long, chairman of the full Finance Committee, who showed up especially to question Califano. Long was still interested in pilot demonstration projects, but held out the possibility to Califano that he might be willing to go along with a comprehensive national program if he was convinced that employable welfare recipients were working and would have very strong incentives to stay in their jobs. In closing, Long commented to Califano:

> I personally am pleased about the way in which you are going about it. If you did what some people would like you to do, you would go back to the Department, take that old Family Assis-

---

*Califano was in error. An offset for the wellhead tax had never been included in the cost estimates.

†Carter's principle stated that the "growing financial burden on state and local governments should be reduced as rapidly as federal resources permit."

tance Plan, call it something else—just change the name of it, and maybe change about one paragraph of it—and come charging back up here saying, "Here is our welfare plan and this is what we are committed to do and we want Congress to vote it through."

I do not think we would pass it. By the time you get through, you might muscle it through the House; that would not be easy though. Mr. Ullman is chairman over there now. He tends to agree with some of us over here that, if you can put people to work, you should not have them sitting there doing nothing.

But assuming you could muscle it on through the House, when you got to the Senate, you would be in for a very rough time. And, when you were all done, I think you would have gotten about the same results as Mr. Nixon did. After two years, you would find yourself back at the drawing board trying to work out something better.

I think you will have more success if you take this approach: Look at what your objectives are; look at the objections which have been raised in the past and consider other alternatives. And be ready to make changes in your program when you find something wrong with it. Then, you can bring us a plan that makes sense, that will enable people to lead better lives, and that the majority of the people in this country can applaud. If you can do that, I would enthusiastically support that plan, and I think a majority of the House and the Senate would also support it. . . .

In Senator Moynihan you have a good leader—a true diplomat to lead the charge for you when you get your plan together. If he cannot sell it, it is because the product is no good. I would hope, though, that this time we can arrive at a product that we are all very proud of.[7]

And Moynihan added:

Mr. Secretary, we could not possibly end these hearings on a more hopeful statement. I trust you realize what Senator Long has said to you.

This effort, that has eluded three administrations, is now yours triumphantly to resolve, to create the right program, and the first word of that program is work and the second is jobs. . . . Senator Long has made an important point. You can produce a bill that will be overwhelmingly approved by this Congress and if you can, you should.[8]

When Marshall appeared before the Moynihan subcommittee the following week, he too received warm kudos from Senators Moynihan and

Long for the strong emphasis on jobs contained in the principles, and he was assured of the cooperation of the committee as long as the program maintained strong work incentives to keep recipients away from welfare. Long again stressed his interest in pilot projects and suggested that a 25 percent marginal tax rate for those expected to work would be appropriate and that the 50 percent used in HEW proposals was much too high. Moynihan, who had once held Packer's position at the Labor Department, told Marshall, "We will follow anxiously the accounts of the titanic struggles going on between the Departments, and once again I say I have a desire out of institutional or personal concern that the Department of Labor will prevail."[9] As one of the primary architects of FAP, Moynihan did, however, drag Marshall over the coals on selected aspects of the jobs program. In particular, he questioned whether the tasks that Marshall planned to delegate to unskilled welfare recipients were realistic ones. Marshall suggested that welfare recipients could perform jobs such as the weatherproofing of low-income homes, the removal of lead paint from the homes of the poor, and conservation efforts in national parks and local communities. Moynihan asserted in response:

> To put it straight out, Mr. Secretary, I have been in the business a long time and I am struck that the list of jobs that are available changes from time to time, but it has been consistent in one respect only. It reflects those things that the professional, upper middle class thinks ought to be done at the moment.
> I congratulate you on coming up with the weatherization of low income homes. That is sure to be a thoroughly fashionable thing in Georgetown. . . . I am quite serious about this. . . . In a friendly spirit, I am saying weatherization of low income homes is, first of all, carpenter's work.
> *Marshall*: You do not have to be a skilled carpenter to do it.
> *Moynihan*: You had better be when you are on a 14-foot ladder.
> . . . What does lead paint removal involve?
> *Marshall*: I am told by the experts it takes you about a week to learn how to remove the paint.
> *Moynihan*: Do you burn it?
> *Marshall*: I really do not know all that they do.
> *Moynihan*: Let's find out. . . . On the Park Service, forest work is serious work, dangerous work. I guess, next to mines or after mines, it has the highest accident rate in the country. Injuries are first in forestry and second in mines, or first in mines and second in forestry, which is it? Mr. Packer do you know?
> *Packer*: No, sir.
> *Moynihan*: Find out.[10]

After Moynihan went on to raise the unlikely prospect that welfare mothers would be working in national parks, a chastened Marshall conceded, "We have just started working on this and have not worked out the details, but we will have worked out all of the details on all of these jobs before we propose it as a plan."[11]

HEW VERSUS DOL: ANOTHER ROUND

While Califano and Marshall were assuaging congressional concerns, HEW and DOL staff were involved in intense negotiations over the benefit structure of the plan. At Carter's order, HEW and DOL had roughly two weeks to settle their differences and return with a compromise plan. During the first week of May, HEW focused on identifying alternative welfare approaches that would maintain as much of a commitment to comprehensive cash coverage as possible, yet still be consistent with a large full-time jobs program and an earned income tax credit. Packer, for his part, continued during the first week to send the ISP staff variations of his original plan for costing out and analysis of advantages and disadvantages.

ISP staff were worried that Barth might acquiesce to Packer's demands for a two-track system. Following the announcement of the principles, which ISP staff had viewed as an HEW "defeat," Barth had soundly reprimanded a staff member for circulating a note that inveighed against making compromises with DOL. In a letter to the staff member, Barth declared with some solemnity:

> Let me make explicit that we have been directed by the President of the United States and the Secretary to examine a wide range of welfare reform options that could appeal to a wide range of persons and groups. Your job as a civil servant and an analyst is to provide analyses of these alternatives: costs and benefits, pros and cons. It is decidedly *not* to proselytize your colleagues against participating in such an endeavor.
>
> The hallmark of the professional policy analyst is the ability to provide the elected and appointed officials to whom he or she reports with objective information. This could include analysis of plans that may not appeal to one's private social and political code. In performing such analyses, one has the dual responsibility to be responsive to one's supervisors and honest with oneself.
>
> You are well aware that these few weeks are a sensitive time in the search for improvements to the American welfare sys-

tem. I must say that I find your circulating the May 2 note at this time to display very poor judgment indeed.

Barth's position, by his own admission, was changing. As he recalled:

> I never thought that the president would make the commit-ment to enough jobs to make the job strategy meaningful. What I was looking for in the early stages was a way to use a politically feasible commitment to jobs, to make the rest of the package, the cash parts of it, politically feasible. My opposition to jobs was an opposition to proposing things that I thought were out of the ball park—I was wrong—I misjudged the ball park. Once it became clear that the ball park was going to include that kind of commitment, I was quite willing to play in it. . . . I was probably less opposed to jobs than some people on my staff.

The HEW plans maintained the original commitment to comprehen-sive cash coverage, usually in a slightly disguised form. For example, one of the six HEW plans was to have a two-tier structure using a greatly expanded EITC (see Figure 2). In this plan, the NETW and ETW groups are separated at zero earnings, but after the EITC hits the kink point, the two plans are indistinguishable. Since families taking a guaranteed job at minimum wage would be making $5,200 a year (well past the kink point), HEW would hardly be sacrificing any equity objec-tives. This thinly disguised NIT and other plans like it were not received

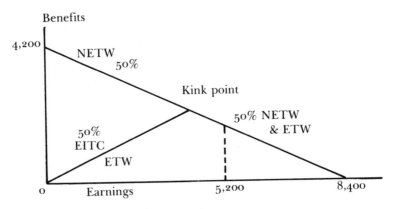

FIGURE 2
Benefit Structure for Two-Parent Families

NETW: Not expected to work
ETW: Expected to work

enthusiastically among DOL planners. As an alternative, DOL planners proposed a classic two-tier system with a very low marginal tax rate for the ETW, as shown in Figure 3.

DOL had departed from its original proposal in that it was now willing to guarantee an annual minimum income ($2,100) for those expected to work. Although $2,100 was surely not a beneficent sum, the original DOL proposal had not offered any guaranteed income—only a PSE job ($5,200), plus an earnings supplement from an EITC (roughly $1,500). DOL willingness to offer a cash guarantee was, in effect, a concession to HEW concerns about the viability of the jobs program. Despite this compromise, the DOL planners remained committed to categorizing the welfare population: their two-tier plan clearly delineated two groups of welfare recipients, with equity maintained within those two groups but not between them, as in the HEW proposals.

On May 9, Packer and Aaron met to discuss the DOL plan (with variations) and the six HEW options. Few compromises were ironed out during the course of the meeting, the discussion turning instead to a consideration of the constraints that each welfare reform option would have to conform to. The next day (May 10) Packer outlined in a memo to Aaron constraints on the size of the wage in PSE jobs and the financial "wedge" that would make private-sector employment more profitable than public employment. He continued to stand firm on the use of a large EITC and suggested that the maximum marginal tax rate for the lower tier of any two-tier system be 30 percent. Aaron was unwilling to accept the two-tier system that Packer was proposing, so Packer decided

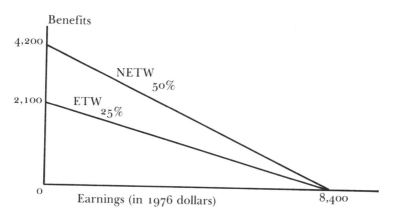

FIGURE 3
Benefit Schedule for Families with Children

to send his proposal directly to Califano via Ray Marshall and began preparing a memo to that effect.

While Packer worked on presenting the case for a classic two-tier system, HEW began zeroing in on one of the six options it had distilled. This option, a "modified Mega" plan, was a modestly altered version of the "Mega" welfare reform plan, which had been internally developed in 1972, during Elliot Richardson's tenure as secretary of HEW. The slightly modified version of Mega, which was presented to John Todd by staff members who had worked on Mega, is diagrammed in Figure 4.

The HEW plan had lower marginal tax rates than the DOL two-tier plan up to the point of the earnings disregard, but had higher marginal tax rates after $3,600 of earnings (50 percent to 30 percent or 25 percent). The average tax rates, however—the tax rate, for example, on the decision whether or not to take a job (rather than the tax rate at the margin)—were lower in the HEW plan than in the DOL plan.* Although Packer and his staff were concerned that the marginal tax rates be kept

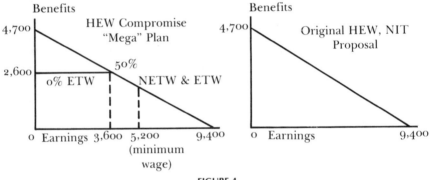

FIGURE 4

Two-Parent Families

*The average tax rate is the reduction in earnings ÷ reduction in income between two points. Thus the marginal and average tax rates are the same when the tax rate is constant (50 percent or 25 percent, etc.). However, in the Mega plan, the tax rate is not constant. The marginal tax rate is 0 percent from $0 to $3,600 of earnings and 50 percent thereafter. For someone with no income, therefore, the average tax rate on taking a minimum-wage job is lower in the Mega plan than in the classic two-tier system. In Mega the average tax rate was 0 percent on the first $3,600 of earnings; between $3,600 and $5,200 of earnings the recipient would lose $800 of benefits. The average tax rate on a job would therefore be 800 ÷ 5,200 = 15 percent (versus 25 percent in the classic two-tier system). Put less technically, HEW was pointing out that someone who had no income would receive more total income (wages and benefits) by taking a job under Mega than they would under the DOL proposal.

low, Packer (much more strongly than his staff) believed that the average tax rates were at least as important as marginal tax rates in generating work incentives, and he was concerned that the average tax rates were too high in the two-tier plan.

When dealing with Packer and DOL staff, HEW sold its plan on the basis of the low average tax rates and the low guarantee being supplied to those expected to work. Internally, however, ISP staff proudly dubbed the plan the "no-compromise compromise." ISP staff assumed that families would start on the upper tier until a job was offered; if a job was not available, families would stay on the upper-level NIT, but if a job was available, most families' earnings would place them past the $3,600 earnings disregard onto the upper-level NIT tier anyway. In short, as far as ISP staff were concerned, the proposal maintained HEW's original commitment to the universal coverage of an NIT.

On May 11, Frank Raines and Jim Parham met with senior HEW staff at a meeting that Packer had planned to attend but had to miss at the last minute. White House staff, who were partly responsible for ensuring that President Carter's deadline be met, were anxious to find a way to resolve HEW-DOL disagreements. John Todd recalled what happened at the meeting:

> We had this meeting in the undersecretary's conference room; we were basically doing some background things, trying to get out of this bind. At the end of the meeting, we're down to a very few people here, Mike turns to me and says, "Why don't you show Frank and Jim what we were talking about the other day as a way out of this thing." Frank had an old PCL paper and I drew how everything worked and talked it over with Frank and Jim. They were genuinely enthusiastic. It was as if they couldn't find a way out of the box they were in and they saw something, whatever flaws it may have had, which indicated to them that there might conceivably be a logical way out. So because of their enthusiasm we started to do the staff work very heavily on our end.

The White House aides were especially enthusiastic about HEW's two-tier plan because it gave them reason to be optimistic about the congressional course of the plan. As Frank Raines recalled:

> Bert [Carp], Stu [Eizenstat], and I went up to a meeting that Moynihan had set up with [Senators] Ribicoff and Long. He was trying to get them on board and one of the reasons we liked that two-tier system was that Long said that he didn't want all these people getting on welfare. He said, once you give them this cash, they'll never take a job. You'll never force them into a

job and they'll find all these reasons not to work. If you put them in a restaurant they'll drop all the dishes, or whatever. That's why the two-tier system made a lot of sense to us because we could say to Long, "Look these people aren't going to get this big benefit from the beginning. They're just going to get this smaller benefit. . . ." After that meeting we felt a little more optimistic that maybe Long could be brought along.

While ISP prepared a presentation of the "no-compromise compromise" plan (which would document that the plan could be done at no higher initial cost), Packer, who was apparently not fully aware of the sudden White House interest in the plan, prepared a memo from Marshall to Califano on the classic two-tier plan, which would be offered as DOL's "compromise" with HEW. In a memo of Friday, May 13, Marshall sought Califano's approval on the two-tier plan:

> We may have to wait well past the president's deadline if you and I delay seeking a compromise until the assistant secretaries involved reach agreement. Fortunately, there seems to be one way to cut the difference between us right down the middle. Although I am still convinced that our original design, which relied on the Earned Income Tax Credit (EITC) was the better plan both programmatically and politically, it is clearly imperative for us to come to an agreement very quickly. . . .

> *Those Not Expected to Work*

> The $4,700 guarantee would apply only to those *not* expected to work. I think this is much too close to the $5,200 that a minimum wage job would provide. I am also sure, after my dialogue with Senator Long, that he will likewise think so. I am willing to accept this reluctantly as a compromise, but it does not seem to me to be wise to go *any* higher than $4,700. Moreover, these families should not receive EITC benefits. If this proves administratively infeasible, then the Negative Income Tax (NIT) benefits should be correspondingly reduced.[12]

Marshall went on to discuss the expected-to-work group and the basis for the "only reasonable compromise" that could be made:

> The most important area of difference between us is the guarantee for those expected to work (and in all of this, we are talking about a family of four with two parents and two children). Our original plan was to provide cash assistance to this group through an EITC. Therefore, the "guarantee" for those expected to work would be zero. Your proposal was to keep the guarantee the same for both groups or guarantee $4,700. The

only reasonable compromise is to split the difference and provide a guarantee of $2,350 (in 1978 dollars or $2,100 in 1976 dollars). In my experience as a negotiator, this splitting of a difference is the only way to end what otherwise always turns out to be interminable and never ending negotiations.[13]

Contrary to ISP staff information, Marshall was not even considering starting a family on an upper tier (until a job became available). Instead, Marshall was claiming that a family would start on the lower tier, conceivably moving up to the upper tier only if a job did not become available. On grounds of equity, HEW argued that families should not be punished simply because a job was not available, but Marshall and much of the DOL staff were concerned that the attractiveness of the upper-tier benefits would make it well nigh impossible to return families to the lower tier, a point that Russell Long had also pounded home to Marshall in hearings on May 12. For this reason, and for the high marginal tax rates contained in the HEW two-tier plan, Marshall opposed the revised Mega structure.

In spite of Marshall's reservations, however, an "agreement" to go with HEW's no-compromise compromise was reached between Aaron, Barth, Todd, Packer, and DPS at an afternoon meeting in Bert Carp's office on May 13. John Todd recalled how the "agreement" was achieved:

> Carp opened up the meeting in his office saying it was his understanding that we had something that worked, that achieved what DOL wanted to do, etc. He then said something to the effect that if he were the Department of Labor he would accept it, indicating that they would really have to undergo an appeal process against virtually everybody else's judgment if they weren't willing to accept it. Then he turned to me and said that he was counting on my assurance that the whole structure was going to fit and was going to work, and that I had until Monday to certify to him that that was in fact the case. . . . The key groundwork for the compromise had taken place two or three days earlier [in the meeting with Raines and Parham].

ISP staff observed that Carp's sudden forcefulness represented a change of tactics on the part of the Domestic Policy Staff:

> This was the first time that anybody started putting pressure on either side to really resolve their differences. Now for the first time somebody came in and twisted an arm. That was Bert Carp. . . .
>
> We had maybe less than a week till Carter had promised to circulate his proposal. Califano kept encouraging Aaron and

Barth to reach an agreement because he really didn't want to have to go back for a presidential decision on this kind of technical issue. Aaron and Barth went over and sold Carp on the revised Mega structure and Carp was ecstatic; he almost embraced John Todd and kissed him on both cheeks he was so happy that HEW had come up with this new plan. Carp announced it the next morning, Arnie's jaw dropped, and they ram-rodded it. Arnie wasn't all that happy with the solution, but he had no counter at that point.

Carp subsequently admitted, "We did crack heads a little bit, but it was being done at the personal request of Califano and Marshall. We felt the agreement left the Labor Department with 90 percent of what they wanted on the jobs side, and HEW 90 percent of what they wanted in the cash program."

In a memo to Carter the next day, a relieved Eizenstat indicated that the "agreement" that Carp had pushed through was a tenuous one, which the president could help strengthen by extending his personal congratulations to Secretaries Marshall and Califano:

> I think you will be very pleased by the progress which has been made since your last meeting with Secretaries Califano and Marshall on welfare reform. As you may remember there was a Labor plan and an HEW plan.
>
> At the request of Secretary Califano, I have gotten Assistant Secretary Packer of the Department of Labor and Assistant Secretary Aaron of HEW and their staffs together on several occasions for very detailed negotiations, along with Bert Carp and Frank Raines on my staff. I have also involved Tom Joe.
>
> As a result of these sessions, Labor and HEW have essentially agreed on one plan. We will have a memorandum to you by the end of this week on this plan which is essentially a "no-cost option."
>
> In order to help this agreement "stick" you might applaud Secretaries Califano and Marshall and their staffs at the Cabinet Meeting on Monday for the spirit of compromise and conciliation which has brought about this "agreement."[14]

Califano and Marshall, however, hardly needed any encouragement to make the agreement stick. Califano, for example, was still more preoccupied with the total sum of monies that would be available for welfare reform than with the intricacies of resolving interdepartmental debate. As one ISP staff member recalled, "The secretary never looked at the entire benefit structure of the plan, didn't approve it, didn't have any interest in it." Marshall was similarly acquiescent. In short, the Carter welfare reform plan, which the president would be presented with in a few days (in a joint HEW-DOL memorandum), germinated from HEW staff, was engineered by forceful junior-level White House staff, was belatedly agreed upon by the assistant secretaries, and was only pro forma reviewed by Secretaries Marshall and Califano.* As Marshall recalled, "there were some details—I forget exactly what they were—that Joe and I worked out over the phone."

DISSONANT VOICES

Elsewhere the plan received more critical scrutiny. The Wednesday following the Friday meeting, Tom Joe (whose comments were solicited by White House staff) dashed off a memo to Eizenstat to register his disapproval. Joe, whose triple-track plan had been thrown out by HEW and DOL several weeks earlier, was quick to pick out the same point that HEW was privately jubilant about—that the plan was a variation of a negative income tax. Joe wrote:

> Although all of us are encouraged by the recent movement of HEW and DOL toward a compromise position on welfare reform . . . the president needs to fully understand what is being proposed before he accepts it and not do so only because it is the product of an agreement between HEW and DOL. . . .
>
> The proposal, in an attempt to produce a consolidated cash payment system that provides comparable benefits to both groups (those expected and not expected to work), applies a flat 50% benefit reduction rate to earned income in both tiers. That is, in my opinion, illogical and makes the total proposal a thinly disguised comprehensive negative income tax system. . . . The cash assistance provision of the proposals are structured as they have been because it is assumed that the manpower system will fail to provide jobs in significant numbers. This perpetuates the existence of the manpower system as an adjunct and not an indispensable part of total reform.[15]

Jodie Allen, vice-president of Mathematica, who had been advising Packer and preparing cost estimates for DOL, was similarly disillusioned with the plan. In a May 19 memo to Aaron and Packer (which was also

---

*This is in stark contrast to the official story handed the *National Journal* in July 1977. According to administration officials, the May 19 agreement on a welfare benefit structure was engineered by Charlie Schultze working directly with Califano and Marshall, and thus constituted a "model" of efficient "Cabinet government" (see "Sometimes the Concept Works," *National Journal*, July 16, 1977, p. 1106).

sent to Parham), she pointed out the weak work incentives in the plan, which would result from high marginal tax rates past the earnings disregard and the high guarantee ($4,700), which was only $500 less than the income from a full-time minimum-wage job. Allen flatly observed:

> You will be open to justifiable criticism that what you are really trying to put across is a high guarantee, high tax rate universal NIT in disguise. With increasing Congressional knowledge and analytic support, I doubt that this sort of back door approach would succeed and it might simply build animosity for the NIT rather than assuage it. And this approach seems to fly in the face of a clear Presidential preference for a meaningful job guarantee.[16]

Allen went on to point out that the benefit structure was hardly the model of simplicity that everyone had supposedly been striving for during the previous months. The benefit schedule depicted in Figure 4, for example, operated at entirely different levels for unrelated individuals, childless couples, and the aged. As Allen bluntly commented:

> The benefit structure is Byzantine. Ask Bob Finch or Elliot Richardson how easy it is to explain a simple NIT with a flat 50% benefit reduction rate to a Congressman. Then try explaining Mega with its changing guarantees, shifting disregards, extra benefits for the first child, additional bonuses for welfare mothers, kickers for the ABD [aged, blind, and disabled] which in turn differ depending upon the size and composition of the recipient unit, etc. I'm afraid that, rightly or wrongly, the plan will lend itself to easy mockery—This is a simplified benefit structure?[17]

Concerns like these prompted Packer to write to Aaron:

> As we have not been able to communicate by phone today [the Monday following the Friday meeting] I thought it wise to get you this memorandum of understanding (or misunderstanding) before you meet with Secretary Califano this evening.
>
> At the meeting held in Bert Carp's office on Friday, we agreed only on a basic structure for the benefit system. The administrative arrangements and benefit levels are yet to be determined (as indicated by the differences between the document passed out at the Friday meeting and the draft of the Presidential memo). I have no authority to go beyond the compromise set out in Friday's memorandum from Secretary Marshall to Secretary Califano. The following lists six decisions that are yet to be made. I am not sure that any but the first issue has to be decided prior to the state-by-state discussions of the pro-

posal. There may be some substantial advantages to postponing them for a few weeks until cost estimates are more refined. You should be advised, however, that the Department of Labor has *not agreed on these six issues.*[18]

The one issue that Packer insisted had to be reworked before going back to President Carter with the plan was the "flip-up, tier-drop" question— that is, HEW's presumption that a family would start on the upper tier and remain on it until a job became available. Packer was insistent that they start on the lower tier in order to ensure the attractiveness of the jobs, and the philosophical distinction between those who were expected to work and those who were not. He wrote:

> What are the rules and procedures by which those required to work are allowed to become eligible for the higher track? What rules and procedures will be followed to return to normal oper-ating status? The arrangements as specified in your draft memo describe a single track NIT with a work test. *This is no compromise and absolutely unacceptable.* This issue is clearly crucial and should be further clarified by the two Secretaries before we go to the President.[19]

When Packer, Aaron, and Eizenstat met on May 18, the "flip-up, tier-drop issue" remained unresolved and was left that way in the eigh-teen-page outline of the welfare reform plan that Califano forwarded (with Marshall's concurrence) to the president on May 19. Califano did note:

> Our ability to create jobs for this many low-income persons remains unproven. As a result, this part of the program should be phased in slowly and monitored carefully. No overall goals should be set. A cautious strategy will avoid the risks that a successful effort to create new jobs will be criticized for missing an ambitious goal.[20]

Califano also noted that, of the "first order" issues, the integration of Medicaid (which the administration preferred to deal with in the context of future national health insurance legislation) had not been resolved; until it was, it would create a Medicaid "notch" in the welfare program. Apart from these two issues, however, he mentioned few substantive difficulties, barely touching on such sensitive topics as who would be better off or worse off under the plan. Even the differences that re-mained between HEW and DOL vanished, for the most part, from the text of the memo. A member of the HEW staff who was familiar with the preparation of the memorandum noted in an internal HEW memo:

My own impression of the agreement (which Mike [Barth] shares) is that very significant issues have been papered over* in order to avoid premature presentation to the President. The hope is that, if the President accepts the HEW/DOL agreed-upon structure, the issues can be settled between us and DOL by later negotiation.[21]

In the joint memorandum Califano and Marshall explicitly outlined for Carter how they envisioned the "later negotiation" process would work:

NEXT STEPS

Information to be Developed

Using the program outlined above as our work hypothesis, we will, if you approve, move forward on the following fronts:
- We will go state by state to determine the impact of the tentative welfare reform package on recipients and on States and localities;
- We will begin to take detailed soundings on Capitol Hill to determine the state of the political waters (for example, membership in the House—and on the Ways and Means Committee—has changed substantially since the last welfare reform fight);
- We will get reaction from governors, mayors, recipient groups, and other interested parties;
- We will review—and make more explicit—the basic components of the plan, and pay special attention to the refinement of our current cost model. . . .

Per your instructions, we intend to complete the next round of information gathering and analysis within four to six weeks.

Starting in mid-June, we will construct the complete legislative package. At that time, we propose that you become involved in the process again—to review the state of our present proposal and to provide additional guidance on other outstanding issues of significance. At that time, we may also be able to make a convincing case for some additional funds.[22]

Califano's prime concern remained making a "convincing case for some additional funds," but he voiced this concern in a more subdued

---

*The long lists of issues that had been discussed during April and cited in Califano's memos—the nature of the administrative apparatus, the proper use of the earned income tax credit, state-federal relationships in the new system, and so forth—remained largely unresolved.

fashion than in earlier memos. The list of offsets in the memo did not, for example, include the wellhead tax that Califano had tried to sell in congressional hearings two weeks earlier. He had added no new offsets to the list and he even expressed reservations about some of the existing ones. He observed, for example:

> Currently, UI program expenditures are declining as the economy expands. Therefore, the availability of this amount is questionable. . . . Our cost estimates fold in $1.3 billion in extended UI, which reflects current expenditures under that program. While most expenditures for this program would phase out at the assumed 5.6% of unemployment rate, we are assuming that money, currently being spent for these purposes, is available for our reform proposal.[23]

Thus abandoning the desperate scrambling for offsets that had characterized previous memos, Califano chose instead to emphasize the momumental political difficulties the proposal would face if left at zero cost.

> The proposal also contains some very important—but highly controversial—technical changes from current welfare practices. *These departures lower the program's cost significantly by reducing payments to many current recipients.* The changes are intended to count income and provide assistance on a fairer basis to those most in need. But they will work some hardship by eliminating or reducing the benefits of some current recipients. Therefore they will engender controversy and significant opposition. But the economies they realize are necessary if structural reform is to be achieved with no higher initial cost.
>
> *Change in the Definition of an Eligible Unit: The "Filing Unit"*
> The new program changes the definition of the group of people—the household or "filing unit"—that will be considered in counting income and determining need. At present, AFDC and SSI have a very "narrow" definition—usually an individual, couple, or single parent with child. The resources of the total household in which a recipient lives are not counted. *By moving to a broader filing unit definition—all relatives living together—we focus cash assistance more precisely on those most in need. But we also cut off benefits to many present and potential recipients of current programs* (especially SSI recipients living with relatives) and lower the benefits of others. *The aged and disabled are likely to oppose this change most strongly.* To hold them harmless (which I personally prefer) would cost about an additional $1 billion.[24]

After warning Carter of the dangers of lowering the benefits for the aged and disabled, Califano closed the memorandum with a bleak portrayal of the proposed plan. Califano, apparently, wanted to be sure the president knew what a zero-cost plan would mean:

A Final Note

The politics of welfare reform are treacherous under any circumstances, and they can be impossible at no higher initial cost, because it is likely that so many people who are now receiving benefits will be hurt.

The states are our natural allies in welfare reform—most members of Congress would still prefer not to deal with the subject at all—and there is virtually no relief in this proposal for governors and mayors. In addition, there will be problems in cutting benefits for the aged, disabled, and the blind, and there will be disputes over our ability to put a significant number of the 3.4 million mothers on welfare to work.

I suggest that we stress to the states and to the Congress that we are only presenting a working plan and that we are engaging in this process before submitting legislation in order to assess impact and to determine what improvements are necessary to make the plan work fairly and effectively for all—beneficiaries, states, cities, and taxpayers.[25]

The joint memorandum describing the plan was forwarded to President Carter on May 23 along with short memos from Watson and Parham, Charlie Schultze, and a cover memorandum from Eizenstat, Lance, and Schultze. Schultze emphasized essentially the same concerns about the inflationary impact of the program that had preoccupied CEA throughout the debate. Schultze was particularly adamant that the wages paid under any jobs program be the minimum, and not—as Marshall had been urging—the prevailing wage, and that no commitment be made to "assuring" the creation of a specific number of jobs.

The Watson and Parham memo was of an entirely different nature, focusing upon the political difficulties the plan would face, rather than on the substantive economic problems it might create. As they observed:

The cash assistance part of the plan is a guaranteed income scheme which will, if implemented, result in having several million heretofore ineligible families receive a federal check each month. Even at the minimum levels proposed, the percentage of the population receiving some such benefit will be quite large in some states. For example, the $9,400 break-even point constitutes approximately 70% of the median family income in

Georgia. I believe that that consequence has very serious social and political implications.[26]

Watson and Parham closed by resurrecting for consideration Tom Joe's triple-track plan (which had been abandoned by both HEW and DOL several weeks earlier) as a means of circumventing the difficulties posed by large-scale expansions of the "welfare rolls."

The Eizenstat-Lance-Schultze cover memo was the only piece of information submitted to the president that attempted to distill the remaining HEW-DOL disagreements and additional crucial issues that were still unresolved. They wrote:

> We believe this agreement represents a sound basis for discussions with the Congress, state and local governments and other interested groups. It does not represent a complete proposal, and another round of detailed Presidential decisionmaking in late July will be required before legislation can be submitted to Congress in August.
>
> The memo itself reflects four areas in which precise agreement has not yet been reached:
> - The precise number of jobs that will be required.
> - Whether some upward flexibility from the minimum wage should be allowed.
> - The precise levels of assistance in the track for those required to work and in the track for those not required to work.
> - The precise allocation of funds between employment programs and income maintenance.[27]

Eizenstat and his colleagues went on to note a variety of other unresolved issues:

> In particular, you should know that this plan makes *no explicit provision for fiscal relief.* While complete statistics are not yet available, the effect of the plan is to provide relief in low benefit states and, in all probability, to maintain or increase the burden of high benefit states such as New York and California. We will prepare a full briefing for you on this question when specific data and options are available.[28]

They concluded with some public relations advice:

> The plan as outlined in the attached memo will, of course, become public as soon as Secretary Califano and Secretary Marshall begin to discuss it with interested parties. It is important to coordinate the plan's release to the press in a manner that (1) avoids an initial round of press reports based on the reactions of others rather than our own presentation, and (2) does not upstage your announcement of principles on May 1.

One way to approach this problem might be for Secretary Califano to make himself available for a detailed briefing of key reporters early next week, perhaps on Monday or Tuesday.[29]

In view of the voluminous output of his advisers, Carter's response at this point in the welfare debate began to look a little laconic. Reacting to Parham's and Watson's concerns that the plan would add millions to the welfare rolls, Carter wrote on the corner of the memo, "Jim [Parham], Stu [Eizenstat], and Charles [Schultze]—This concerns me also, J.C." His occasional comments in the margins of the joint memo and the cover memo from his advisers suggest that Carter considered the breakeven ($9,400) too high and hoped to reduce the basic benefits (as suggested by HEW-DOL) by integrating the EITC into the cash assistance structure; it is unclear, however, whether Carter understood that enlarging the EITC could actually effect the goals Parham and Watson sought—that is, cutting down on the welfare rolls. Responding to Schultze's memo, the president agreed with both of Schultze's points: wages in the job program would be minimum wage and families would not be "assured" a job as under job entitlement schemes. But by far the most detailed written directive the president supplied to his advisers was on the Eizenstat-Lance-Schultze memo. Assenting to Califano's request to raise the benefit levels for the aged, Carter wrote: "Need to reduce payment level to accommodate hold-harmless for aged in homes and others. Leave some other leeway regarding current costs if possible until hearings, etc., underway.—J.C."

The president's ready acceptance of the plan may have been as much a function of his trust in Califano, Marshall, White House staff, and his own understanding or misunderstanding of the plan as it was a function of the manner in which the plan was presented. Disagreements and unresolved issues had been quickly passed or papered over; unlike earlier crucial moments in the development of the process, no meeting had been called to discuss the details and ordering of the plan. Carter had essentially been presented with a *fait accompli*. When Carter's comments arrived at HEW on May 24, HEW lowered the basic benefit one hundred dollars on the cash assistance tier to allow for more generous benefits for the aged, and the next day Califano announced the plan and the consulting process for its future development.

PUBLIC REACTION

When Califano announced the plan on May 25, he used the word "tentative" five times and the phrase "working plan" several times in the first three pages of his remarks. Apparently attempting to forestall criticism from the states for the austere levels of fiscal relief contained in the plan, Califano modestly observed:

> We recognize that Washington, D.C. is not the final repository of wisdom. We do not have all the answers, not even the questions. That is why over the coming weeks we will assess our tentative working draft by going over it on a state-by-state basis. . . . I *should emphasize that no final decisions have been made on welfare reform.* We view the next several weeks as a critical period in which to refine or alter the proposal that the President will ultimately send to Congress.[30]

Califano refrained from commenting on the lack of state and local fiscal relief, but—reflecting on the difficulties of the PSE program—noted, "I think it'll take everything we have to provide 1.4 million jobs . . . and you'll notice we said we'll do everything we can to *attempt* to produce them."[31] A disappointed Califano also admitted that President Carter was "standing firmly" behind the no-higher-cost constraint.[32]

Editorial reaction to the program was generally favorable and often typified by comments such as those that appeared in the *Chicago Tribune,* which reported that under the new plan "hundreds of thousands of persons now on relief would be required to accept jobs or lose a large part of their public assistance."[33] The *New York Times* reported:

> Unlike the current welfare system, the proposed plan appears to provide significant incentives for the poor to work. For instance, a mother with three teenage children would receive only $2,300 in federal payments. If, however, she took a job in private enterprise she could get a total annual income of $6,800. . . . If the job were on the government payroll . . . she would [get] a total income of $5,850.[34]

Elsewhere the *Times* noted, however, that welfare experts in Congress and outside the administration were skeptical that a humane benefit structure and ample fiscal relief could be provided at no new added cost.[35] Timed with Califano's announcement of the plan, an administration official had leaked a copy of Califano's May 19 memo to the president to the *Washington Post,* which promptly printed portions of the memo wherein Califano stressed the political obstacles to a no-cost reform proposal and the limited local and state fiscal relief in the plan. An anxious Senator Moynihan queried in a speech on the 27th:

> What animates the Administration? An indomitable innocence or a profound cynicism? Are they sending us a welfare program that will do such injury to welfare recipients that we will

not enact it? Are they sending us a program that provides no relief to states and local governments—relief that has been solemnly pledged by the President—such that state and local governments will urge us not to enact it?[36]

The president, however, stood firm behind the zero-cost constraint, despite the admonitions from Moynihan, Califano, and others to drop it. In a response to a question at a press conference on the 27th, Carter commented:

> The basic premise on which this proposal has been evolved has been no additional cost above and beyond what we presently spend on welfare, plus training and employment programs for those who might go on welfare. Later, if we see that we have additional money, we can expand the program or directly re-duce the amount paid by local and state governments. But in the evolution of the program itself, one of the requirements I have laid down, which is a tight constraint and a necessary discipline, is no additional cost above what we have now.[37]

Besides criticism of the no-cost constraint, the administration was also attacked for using the "highly controversial technical changes" that Cali-fano had outlined in his memo—that is, expanded filing units and ex-tended income accounting periods. These technical changes, which had been argued for primarily on philosophical grounds within the adminis-tration (where they were perceived as a more accurate means of assess-ing need), were soon depicted in the media as a punitive trick on the part of the HEW technicians to lower the cost of the proposal. Although both the *Washington Post* and *New York Times* had been slipped copies of the portions of Califano's memo in which the changes had been de-scribed on May 26, it was not until a week after the plan was announced that the stiffer eligibility requirements achieved real notoriety, apparent-ly because of the efforts of some administration officials to scuttle them. A front-page story on June 2 in the *New York Times* began:

> The Carter Administration's plan to revise the nation's wel-fare system is designed to save billions of dollars by tightening the eligibility requirements for public relief, according to Administration officials familiar with the proposal.
> Under the plan, benefits would be withheld from many chil-dren who live with grandparents and from some people who work on and off through the year.
> Among those who would apparently suffer most would be unmarried teenaged mothers and their children and families dependent on seasonal work, such as construction jobs and employment in the canning industry. . . . The officials, who did not want to be identified by name or position in the govern-

ment, acknowledged that the main reason for proposing that eligibility requirements be tightened was that it seemed to be a way to meet President Carter's mandate that the new welfare system cost no more than the present one. They said that the technical changes in eligibility rules could save the federal government $3 billion a year.[38]

Stories of a similar nature appeared in the *Washington Post* and *Washington Star* but did not seem to faze White House officials. On the contrary, some aides to the president were more concerned that the plan would ultimately be perceived as not going far enough in cutting recipients from the rolls. As Jim Parham wrote to Aaron and Packer on June 6:

> Probably you saw the attached memorandum [Parham's memo of May 23] with the President's comment. The concerns discussed in the memo continue.
>
> Despite the headlines in the *New York Times* and the *Washington Star* which depicted our tentative plan as reducing benefits (which it does for certain individuals), it seems to me that the issue of expanded eligibility will be the more volatile political problem. It seems to me we should do everything we can to project our plan as drawing as tight a line as possible around the residual welfare group and explain them as people who *ought not* to be required to work.[39]

THE INTERNAL PLANNING PROCESS AND KEY REMAINING ISSUES

As part of the effort to coordinate the upcoming decision-making process, HEW, DOL, and OMB drew up schedules indicating when particular unresolved issues should be decided and by whom and the agencies responsible for preparing issue papers. Attempts to coordinate a strict decision-making process soon dissolved, however, into a general agreement to let HEW and DOL thrash out issues with the states during June, deferring unresolved issues for July. The remaining issues would be settled—at least as many as possible—at a meeting early in July between the assistant secretaries and senior representatives from other appropriate agencies, before the plan was presented to President Carter in late July for approval and any alterations. The decision-making process in effect was to "go on hold" during June, while the agencies consulted with the states. Califano acknowledged that he was one of the prime boosters of state consultation. As he recalled:

> The Department [HEW] was terrible with the states. It didn't pay any attention to them, handed down edicts from on high,

and so on. One of the larger lessons I hoped would come out of this [effort] in the Planning and Evaluation Office was that they would spend more time with the states, that is, the states would become more a part of the priorities they picked to study.

Some idea of the principle issues that remained following the May 25 compromise can be gained by examining the list of issues appended to Califano's May 19 memo to the president:

- *The role of State Supplements.* Should the federal agency that administers the cash assistance program also administer state supplements? Should the federal government "hold harmless" states for state supplement expenditures that exceed the state's old share in AFDC plus SSI state supplements?
- *Fiscal Relief.* Should more resources be devoted to the basic federal program to increase the limited fiscal relief to states (assuming the states have supplement programs) in the current proposal?
- *Regional Cost-of-Living Differentials.* It is generally agreed that some adjustment of benefits to reflect living cost differences among areas could be desirable. The amount of any such adjustments, and the manner of measuring and implementing them, are complex issues on which there is currently inadequate information.
- *Inflation Proofing (Indexing).* Should benefits be automatically adjusted to reflect changes in the cost-of-living?
- *Relationship to Medicaid.* Currently, cash assistance and health care are closely linked. Reforms in eligibility for Medicaid and possibly in the program itself will have to be addressed in the next month before any legislation can be prepared.
- *Relationship to Social Services, Including Day Care.* Delivery of cash assistance and social services, including day care, are intertwined in the AFDC program. The relationship between the new cash assistance and jobs programs and the need for social services has not been resolved.
- *Puerto Rico, Guam and the Virgin Islands.* Should these outlying territories be included in the new program?
- *Institutional Population.* Should individuals in institutions such as long-term care facilities, be covered by the new system, or should they be categorically ineligible and covered in special programs that are oriented to institutional settings?
- *Assets Test.* Should an assets test be applied to those units where income exceeds the disregard?
- *Work Requirement for Single-Parent Families.* Should single-parents with no children under 14 (or 12 or 6) be required to work?[40]

In addition to these issues, the "flip-up, tier-drop" issue still required resolution and the entire administrative structure of the program needed to be worked out. Although Carter had indicated his opposition to the use of prevailing wages in the Schultze and Califano memos of the previous week, the issue was reopened on May 27 (two days after Califano's announcement of the plan) by Marshall with Carter's assent.

The key concern that summer, however, would be the one that Califano had placed at the top of his list—the role of state supplements in the program. The manner in which states could supplement the basic federal payment in the program would ultimately determine how the program would be characterized, since the addition of state welfare payments would, in effect, determine the marginal tax rates, basic benefit, and breakeven points of the welfare program.

Even as the tentative benefit structure was put before the press, the issue of state supplementation was being raised by the CEA, DOL, and OMB staffs. One problem with the existing HEW-DOL compromise plan was the fact that it had inordinately high marginal tax rates. Although the tax rate (past the earnings disregard) was nominally set at only 50 percent, the cumulative marginal tax rates (when the effect of other programs on welfare recipients such as the employee's share of social security tax, the phase-down portion of the EITC, and crossing the income tax liability threshold were considered) could easily mount to between 70 and 85 percent for families with children. These excessively

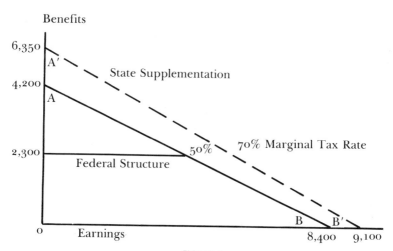

FIGURE 5
State Supplementation and Work Incentives

high marginal tax rates would probably be forced into even higher ranges by the addition of state supplementation. States that wished to supplement the basic benefit up to the poverty line, for example, so as not to make current recipients worse off, would not be similarly disposed to expand the range of welfare payments to a higher breakeven (which would be target inefficient, since welfare payments would then be going to middle-class citizens). That is, as Figure 5 shows, if a state wants to raise the basic benefit (A) to the poverty line (say A') it will simultaneously wish to have B' remain as close to B as possible, so as to reduce the range of welfare payments and the sum of state monies being paid out in the welfare system. This makes the slope (and thus the marginal tax rate) of A'B' much greater than the original 50 percent AB reduction rate.

THE STATE MEETINGS, JUNE

The two-tier structure that Califano unveiled on May 25 raised a number of concerns for state welfare representatives, who voiced these concerns repeatedly during a series of ten meetings of the HEW "regions" in Washington, D.C. As Barry Van Lare, chief lobbyist for the New Coalition explained it, the primary focus of state concerns appeared to be the job program and its potential impact on state fiscal relief:

> The issue we were raising from the state point of view was that we were not convinced that we would ever see the number of jobs that would be necessary to guarantee employment; accordingly we were very concerned that a guarantee of $3,300 or $2,300 for the intact family was not a sufficient safety net and wanted that guarantee higher, something perhaps like the AFDC benefit levels in New York and Michigan in 1977. Labor's concern was, if you start the family at $5,000 and say we want you to take a $4,200 job, there wouldn't be sufficient incentive for the family to take that job.
>
> Basically we felt the payment level was too low to be politically feasible in states which had an AFDC-UF program. The financial impact of that could have been disastrous in New York, Michigan, or Massachusetts; for people who are currently depending on welfare, it's pretty hard to make the drop from $5,500 to $4,800. Our position was, if you are convinced there will be jobs to support these people, then write it as a guarantee. The federal government was saying, "Well, we are convinced but we don't want to write it as a guarantee." So we insisted that they expand and revamp the emergency needs program for people for whom a job could not be found.
>
> The other concern was the way the benefit reduction rates

worked. The system was structured so that as the income of the case increased, the percentage of benefits being provided by the states and localities increased. We were very concerned that, if we were being forced into a higher breakeven, the federal government not take itself out of the system at $8,000 and say: "Tough luck states. You deal with this middle income population at 100 percent state cost." So we talked to everybody on fiscal relief. We did not think that a zero-cost plan was feasible. From a state and local perspective there needed to be new money in the program and we took that position quite strongly at the White House and with the department.

State concerns came through clearly in the first few meetings between state and local representatives and representatives of HEW and DOL. The meetings usually opened with an introduction by Aaron, and a description of the tentative proposal and cost estimates (the cash portion by John Todd, the jobs portion by Jodie Allen),* which was followed by a description of unresolved issues and options for their resolution by Barth. After a recess for lunch, state and local officials could return to give their gripes about the program. The first of these meetings, on June 1 and June 2, were attended by representatives of most of the high-benefit states, who quickly aired their dissatisfaction with the zero-cost restraint. Aaron reported to Califano on June 6 that state reactions were qualifiedly positive. But he also noted:

> As we expected, opposition to zero net cost came through loud and clear. This was muted only somewhat by our pointing out that the allocation of $5.4 billion of Title VI CETA funds due to expire at the end of FY 78 to this program really means that it is not zero cost. We did not mention the similar status of $1.3 billion of 26–39 week UI benefits. This is because the President has not as explicitly signed off on these funds.
>
> Two features of the proposal—the broad filing unit and the long accountable period—were broadly criticized and there exists the presumption that these were so developed only to save money. Clearly the *New York Times* and CBS News share the

*Allen left Mathematica in June to become a special assistant on welfare reform for Secretary Marshall. Allen soon became Packer's expert on welfare reform. As Frank Raines recalls, "Arnie was at a real disadvantage on the income side. They didn't know the computer model or the interaction of various income programs. That's when they brought in Jodie who knew all that stuff and who could immediately say, 'Well, wait a minute. That criticism of ours isn't unique to ours, it's also in your plan.' Before that, anytime Labor came up with something HEW could tell them twenty things wrong with it. Labor was stuck until Jodie got there; they didn't know that ten of those twenty criticisms also applied to the HEW program."

same misperception. We are preparing materials on this issue for Public Affairs and for distribution at succeeding meetings that will, I hope, explain why one could favor these features for reasons other than cost savings.

Other points of interest:

- Any plan without a hold-harmless is thought to be a non-starter. We had very useful discussions of how these might be structured. Medicaid is, of course, a real problem here since it is the states' real concern. There is some interest in using state supplements to adjust for regional cost-of-living differences.
- The jobs program, which was not well presented, was negatively received. Part of DOL's problem is that they have not yet developed the program. State and local officials were concerned that prevailing wages must be paid (this would wreck the cost constraint and pain Charlie Schultze).[41]

The second report, which the secretary received on June 20, was written by Barth and summarized information that HEW had gathered from meeting with officials from twenty-five additional states. The report was again generally optimistic. Barth observed:

> Several issues are consistently raised in the meetings. They fall into these groupings: administration, State supplements, Medicaid, jobs, and definition of the filing unit. . . .
>
> *Jobs*: This subject brings the most consternation from many state and local officials who think the minimum wage is too low, who doubt that enough of these jobs can be created, and who see the proposal as a threat to municipal unions. In some cases, it is against State and local charters to pay wages that are below the prevailing wage. Part of the problem is the lack of responsiveness by DOL on these issues. Clearly, some creative thinking will be needed to overcome the legitimate concerns of the program officials and unions. In general, the low wage Southern States did not share this concern. Only Birmingham, Alabama, complained about the minimum wage being too low.[42]

Fiscal relief continued to be a critical issue and the zero-cost constraint a basic stumbling block:

> *State Supplementation*: The high-benefit States (California, Michigan, New York, Massachusetts, and Vermont) are concerned that no fiscal relief may be forthcoming in a zero-budget increase proposal. They fear also that the expanded filing unit will result in the States having to pick up the cost of those recipients made worse off by the new Federal program.
>
> We are trying to develop a scheme that will permit States to

supplement if they wish and in a way that is consistent with the Federal rules (known as "congruent supplementation"). Also important here is some sort of hold harmless. Our ability to work something out with the States depends critically on the availability of some additional funds. It could require in the neighborhood of $4 billion to fund a proposal acceptable to the States.[43]

In closing the memo, Barth summarized what he saw the intent of state consultation to be. Realizing that suggestions from states were likely to make the program more complicated rather than less, Barth suggested—or, at least, seemed to be suggesting—that a simple proposal might ultimately turn out to be politically infeasible:

Let me close with a perspective on what we are doing and what we might accomplish. We have developed a system that is considerably simpler than the current set of programs, while not being simple in the absolute sense. The tentative proposal cannot be described in two pages, but it is not yet eight feet of procedure manuals. We continue to receive two conflicting views: (1) keep the program simple; and (2) build in provisions that meet this or that special need. If the ultimate proposal is about as simple as the current, tentative version, we will precipitate a national debate on whether or not the nation really wants a simplified income maintenance system. Indeed, we have already begun this debate. That seems to me a good thing. It may be that when the implications of a simpler system are fully perceived, such may not be desired. If so, then we can all stop talking about the "mess," and stop reorganizing. If, however, the desire for a simpler system is clear-cut, then we will have built a real consensus for ultimate reform, which under any circumstances would not be obtained immediately. The meetings to date suggest that we would do well to continue to walk the delicate line between simplicity and political feasibility, while remembering that each exception would cost us dearly in administrability and public understanding.[44]

At the Department of Labor a very different picture of the state meetings was emerging. In reports to Allen Gustman, Packer's assistant, Jodie Allen stressed that the problematic portions of the proposal were the welfare portions. On June 9, Allen reported: "Concerns raised related to: the filing unit and income accounting features of the income maintenance program; whether Medicaid would be available to all PSE and welfare participants . . . and what will happen to current [CETA] enrollees as the program is retargeted."[45]

On June 15, Allen reported, "the meeting with representatives of

Region 9 (far west) state and territories like the earlier meetings was devoted primarily to discussion of the welfare aspects of the plan."[46] On June 30, Allen reported:

> On the Income Supplement side, the following now familiar criticisms were perhaps more frequently and clearly stated than in any of the earlier meetings I have attended. *These concerns are very serious and deserve close attention.*
>
> (1) Federal Administration of Cash Benefits—no state present from Virginia to Pennsylvania thought this was a good idea. They said that: SSI has been a disaster; it has simply increased their administrative burden; *the error rate is much higher in SSI than any state run AFDC program*; the AFDC / working poor population is far more difficult to deal with than the SSI population so that federal error rates will be even higher; state administration is cheaper because state salaries are lower than federal; federalization of AFDC administration is inconsistent with and loses the benefit of all the efforts which have been and are being made to improve state welfare administration.[47]

Going on to note state and local dissatisfaction with the lack of social service support and certain day care provisions, Allen reported frankly:

> Virginia feels that the program is not consistent with Carter's campaign promises and has not been candidly discussed particularly in two [*sic*] regards.
> 1. The extension of a guaranteed income to whole new classes of people has not been made explicit.
> 2. Federalization of administration is inconsistent with emphasis on local variation, improvement of state administration.
> 3. Work incentives are very weak.
>
> Pennsylvania said they would lead a protest march over federal administration if they had to.[48]

The problems Allen noted with the jobs side of the program revolved less around the substance of the proposal (such as the nonexistent delivery mechanism) than around an inevitable regional problem: the level of wages. As Allen recalled: "The high wage areas were saying the wage was too low, and the low wage areas were saying, 'My God, you're going to wipe out our labor force.'" At a subsequent meeting, dominated by New York City welfare departments and municipal unions, Allen encountered more serious resistance to the jobs component of the proposal. She reported on the 24th:

> [The] most fundamental problem is that the big cities, such as New York, Newark, have, contrary to statutory intent but un-

surprisingly, used CETA Title VI funds to support regular municipal services employees (who, in New York City have been fully unionized) and are going to fight as hard as possible to keep their high wage jobs paying pension contributions and union dues.

They feel that a zero-cost based welfare reform is just taking money from poor people to give to other poor people and the job component is just a scheme to take their CETA money and give it to a bunch of people "out west."

Fiscal relief (and maintenance of current benefits) is, as expected, their major overwhelming interest.[49]

The state and local consultation process apparently succeeded in clarifying state interests for the HEW and DOL planners, who privately modified the May 19 proposal to meet state concerns in a number of significant ways in the month following the meetings. Important changes that would be recommended to President Carter in late July included a narrower filing unit, an expanded emergency needs program, a mixed administrative system (states would have the option of handling the intake function), and alterations in the benefit structure that would provide high-benefit states with fiscal relief and low-benefit states with a way around raising their benefits and the total sum of state monies paid out for welfare.

According to a note Barth sent to ISP staff, Califano briefed a number of governors at the White House on July 9 on changes in the reform plan that HEW was considering and "received a number of compliments for the manner in which we have dealt with the states. . . . The secretary later told me that we deserve part of the credit for a new partnership between the federal government and the states."[50] Speaking on the states' behalf, Van Lare similarly observed:

We got good representation from those groups [local and city governments] and I don't think that any state didn't come to a meeting. All of them were involved in one way or another. We had very frank and sometimes antagonistic discussions. But there was a sense on the part of the states that they had conveyed some information and that the federal analysts had gained some understanding of these problems. . . .

Most of the alterations that we proposed, and HEW subsequently accepted, made sense from a programmatic viewpoint. That is, the consulting process was very straightforward; we didn't have to do a lot of politicking to get what we wanted and HEW kept us pretty well informed about the changes they were making.

It was a good process. It was a large investment of time but it was a real benefit in terms of the states' understanding of the cost estimates and the federal government understanding some of the administrative difficulties and complexities of the system.

CHAPTER EIGHT

The Informal Cabinet

BY JULY 1977, THE CARTER ADMINISTRATION HAD CREATED THE ROUGH outlines for a comprehensive welfare reform proposal in preparation for its August announcement of the plan. The administration was committed to consolidating a number of existing welfare programs into a single cash program with universal cash coverage and had decided to tie reform of the welfare system to that of the manpower system by creating an unprecedented 1.4 million jobs for welfare recipients. Fundamental decisions remained, however, concerning the nature of state supplementation, the size of the earned income tax credit, the level of wages for the job slots, the selection of cost offsets, and the size of the filing unit. In addition, the entire administrative structure of the cash and jobs sides of the proposal was in skeletal form. Essentially three decision-making forums evolved in response to the need to fill out the details of the plan. They were: first, an internal HEW group known as the Aaron-Cardwell meetings,* which would deal primarily with secondary policy issues and administrative planning related to the cash portion of the program; second, an internal group at DOL that would attempt to create an administrative system that could deliver 1.4 million jobs to heads of families on welfare; and, third, a group of high-level officials from various agencies, mostly at the assistant secretary level, who would decide the fundamental issues that remained before the July 28 briefing with President Carter. The pace of work would be frenetic. During most of July, many HEW and DOL staff members worked eighty to one hundred hours a week to ready the plan for presentation to the president.

---

*James Cardwell was a career bureaucrat who had risen to the directorship of the Social Security Administration.

173

THE INTERNAL HEW GROUP

In late June, Aaron and Cardwell—who had not been seeing eye to eye on the question of which of them should have the lead responsibility for implementation planning—were joined by a mediator: Dan Marcus (deputy general counsel in the Office of Counsel) who in late May had been ordered by Califano to become involved in welfare planning. Serving the Aaron-Cardwell-Marcus group, or HEW "tea parties," as they were subsequently labelled, was a group of a couple of dozen staff members—half from the Social Security Administration (SSA) and half from ASPE—who worked under the direction of Wray Smith, Aaron's "technical director" in ASPE. Smith's staff would prepare brief documents on various issues for "tea parties," and staff members would occasionally make presentations to members of the group (that is, the three principals, Aaron, Cardwell, and Marcus, and their aides).

Although the group was nominally set up to plan for implementation, it quickly became a key forum for decision-making on policy issues too. There were two reasons for this development. One was simply that administrative planning could not be done if policy decisions were not in place. As Aaron recalled:

> In June, Barth sent out a work calendar and then a few days later Wray Smith sent out his list of decisions, and Barth's calendar fell apart and we ended up working according to Smith's. Barth, I'm sure, had no regrets; the role that he and his office played was not diminished in the slightest. The administrative issues simply became the organizing device.
>
> The fact is that in order to think intelligently about administration, you've got to know each step of the process. You've got to be able to write the manual that will tell the worker what questions he has to ask and, when he gets an answer, what to do with them—that's a powerful organizing discipline through which analysts seldom go. . . . The administrative group sucked up major decisions into its ambit.

The chief reason for the expansion of the "tea parties" into a policy-making forum was Califano's flagging interest in the details of welfare reform. Originally it was intended that the dozens of issue papers ISP staff were churning out would be sent to Califano, who would read each and then sign off on each issue. However, as Cardwell recalled, "Califano was getting inundated and felt he was knowing material which he didn't need to know. So he started to use Heineman [Califano's executive assistant] as a shield."

Another senior HEW aide observed:

They had a lot of briefing sessions for Califano in the spring and then he lost interest in it for a while. He tries to keep his hand in everything so he doesn't have a lot of staying power on any single issue. I always felt that the administrative planning thing was a smokescreen to have the policy decisions get made and presented to the secretary.

Thus, it happened that decisions would be made in the tea party and presented to Heineman, who would decide which issues should be presented to the secretary as well as determine the format of presentation. As Aaron explained,

The tea party decisions were passed on to Califano for approval but he basically didn't look at many of the details. They were flown by him. By that time Heineman was beginning to emerge as able to speak pretty much with the secretary on a lot of issues—not the major ones—but it had gotten to the point where Califano would look at Heineman or get pre-briefed by Heineman. If Heineman told him that it was okay and not to worry, he would say okay and not worry. If Heineman told him that here was an issue that he needed to worry about, then he would be concerned.

As Todd summed it up, "It couldn't have been more than three or four decisions that went to the secretary. Most of them just went for confirmation." As Califano himself explained:

I felt it was done. I testified and then I figured it was my role to get the damn thing done on the Hill. I had made in my own mind most of the decisions. I didn't think they needed me, they were functioning, they knew what I wanted, and Heineman, Aaron, and Barth were a good mixture. Ben brought skills in communication, relevance, and sharpness, and Aaron and Barth brought enormous analytic skills.

The one subject on which Califano did seem to have a clear-cut viewpoint was the necessity of making the program attractive to congressional conservatives and the public. As Todd recalled:

He [Califano] had strong views on wanting to improve the adequacy of the program for people and recognizing the essential political fact that we were not going to achieve that, unless we convinced the American public that we were going to run an efficient system which would have a lot less error and fraud; we were going to take people who could work and make them work. He had an impatience with liberals who simply wanted more adequate benefits. He felt they were not going to aid the recipients they were trying to serve by persisting in those attitudes, and that people like Senator Long had very legitimate grievances, which if you simply dismissed as being anti-recipient, you were doomed to failure.

Califano's interest in a stringent program apparently affected the outcome of two issues. During June, HEW and DOL had continued to debate the "flip-up, tier-drop" issue, that is, at which tier a family with a member expected to work should start if a job was not available. DOL felt it was crucial that the family start on the lower benefit schedule to ensure that receiving a minimum-wage job would remain an attractive offer, while HEW staff were determined that any family for which a job was not available should start receiving higher benefits. Califano, however, eventually acquiesced to the DOL position. As Dan Marcus recalled, "The Secretary decided to throw in the towel on that one. He felt it was important that the program contain tough work requirements, provisions that would win conservative as well as liberal support." Califano was concerned, for example, that the HEW position might lead to administrative headaches and an unnecessarily generous program. As he recalled:

> To knock somebody from the upper tier to the lower tier would require a hearing and I was afraid that would create an enormous administrative bureaucracy along the lines of the Social Security Disability Program. We'd end up with this massive morass of administrative law over whether or not an individual should be knocked from a tier, and it's a helluva lot easier to go up than it is to go down. That's basically why I did that—you'd never get them off the upper tier.

Califano's insistence on tough provisions to combat fraud and error also appear to have been partly responsible for maintaining an assets test in the new system. As Cardwell recollected, "Califano was ironically more concerned about fraud than Weinberger [who had a reputation as a fiscal conservative], because public concern over error rates had greatly increased since the Income Supplement Program." Wray Smith similarly observed:

> He was perhaps more preoccupied than all of us with the notion that you can make a very large savings by pursuing fraudulent use issues. There are savings to be had, the question is how far you can drive these rates down and what savings you could reasonably claim. . . . In discussing assets rules, he said he wasn't going to stand for the welfare Cadillac situation.

Apart from these two issues, Califano apparently did not have much impact on the development of the plan during June and early July. The tea parties, operating at some distance from Califano, followed a harrowing schedule for multimillion-dollar policymaking, as the synopsis of key decisions given below indicates. (One staff member described the process as "the way decisions got made during the French Revolution.")

June 28: First, the group left Medicaid with existing eligibility rules, rather than opting for an interim plan (while hoping to pass National Health Insurance in spring 1978). Second, benefits would be indexed to the Consumer Price Index. Third, assets would be tested by imputing some fraction of assets to income rather than by a strict cut-off limit. Finally, Puerto Rico and other territories would have the same structure but lower benefit levels.

July 1: ISP staff argued for full federal administration of program; Cardwell argued that states should have an option of handling the intake function; no agreement was reached on a preferred model. Estimates were supplied for treating the aged, blind, and disabled (ABD) as a separate filing unit, thus making for a narrower filing unit that would protect the ABD population. The group also recommended that problems involved in pricing out housing subsidies might be unmanageable.

On July 2, at a briefing, Califano approved decisions on Medicaid, separate filing status for ABD, and the assets test. Persuaded in part by Cardwell, Califano decided that the federal government and the states must both participate in the new system. Califano indicated several other preferences: First, there would be no regional cost-of-living variations; the problem would be considered under the state supplementation issue. Second, he agreed to a retrospective accounting period of from three to six months. Third, as recommended by the staff, parents without children under age twelve would be expected to work. Fourth, more information would be required on indexing and on how nominal versus real benefit levels are affected over time. Finally, families expected to work would not start on upper tier (the DOL position). DOL would have three to five weeks to find them a job before they would flip up.

The hectic schedule continued through July:

July 5: ISP recommended a six-month accountable period, which Cardwell argued was unadministerable. Since no agreement was reached, options would be presented to the secretary. In addition, a monthly retrospective reporting of income (unlike prospective reporting in the current system) was recommended.

Meetings on July 12 and 13 were devoted to the state supplementation issue and important cost tradeoffs that should be presented to President Carter:

July 12: First, a decision was made to recommend dropping the basic benefit level and using the money to pay a percentage of costs of congruent state supplements—that is, to reimburse the states at a high rate for benefits up to the original benefit level and at a lower percentage beyond that level. Second, agreement was reached on federal rules for congruence (that is, common assets tests, filing unit, accountable period, etc.). Using supplements that were congruent with federal rules, states could choose their breakeven and choose benefit levels and tax rates from federally constrained ranges. Third, the group agreed to recommend to Secretary Califano that no "maintenance of effort" on the part of the states would be required (to protect recipients from being made worse off). Fourth, there was a discussion of "hold-harmless" provisions that would ensure that states would not spend additional money in congruent supplements over expenditures in the old system. If any grandfathering of recipients (maintaining current benefit levels) would be permitted, it would only be for the current SSI recipients.

July 13: Concerning marginal dollars and cost tradeoffs, the group recommended: family-based filing units, an increased emergency needs program, and an expanded EITC. Several other possible additions, such as grandfathering AFDC recipients and moving to a shorter accountable period (three months), were not recommended. In addition, they recommended that housing subsidies be disregarded in calculating costs of the plan.

Meetings on July 15, 19, 21, and 22 were devoted primarily to ironing out discrepancies in ASPE and SSA administrative cost estimates. On July 25 the memo summarizing the plan was sent to the president.

THE INTERNAL DOL GROUP

On May 26, Packer and Ernest Green (the assistant secretary of the Labor Department's Employment and Training Administration) had circulated a memo establishing a small "Welfare Reform Group" at the assistant secretary level, to meet twice a week. During meetings in June, the group finalized DOL's position on the flip-up, tier-drop issue and considered various options for the manpower delivery system that would deliver the promised 1.4 million jobs to the poverty population. The DOL Welfare Reform Group meetings, however, were less formal than the HEW tea parties, appeared to be largely controlled by Packer, and did not develop into a genuine decision-making forum. Minutes of the second meeting, for example, stated: "Several people expressed the need to distribute drafts prior to meetings so participants can have an opportunity to review them. Nick Edes [deputy undersecretary] was concerned that a complete calendar be established for the purpose of determining the schedule of work assignments and decisions that must be made by the committee."[1] Similarly, a rough HEW issue paper that was forwarded to Bert Carp, Frank Raines, and Jim Parham on June 29 by Heineman commented in passing that "the [DOL Welfare Reform] group was established to consider policy issues, but has made no decisions yet and may not develop into a decision-making body."[2]

The problem with the Reform Group was that an internal battle had erupted within the department over control of the manpower delivery system that apparently could not be settled within the confines of the group. The state Employment Services, the local CETA prime sponsors, and the administrators of WIN all wanted to be in control of the new system. On July 7, Packer and Green sent Marshall a memo summarizing five options the Welfare Group had considered, but recommended that he "delay making a choice until those consultations [with Congress and interest groups] have moved further along."[3] (The options differed primarily in the amount of control over job delivery that would be ceded to state or local governments and in the amount of program consolidation sought—that is, the degree of reliance on existing systems in a reformed delivery mechanism.) Following the July 7 memorandum, a decision was made privately in mid-July by Marshall, Packer, Green, Dick Johnson (DOL legislative assistant), and Bill Spring (Domestic Policy Staff) that the CETA prime sponsors would be responsible for providing subsidized jobs and training.

The late date of the decision, however, precluded developing reasonably detailed administrative outlines of the jobs program before the August announcement. As a result, one senior HEW official bluntly noted, "The administrative work behind the jobs program was probably the shoddiest part of the proposal." Packer, for example, informed an OMB official the day before the presidential briefing that the administrative costs of the jobs program would be $500 million, but admitted that this was a "plug" (a crude estimate), based on overhead costs in the small WIN program.* Similarly, DOL officials "forgot" to inform HEW of this cost estimate until the very last minute in August. Commenting on DOL's eleventh-hour provisions, a consultant to DOL admitted, "You can complain all you want about HEW's cost data but, boy, DOL really went by the seat of their pants."

---

*Part of DOL's problem was that, when Allen left Mathematica to join DOL, the department lost the capacity for getting independent cost estimates, due to her potential conflict of interest.

THE INFORMAL CABINET

In July, a group that could be labelled the "informal cabinet" met three times to decide key welfare issues, twice in mid-July and once following the presidential briefing. Members of the group, who were convened by the Domestic Policy Staff, included Aaron, Barth, Todd, Heineman, and Marcus from HEW, Packer, Allen, and Gustman from DOL, Charlie Schultze, William Nordhaus (member), and Bill Springer (staff) from the CEA, Sue Woolsey from OMB, Stu Eizenstat, Bert Carp, Frank Raines, Bill Spring, and Jim Parham from the White House. Tom Joe apparently was the only outsider. The group first met in the vice president's conference room on July 16 to discuss the use of the earned income tax credit and the nature of state supplementation.

STATE SUPPLEMENTATION

One decision on state supplementation had been made prior to the meeting. At the suggestion of John Todd, HEW had lowered the basic benefit in the program from $4,700 to $4,200 (from 75 percent to 65 percent of the poverty line), providing for federal cost-sharing of state supplements above the $4,200 benefit (75 percent back to $4,700 and 25 percent from $4,700 up to the poverty line). (HEW lowered the benefit from $4,200 in 1976 dollars to $4,200 in 1978 dollars.) This scheme permitted states to pay lower benefits as appropriate for local economic conditions, and would increase chances of fiscal relief to high-benefit states, as well as the number of welfare recipients. The issue, however, of how the states could supplement the basic federal benefit remained unsettled.

As was noted earlier, the May 19 proposal had very high cumulative marginal tax rates, which were likely to rise with the addition of state supplementation. At the Department of Labor, these high marginal tax rates created tremendous concern over whether a job program would be viable. If recipients could only keep fifteen to twenty cents of each new dollar they earned, it seemed that they would be unlikely to leap at the offer of a job, especially if the job paid little more than welfare. To address this problem, Packer and Jodie Allen recommended that states be allowed to supplement payments only for unemployables. DOL's initial position vis-à-vis state supplements is diagrammed in Figure 6.

The high-benefit states, however, wished to continue supplementing families with an employable member for whom a job could not be found, up to the poverty line or close to it. The states saw no reason to limit the guarantee for two-parent families simply because they had been unable to find a job and were afraid of the political fallout they would receive

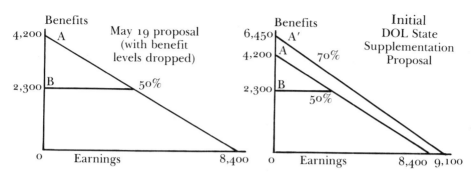

FIGURE 6

The Federal Benefit Structure and DOL's Proposal for State Supplementation

Federal Structure:
  A: Not expected to work, expected
     to work flip-ups (for whom a job
     could not be found)
  B: Expected to work

State Supplements:
  A': Not expected to work, no flip-
      ups allowed
  $6450 = poverty line

from lowering recipient benefits. HEW ultimately came out in a similar position to that of the states. Initially (in June), HEW contended that state supplementation was not the federal government's concern. As Aaron remarked in a June interview in *Public Welfare*, "I think that there should be a national minimum benefit and that if states wish, they should be allowed to provide supplements."[4] Characterizing the HEW position in retrospect as "a bit naive," one ISP staff member recalled:

> For four or five months we'd been playing back and forth with the Labor Department trying to figure out what the program is going to look like. So we come up with this program [the May 19 proposal] which will affect benefit levels in Mississippi, Louisiana, Georgia, South Carolina . . . ten states! Ten states that aren't worth spit in terms of the nation's population! It's not the program that will exist in California, Illinois, New Jersey, New York, and so on.
>
> HEW's attitude was we'll fund the federal guarantee, that's sufficient to give every state some fiscal relief, and the states can continue to supplement under their old AFDC rules, or, in effect, have some congruent rules. Essentially we argued that the sups are the state's business.

Recalling HEW's position, Jodie Allen stated:

They were very fond of talking about this shadow program which underlay the real world. In other words, the federal government suddenly comes in and instead of paying 55 percent of the whole average benefit it now pays 100 percent of the basic benefit. The shadow program is this mythical $4,200 guarantee with a 50 percent tax rate which actually would have operated in only eleven states because of supplementation. They liked to talk about their caseloads and everything else in terms of that underlying program. HEW's idea was, "Well, we set up this federal program, it has all the proper incentives, the fact that it only operates in eleven states in the South is not our business." We said, "Wait a minute, that is just a sham, if you're going to have a program it's going to have to be an integrated one."

The shadow program was like full employment; it's an interesting concept, but as far as the number of people coming through the door, you have to look at the total system. Essentially, the federal structure was a change in the matching rate and the structure of the matching rate, so the supplementation was actually the program. In the end, that's what we fought the hardest over because we were very concerned about the work incentives. . . . We realized that if you're going to spend all this money for jobs, for heaven's sake, don't at the same time construct a system that makes it crazy for a person to take a job. That's what the big fight occurred over.

DOL's disillusionment with the HEW position was shared by OMB and CEA staff, most importantly by Bill Nordhaus, one of the three members of the Council of Economic Advisers. Nordhaus, who had been skeptical of the jobs program, nevertheless felt that "it simply didn't make common sense to tax poor people at those high tax rates."

Faced with pressure from DOL, Domestic Policy Staff, and Nordhaus, HEW took the position in early July that, if the federal government was going to constrain state supplementation, employables for whom a job could not be found should at least be able to receive supplementation equivalent to the unemployables. Trying to calm fears about work disincentives, they proposed eliminating the EITC and replacing it with a 5 percent reduction in the benefit reduction rate across the board, then placing a limit on marginal tax rates for state supplemented employables and unemployables at 60 percent. HEW's position is diagrammed in Figure 7.

HEW hoped to maintain the Mega structure when state supplements were added (B'A' vs. BA), even though they realized that doing so

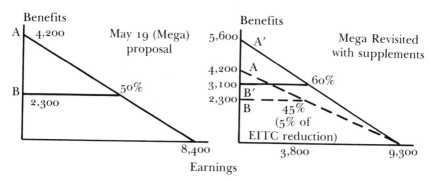

FIGURE 7
The Federal Benefit Structure and HEW's Proposal for State Supplementation

would produce high cumulative marginal tax rates.* As John Todd expressed in his July 13 proposal on state supplements: "The distance between the income support [A and A'] tier and the earned income supplement tier [B and B'] would increase in the same proportion as the basic benefit level. The disregard would be set at the level necessary to provide equal benefits on the two tiers at earnings levels above the disregard." HEW, in short, hoped to maintain the disguised version of the negative income tax they had worked out in May. At a minimum, they wanted to grant employables for whom the jobs program was not working the right to the same amount of support.

At the meeting on July 16, Aaron, Barth, and Todd bantered back and forth with Packer and Jodie Allen in an attempt to find a compromise. HEW argued that there should be no special limitation for supplementation to two-parent families with employable members since any limitation would put too much reliance on a yet-to-be-proven jobs program. Furthermore, they argued, there was no reason that two-parent

---

*The limit of 60 percent would apply only to the welfare program: the tax rates of other programs that might affect welfare recipients could cause the cumulative marginal tax rate to rise to the 80–90 percent range.

families with young children should receive less supplementation than single-parent families with young children, who were classified as "not expected to work." Packer and Allen retorted that allowing two-parent families to receive high cash benefits amounted to assuming that the jobs program would fail—and would, in fact, guarantee that it did so. They argued that, if the government was going to be involved in massive job creation, the effort should be predicated on the notion that the program would be a success, not a failure.

The HEW-DOL disagreement was finally settled by a compromise solution put forth by Bill Nordhaus. The "Nordhaus lines," as they would later be labelled, did allow states to provide some supplementation to expected-to-work two-parent families, but it constrained the marginal tax rate for these families to 52 percent, whereas the unemployables could face marginal tax rates up to 70 percent.

The 52 percent was arrived at because HEW was insistent that states at least be able to supplement two-parent families up to 75 percent of the poverty line: since everybody agreed there should be a common break-even for the state supplements (in this case the tax entry point), Nordhaus picked the two parameters (that is, 75 percent of the poverty line, or $4,722, as the basic benefit, and the tax entry, $9,080, as the break-even), and figured the limitation on the marginal tax rates by dividing the two figures. For the "unemployables," the 70 percent was similarly arrived at by setting the limit for the basic benefit near the poverty line and the breakeven at the tax entry point. The compromise, which is diagrammed in Figure 8, was clearly one that was resolved in favor of the Department of Labor.

As the darkened lines indicate (A''B'), what had been just nominally a two-track proposal became a genuine two-tier system—similar in fact to what DOL had proposed in May—once state supplementation was added. That is, a family member working at the minimum wage in the federal proposal would have a total income at point C, as would a family without a member expected to work. Once supplementation was added, however, the upper tier in the federal system was split into two tiers (A'A'')—one for employables and one for "unemployables" (including single-parent families with young children). Thus, the federal government would provide more income supplementation, for example, to single-parent families with young children than to two-parent families with young children—the difference between C' and C''. In the eleven southern states, where no one received benefits higher than $4,722, the integrity of the federal structure was maintained, but in higher-benefit states the two tiers went unmerged. In short, in order to create stronger

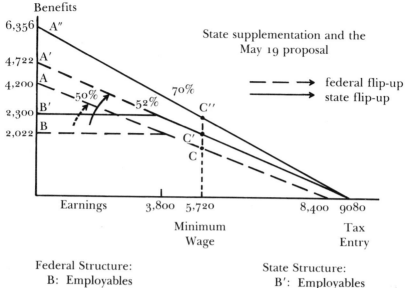

Benefits

State supplementation and the
May 19 proposal

- - - → federal flip-up
——→ state flip-up

Earnings   3,800 5,720   8,400 9080

Minimum   Tax
Wage   Entry

Federal Structure:
  B: Employables
  A: Unemployables,   employables
      who are "flipped-up" (i.e., after
      a job cannot be found)

State Structure:
  B': Employables
  A': Employable flip-ups
  A": Unemployable

FIGURE 8
Benefit Structure of the Program for Better Jobs and Income

work incentives, the proposal allowed large benefit disparities to exist in high-benefit states between some single- and two-parent families, and raised political difficulties for states that would have to explain to two-parent families why their benefits were being substantially reduced.

For some ISP staff members, sacrificing these equity objectives and reintroducing some of the very categorization that they had valiantly sought to eliminate was quite depressing. As one ISP staffer noted, consultation with the states seemed to produce changes in the proposal that were making it increasingly like the system they were trying to reform:

> The state supplementation saga unravelled everything HEW had stood for. One of the reasons we went with the no-compromise–compromise plan [the May 19 proposal] was that we saw no reason that a family's supplementation should differ when their earnings were equivalent. What did we do in the

state supplementation decisions? We completely undermined it, *and* we undermined it with federal cost sharing.

We ended up reducing the benefits that go to everyone—that is, benefits that go to people in the poorer states, from 75 percent of the poverty level—a munificent sum to begin with— to 65 percent of the poverty level, in order to finance federal sharing of state supplements. In essence, when you look at the bill we put out, you come back to a slightly different formula than we have under AFDC. You still have federal matching of state funds over some benefit ranges, you have differences in benefit levels from state to state, you have discrepancies be- tween families with similar needs, and differences in the amount that the federal government is contributing to people in different states. But it's not even a question of saying, if the states want to undermine it, that's their business—100 percent on their own nickel—we don't say that. It's our money, federal money!

Aaron was also disappointed by the outcome of the state supplementa- tion saga. He left the all-day meeting exhausted, feeling as though he had won the May 19 battle but lost the war.

THE EITC

The other major topic of discussion at the July 16 meeting was the earned income tax credit. In the May 19 proposal, the small EITC had been left as it was under existing law. Figure 9 depicts the parameters of the credit. The tax credit phased up at a rate of 10 percent up to $4,000,

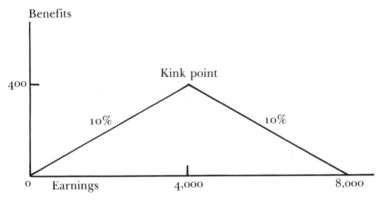

FIGURE 9
Existing Earned Income Credit

the "kink point," at which there was a maximum credit of $400. From the kink point, the credit phased down, again at 10 percent, to $8,000, where the credit was eliminated.

During June and July, HEW argued that the EITC should be eliminated from the program, even though it had been specifically cited in Carter's principles. HEW pointed out that the EITC would lower marginal tax rates by 10 percent while phasing up, but that beyond the kink point of $4,000, where marginal tax rates had an important impact on work effort, it would raise them by 10 percent. Furthermore, they contended, administering the EITC outside of welfare simply added needless complexity to the income security system. They preferred instead to lower the marginal tax rate across the board and change the EITC into a work expense deduction (which would extend the earned income disregard).

Packer responded to the first objection in early July by proposing a greatly expanded EITC, where the phase-down portion of the EITC would not begin until the welfare breakeven, thus obviating any work disincentive effect the EITC might cause for welfare recipients. Packer also pointed out that, by expanding the EITC and thus increasing cash assistance to recipients outside the welfare system, the amount of "welfare" given to recipients could be reduced; this would lower the breakeven and the number of people treated in the welfare system. In a July 1 memo to Aaron, Packer emphasized the political attractiveness of his approach, as well as some substantive advantages (that is, ways to improve work incentives):

> As you know, Senator Long is interested in expanding the EITC. Moreover, our early indication that Senator Long would disapprove varying the EITC by family size appears to be incorrect. He had not thought about it before and his initial reaction was favorable.
>
> An expanded EITC would permit us to better achieve three important objectives in welfare reform.
> 1. Increasing the income payments through the EITC would permit an offsetting reduction in payments through the negative income tax (NIT) and would thereby release funds that could be used for fiscal relief. The welfare reform program would still be at zero cost on the spending side but would be much more acceptable to the States.
> 2. Paying more income through the EITC would reduce the number of people on welfare without substantially reducing the total income of working poor. This will allow us to meet the concerns of Jim Parham, Jack Watson and others about

the number of people receiving welfare type payments. (Our estimates indicate that under the current proposal, 35 to 40 million people would be eligible for a welfare type transfer.)

3. Integrating tax and welfare reform as described in the enclosure would reduce tax rates over the range where it affects the work incentives for many of the working poor.[5]

HEW remained unconvinced by Packer's arguments. They pointed out that the phase-down portion of the EITC (beyond the breakeven) would make welfare reform the vehicle for a tax transfer to middle-income families. They noted again that maintaining the EITC would also not serve the aim of program consolidation. Nevertheless, support for an expanded EITC continued to swell during July. Independent of DOL, Carter aides Watson and Parham, Bert Carp, and Charlie Schultze also threw their weight behind expanding the EITC. As Ben Heineman explained in a July 7 memo to Aaron and Barth that recounted a conversation Carp had with Packer that morning:

Arnie made it sound like Henry Aaron was very interested in the possibility of altering the benefit structure along expanded EITC lines. Carp was interested too, despite what he had said to me this morning. . . . We should have a very brief and rough paper for JAC, Jr. [Califano], on this by Saturday morning July 9, not for decision but rather for information. He should understand the surface attractiveness of this proposal and its drawbacks. Carp is right that we have to be able to draw out of tax reform some extra $$$.

This may not be easy to beat back unless we have some real ammunition to use on Carp/Schultze.[6]

Reacting to the growing support for an expanded EITC, HEW officials emphasized to Packer and Allen that Treasury was strongly opposed to the EITC. Packer, who had worked with the assistant secretary for Tax Policy, Laurence Woodworth (when Woodworth was the chief of staff of the Joint Committee on Taxation), was surprised to learn of Woodworth's opposition and decided to speak to him about it. Following a memo on the expanded EITC forwarded to Woodworth on July 8, Packer decided to meet with Woodworth before the all-day Saturday meeting on July 16.

In the interim, he was also taking his case elsewhere. In a July 16 memo to Marshall, Packer suggested that he speak to Califano and, if necessary, to the president about expanding the EITC. He wrote:

I want to convey my concern about welfare reform. The cash assistance structure being developed by HEW has serious problems. When we agreed to a compromise cash structure in early May, we recognized that this structure would reduce work incentives and would result in a significant increase in the welfare population. Since that time, we have addressed the issues of State supplements, Medicaid, and tax integration. Including these issues in the analysis indicates that the program's problems are worse than we originally feared. In addition, HEW has not only rejected the opportunity to mitigate these problems by expanding the Earned Income Tax Credit (EITC), but in their recent revisions of the plan, have proposed eliminating the EITC entirely.

For these reasons, which we elaborate on below, I recommend that you express our doubts about the current benefit structure to Secretary Califano and, if necessary, to the President.[7]

Securing Marshall's approval on the same day, Packer dashed off a memo to White House staff that not only proposed an expanded EITC but also suggested that an alternative benefit structure be employed. HEW staff were enraged. Ten days before the plan was to be presented to the president, here was Packer attempting to re-open issues that had been the subject of months of intense negotiations between the two departments.*

Packer noted in the memo that his plan would lower marginal tax rates and "result in a 17% reduction in the welfare population compared to a ¼ increase that would result from the [Mega] design." He closed by suggesting:

> Whether or not the Administration finds the[se] arguments convincing, Congress clearly will. Senator Long and Congressman Ullman are likely to think the earned income tax credit should be expanded and will go ahead and expand it. If the Administration's program has no place in it for an expanded earned income tax credit, we are likely to lose control, particularly if Senator Long places the earned income tax credit in the tax reform bill.
>
> If the Administration's position builds upon an expansion of the earned income tax credit, then we are more likely to be able to fashion the ultimate system. Otherwise, we are going to be making compromises from a position of weakness while both Secretary Califano and Secretary Blumenthal explain why there is no place for the earned income tax credit in either tax

---

*By greatly expanding the EITC, Packer cut down the welfare breakeven for a family of four to $7,750. He also eliminated the earnings disregard and opted for a steady, low marginal tax rate on the expected-to-work tier (35 percent) and raised tax rates for the not-expected-to-work (until the two tiers merged at $4,400).

reform or welfare reform. Strategically it seems sensible to accommodate the strong wishes of Senator Long if we can do so without coming out with a much inferior design. When, as in this case, the design can, in fact, be enhanced by going along with Senator Long's predilections, it would seem desirable to accommodate him.[8]

To ensure that the need to expand the EITC was brought home to the White House staff, Tom Joe also sent a long memo to Eizenstat, strongly urging him to adopt DOL's suggestions.

Such was the context for Packer's morning meeting with Woodworth. Jodie Allen's recounting of the meeting and the subsequent discussion of the EITC that afternoon indicate that lines of communication regarding the plan were somehow badly crossed:

> We went over to see Larry that morning before the meeting. Arnie starts off by saying, "Look I understand you have a lot of problems with this EITC. Let me tell you why I think it's a good idea. "Larry interrupts him and says, "You don't have to tell me this. I've always considered myself one of the fathers of the EITC when Mike Stern [head of staff, Senate Finance Committee] came up with this idea. I helped to put it together and I've always had good feelings about it . . . there are certain administrative problems but I don't think they are insurmountable and we'll just have to face them." I'm sitting there and my mouth is dropping open because we have been told consistently, for a month, by HEW, that Treasury was dead opposed to this thing.
>
> So we go over to the meeting at the White House, two or three things are said, and then Henry Aaron says, "Let's abolish the EITC." We retort that it's a good idea and add that Treasury does too. Aaron responds, "No, they don't. They want to get rid of it." Arnie says, "That's funny, I was just over this morning talking with Larry Woodworth and he thought it was a good idea." Henry says, "That's not true." I say, "Yes, it is true. I was there." Stu Eizenstat looks at me and asks, "What did he say?" So I repeated it; it was almost embarrassing to have to say that Arnie wasn't lying.
>
> Stu was a little taken aback and said, "This is really interesting—that's the first time I've heard that." Then this great battle erupts which Stu interrupts to say that he'll have Larry come over in the afternoon. . . . Well, when he came over, he not only repeated what he said to us, he came on more affirmatively. After that, the argument came to be how big the EITC should be and who should pay for it, rather than whether it should exist.

Having lost the fight to eliminate the EITC, HEW soon joined suit to argue for a large EITC that would at least lower marginal tax rates. (HEW and DOL agreed to recommend an EITC that phased up at 10 percent all the way to the tax entry—$9,100—and 15 percent down, ending at $13,000.) The size of the EITC was apparently agreed on at the second "informal cabinet" meeting on Wednesday, July 19, which was devoted primarily to discussing limitations on the level of wages in the jobs program. Nordhaus and Packer hammered out an agreement that provided some limited upward flexibility from minimum wages but that also explicitly capped the number of jobs the government could provide, even during a recession, at 1.4 million.*

Schultze recalled the informal cabinet discussions with some chagrin:

> Nordhaus and the other members of the group sat around for months, or so it seemed, drawing lines and trying to integrate Labor's and HEW's programs. The thing got so goddamned complicated that nobody in the world but the three or four people who put it together fully understood it, and I doubt if they did fully. It was clear to me that selling the plan to the Hill would be an incredible task.

Other participants remembered the two meetings were characterized by the "experts" (particularly, Aaron and Packer) trying to upstage one another. One participant commented: "Packer and Aaron were like kids arguing back and forth. A lot of it was silly nonsense. . . . There was a lot of one-upmanship in those meetings." A White House aide suggested that "they threw Heineman in there to make sure this wasn't just a personality struggle, because Packer and Aaron were in an ego-struggle." Reflecting on the meetings, another source observed:

> My impression of the whole group was that it had a crazy dynamic. There was something fairly troublesome about that group of people getting together and it had to do with their "out-machoing" each other. You know, I know more about this issue, and I can shout louder than you can. Arnie and Mike [Barth], for example, they're screamers. I found it difficult to sustain that level of fury for an extended period of time.
>
> To the extent that there was a moderator, it was Bert Carp. Coming from the Hill and being quite accustomed to commit-

---

*The wage rate would be the state or national minimum wage, whichever was higher. This could be supplemented up to 10 percent over the national minimum wage if the cash assistance tracks were supplemented too. Also, 15 percent of the PSE workers could be paid a 25 percent premium for being "work leaders." PSE jobs only lasted one year, however, and were available only after a five-week unpaid job search.

tee meetings there, he was not at all concerned about the fact that the way these things seemed to work was that you had a six-hour meeting, and whoever got worn down lost. I found myself very bothered by the ethos in the meetings and the notion that this crazy dynamic should be decision-making.

One tool employed by DPS to limit disagreement was to control the membership of the group. As a Domestic Policy staff member subsequently admitted:

> We made sure Heineman was there because we came to realize that he was the only person at HEW who could speak for the secretary. We tried as much as possible to freeze OMB out of the process because we knew they were going to oppose the plan; they were concerned over its costs, so we wouldn't always invite them to meetings. Similarly, we would rather invite Schultze than Nordhaus, because we knew Charlie was more sympathetic to welfare reform. We would invite Woodworth rather than Blumenthal, because he was more liberal with Treasury's money, and so on.

Apparently Carp's ultimate tool for resolving a heated disagreement was the threat that an issue might be presented to the president. As Frank Raines recalled:

> We would far less say, "Look, this is the way it's going to be," than "If we can't resolve it here, why don't you guys write up a decision memo for the president and we'll send it in and ask him to decide." It wasn't necessary to invoke our authority and we didn't see our role as that. We were playing the honest brokers, but we would also invoke the possibility that the president might decide, and that made them more than willing to look at compromises.

CHAPTER NINE

The Plan
Makes
Its Debut

THROUGH MUCH OF JULY 1977, HEW AND DOL WERE PREOCCUPIED WITH forging sufficient agreement to enable them to draft a joint memo to President Carter describing the program. This task appeared complicated enough to prompt Barth to draw up a "decision flow" chart merely to arrange the four "lists" of people within HEW who had to read the memo. The portion of the memo that would explain the jobs program was relegated to DOL, with the cash assistance portion written by Aaron, Barth, and Marcus, and subsequently rewritten by Heineman. The first half of the memo, which described how the program operated, combined the HEW and DOL portions, while the second half discussed the costs and impact of the proposal and outlined the case for additional funds above the zero-cost restraint. The costs of the proposal would fuel major interdepartmental debates during July.

COSTS OF THE PLAN

During July, intense public pressure was brought on the Carter administration to lift the zero-cost spending limitation. The pressure had begun to build during June, when high-benefit states indicated their strong disapproval of the zero-cost limit. Criticism also came from the AFL-CIO and representatives of welfare recipients. Although the unions had faded from the picture somewhat after Tom Joe's triple-track proposal had been eliminated in April, they remained strongly opposed to creating jobs at the minimum wage; they could not, however, as Jodie Allen observed, "really come out against large-scale employment programs." Also, as Tom Joe noted, "The elements of triple-track [the EITC, the jobs program] were there, even though they were packaged wrong, so they used that to put off the unions."

Bert Seidman, the AFL-CIO spokesman on welfare, was quite clear, though, about the impact of Carter's zero-cost constraint. As he wrote Califano on June 2, "While I think we have some fundamental disagreements on the structure of the proposal, the removal of the 'given,' zero-cost, would change the impact of the proposal considerably. As I said at the public meeting of the consulting group at which you presided, zero-cost means taking from the poor to give to the very poor."[1] Henry Freedman, the director of the Center on Social Welfare Policy and Law and a member of the consulting group, echoed these sentiments:

> It is clear that the program proposed will not provide equal aid to all poor people at the same level of need, and that it will not provide adequate benefit levels for all that are aided. The major reason for this fundamental inadequacy is that the President had stuck to this May 2 decision that any new program must not increase federal expenditures. He has tied this decision to his overall decision to make balancing the budget by 1981 his highest priority. . . . It seems clear that there is little hope for total elimination of these inadequacies unless the requirement that the program be held within the level of federal expenditures for current programs is removed.[2]

Unaware of whether these protestations were having any effect in HEW, organizations concerned with the cost stricture decided to take their case directly to the president. On June 23, a letter sponsored by the Center for Community Change was sent to Carter with the signatures of representatives from twenty-nine organizations, including the AFL-CIO, the United Auto Workers, the American Federation of State, County, and Municipal Employees, the American Public Welfare Association, the National Urban League, the Americans for Democratic Action, and a number of religious and social worker groups. The signatories stated their preference for the creation of fewer jobs at higher wages and their adamant opposition to the zero-cost restraint. They inquired:

> We cannot understand why you have imposed a specific condition on the development of a solution to the welfare problem which has not been imposed on any major area of federal responsibility. To our knowledge you have laid down no such hard and fast limitation in such areas as transportation, defense, health, tax reform, energy or farm programs. In every case, of course, we share your hope that costs can be kept down. But in each case, the level of expenditures will be and should be determined on the merits and the needs that can be demonstrated and supported. Why should the one program which is most crucial to the welfare of the poorest and most disadvantaged among us be singled out for an arbitrary ceiling based on current expenditures?[3]

Receiving no response from the White House, the Center for Community Change released the letter to the press on July 7. When portions of the letter were printed in the *New York Times* and the *Washington Post*, the only White House response was "no comment."

In the face of growing public pressure over the zero-cost constraint and the absence of any sign of flexibility from the White House, a desperate scramble began within the government to locate additional offsets to the cost of the plan. The offset merry-go-round began on July 7 with a memorandum from Carter to Califano, Pat Harris (secretary of HUD), and Charlie Schultze. In the memorandum, which Bert Lance had written and asked the president to sign, Carter stated:

> During our discussions on the 1979 budget, OMB raised the issue of welfare reform and its implications for federal subsidized housing programs. This is a matter which warrants our careful consideration as we proceed with the development of a welfare reform initiative.
>
> Accordingly, I have asked Bert Lance to take the lead in developing a more detailed analysis of the issue, including alternative ways in which housing subsidies and the welfare system might relate to each other. I hope each of you will contribute to this analysis and indicate your recommendation as to what the relationship between these programs should be.[4]

A preliminary draft of OMB's paper analyzing the housing subsidies issue was completed on July 7. The paper was prepared by William Hamm, deputy associate director of OMB's Housing, Veterans, and Labor section, who, in the words of one CEA staff member, "was really out to get HUD's subsidized programs and had been since 1972." The analysis presented in the paper clearly suggested that the $4.9 billion in housing subsidies constituted an inefficient and inequitable method for assisting welfare recipients. The paper stated, for example:

> Households with incomes at or below 80% of the median income for their area are eligible to participate in renter-oriented housing subsidy programs. This included approximately 27.5 million households (versus 9.7 million expected to qualify for cash assistance under welfare reform). . . . Of those eligible, only 8% now receive housing subsidies. At the current program level, coverage would increase by about 1.25 percentage points annually. Of those households earning less than $6,000 (the poverty line for a family of four is $5,850), one out of every 13 currently receives benefits under the subsidy programs. . . .
>
> OMB acknowledges that redistributing housing subsidies to all who qualify under welfare reform would reduce significant-

ly the average subsidy per current recipient. OMB believes, however, that the resulting distribution of benefit would be far more equitable and would leave the great majority of poverty level households better off as a result. . . . Most families can obtain decent housing for less than it costs the government to obtain it on their behalf [and] most families would not choose to devote the full amount spent on their behalf under the subsidy programs to housing if they were given cash instead. Consequently, housing subsidies do not improve recipient welfare as much as would an equivalent amount of cash.[5]

The discussion draft closed with three alternatives: (1) continue housing subsidy programs without regard to welfare, (2) continue housing subsidies but reduce welfare benefits paid to program participants accordingly, and (3) for those already participating in housing programs, offset welfare benefits as in alternative 2, and reduce the annual level of new subsidized housing starts from 400,000 to 50,000 units. The draft was circulated to HUD, HEW, CEA, and DPS for comments, with a final draft to be ready for President Carter on July 20.

The discussion draft met with outrage at HUD, where it was seen as a blunt instrument for killing HUD housing assistance. During April and May, HEW officials had assured HUD that housing assistance would not be part of their welfare plans. On May 26, HUD officials had met with Hamm and were told again that the administration was not evaluating housing subsidies in the context of the welfare effort.[6] In early June, OMB had presented Carter and Harris with several options for modifying housing subsidies as part of a preview for the fiscal 1979 HUD budget; Harris reportedly expressed her "vehement opposition" to any cashing-out of housing benefits, but assumed that the options were only being raised in the context of the budget review and not the welfare reform debate.[7]

Instead of attempting to put together a joint memo with OMB at this late date, senior HUD officials decided to try to scuttle the review effort by leaking a copy of the paper to the press. On July 13, Pat Harris met with White House aide Hamilton Jordan and privately lodged a strong protest against the "proposal," which had never, in fact, been formally made.[8] Apparently not receiving much encouragement from Jordan, the discussion draft was leaked to the *Washington Post*, which blazed forth with a front-page story beginning: "A major battle has erupted within the Carter administration over a proposal that virtually all federal housing subsidy programs be scrapped to provide money for welfare reform."[9] According to the article, Califano had discussed the matter with Harris and told her he was "100% behind OMB's position."

Califano had apparently adopted this posture against strong warnings from Henry Aaron (and HEW staff). As Aaron recalled:

> When the issue came up I recommended that we not touch it. I said, if you do this, the housing people are going to come down on you like a ton of bricks and you're going to lose. More important, there is a budgetary issue of how you treat the housing subsidies of people presently in subsidized housing, in computing their welfare benefits, which you really do want to make an adjustment for.

Califano, it seems, decided that he actually had little to lose by letting it be known that he supported cashing-out. As Frank Raines suggested:

> Califano saw it as an easy way to save some money. He was willing to portray it although he knew it would never happen. He wanted to find anything he could to show the president that he was reducing the cost. So he used cashing out subsidies as an issue, but I don't think he ever thought it was a completely viable thing to do.

Once HUD released the memo to the press, congressional backers of housing programs, White House aides, and members of the building industry began to flood OMB and the White House with complaints.* Bert Lance promptly decided to drop the issue altogether, after which Califano announced that he was considering a special tax of 15 percent to be placed on welfare recipients in subsidized housing. This proposal also brought an angry squeal of protest from HUD, which characterized Califano's proposal as "robbing the poor to pay the poor."[10] In a private meeting with New Coalition representatives and several governors on July 20, Califano indicated that he did not believe imputing the value of housing benefits was worth the political hassle and so would forego all the OMB options and merely request that the $400 million of savings HUD would accrue from reform—since owners and renters of subsidized housing would receive more cash assistance after reform†—be an offset to the cost of the program. Following the meeting, Califano held a

---

*Sue Woolsey recalled: "During that whole funeral everybody was inundated by calls, letters, furious telegrams, requests. Not one was from a poor peoples' organization. It was unbelievable—the mortgage bankers were in it, the building contractors were in it—it was clear to me by the end of that, who benefits from that program."

†Rents paid by tenants in subsidized housing are based on 25 percent of tenant income, with HUD making up the difference. If tenant income rose, HUD would be able to reduce its subsidy.

press conference to air his decision not to push for any of the OMB options and stated:

> The OMB staff memo suggested that housing subsidies be [cashed] out as part of the welfare program; that [will] not be done. . . . I'm not unmindful of the [imputation] issue but we're not going to solve it in this particular proposal. . . . The issues related to housing will be discussed in the 1979 budget process between OMB and [HUD].[11]

In his July 25 memo to the president, which described the plan, Califano requested the $400 million of savings be given to the reform effort, but refrained from recommending a tax on recipients, stating: "My best political judgment is that the misery is not worth the fight . . . but some of your advisors do not agree with me. On the merits, most (except HUD) would impute something as a matter of equity."[12] Pat Harris, however, found even this retrenched position unacceptable. In a memo to President Carter on July 26, she attempted to rebut assertions that housing subsidies were inefficient and attacked OMB "premises" and HEW "proposals" (which premises and proposals had never been presented to the president):

> Each of the HEW proposals to redirect housing expenditures to welfare reform rests on a false premise that provision of subsidized federal housing is "inequitable." This is untrue. All potential recipients (i.e., housing deprived income eligibles) have equal access to the federal housing programs; budgetary constraints simply prevent HUD from serving all eligible households immediately. . . .
> Apparently even HEW now rejects the original proposal to eliminate subsidized housing programs and distribute the funds made available to all persons eligible for welfare payments. This proposal would have virtually eliminated the possibility of any improved housing supply for poor people.[13]

Carter, perhaps somewhat taken aback, wrote in the margin of the memo that HEW had "never made" such a proposal. Even if a full-scale cash-out had been proposed, however, it was clear the president would not have been interested. (In a speech in Yazoo City, Mississippi, on July 21, Carter had stated that he would not "do away with the housing program." He did note that the government was spending money on "just a few people when many more hundreds of thousands of American citizens go without housing subsidies.")[14]

Harris' memo went on to attack Califano's idea of taxing those recipients with subsidies, a notion which Califano had suggested but not recommended, and then closed with a plea that any savings in HUD programs attributable to welfare reform be given to HUD:

> The "fiscal dividend" emerging from assisted housing programs, that is, the amount that housing subsidies are reduced as a result of the increase in tenants' income because of increased welfare payments, should be used (in accordance with HUD's mandated housing goals) to expand the coverage of current housing programs rather than be earmarked for welfare payments. . . . Without the use of these "savings" resulting from welfare reform, the housing programs will require significant budget increases just to maintain current program levels.[15]

Having just argued that savings from welfare reform should be used to supplement HUD programs, Harris closed by stating, "I urge you to consider the housing policy of this Administration as an issue in its own right and not as a means of providing additional funds for welfare payments."[16]

Stu Eizenstat was sufficiently disturbed by this memo to attach a cover memorandum to the president:

> I think you should be aware of the following points while reading Secretary Harris' memo:
>
> (1) To the best of my knowledge, no one at a higher level in this Administration has ever proposed a massive cashing out of housing programs. It was simply one option put forward by joint OMB staff in the joint OMB-HUD study of housing policy which you requested during the OMB Spring Review.
>
> (2) The welfare/jobs proposal will increase the income of low-income Americans. Since recipients of subsidized housing receive subsidies based on income, expansion of the welfare program will result in savings to HUD. Secretary Califano does recommend that these increases—on the order of $400–$500 million—be returned to HEW. . . .
>
> (3) In addition, a strong case can be made for counting a modest share of rent subsidy payments (perhaps 15%) as income for purposes of computing benefits under the new welfare system. . . . A moderate imputation could better integrate HUD subsidy with the welfare reform proposals and somewhat reduce the discrepancies in transfer payments between those who receive only welfare and those who receive both welfare and housing assistance.
>
> However, my understanding is that Secretary Califano and Bert Lance do *not* intend to recommend this approach to you, nor, in the light of events, do I. It is not worth the political fight.[17]

In response to Eizenstat's last paragraph, Carter bluntly queried "Why not?" But lacking the support of his key advisers, he ultimately decided not to impute recipient benefits and to allocate $500 million in savings to HEW. So ended the opportunity for a meaningful discussion of the relationship of housing subsidies and welfare reform.

MORE OFFSETS: EXTENDED UNEMPLOYMENT
INSURANCE, MEDICAID FRAUD, WELLHEAD TAX, EITC

The search for offsets by no means ended with the resolution of the subsidy debate; during June and July, Califano and his advisers decided to add several offsets to the list. First, the $1.3 billion of extended unemployment insurance (UI), which might be folded in under the reformed system, was given the status of an official offset. The UI offset had been used in calculating the cost of the May 19 plan, but had never been formally approved by the president. In fact, in the May 19 proposal, Califano had stressed to Carter that its availability was "questionable": since the Labor Department would have to design and pass legislation that would change the unemployment rate "trigger"* in extended UI, so, that, at the anticipated unemployment rates, extended UI expenditures would decline to zero. In June, the president still had not approved the offset, and there is no indication that he did so in early July. When the plan was sent to Carter on July 25, however, the $1.3 billion figure was in the list of offsets, since it had been an "assumption" in the May 19 proposal. No problems with the offset were mentioned by Califano this time.

Califano also decided to add another offset to the May 19 list. In early July, Califano received a report indicating that management changes in HEW programs could cut down fraud, essentially in Medicaid, and save the department one billion dollars. After reading the report, Califano decided to allocate $400 million of the potential savings to the welfare effort, although Medicaid would be unchanged by the welfare reform gambit. This offset was also added to the list sent to Carter on July 25.

Welcome relief also came the department's way from Bill Nordhaus, one of the three members of the Council of Economic Advisers. In early May, Califano had announced at congressional hearings that those portions of the wellhead tax that were rebated to welfare recipients would be used to offset the cost of the welfare program. This, too, was a questionable offset since the wellhead tax legislation (which was part of

*Regular unemployment insurance covers the first twenty-six weeks of unemployment. Extended UI, which is only available in areas experiencing high unemployment rates, covers from twenty-six to thirty-nine weeks.

Carter's energy bill) had not in fact passed Congress. In the May 19 proposal, Califano had refrained from including this in the zero-cost base, apparently because William Morrill (who was helping James Shlesinger set up the Department of Energy) was concerned that the objectives of the energy bill might look like they were being deferred in order to finance welfare reform, a possibility that also disturbed GOP Chairman Bill Brock and the Republican congressional leadership. Aware of the desperate scrambling going on at HEW for offsets, Nordhaus wrote Aaron on July 21, suggesting that it would be permissible to use the wellhead tax as a $1.3 billion offset:

> I am concerned to inquire whether the welfare reform effort has taken account of the proposed energy taxes and rebates. According to Treasury estimates, the *wellhead tax* will be available for per capita rebates slightly under $50 per year from 1980 on. According to both public pronouncements and private discussions, it was very clear that this would be available to both taxpayers and non-taxpayers. . . . To be safe, therefore, you should count on administering in the order of a $45 per capita rebate in the welfare system.
>
> I do not recall that it was ever explicitly stated that the $45 per capita (or whatever) would be "given to" the welfare program. On the other hand, it is hard to see how else it can be administered and credited.[18]

Nordhaus went on to observe that several other potential tax credits derivable from tax and energy reform efforts could not properly be considered as welfare offsets, since either they were unlikely to pass Congress or were planned to be given only to taxpayers. He did raise the possibility that the $250 per capita credit, which Treasury was considering as part of the tax reform package, might be made refundable and also given to non-taxpayers, in which case it might serve as an offset to welfare, like the wellhead tax.

The Treasury Department, however, was not interested in underwriting the cost of welfare reform at the expense of its tax reform package. In fact, a major ruckus had broken out within the administration over who would pay for the cost of expanding the EITC, the phasedown portion of which would go to middle-income taxpayers. Although there was some debate over just how far to expand the tax credit, the primary difficulty was getting Treasury to acquiesce to paying for part of it. That is, HEW was willing to foot the bill for expanding the credit as long as it was being given to welfare recipients, but it had no intention of paying for rebates given to taxpayers whose income placed them beyond the tax entry point and thus placed them in the domain of the

Department of Treasury. In a memorandum to President Carter on July 28 Secretary Michael Blumenthal suggested that this $7.4 billion expense (the HEW estimate was $3.3–4.3 billion) not be deducted from his tax reform package. He noted:

> *The increase in the earned income credit is not needed to provide a well-balanced tax reform program.* With the $250 tax credit, we have already proposed a reduction in the effective rate for those with income under $5,000 from 0.3% to −0.2%, and for those with incomes between $5,000 and $10,000 from 5.5% to 4.3%. This presents a significant reduction in the tax burden in these categories. *We understand the need under the welfare program for a reduction in the high marginal tax rates of the various programs, but this is clearly a cost of the welfare program, not of tax reform.*[19]

The issue of how to treat the cost of the expanded EITC would not be settled until a week before the welfare package was released.

Many administrative officials, recalling the scramble for offsets, expressed some reservations about the wisdom of employing the zero-cost restraint as a tool to keep down the cost of reform. Frank Raines suggested:

> In our discussion of the offsets we considered whether this would be viewed as an attempt to slide things by people. We all agreed that "yes, these aren't additional costs because they are things that we've intended to spend elsewhere and we are just spending them here." In part, it was maybe a matter of our getting ourselves in that mind set, and in part it was a response to the president. He obviously didn't start this looking for a $12 billion welfare plan. For most of those offsets it was made clear to him what we were doing, and he signed off independently. . . . In a real zero-cost plan, you can only make marginal changes. If you want a reformed structure, it's going to cost extra money. No one was willing to insist on that to the president, because they were afraid he would say, "Forget it."

Charlie Schultze commented:

> My view was that there is no way you could put together a zero-cost program and progressively reform the welfare system, but conversely that it wasn't a bad ploy to put the heat on Califano (who didn't particularly worry about big budget numbers) to make sure he didn't treat the budget as his oyster. I thought the zero-cost goal was silly as something you really meant, and I'm not sure the president understood that. Califano was clear that Carter was putting the heat on, and so, then

the endeavor became how do you count and which shell was the pea under.

In order to meet the zero-cost goal we employed all these phony offsets. . . . The decision to use '78 dollars really resulted, I think, from being so close to, so familiar with an issue that it was never examined. We got used to thinking in '78 dollars and often dropped the term "in '78 dollars" when we were talking about the cost of the program. The minute you go public, and the first critic says, "What are you doing?" it becomes obvious you can't tell people in 1981 this is going to cost x. Once in a while, when you get outside a group that was working on an issue, some blinding point you had never thought of becomes clear and you kick yourself and say, "Why the hell didn't I think of that?" This was a clear case.

Aaron, like Raines, stressed that there was a certain "mind set" that seemed to prevail in the consideration of offsets:

The zero-cost device was good in one sense and led to disaster in another. It was good in that it forced everybody to think tight and small in a way that analysts, especially liberal analysts, are not inclined to do. Consequently we ended up with something which was tighter than it otherwise would have been. And that was good.

It was a disaster because it led us into taking a number of offsets in order to meet the zero-cost constraint or just go above it, things that were indefensible once we hit the street. We ended up claiming the CETA offset, the wellhead tax, and things like that. You could go down the list and there was about eight billion dollars' worth or so which you couldn't defend with a straight face.

This was a cooperative venture between us and the White House. We were given a constraint, zero-cost, subject to which, comprehensive reform was impossible, unless you claimed those offsets. We were locked into a mind set centered on these offsets. . . . It was a kind of innocent duplicity.

The duplicitous aspect of the endeavor was explicitly acknowledged, at least among ISP staff. One member, for example, who worked extensively on the preparation of the cost estimates, divided offsets into class A and class B offsets in an August 4 worksheet on costs that he prepared for his superiors. Offsets that were a direct result of the imposition of the program—that is, the folding in of AFDC, SSI, and food stamps— were not, of course, in question. Those offsets, which resulted from indirect effects of the program he classified, appear below:[20]

Class A Offsets		*Class B Offsets*
	(In billions of dollars)	
.5	Reduction in HUD Outlays	5.5	CETA
.3	Increase in Social Security Taxes	.7–1.3	Extended UI
.4	Decline in Regular UI	.4	HEW Savings from Fraud
.4	Replacement of WIN	1.3	Wellhead Tax
1.6	TOTAL, Class A Offsets	7.9–8.5	TOTAL, Class B Offsets

Additional Federal Outlays in New System	12.25
Minus Class A Offsets	− 1.6
	10.65
Minus Class B Offsets	− 7.9–8.5
Added federal cost	2.15–2.75

Explaining the list, the analyst noted:

The class A offsets are what we called real offsets. The other ones are fake or phoney. All of the class A offsets are definite effects that will come about because of the imposition of the program. If you give people more money and jobs, there will be a decline in regular UI benefits paid out. If you give people more jobs, they will pay more social security taxes. If you give people who are in subsidized housing more money, the amount of money HUD will have to spend will diminish.

Now the class B offsets are the ones that do not result directly from the imposition of the program. The phoniest one of the bunch is the fraud offset. The secretary said he was going to dream up ways of cutting fraud in the Medicaid program by one billion dollars. He then says, "Ah, ha! Well, here I have this one billion dollars and since I found it, it's mine to spend, and I'm going to spend four hundred million of it to help finance this program."

With extended UI, the Labor Department was sent off to come up with legislative proposals which would cut reliance on extended UI. Supposedly since that would dry up, we would have those monies for this program. They never produced the proposals, so, even if it was imaginable in the first place, it was always kind of a dance of the veils.

The CETA offset was really the most complicated one. The administration said, "We have this big CETA program and if you assume that it's going to be reauthorized at the same level, you're going to need less CETA, because we'll have introduced this big jobs program, and therefore you can count the reduction in CETA as an offset." Well, the number of dubious assumptions there is fantastic. First of all, CETA was only authorized to run to 1979. You can't take it as an offset because there is no law saying the program will even exist. The other side of it is that, even if you grant the assumption that it will exist, there is nothing to assure you that, in the absence of the Program for Better Jobs and Income, it will be as large as it was in 1978.

The wellhead tax is probably the most justifiable one on the list. We asked the president if the wellhead tax wasn't passed would he come up with that amount of money from another source. He essentially didn't say no; he said, "Ask me when that happens." So you might be able to make a plausible case for that. But as you can see, without the class B offsets, a two to three billion dollar option becomes an eleven billion dollar one.

Concerns about the offsets, however, were not merely voiced at the lower levels of government. In a memo to Carter on July 27, the day before the presidential briefing, Sue Woolsey, signing off for Bert Lance, decided to blow the whistle on the planners. (Except for some complaints at the staff level about biases in the model HEW was developing, OMB had been almost entirely absent from the cost-estimating procedures after Lance had lost the struggle in April over the CETA offset.)* Lance's memo stated:

> *Costs.* The Secretary is now $3.3 billion over the zero cost base, in 1978 dollars. Moreover, when allowance is made for the inevitable overpayments and less optimistic assumptions, the cost of the current design is at least $2.5 billion higher than HEW estimates. This is a significant amount for the budget to absorb, and ignores the cost of an expanded Earned Income Tax Credit (+ $7 billion, according to Treasury) and the program enhancements (+ $2.8 billion) that the Secretary asks you to approve. If the cost of the expanded EITC cannot be absorbed within the allowance for tax reform and the program enhancements are added in, you may have a $16 billion budget problem on your hands.[21]

Lance went on to point out that, because of time constraints in building the cost model, the cost estimates had all been done in 1978 dollars

---

*There were at least two reasons for OMB's absence from the proceedings. One was that, with the arrival of the Carter administration and its concomitant emphasis on cabinet government, the influence of OMB declined generally. A second reason was that Bert Lance was plagued by scandals with regard to his personal finances and so, as Sue Woolsey observed, "As the summer wore on, he became virtually invisible in the process."

and so might not accurately reflect the cost of the program in 1981, when it would be in place:

> *Budget Impact.* The real issue for you is not the hypothetical 1978 cost of the proposal, but rather the out-year costs in the context of a balanced budget. The planners have made no estimate of how social and economic changes that are likely to occur between now and 1981 (e.g., population shifts, labor force behavior, inflation, etc.) will affect the cost of welfare reform. While this is a very complex task, it simply must be done. Even without these calculations, however, it is clear to me that the added cost of welfare reform could absorb at least half and maybe all of the 1981 balanced budget margin of $13 billion. . . . Phase-in plans have not been developed and estimates for actual outlays or comparison with current program costs in FY 1979–81 are not available. Indeed, the cost uncertainties involved are enormous.
>
> The budget affordability of the welfare reform plan depends on how much of the base or margin you wish to commit. In terms of budget planning, however, it would be preferable, to make no more than modest commitments above a true "no cost" level at this time and then to proceed as funds become available from revenues or economies.[22]

Lance and Woolsey were sufficiently concerned about the cost estimates and the lack of administrative detail in the plan that they suggested postponing a full announcement in August:

> A detailed message for the first week in August can be prepared based on the July 25 proposal, subject to your decisions at the meeting on the 28th. However, I cannot with confidence assure you that the concerns I have noted above and in the attached paper can be dealt with adequately by then.
>
> The key decisions you must make now if we are to meet the August timetable are (1) how much additional money you are willing to commit to this effort, and (2) what enhancements and attendant acceptability do you expect in return. I do not believe the analysis done to date is adequate to allow you to do that.
>
> I therefore recommend that the early August announcement stress the basic structure of the benefits and the system of incentives to work, which have been the focus of HEW and Labor Department efforts until now. . . .
>
> During August, I suggest that the Departments be asked to come back to you with
> - better cost estimates including a fuller development of the relation of the welfare system to tax reform, and
> - more detailed options on the administration and fiscal man-

agement of both the cash and employment and training systems.[23]

In an attachment, OMB methodically laid out for Carter its differences with HEW over the costs of the program. Their first table showed the difference in proposed base costs:[24]

Program ($ billions)	HEW	OMB Staff	Comments
AFDC	6.6	6.4	
SSI	5.7	5.7	These amounts
Food Stamps	5.0	5.0	will reduce
*Unemployment Insurance 27–39 weeks	1.3	—	the estimated budget margin if the President
Earned Income Tax Credit	1.3	1.3	now decides to include them.
CETA & WIN	5.9	5.9	
Subtotal:	25.8	24.3	

*Major issue.

Program ($ billions)	HEW	OMB Staff	Comments
*HEW Management Improvements	.4	—	Estimated Fraud and
*Wellhead Tax	1.3	—	Abuse Savings.
*Reduced Subsidized Housing Benefits	.4	—	Availability is Questionable.
HUD Budget Savings	.55	.55	Potential 15%
Social Security Revenue	.3	.3	reduction in cash benefits
UI Savings	.4	.4	for housing beneficiaries.
Total, Proposed Base	$29.15	$25.55	

*Major issue.

The proposed base costs differed by around $4 billion, with extended UI and the wellhead tax accounting for most of the difference. OMB went on to suggest that the program costs were understated by as much as $10 billion:[25]

HEW Program Costs ($ billions)	28.9	Excludes Earned Income Tax Credit revenue loss of $3–4 billion above the cash assistance breakeven point.

OMB Add-Ons

Overpayments and Payments to eligibles	1.5
Asset test	1.0
Veterans pension offset	.3
Earned Income Tax Credit (based on initial Treasury estimates)	7.0
OMB Staff Estimates:	38.7

In estimating program costs, OMB emphasized the expanded earned income tax credit as the single largest component in the differences. The $7 billion Treasury estimate that OMB used was a subject of dispute, however, with HEW estimating the expanded EITC as costing between $3 and $4 billion. When Treasury subsequently dropped its estimate to accord with HEW's several days later, it looked like Woolsey had pulled out her hammer on the wrong topic. The memo brought an angry response from HEW and White House staff who could not understand why OMB had waited until the last moment to complain about the cost estimates. As Califano remarked, "That's classic. That's all OMB ever did on these programs."

The memo also stirred a reaction in the Oval Office: As one White House aide recalled, "The president was concerned by the memo, but we made it appear that these were far outside possibilities and unlikely to occur. But basically it was too late. We had this deadline." In the wad of material that was forwarded to Carter by his advisers to describe the plan, no one else raised questions about the legitimacy of the offsets. Recalling the reluctance of Carter's advisers to raise questions about the cost estimates, one White House aide later labeled it, "a certain conspiracy of silence."

THE MONSTER MEMO AND REACTION TO THE PLAN

On July 25, Carter received the joint HEW-DOL memorandum describing the welfare plan. The "monster memo," as it was called, had sixty-two single-spaced pages of text, and had thirteen tabs attached to it totaling another seventy-five pages. (The president apparently read the memo from cover to cover.) The memorandum had a brief introduction that outlined the text for the president and stressed the importance of including the expanded EITC in the package. Califano wrote:

> Given the long and complex history of welfare in this country, and given the important role states have traditionally

played in providing assistance to the poor, the proposal is not as simple or as equitable as it might be if we were designing a wholly new system of work and cash assistance for the low income population. But it is a significant advance over the welter of anti-work, anti-family and often inadequate welfare programs for the poor. And it establishes a sound structure for future reforms. . . .

We propose a significant expansion of the Earned Income Tax Credit —it should rise steadily to the entry point of the positive tax system. . . . *And there is near unanimity within the Administration that the political viability of welfare reform turns on the inclusion of this enlarged EITC in our proposal.* Its cost below the tax entry point— approximately $0.3 billion—is included in the zero-based estimates. But the $3–$4 billion in additional cost above the tax entry point will have to be met with dollars from tax reform.[26]

Califano went on to note that the primary addition to the May 19 proposal was the structure of state supplements and that it would be necessary for Carter to approve several other additional expenditures before a reasonable proposal could be sent to Capitol Hill:

The Case for Additional Funds

We set out various strategies for using additional expenditures and making additional program modifications that we consider important to the integrity of the proposal. We suggest that other sources of funds, such as revenue from the wellhead tax and savings from HEW programs, be included in the "no higher initial cost" expenditures base. Expansion of the zero base total will allow us to fund certain alternatives in both the jobs and cash assistance programs that will substantially enhance the political attractiveness and equity of welfare reform. . . .

If you approve our proposed alterations, and the attendant increase in expenditure and/or tax reductions, I believe that you can send to Capitol Hill a welfare reform proposal that will be a strong and sound beginning to the lengthy Congressional and public considerations of this vexing subject.[27]

The next thirty pages of the memorandum methodically laid out the details of the cash assistance and job portions of the program, especially changes from the May 19 proposal. The reduction in the basic benefit, federal cost-sharing of state supplementation, constraints on state supplementation and the concomitant benefit disparities between single- and two-parent families, the decision to leave Medicaid out of the welfare package, and the agreement to provide some upward flexibility from the minimum wage were all decisions presented to the president, although his approval of them was not requested. The proposed changes in the program design that required his decision were:

		($ billions)
1.	Additional offsets	
	HEW savings from program to combat fraud	.4
	Wellhead Tax Revenues	1.3
	HUD budget savings (not imputation)	.55
2.	Program Changes—Additional Funds	
	a. Enlarged EITC	.3
		($3–$4 billion to tax reform)
	b. Federal Sharing in State Supplementation of PSE wages (in order to provide greater incentive for a state to put a family on the expected-to-work tier)	.16
	c. Allow homes with "informal" foster children (i.e., living with aunts, grandparents who are not legally responsible for the child) to file for benefits	.2
	d. Grandfather (i.e., hold at current benefit levels) federal portion of SSI benefits for existing recipients, in order to minimize any worseoffness that will occur as a result of reform	.1–.3
	e. Move to narrower family-based filing unit (would protect many AFDC recipients from being made worse off)	.6–1.0
	f. Increase funding for Emergency Need Program, (to ensure state protection against inadequate federal supply of emergency assistance)	.4
	g. Deduction for Child Care Expenses (provides stronger work incentives, similar to AFDC program)	.5–.8

Total Additional Offsets: 2.25
Total Additional Costs: 2.3–3.0
Program Cost: 0–0.7

The second half of the memo provided the rationale for the new offsets and program add-ons, and contained the first detailed breakdown of what recipients would be made worse off or better off and state-by-state fiscal relief that had been compiled for the plan. As the memo suggested, the plan provided considerable fiscal relief* at the expense of benefits to a very large number of current recipients (especially those in the AFDC program). The memo stated:

> The benefits of 6.3 million AFDC recipients (out of a total 15 million recipients in 1975) will increase by $1.9 billion—or an average of $300 per recipient. *Nearly two-thirds (64%) of those AFDC recipients who gain had pre-reform incomes below the poverty line, and 27% of them will move above the poverty line as a result.* . . . We estimate that the benefits of 6.5 million current AFDC recipients will decrease by $2.7 billion—an average of $400 per recipient. Of this group, 75% had pre-reform incomes above the poverty line. 900,000 will fall below the poverty line as a result.[28]

The fact that the majority of AFDC recipients would be made worse off by reforming the system was of special concern to Carter aides. At the Department of Labor, however, Packer was relatively pleased with the plan. In a confidential memo to Marshall on the 25th, he wrote:

> Although I still believe that our design of the cash assistance system is considerably better than the one put together by HEW and described in their portion of the memo, we have come out in pretty good shape.

Jobs

> Most important, there is implicit commitment to find a job for principal earners in all families with children within five weeks generally and within eight weeks in all but exceptional circumstances. Although this commitment is substantially less than a guarantee and may not be honored if the demand for these jobs is substantially underestimated or if the economy is in a recession, *there is a commitment to provide 1.4 million jobs to meet the goal.* In a sense, this defines full employment along the lines that you have stated so often; that is, full employment is a situation in which no one has to look for a job for more than a specified period. The specified period is now defined as eight weeks and the definition is restricted to principal earners in families with children. . . .
>
> As long as the CETA Title VI build-up continues in an acceptable fashion, DOL will do very well with the welfare reform proposal before the Congress.[29]

---

*Estimates of fiscal relief were actually in 1975 dollars and had not yet been "aged" to 1978, much less 1981, dollars. Even in 1975 dollars, however, the estimates were very generous: New York and California, for example, would have received $859 million and $864 million respectively.

In a memo to Eizenstat on the 27th, Tom Joe gave a far less sanguine evaluation of the plan and recommended postponing its announcement for a month in order to make further changes. Joe argued that the planning process had been a chaotic one without clear goals:

> The proposed plan has resulted from an attempt to preserve a negative income tax structure as the basic and primary mechanism of welfare reform. The planning process from which the direct plan emerged was disorganized, and did not establish clear objectives for the reformed system. Rather than thoroughly reviewing the nature of the current system, identifying its problems, addressing these problems within a clearly defined policy framework, the planning effort pursued a design subject to little real debate on its ability to accomplish fundamental goals. Cursory debate about fragmented and disjointed issues (such as filing unit, accounting period, marginal tax rates, etc.) has dominated the time and energy of everyone concerned. The proposal was not built inductively from a clear identification of what the existing system and problems are, but seems to have developed from a predetermined conceptual commitment to use a single cash assistance mechanism. Under pressure from the White House, the Department of Labor and other sources, the earned income tax credit has been added to the final plan. . . .
>
> Although initially it might have been argued that the negative income tax (NIT) structure would at least lead to a clear and administratively simple program, the result is the most complex plan of all. The plan treats and rewards people very differently, making many distinctions among people on the basis of family composition. Thus, singles and childless couples are treated differently from one-parent families, who are in turn treated differently from two-parent families—and within each group, those expected to work are treated differently from those who can't work. The result is a program which produces multiple benefit packages, unjustified inequities, administrative complexity (if not chaos), and which, in effect, maintains as many, if not more, different categories of recipients as the maze of programs it was designed to replace. In the series of recent planning meetings, a major problem has surfaced in just trying to communicate the complex and confusing elements of the plan, let alone figure out how to administer it. . . .
>
> The primary analytic emphasis has been on trying to accommodate the diverse goals of welfare reform within the NIT,

and secondary attention has been given to what is the most important aspect of welfare reform—providing real and productive job opportunities for people, and making DOL accountable for producing these jobs. . . . As far as I'm concerned, this is contrary to everything the President has said on the welfare issue, including his May 2 statement of principles. . . .

The most serious consequence of all of the above is that the welfare reform plan ends up disadvantaging many of those people who are currently helped and who we in fact want to help. Somehow the concerns of the needy and the dependent got lost in the technical aspects of the process.[30]

Joe's concern about the damage the plan would cause for current recipients was echoed in memos sent to Carter on July 27, the day before the presidential briefing: on that day Carter received Harris' memo (with Eizenstat's cover note) inveighing against offsetting welfare costs with HUD savings, OMB's memo on problems in the cost estimate, memos from Charlie Schultze and the Domestic Policy Staff on the plan, a memo from Eizenstat summarizing the agenda and key issues in the upcoming meeting, and a memo from Jim Parham. Parham was quite disturbed by the HEW plan and informed Carter in no uncertain terms that the proposal was simply too parsimonious. He wrote:

Almost exactly eight years ago—after six months in office—President Nixon announced his plan for welfare reform. For a family of four, it included a basic guarantee of $1600 per year, a $720 per year ($60/month) earned income disregard, and a 50% benefit reduction rate on additional earnings. He called his plan "workfare," included a strong work requirement, but no public service jobs. According to Tom Joe, the plan included a pledge that no current recipient would be hurt. The final version considered by the Congress provided a minimum benefit of $2400 for a family of four, to be accomplished by a cash out of food stamps.

Adjusted for eight years of inflation, the guarantee discussed by President Nixon may turn out to be relatively more generous than the plan submitted to you this week.

In addition to the above, you should note that our proposed plan:
- admits to making "worse off" over nine million current recipients (some say the figure is higher), over 2.4 million of whom are acknowledged to have had pre-reform incomes below the poverty level;
- causes 1.9 million persons to fall below the poverty level;

- terminates eligibility for 6.5 million persons;
- makes "worse off" many recipients who are working and utilizing the work incentive provisions of current programs, although fiscal relief at $4.6 billion is proposed to give states the "option" of lessening the "worseoffness" of recipients;
- targets $3 billion of tax expenditures in the revised EITC toward families with incomes above the plan's breakeven point.

Admittedly, such comments as those above put the worst face on the plan, but the point should be clear.

Given the constraints imposed upon them, the planners have performed brilliantly and have worked to the point of exhaustion. In spite of this, however, *my advice is that you reserve judgment on the plan and continue, after giving the planners a few days off, to seek more feasible approaches to [this problem].*[31]

The memo from the Domestic Policy Staff (Eizenstat, Carp, Raines, and Spring) also pointed out the "worseoffness" problem and suggested that an alternative could be developed that would lessen fiscal relief and provide more aid to recipients. They made a few recommendations along these lines and strongly urged that HEW be directed to explore the options (using their computer capability) in very short order.

As with Parham, Eizenstat and his colleagues wanted to be sure Carter did not rush his decisions just to meet his deadline:

In light of the fact that Congress will be in recess after August 6 for one month, you may wish to postpone submission of the plan until immediately after Congress comes back in early September, *if* you are not completely satisfied with the HEW-DOL proposal. There are some hard choices which are presented to you and the HEW computer remains somewhat in a state of flux with respect to costs and impact both on states and individuals. If you cannot accept the earned income tax credit recommendation, and I would urge that you do accept it, then a postponement is most certainly necessary. The welfare reform proposal will be one of the most important decisions you make in the next four years and a few additional weeks might clarify any questions which you may continue to have after Thursday's meeting.[32]

The DPS essentially agreed with the HEW recommendations for cost add-ons.

Schultze felt that the welfare package would be ready for presentation

*Parham went on to suggest that the president reconsider triple track and consider three separate legislative packages, one for the working poor, one for the jobs component, and a third for the residual welfare population.

in August subject to two changes. Rather than stressing problems from the vantage point of recipients, Schultze emphasized the need to remove any inflationary seeds from the program. Schultze insisted again that the wage of the jobs be kept as close to minimum wage as possible and that an explicit cap of 1.4 million be provided on the number of jobs the government would provide. He was also strongly opposed to indexing and thought the expanded EITC unnecessarily generous.

The final memo Carter received was Blumenthal's note advocating that the full cost of the expanded EITC be charged to welfare reform.

THE PRESIDENTIAL BRIEFING AND THE JULY 30 MEETING

On July 28 at 5:30 A.M., President Carter sat down at his desk for three hours of study of the various memoranda submitted to him on the welfare reform plan. That afternoon, Califano briefed the president on the plan at a two-hour meeting attended by Aaron and Todd from HEW, Marshall and Packer from DOL, Eizenstat, Carp, Raines, and Parham from the White House, Schultze from CEA, Blumenthal and Woodworth from Treasury, HUD Secretary Harris, Sue Woolsey and Bo Cutter from OMB, Vice President Mondale, and Tom Joe. The meeting lasted roughly two hours. For most of the time, Califano ran the president through the plan, with Carter occasionally interrupting to ask questions. Potential trouble spots with Congress, such as problems of integrating Medicaid and requests to lower the age of the youngest child (before the mother would be required to work), were duly noted and passed over. Marshall recalled that the president seemed "to have greater reservations about the cash side than the jobs part; he was pleased with the jobs program."

OMB's problems with the cost estimates were also voiced by Bo Cutter, but with Califano, Marshall, Schultze, and Eizenstat supporting the plan, the challenge lacked force, especially once the decision to allocate the cost of the expanded EITC above the breakeven to Treasury appeared to be settled.* Schultze pointed out to Carter that, "from the standpoint of tax reform, on a scale of ten, this EITC might rank an eight, and from the standpoint of welfare reform, it also probably ranks an eight, but you're getting 16 through one instrument." Schultze's comments, as Aaron recalled, "more or less swept the day and set up the atmosphere for getting a compromise proposal." With the cost of the expanded EITC settled, Califano, Aaron, and Todd took turns explaining the rationale for each offset to the president. As Bert Carp recalled, "We

---

*The single largest component ($4 billion) in the differing HEW and OMB estimates was the cost of the expanded EITC.

explained to the president that our offsets might be disputed and Joe [Califano] made the point that, as these bills get recosted, they always grow. The President understood that." As another attendee recalled, Carter "understood quite clearly the issues involved in taking the offsets—especially the major ones, CETA, wellhead, the allocation of EITC costs, and perhaps the extended UI offset."

Carter reserved his most intense questions for the close of the meeting, when Califano explained the need for additional funds. Carter appeared to be contemplating his advisers' comments on the trade-off between fiscal relief and recipient well-being, but did not specifically discuss the issue. He also did not give approval to any of the specific add-ons, but did indicate that he might be willing to spend some additional money if he was convinced the changes were necessary. He instructed HEW to reconsider alternative ways of modifying the "family-based" filing unit to make it less costly and more reflective of the efficiencies of living in a larger household. He gave HEW, as one participant explained, the "Washington Monument" litmus test:

> The president asked us how much could be saved by reducing the basic federal benefit and, if no additional monies were available, would we prefer to keep our proposal benefit levels and not have any of our proposed program modifications. That is, he was saying, would you want to consider reductions in the benefit structure as a possible cost saving device, to make funds available for other program changes.
>
> He understood that the changes we had proposed were very attractive but he wanted to be sure that we weren't using them to conceal some marginal aspects of the basic program. He was using the "Washington Monument" budget technique—that is, if you say to the Interior Department, "You may have to take a 5 percent cut in appropriations, what's the first thing to go?"— if they respond "the Washington Monument," you're unlikely to pursue the budget cut.

The meeting, as John Todd recalled,

> was generally one of good will. The president seemed pretty enthusiastic about the plan and Joe did a good job of presenting it. There were no major issues of contention between people; the plan had been pretty well worked out before the meeting. The president did ask some tough questions, so we had a lot of work to do in preparation for the next meeting.

The next meeting was on Saturday, July 30, and was attended by most of the president's key advisers but not Carter himself. The meeting, which was chaired by Eizenstat, was another all-day affair, and produced several changes in the proposal, the most important of which limited fiscal relief to the states along the lines the Domestic Policy Staff had suggested, and freed up roughly $2 billion of additional funds for the proposal.

The generous fiscal relief called for in the plan caused a special problem for the administration in regard to the southern states. The $4,200 federal national minimum would be higher in southern states than existing benefits, which meant that those states could eliminate what meager benefits they were providing (which were already proportionately far less than high-benefit states). Also, since states would have the option to administer intake in the system, there would be no incentive for these low-benefit states to be cost efficient. In this sense, the proposal would look like Carter's payoff to the South, and it raised fears among organized labor and liberals that recipients in southern states were going to get the bad end of the bargain. At the suggestion of Tom Joe, and the insistence of Bert Carp and Frank Raines, who were determined that the southern states not "walk away" from the system, a "maintenance of effort" provision was incorporated into the proposal, which required states to pay 10 percent of the cost of the basic federal benefit.

The maintenance of effort provision, however, would have meant that some southern states, such as Mississippi, would have had to triple or quadruple their current welfare budgets. Since this was clearly unacceptable, the planners put in another provision, again mostly based upon a suggestion by Tom Joe, which would place specific limitations on fiscal relief, phasing it in over the course of several years. This "hold-harmless" provision assured that no state would be required to pay more than 90 percent of its current expenditures, but mandated that states contribute at least 90 percent of their welfare expenditures in the first year, 60 percent in the second, and 30 percent in the third. By effectively limiting the amount of fiscal relief during the first few years of the program, the planners created extra funds to compensate for those recipients who would be made worse off. As Eizenstat, Califano, Marshall, and Schultze stated in a memo to the president the following day:

> We recommend adoption of this approach. Secretary Califano believes *strongly* that we must make every effort to deal with the "worseoffness" problem, especially for those below the poverty line, even at the cost of *initial* year fiscal relief.
> The advantage of this new proposal is that, without increasing the Federal cost of the program, it permits short-term protection of AFDC recipients, and creates a gradual transition to the new system for them. By the end of the third year, States

and localities will have as much fiscal relief as originally proposed and AFDC recipients will be in the same posture; but
their burden will be eased by the transition. This will also help
blunt the expected criticism of the worseoffness problem our
proposal creates.[33]

As might be expected, HEW strongly preferred the maintenance of
effort and hold-harmless provisions to any reduction in recipient benefits. The memo stated:

> Not only would a reduction in the basic Federal benefit in-
> crease worseoffness (in a plan with nearly nine million recip-
> ients potentially worseoff) and reduce fiscal relief, it would
> lead to sharp attacks on the plan from liberal groups. A central
> problem with the reduction is that it would make benefit levels
> for the expected to work group *lower* in many instances than
> benefits provided under the current food stamps program.
>
> We believe that a far better way to save money within the
> present program structure is to require States to pay 10% of the
> costs of the basic Federal benefit (i.e., 10% of $4200 for a family
> of four). This measure would *save $1.8 billion*.[34]

Carter's advisers also made recommendations or decisions on several
other issues. Pushed by Charlie Schultze and the Treasury Department,
Eizenstat, Califano, and Marshall agreed to lower the phase-up and
phase-down rates to reduce the expense of the EITC.* This also meant
there would be less tax money going to welfare recipients than in the
July 25 proposal, but more going to middle-income taxpayers, who
would not experience quite as high marginal tax rates as a result of the
lowering of the phase-down rate. Schultze also insisted, over the opposition of Tom Joe and Aaron, that the issue of indexing be brought before
the president.† Finally, HEW, OMB, and Labor agreed on the costs and
offsets to the program. A paragraph in the draft of the memo that
requested Carter to pass on the availability of extended UI expenditures

---

*The July 25 proposal was for an EITC that phased up at 10 percent to $9,070 for a family
of four (that is, a maximum credit of $907) and phased down steeply at 15 percent, ending
at $15,119. The July 30 EITC phased up at 10 percent to $4,000 (as under existing law)
and, at a lower rate, 5 percent, from $4,000 to $9,070 (that is, a maximum credit of $654).
It also phased down at 10 percent rather than 15 percent. When indexed to 1981 dollars,
this EITC would reach a peak around $11,000 and phase out at the $18,600 mark.

†Schultze opposed indexing because he felt it would eliminate the possibility for discretion-
ary charges in benefit levels and might create a dangerous inflationary seed in a still-
untested program. Aaron and Joe contended that it was inhumane not to assure the poor
that their real incomes would not decline during inflationary periods.

was deleted, and of the only remaining contested offset, HUD savings from welfare reform, all except HUD agreed that it should be employed to offset the costs of the program.

The end of the memo restated the need for the seven add-ons Califano had requested at the briefing with the president and laid out a decision checklist for Carter. Carter's advisers stated:

> We believe that the *first four program modifications* are essential to the political viability of the welfare reform proposal, and strongly urge their approval. There cost totals $1.56 to 2.1 billion. . . .
>
> Two of the first four proposals—the adoption of a modified family-based filing unit and a standard childcare reduction— would have a substantial impact on the single biggest problem of politics and equity presented by the basic proposal: The number of existing AFDC recipients who will be made worseoff (assuming only congruent supplements) by the new plan.
>
> If these proposed changes are adopted, the number of AFDC recipients made worseoff is reduced from *6.2* million to *4.5* million; the total amount of the reduction in their benefits would decline from $*2.6* billion to $*1.8* billion; their reduction in disposable income would decline from $1.9 to $1.3 billion.[35]

Attached to the joint memo was a cover memo from Eizenstat, which also emphasized the need to put additional funds in the program:

> This plan is the most frugal possible. You "no cost" directive has had an exceptionally good impact from a discipline standpoint. The plan puts primary emphasis on jobs, with cash assistance improved by including, on a national basis, for the first time, intact families.
>
> The first 4 add-ons suggested in the memorandum are very important, if there is to be any chance to sell this program and to be perceived as dealing compassionately with current recipients. However, you should recognize that some black and liberal leaders will nevertheless criticize the plan as inadequate in fiscal relief, benefit levels and wages.[36]

Eizenstat went on to note the tenuousness of the CETA offset for the umpteenth time:

> It is important to recognize that the 1.1 million public service jobs in the plan are affordable only because these "minimum wage" jobs will supplant the 725,000 "prevailing wage" CETA jobs which we will have in FY 1978 as part of the stimulus package and which are designed to terminate thereafter. One

concern is whether Congress will be willing to phase these out, particularly if unemployment is still high by then. This, of course, is a battle for another day.[37]

Carter was quite willing to defer that battle. Although his advisers had hardly gone out of their way to stress the problematic nature of the offsets, they had pointed out to him at various junctures the difficulties that might arise, and why the offsets were not part of standard budgeting procedures. Ironically, in searching for a genuine zero-cost base, Carter, in the words of one HEW staff member, had become "the biggest game player of them all." Somehow the planners and the president had convinced each other that these were legitimate offsets to include in a zero-cost base, and any impulses to dissent had effectively been stifled.

Carter was apparently pleased by the changes the July 30 meeting had wrought in the plan. His marginal comments on the July 27 Domestic Policy Staff memo and Parham's note indicated that he wanted less fiscal relief in the plan and less recipient worseoffness, and considered that hold-harmless, maintenance of effort provisions might be a good way of reaching these ends.* He also indicated on Schultze's memo that benefits should not be indexed and that the EITC, as then structured, had been unnecessarily generous. Regarding the cost add-ons, Carter took the advice of Jim McIntyre, offered in an August 1 memo (signing off for OMB Director Bert Lance), that he accept the first four cost add-ons and reject the remaining three.†

The last-minute addition of the hold-harmless, maintenance of effort provisions was not warmly received at HEW. There were questions about just how enforceable the provisions were, what kinds of state expenditures on welfare would be considered appropriate in calculating the hold-harmless, and so forth. The provisions when fully spelled out were also extremely complicated. Both Aaron and Dan Marcus (who would draft the congressional bill during August) admitted that the provisions were "virtually impossible" to understand. Marcus commented:

> Aaron, and to a lesser extent Barth, were very opposed to those provisions. They had the true welfare reformer's view, that when you make a clean cut with the past, you establish a new,

---

*Carter also approved the minor change in the "family-based" filing unit, which was made to account for the efficiency of being in a larger household. In households where two or more filing units lived together, only one was eligible for the $800 "head of household" bonus.

†The three add-ons rejected were for federal sharing of supplementation of PSE wages, premiums for work leaders, and an increase in emergency assistance.

clear, simple, streamlined system. If you start burdening it with complicated grandfather, hold-harmless, maintenance of effort provisions, you destroy the beauty of reform. . . . I felt strongly that with another couple of months we might have avoided some of those messy things and had a cleaner, simpler bill.

Heineman was also disturbed by some of the last-minute changes and commented to a staff member: "I have this vision of Joe Califano and Jimmy Carter flying over Washington in a B-1 bomber. They open the bomb bays and drop out one of the biggest turkeys Washington ever saw." An ISP staff member similarly observed:

> The compromise with Treasury and Schultze created this funny EITC, which was really rather insignificant in terms of the entire benefit package people would get. It had all the disadvantages of the large-scale EITC and really none of its advantages; people weren't getting that much from the credit, they still had to troop down to the welfare office for most of their benefits, and it had a very high phase-out point. Soon after the plan was released we started getting the Jane Quinn Bryan pieces [a financial reporter]: "Look what reform has wrought—welfare for the middle class."
>
> Then we also had the hold-harmless, maintenance of effort provisions, which formed these wonderfully convoluted passages in the bill, which I don't think five or six people in Washington understand. Two or three, however, are lobbyists for state and local governments; this just became a plaything for the lobbyists.

LONG AND ULLMAN: MORE LAST-MINUTE CHANGES

Before releasing the proposal, the administration decided to try and clear up any major trouble spots the proposal might raise for Senator Long and Congressman Ullman. The morning of the presidential briefing (July 28), Carter had called Long to talk over the plan with him. Long's reactions were not entirely favorable. In a handwritten note, which was forwarded to Eizenstat, Watson, and Schultze, the president indicated Long's problems with the plan.

Senator Long
a. Mother/child—job available—mother not take job until 14 years old, ridiculous. Number children important.
b. People who can/should work claim falsely job not available. Should say certain people should *not* work (mother with 3 children) equals 250,000 jobs now available in WIN.
c. Needs to see Califano.

Califano met with Long the following day. In a memorandum to Carter on August 1, he told the president:

> Long seemed to respond generally favorably to much of our proposals, with two big and strongly-held differences:
> 1. Long would require single-parent family heads to work if the youngest child were six years or older. Our proposal requires such individuals to work where the youngest child is 14 years or older. He argues that if you lower the age to six, you are taking almost half the people off AFDC, whereas lowering the age to 14 only gets about ten percent.
> 2. Long likes the two different tiers, but he would never permit those on the expected-to-work tier to flip up to the not-expected-to-work tier. Our proposal *does not* permit childless couples and singles to flip up. It *does* permit families with children to flip up where there are no jobs available.
>
> Long was concerned about the difficulty of returning flipped-up families to the lower, expected-to-work tier, once they got a taste of the higher benefits. . . .
>
> Long particularly liked the expansion of the EITC, the consolidation of the cash program on one computer, and the emphasis on jobs.
>
> Long would prefer a program with lower benefits for everyone, even requiring mothers with children *under* six to work (at least in sheltered workshops, part-time) to get their AFDC benefits. He said at one point that he would give us $5 billion more if it were to pay these mothers for working.
>
> Clearly, whatever plan Long's committee receives will come out much more conservative than it goes in.[38]

Califano also met with Ullman, who had strong reservations about the plan, too. In the same memo he reported:

> Ullman's reaction to our proposals is less clear than Long's. Ullman likes the centralized computer for the cash program and he likes the jobs component.
>
> Ullman expressed four strong reservations:
> 1. Like Long, Ullman would require single-parent family heads to work if the youngest child were *six* years of age or older. He said that is where Congress will come out.
> 2. Ullman does not like paying government cash to individuals who are employed. I think he recognizes the need in terms of preserving incentives to work, but he prefers trying to do this by additional tax credits for employers (along the lines of the tax credit he placed in your fiscal stimulus legislation), or by paying cash to employers to pay employees. In the case

of public service jobs, Ullman would try to solve the problem by a grant to the state.

3. Ullman does not like any payments geared to the *size* of the family of *working* parents. In his heart, I think he opposes all payments geared to the size of the family, believing that these payments encourage poor people to have children.

4. Unlike Long, Ullman does not like "makework" jobs where people just sit at courthouse desks.[39]

Califano closed by giving his appraisal of the course the two men would likely pursue in the upcoming debate:

> Ullman has a much less clear perception of what we are doing than Long. He is also a much weaker leader. For example, Ullman harbors concern about objections to folding in the food stamp program, does not fully appreciate why it is important to temper the earned income tax credit, has little interest in the pro-family aspects of the plan, and seems skeptical about our ability to create 1.1 to 1.4 million jobs.
>
> My bottom line sense of the two Chairmen is this: Long is moving off the pilot plan approach and is likely to be willing to deal; Ullman, still burned by the FAP fight, has no stomach for welfare reform.[40]

Carter directed Eizenstat to investigate how the revisions Long and Ullman desired would affect the program. Reporting back on August 2, Eizenstat and Raines contended that Ullman's suggestion (that benefits for employed individuals not be conditioned by family size) would "fundamentally alter the incentive structure of the proposal you have approved." They pointed out:

> [This] change would upset the work incentives in the plan. Small, two-parent families would have a smaller work incentive than larger families. It would also permit many situations where someone on the upper tier would have more *income* than someone on the lower tier even though they had the same *earnings*. This is one of the problems the reform was meant to correct.
>
> By making the upper tier still more relatively attractive than the lower tier, it exacerbates the problem which concerns Senator Long: how do you make the jobs program work if there is a real incentive to avoid the jobs and get on the higher tier. . . .
>
> The change would reintroduce many perverse incentives for families to split up. . . .
>
> Chairman Ullman would agree with us that these results are undesirable. Rather than modifying the proposal at this point,

it would be better to proceed with the approved plan and tell the Chairman that we will be happy to work with him to see if some other change could be made which would assuage his concerns.[41]

Ullman, however, was not so assuaged when he met with the president at the White House on the morning of Wednesday, August 3. Carter showed no interest in eliminating family-sized benefits, and when Ullman met with reporters afterward, he indicated that it would be best for Carter to hold up on the scheduled end-of-the-week submission of his proposal to Congress.[42]

The administration had more success in finding a compromise in response to Long's criticisms, which were given national coverage when Long commented on the CBS Evening News telecast: "You shouldn't have some poor soul come in with a little child and live her entire lifetime on the welfare rolls. You ought to improve the condition of that person's life so that they [can] move away from dependency." On that same day, Eizenstat, Carp, Raines, and Spring wrote in a memo to the president that Long's concerns "can be accommodated but must be modified because of the following problems":

- It would require creation of 900,000 additional public service jobs, at a cost of roughly $6.7 billion.
- It would require the creation of perhaps 1.8 million additional day care slots, at a cost of perhaps $1.6 billion.
- Under our plan these women are expected (and provided strong incentives) to work part-time. Requiring them to work in full-time employment would appear to have a "vacuum cleaner" effect, reducing the secondary part-time and seasonal labor force.
- A work requirement at age 6 (while popular with the majority of the Congress) will be an additional major rallying point for liberals who oppose the program. These liberals are an important part of your constituency and it would be unfortunate to have a program which both consumes a substantial share of our budget margin and alienates liberals.[43]

The Domestic Policy Staff recommended the following compromise:

Require women with children between ages 6 and 14 to register with the employment service and to accept part-time work which does not interfere with after-school care of children. (These women would continue to be eligible on a voluntary basis for full-time employment and would have incentives to take advantage of it.) This approach has substantial advantages:

a. It establishes age 6 as the starting point of the work requirement.
b. It avoids the day-care problem. Providing day-care to a woman with 3 children so that she can take a full-time job at the minimum wage is simply not a cost-effective proposition, and numbers of child development experts will agree it is harmful to the children and destructive to the family as well.
c. The pattern of secondary labor market participation by these persons (strong at present) would continue.[44]

Stressing that Long was likely to remain interested in providing tax incentives for employers to hire recipients and uninterested in expanding coverage to two-parent families, Eizenstat and his colleagues concluded:

> Against the background of his long and deeply held opinions, we believe tough negotiations with Senator Long are inevitable. We would urge that there be a clear *quid pro quo* for any further concessions—especially since Senator Long emerged (somewhat unfairly) as the chief villain in the eyes of the liberals during the last round of welfare reform.
>
> The chief *disadvantage* of the alternative approach we propose is the *incentive that it provides to have additional children.* Any woman whose oldest child is approaching age 6 will clearly face this incentive. The same incentive is present in the existing AFDC program where a work requirement is currently imposed at age 6.
>
> Therefore, while the alternative approach that we have suggested would be more attractive from a political and legislative point of view, it is less attractive than our original proposal from a policy standpoint.
>
> We have talked with Senator Long's staff and they believe the approach we have advanced would be acceptable on this issue—but that Senator Long will push for a program along the lines he has advocated for the past few years.[45]

When Carter met with Eizenstat on August 3, he indicated a willingness to commit additional funding to meet the increased need for job creation and day care that would result from lowering the age from fourteen to six. A memo from Eizenstat and Carp the following day indicated the cost of the proposal on the jobs side would be $700 million, plus $200–$500 million for increased day care facilities. The president met with Long that morning, and Long seemed pleased by the compromise. Later that day, however, both Long and Ullman suggested delaying the plan to work out further compromises.[46] Carter agreed to defer announcing the plan for one day, since Speaker of the House Tip O'Neill (D–Mass.) was concerned that representatives who objected to portions of the welfare package might threaten to vote against the pending energy bill in order to pry last-minute concessions from the administration.[47] Carter was determined, however, to make his announcement the following day.

A first draft of the message was done at HEW and forwarded by Heineman to Carp and Raines on Wednesday, August 3. Raines and Carp subsequently rewrote the entire draft, leaving the table of costs and offsets that HEW had provided in the message. They spent most of Thursday evening and Friday morning going over the draft with Eizenstat. On Saturday, August 6, 1977, in a national telecast from an agricultural experiment station in Plains, Georgia, President Carter announced his proposal for comprehensive reform of the welfare system, christening it the Program for Better Jobs and Income (PBJI). The plan, he said, would cost an extra $2.8 billion.

CHAPTER TEN

Postscript: The Price of Reform

IN JANUARY 1977, JIMMY CARTER HAD ANNOUNCED THAT HE WOULD have a plan to reform the welfare system ready by May. Unable to bridge interdepartmental differences by his May deadline, however, Carter had settled for announcing a set of uncontroversial principles that would guide the upcoming reform effort, and boldly declared that "the most important unanimous conclusion [we have reached] is that the present welfare system should be scrapped and a totally new system implemented." On August 6, 1977, at a nationally televised press conference, Carter unveiled the Program for Better Jobs and Income (PBJI)—his plan for comprehensively reforming the welfare system. In choosing to push a bill that linked welfare reform to a restructuring of the manpower system, Carter (and Califano) had passed over the advice of Assistant Secretary Arnold Packer (DOL), Congressman Ullman, and others who had suggested that an incremental approach—separating the jobs and welfare portions into two bills—would have a better chance of getting through Congress.

PBJI never reached the House floor. After several attempts to create a compromise bill failed, the administration unveiled a second plan on May 23, 1979, roughly two years after Carter and his advisers had unanimously agreed on the importance of comprehensive welfare reform. Carter made no public statement that day, but, as the *New York Times* reported, "to underscore [the administration's] seriousness about this proposal . . . a briefing [was held] for reporters by Stuart Eizenstat, Joseph A. Califano, and Ray Marshall."[1] Carter's advisers announced that the administration was requesting rather modest reforms, which would be sent to the Hill in two bills. In background material explaining the bill, HEW analysts included (on page 56) a comparison of PBJI with the new proposal and gamely observed:

President Carter's analysis of the welfare situation and the need for reform is as correct today as it was in 1977. This proposal goes far toward meeting that need. Even during this period of fiscal stringency, we can do no less. We are proposing a set of programmatic changes that is not comprehensive, yet makes the most essential changes and lays the groundwork for further needed reforms.[2]

The withering of the administration's more grandiose aspirations did not come as a surprise to past participants in welfare reform debates (or, indeed, even to observers of the Carter administration), but the disintegration of the reform effort had followed a path strangely unlike that of previous efforts.

THE HONEYMOON PERIOD

The Program for Better Jobs and Income initially evoked a limited range of responses, most of which were quite favorable. Within the administration, perceptions of PBJI among senior- and junior-level staff were sometimes at odds, with junior officials expressing greater reservations about the planning process. DOL's Jodie Allen felt "PBJI was really an incremental reform, but we kept talking about it as if it was comprehensive, and comprehensive doesn't sell anyway. We disguised it as something nobody wanted." An ISP staffer similarly felt PBJI fell short of genuine comprehensive reform:

> We put in a minimum, mandated something like an AFDC-UF program, put in a different cost-sharing formula with the states, and cashed out food stamps. When all was said and done, that's all we did. One of the strange things that came out of this is that we managed to replicate the current system with a comprehensive one. By trying to make no one worse off, and by trying not to spend additional money, we designed this very complicated structure which essentially replicated the existing one. It wasn't easy to do.
> Califano's image of public policy was simply to get the relevant actors together, refereed by the computer, and throw them the "football." Somehow, whatever gets to the goal line wins, and that's the way it ought to be. Well, the problem is that if that's your image of policymaking, what you end up getting isn't a lot different from what you've already got, because no one can agree on anything but the present system.
> The process that was set up was not consistent with the goal

of reaching comprehensive reform. The problem was the inconsistency between the way Califano approached the problem and what Carter had promised. Califano's approach may be fine for incremental reform, but when you try to use that approach to do something big, you don't get a very coherent proposal, or else you end up recreating the very categorization you said you didn't want.

The initial public reaction to the plan, however, was considerably more promising. As Jim Parham recalled, "We were all surprised at the favorable reception the plan received in the early days. We thought it would be pounced on, but the fact that we spent some extra money deflected much of the initial criticism." Extra funds for welfare did not deflect initial criticism from some conservative Republicans—for example, Senator Carl Curtis (R–Neb.), the ranking majority member on the Senate Finance Committee, labelled the plan a "warmed-over version of what HEW policy planners have been pushing for a decade, a guaranteed annual income"[3]—but PBJI received a generally favorable and sometimes enthusiastic reception in the media, in Congress, and even from some minority organizations. Editorial support for PBJI was overwhelming. HEW reported that out of the 150 newspapers it surveyed, 140 favored the program.[4] Editorial support, moreover, was nationwide, rather than concentrated in a few regions, as the following examples indicate:

> *Washington Post*: This time around there is a better chance that a decent version of welfare reform will be enacted. . . . The administration has done its work well: it has come out in the right place.
>
> *Memphis Commercial Appeal*: In general, the Carter reform package takes the right direction toward making the system more responsible and efficient.
>
> *Los Angeles Times*: [PBJI] offers the first assurance ever given that welfare recipients who can work will never come out behind if they do so. . . . It is going in the right direction, and it recognizes that correcting the worst faults of the current system is the indispensable first step.
>
> *Kansas City Times*: Society should strive toward . . . policies that take care of needs efficiently and promote self-esteem and self-reliance. The Carter proposals would move positively and definitely in that direction.
>
> *New York Times*: Mr. Carter's plan [in many] respects turns out to be bold, intelligent, and humane. . . . Eight years ago, Daniel Moynihan pleaded the cause of the Nixon welfare

reform by urging Congress not to allow "the best to be the enemy of the good." Mr. Carter has offered us the good and it deserves support.

Time: [PBJI's] basic philosophy is clear and commendable: to get people off welfare rather than encourage them to stay on. . . . The basically sound Carter program has a reasonable chance of passage.

Louisville Courier Journal: The [proposal] is pro-family [and] pro-work. . . . The President has given it his best shot. He has done un-Carter like things. He has waited, he has consulted, and he has compromised, all in the hope of getting workable welfare reform through Congress.[5]

Congressional and interest group support was considerable, too. Senator Moynihan observed that PBJI "is a magnificent program and very well-crafted,"[6] and "the most important piece of social legislation since the New Deal."[7] Senator Long stated that the plan had "laudable objectives" and that he was "pleased that some changes were made along the lines I suggested, and I believe it is a better proposal because of that fact."[8] Congressman John Anderson of Illinois, chairman of the Republican Conference and the third-ranking GOP member in the House, observed, "Its general concept of trying to address the problems of the breakup of families, doing something about the escalating cost of welfare, getting people off the welfare rolls and into working jobs where they become taxpayers, instead of taxeaters, those are all principles I can support."[9] Congressman Corman considered PBJI "an excellent blueprint."[10] Strong support for the plan came from the National Governors' Conference and even Vernon Jordan, who, in the aftermath of the New York City blackout, had spent most of the summer excoriating Carter for his neglect of minorities, observed, "We have some reservations . . . but it represents an improvement over the present system."[11] Finally, a Harris Survey taken shortly after the plan's release contended that support for PBJI was "unprecedented"; a 70 percent majority of the public (versus 13 percent) supported it and large majorities supported specific provisions of the plan.[12]

Among senior officials of the Carter administration, optimism ran high as well. In a note to ISP staff on August 8, Barth stated, "Secretary Califano has asked me to pass along to you the fact that President Carter is 'filled with admiration' for the work of the Department in preparing major parts of the welfare reform proposal. . . . I am very proud of the work of the ISP staff and honored to be associated with you. . . . Once again, thank you for one helluva job!"[13] Packer was passing similar congratulations to his staff. In an August 5 note, he told them, "I think [the proposal] has come out quite well for this Department and, much more importantly, for the poor in this country."[14] Califano not only appeared relieved to have the plan finished—he allowed in a *Time* interview that "welfare is the Middle East of U.S. politics, it is the most complicated political and economic problem I have ever dealt with"[15]—but also exhibited excitement about PBJI. Before the plan's release, he had arranged with Tip O'Neill to expedite consideration of the proposal by expanding the Corman Ways and Means subcommittee to include members of other House committees concerned with welfare reform. Appearing on CBS's "Face the Nation" on August 7, one day after Carter had announced the plan, Califano stated with some assurance: "This is the day in which we're finally going to reform the welfare system. . . . This program is going to go through Congress."[16]

THE DEMISE OF PBJI

The warm and sometimes euphoric reception PBJI received at first soon faded. The frenetic pace with which basic portions of the plan had been constructed in July and early August had prevented "outsiders" from fully understanding the details of PBJI,* and, as these details became better understood, they began to stir some alarm. Congressional conservatives like Senator Long were appalled at the number of people the plan would add to the "welfare rolls" and vigorously opposed the extension of welfare coverage to single individuals and childless couples. The AFL-CIO and AFSCME were worried that massive public service jobs creation at the minimum wage would undercut local labor markets; they also felt that the levels of welfare payments were too low. Recipient rights groups, who were baffled and angered by the complexity of the program,† quickly labelled the program "JIP" and

---

*For example, Nezzie Willis—the only welfare recipient who sat on the Welfare Reform Consulting Group that HEW had formed in January 1977 to solicit advice on, and encourage discussion of, welfare reform—knew nothing about the details of the welfare program by August 15 (beyond what she read in local newspapers) because HEW had not bothered to send her materials available in Washington on the plan (see "A Participant Speaks Out," *National Journal*, Aug. 27, 1977, p. 1333).

†As a study for the Center on Social Welfare Policy and Law observed:

"The program seems to have been designed so as to assure that only the few individuals who are able to devote substantial portions of their time to studying it will be able to fathom its complex details.

"Even leaving aside the basic questions of the merits of the substance of the proposal, this incredible complexity is a defect serious enough by itself to call the entire program into question. Those who have created this proposal seem to have lost sight of the fundamental fact that the program is intended to serve real living human beings, not computers. There

argued that higher benefit levels in the program had been sacrificed to help finance state fiscal relief.

Despite these substantive concerns with the plan, the fundamental problem appeared not to be philosophical—as with previous plans—but rather financial: the administration's estimate that the plan would cost only $2.8 billion additional federal dollars came under heavy criticism soon after the plan's release. The first public expression of doubts surfaced on August 7 (the day after the plan was released), during an interview with Califano on "Face the Nation." *New York Times* reporter David Rosenbaum inquired of Califano: "Social programs always end up costing much, much more money than was ever anticipated. . . . Do you have any confidence at all that this program isn't going to cost several billion dollars more than you think it is?" Califano responded:

> I do have confidence, and the reason I have confidence is because we've done this in a very special and unique way. We announced a tentative proposal in early May, and we took our numbers state-by-state and gave them to each state in the Union. We gave them to counties and cities so that they could check them. They came back, checked our numbers. We made all kinds of corrections.
>
> We have the most sophisticated base of information that has ever been assembled on this subject. They're the best numbers we're able to put together. Are they perfect? No numbers in a subject this complicated can be perfect, but there have never been better numbers than there are now.[17]

Despite Califano's assurances, skeptics refused to convert. On August 15, Senator Long held a press conference to announce that it would be "foolhardy" to proceed with PBJI on anything more than an experimental basis: Long felt that, "with some of [our] past experiences to serve as a guide, we had better be prepared for [the] actual cost [of PBJI] to run up to $60 billion or even $120 billion."[18] Califano remained unruffled, confident that differences with Long could be ironed out: "There's always some preparation before people go and dance together," the political veteran explained; "the music is just beginning to play on this."[19]

By the time Califano and members of the HEW entourage testified

is simply no sense in establishing a program which cannot be understood and in which only a few will be able to determine their basic rights" (Adele M. Blong and Timothy J. Casey, *Administration's Welfare Reform Plan* [New York: Center on Social Welfare Policy and Law, Sept. 2, 1977], p. 25).

before the Corman subcommittee in mid-September, the music had acquired a strident tone. Members of the subcommittee, especially the Republican ones, bombarded Califano with questions regarding the cost estimates. As Congressman Skip Bafalis (R–Fla.) bluntly told Califano:

> As I analyze what HEW has come up with, it appears to me that the figure is [closer] to $14 billion, and let me tell you where your figures and my figures differ. In addition to the $2.8 billion which you are estimating as the net increase, you have not included $3.4 billion in the earned income tax credit, you have not included a $1.3 billion figure for the wellhead tax, which does not even exist today, and would not be considered welfare. You have not considered a $1.7 billion unemployment compensation extension; that is not a regular annual cost. You have not included $5.5 billion in CETA funding, which is a countercyclical program; it is not regular annual costs; and you have not included a $3 billion increase in social security contributions which go to the trust fund. Now, when I add those figures up, initially [the cost] is some $14 billion. I think the American people . . . ought to certainly be aware we are talking about a massive new welfare program, not a welfare reform program, Mr. Secretary.[20]

Dan Marcus, who assisted Califano in his testimony, recalled the congressional grilling with some regret:

> The first time the secretary testified before the Corman subcommittee we had charts showing the cost and we just kept getting hit on it. . . . I think we should have seen our way clear to coming in and saying, "This program is going to cost $6 to $8 billion [offsets plus EITC costs] and that's the price for welfare reform with a coordinated jobs program, but it's a price worth paying." Most of the additional dollars were on the jobs side and that was the politically attractive part of the program; that all got lost in the cost controversy.

Califano felt that the distinctive thrust of the program—the singular commitment to massive job creation—was lost for other reasons as well:

> We could have displayed the costs of that program in selling it better if we had put more emphasis on the jobs than we did. In a funny way, part of that may simply have been a function of the strength of my personality versus the strength of Marshall's personality. Once we decided to do the briefings where I would do the cash income and Ray would do the jobs side, that became the dominant thing. You would have to sit there to understand

what I'm saying—I'm not criticizing Ray in any way—but I came on so strong. . . . I was immersed in that program and may well have known more about the jobs program than he did.

Marshall partly agreed with Califano's assessment: "Joe spent a greater proportion of his time on welfare than I did . . . but I always felt the cash side needed more salesmanship than the jobs part, which had the public's support, congressional support, and the support of Russell Long."

On September 21, two days after Califano's testimony, Corman requested the Congressional Budget Office (CBO) to prepare an independent estimate of PBJI. CBO, which Aaron and other HEW officials had initially hoped to include in the cost-estimating procedures before the release of the plan (see Chapter Five, pages 92–93), had, in fact, been left in the dark regarding the cost estimates until the day the plan was made public. As CBO prepared to study the plan, the office gave early indications that its cost estimate would differ sizeably from HEW's, much to the administration's chagrin. John Korbell, a CBO analyst who helped prepare the CBO estimate, recalled:

ASPE [Planning and Evaluation at HEW] was a little naive in the way they thought we would treat the cost estimates. I remember early in the game when we started to develop estimates, certain people over there were saying things like, "Of course you'll look at gross cost, you won't look at the offset issue because that's really a political issue that shouldn't be decided by the analysts."

Another CBO staffer countered: "They weren't naive. They were told to do it and if they could convince us that this was a political decision and not an analytic question we should look into, all the better for them. What could they do otherwise?"

While CBO was preparing its cost estimates, other organizations concerned with welfare reform jumped into the reform price tag fray. In early November, a report on PBJI from the American Public Welfare Association stated:

Many welfare policy analysts are incredulous over the cost estimates [HEW] provided. . . . The Administration arrived at the figure of $2.8 billion additional federal cost not by comparing the cost of current programs *alone* with the anticipated cost of the new program, but by adding several other "offsets" which cannot be fairly described as costs of the current welfare system. . . . The upshot is that $8 billion to $9 billion, or more, is being put into a new welfare system above the amount currently spent on what we call "welfare."[21]

Opposition also came from the conservative end of the political spectrum. The American Conservative Union stated that "the cost estimates have been seriously understated" and suggested that an additional $8.6 billion should be included in the administration's calculations of increased spending over the existing welfare system.[22] Despite such ominous rumblings, administration officials continued to stick to the $2.8 billion estimate. As Carter told a meeting of the Democratic National Committee on October 7: "The cost of the [welfare reform] program is completely compatible with present expenditures, slightly increased, but primarily because of the provision of job opportunities."[23]

On November 29, CBO completed its preliminary cost estimates and forwarded them to Congressman Corman. Corman, who was an enthusiastic supporter of the administration's program, was dismayed to learn that CBO placed the price tag of PBJI at $14.0 billion, or five times the cost estimated by HEW. The CBO estimate had been done in 1982 dollars, which accounted for approximately $4 billion of the difference; the remaining $7 billion was largely attributable to CBO's refusal to consider the CETA VI, the wellhead tax, HEW savings from reduced fraud, and reductions in extended unemployment insurance as legitimate offsets, or to consider the cost of the expanded EITC as chargeable to tax reform.* In early December, Corman urgently requested Califano to supply him with comments on the CBO cost estimate.

Problems with Congress over the cost estimates had not been entirely unanticipated, although early warnings on the subject had been largely ignored by senior management at HEW. For example, in May 1977, after a working proposal had been drafted, Califano requested information on the political history of welfare reform from ISP staff. The paper, which was forwarded to him by Aaron, stated:

> *Pay attention to details.* The FAP opponents were able to use the analytic failings within the Administration's case against the very idea of comprehensive cash coverage. Welfare reform expenditures are held to a higher level of analysis and detailed justification than any other government program. Compare, for example, the relative inattention to the large expenditures involved in both long-term and short-term financing issues of Social Security as opposed to the very detailed attention paid to relatively small net expenditures involved in welfare reform. This suggests that a few months in 1977 will pay dividends in

---

*Some difference in the estimates resulted from different demographic and economic assumptions, but these differences were minimal compared to those which resulted from offsets and 1978 versus 1982 dollar years.

1978–80. It also suggests that HEW cost estimates should be checked with the Governors, Mayors, CBO, Hill staffs, etc.[24]

Similar warnings about circulating cost estimates were being sounded at that time by Jeff Peterson, the HEW Legislative Coordinator for Welfare Reform. In a memorandum to his boss, Dick Warden, the assistant secretary of legislation, Peterson summarized congressional prospects for welfare reform and closed with a warning about circulating the cost estimates:

> Whatever HEW welfare reform package is sent to the Hill should contain not only its own cost estimates but also the cost estimates of other groups such as the Congressional Budget Office, the Ways and Means Committee and the Finance Committee. It is better to have these alternative cost data submitted at the outset than to have alternative data thrown in HEW's face later.[25]

In a memo to Califano on the CBO preliminary estimate, Aaron warned that changes would be necessary in the $2.8 billion figure. Congressmen were demanding that HEW update its 1978 figures to 1982 dollars and OMB was also requesting these figures (by mid-January) as part of the budget review. Changing to a 1982 estimate, Aaron discovered, would up the cost of the plan to approximately $7 billion,* and any of the questionable offsets the administration might consider excluding would raise the cost even further. Aaron suggested the need for one such change to Califano:

> We can argue that the CETA offset was a legitimate part of a FY78 net cost estimate because money was being spent for CETA in that year and we were comparing outlays under H.R. 9030 [that is, PBJI] to actual expenditures in that year. However, we cannot make that argument for FY82. If unemployment is at the official Administration forecast of 4.5%, there will be no need for CETA. Furthermore, CETA expires at the end of 1978. If it is not renewed, we cannot claim as an offset funds that are being spent for an ongoing program. . . . I think we have no choice but to drop the CETA offset. We can explain that it was relevant for our FY78 estimate given its assumption, but would not be a real budget offset in FY82. . . . I am fully cognizant of the fact that all of these changes will increase drastically the advertised cost of H.R. 9030 [to nearly $13 billion]

---

*Part of the increase was due to an inflation factor and part was due to the fact that offsets to the cost of the program did not grow as fast as the costs of the program between 1978 and 1982.

and that this increase will have far-reaching effects. The key is the CETA offset which, in my view, is now indefensible. We can, as the ad goes, pay now or pay later.[26]

With the support of the White House, Califano decided to pay later. In January, HEW unveiled its 1982 cost estimate of PBJI, which placed the cost of the program at $8.8 billion and maintained the original set of offsets that had been announced in August. CBO also completed work on the preliminary estimate released in November, concluding that PBJI would actually cost $17.4 billion, $3.4 billion above its initial estimate.*

Considering that PBJI would involve juggling expenditures of $40 billion and would not start up for almost four years, the estimates of outlays for the program were strikingly similar (only $3.5 billion apart)—hardly surprising given the fact that both CBO and HEW were using essentially the same model to cost out PBJI. The crucial difference came in the offsets and the cost of the expanded EITC: of the $8.6 billion difference between the two, all but $180 million could be accounted for by the CETA VI, the wellhead tax, extended UI, HEW fraud control offsets, and the disputed EITC costs.[27] Pressed to explain why its offsets were legitimate, administration spokesmen contended that using the offsets was simply a political matter and not a budgetary issue. As Frank Raines of the Domestic Policy Staff argued, "Once you get into the business of offsets, it's a judgment call. It's a legislative judgment that the committees and Congress will have to make." At HEW, Ben Heineman and Mike Barth also defended the cost estimate; as Barth pleaded, "If people would look at the outlays, it might in the long run be more enlightening and depoliticizing."[28]

The cost issue, however, refused to depoliticize. The administration's already shaky case was further undermined at CBO by private acknowledgments of half-heartedness and division within the Carter camp. As Bob Reischauer, assistant director of human resources for CBO, recalled:

> Califano was screaming how can we make that [the zero-cost limit]? A bunch of imaginative people were giving him numbers and all the time coming over here and saying, "We're still intellectually honest, we don't agree with any of this, . . . this is absurd, but the secretary says can you think of any conceivable reason how to get this figure down?" So you're asked to come up with crazy numbers.
>
> Of course the problem basically lay with the president. When

---

*The CBO estimate increased primarily because CBO discovered it had overestimated the offsetting amount of receipts from income and social security taxes.

the president says, "Faithful servant, I want a Cadillac and it should only cost $2,000, get it for me and show me the itemized bill" . . . well, PBJI was not an incremental change in public policy and there was no reason why it should have been at marginal cost.

As the debate over the plan dragged on in Corman's subcommittee through January, it became clear that Congress would adopt the CBO estimate and that many congressmen felt that the administration had intentionally placed a deceptively low price tag on PBJI. Nor was the administration's case greatly aided by the lukewarm lobbying effort mounted by the White House. On December 1, the day after the CBO estimate was released, Carter gave members of the Corman subcommittee a "pep talk" about pushing ahead for passage in which he stressed that they should not make expensive additions to H.R. 9030. "It is crucial," Carter told the group of thirty congressmen, "that if the program is ever going to be passed, we've got to have no substantial increase in the total cost of the jobs and income program compared to what we have now."[29] By December 4, however, Carter was omitting welfare reform from a list of administration initiatives that he thought would pass in 1978, and observed in a year-end interview with James Reston only that "we will have good progress made on welfare reform [next year]."[30] Then, in his January 1978 state of the union address, Carter—on the advice of critics who contended that too many complex legislative proposals were being forwarded to the Hill—ranked the order of his legislative proposals in terms of national priorities. Carter cited Senate ratification of the Panama Canal treaties, enactment of comprehensive energy legislation, and a tax reform package as his primary objectives. Welfare reform was conspicuously absent from the list; and on January 25 two senior White House aides were quoted on the front page of the *Washington Post* to the effect that the administration had little hope of passing a welfare reform bill in 1978. This prompted Corman, who had been struggling to get H.R. 9030 through his subcommittee, to query publicly: "Tomorrow members are going to be saying to me, 'What the hell are we doing beating our brains out?'"[31] That evening, Corman, Moynihan, and Califano met in Corman's office and agreed after some discussion that PBJI could be considered by the Senate if Corman could muscle the bill through the House by April 1.[32] The next day Carter attempted to assure Corman of his support by sending him a handwritten note (obtained by the *Washington Post*) in which he expressed his "every hope and expectation" that welfare reform would pass in 1978. "Call on me directly when I can be of help," Carter wrote, "and of course Secretary Califano, other members of the Cabinet, and all who work with us are eager to be continuing partners with you."[33] Jody Powell, the president's press secretary, adopted a more muted tone in commenting that Carter "hopes to see it passed, but he is not laying odds on it."[34]

Corman's subcommittee, primarily at the behest of organized labor, made several alterations in H.R. 9030, that made PBJI slightly more liberal,* and that CBO estimated would raise the cost of the plan to $20 billion. The revised version of H.R. 9030, H.R. 10950, was approved by the Corman subcommittee in early February and sent to the full Ways and Means Committee for consideration, but it was clear by this time that the chairman of Ways and Means, Al Ullman, had no intention of supporting a $20 billion welfare reform plan. Several days before Corman's subcommittee approved H.R. 10950, Ullman attempted to substitute his own bill, the "Welfare Reform Act" (an incremental program with a price tag of about $8 billion), for that of the subcommittee. Ullman's move was narrowly defeated, but he had made his point: he would fight to keep H.R. 10950 from moving through his committee. In the light of such opposition, Corman did not expect Carter's support for H.R. 10950 to mean much to Ullman; as Corman acknowledged, "The President's backing isn't worth much in this Congress; when someone crosses him, he tends to attack them."[35]

Ullman's intransigence was fueled by scheduling problems, as well as by philosophical conflicts. Due to the breadth of the legislation, PBJI had to be considered by several committees, and Rep. Thomas Foley (chairman of the House Agriculture Committee, which had jurisdiction over food stamps) announced he would oppose the cashing out of food stamps and take up the bill only after Ways and Means had considered it.[36] The White House, moreover, was pushing three "comprehensive" legislative initiatives at once—an energy bill, tax reform, and welfare reform—and it was doubtful that all three bills could get through Ways and Means, the House, and the Senate by the end of the session, especially since the reforms touched on sensitive matters in an election year. Several days after H.R. 10950 cleared the Welfare Reform Subcommittee, Califano called Corman to tell him the president had decided to push for tax reform before the welfare bill. Corman commented, "That was when I knew we had been derailed, and I think Joe was just as

---

*The most important changes were: (1) recipient benefits were indexed, (2) the limit on benefit reduction rates (52 percent) on state supplementation for those who were expected to work was dropped, with 70 percent remaining as the uniform rate, (3) the jobs appropriation was made open-ended in place of a cap at 1.4 million jobs, (4) the six-month retrospective accountable period was reduced to one month, (5) the EITC was lowered, (6) states were given the option of administering the program, and (7) greater leeway from the minimum wage was provided.

disappointed as I was." Shortly thereafter, Corman asked Speaker of the House Tip O'Neill to pressure Ullman to give early consideration to welfare reform, but Ullman responded that this would delay tax reform, which he would do only if requested by the White House. No request was forthcoming,[37] so Corman called Stu Eizenstat, who, at Corman's request, arranged a meeting on March 10 with the president, Corman, Long, Ullman, and Califano. Corman recalled:

> We had a brief meeting with the president and got a halfway commitment from Ullman to proceed expeditiously with the welfare bill—to get it out by April 1, I think. Long took the attitude that he wasn't ever going to let the bill go anyplace—no matter when we sent it to him. Carter looked a little frustrated and told them that it was a very high priority in Congress, something he felt deeply about, and asked for their cooperation.

Faced, however, with the structural difficulties of passing comprehensive welfare reform, combined with unrealistic legislative scheduling by the White House and fundamental problems in the presentation of cost estimates, the administration decided in mid-March to drop PBJI in favor of finding a compromise reform measure. As one administration official phrased it, PBJI "was pretty much dead in the water."[38]

THE NEW COALITION BILL AND PROPOSITION 13

On March 22, 1978, a group of bipartisan senators led by Minority Leader Howard Baker (R–Tenn.), Abraham Ribicoff (D–Conn.), Henry Bellmon (R–Okla.), and John Danforth (R–Mo.) introduced in the Senate the Job Opportunities and Family Security Act of 1978, a less comprehensive and less costly program (about $9 billion) for reforming the welfare system.* Appearing before the Senate Human Resources Committee the following day, Califano signalled the administration's willingness to compromise by pointing out that the Ullman Welfare Reform Act and the Baker-Bellmon bill had important similarities to PBJI. Acknowledging that "there is no such thing as a 'perfect' welfare reform proposal," Califano observed that "the introduction of the Ullman and Baker-Bellmon-Ribicoff proposals reflects an emerging consensus for significant reform upon which to build."[39] Shortly thereafter, Carter indicated his willingness to explore the possibility of a compromise bill. White House aides reported that Carter was very dis-

---

*The bill never got out of the Senate Finance Committee.

appointed about turning away from PBJI but feared that the administration would end up with nothing if it adopted an "all-or-nothing" approach.[40]

Califano's acknowledgment of an "emerging consensus" was not merely an invitation to begin negotiating. In fact, his comment accurately reflected a decade of change in the debate over welfare reform. Each of the four welfare plans—PBJI, the amended Corman subcommittee version of PBJI, the Ullman Welfare Reform Act (WRA), and the Baker-Bellmon bill—contained many similar essential provisions. Most important, each of the proposals granted the right of a guaranteed minimum income to poor families with children, a right that had proved to be the fundamental stumbling block in previous debates on welfare reform. Whereas, during the debate over FAP and the Income Security for Americans Act, congressional conservatives had raged over the extension of a guaranteed income, many now found themselves in the ironic position of supporting "incremental" bills (Ullman WRA, Baker-Bellmon) that provided a guaranteed income support system.

The similarities among the bills did not end with the extension of a guaranteed income. Other salient features of the proposals included: establishment of a national minimum benefit level of between 60 and 65 percent of the poverty line for single-parent families with children; extension of welfare coverage to two-parent families with children for the twenty-four states that did not have an AFDC-UF program; expansion of the existing EITC to raise the tax credit over the (maximum) $400 rebate then being provided to some low-income families; expansion of public service employment programs to make work requirements more meaningful; creation of some fiscal relief for state and local governments; and changes in some administrative practices (such as prospective accounting, irregular reporting of income) to make eligibility determinations more equitable and to cut down fraud and error rates.

There were, of course, also significant differences in the proposals. The two "comprehensive" bills (PBJI and the Corman subcommittee version) called for a great deal of program consolidation and extended cash coverage to single individuals and childless couples, and would have created many more public service jobs than the Ullman and Baker-Bellmon proposals, but these differences could not obscure the striking philosophical similarity among the four bills. Their one outstanding difference was the price tags.

The overriding importance of cost in the welfare debate was graphically demonstrated between March and July, when the administration and Congress struggled to find an acceptable compromise plan. At the end of March the administration began negotiations with Corman and Ullman and nearly reached an agreement with Ullman. Agreement was forestalled, however, by the administration's unwillingness to "sell out" Corman, who had fought for the Carter proposal and was insistent that any compromise proposal be passed on by his subcommittee.[41] Negotiations remained at a standstill during April, and by early May there were some indications that Carter was preparing to drop welfare reform. In late April the White House gave Speaker of the House Tip O'Neill a list of ten priority bills on which welfare reform was not present.[42] On May 4, O'Neill announced, after a meeting with Carter, that the president affirmed welfare reform was not on his list of priorities, a sign that O'Neill took to mean there was virtually no chance a major welfare revision could pass in 1978. (Senate Majority Leader Robert Byrd, who attended the White House session with O'Neill, claimed after the meeting that welfare was among the priority items.)[43] When Congressman Rangel brought the news of O'Neill's pessimistic assessment to the Senate Finance and Public Assistance Subcommittee, Daniel Moynihan exclaimed in disbelief, "Oh my God! Do you mean we are going to lose this again?"[44] Informed of Moynihan's and Rangel's remarks, HEW's Barth retorted that "of course welfare reform is not dead for this year."[45] Several days later Barth appeared prophetic. With the aid of the New Coalition,* the consent of Ullman, and considerable prodding from HEW, Ullman and Moynihan reached a compromise. Following a May 16 meeting, they announced that if the New Coalition could put together a bill in three weeks that had the support of Ullman, Corman, and the administration, Ullman would assure the bill a hearing before the Ways and Means Committee. With the help of the HEW computers, HEW and DOL planners† and members of the New Coalition worked out a rough plan in a few days that embraced the common elements of the four proposals.[46]

---

*The New Coalition was an umbrella lobby for the National Governors' Association, the National Conference of State Legislators, the National Association of Counties, the National Conference of Mayors, and the National League of Cities.

†White House involvement was again lukewarm. As late as June 1, the White House had not designated anyone to work with the New Coalition negotiations, leaving the overwhelming burden to HEW. One Carter aide explained that the administration was deliberately pursuing a "soft-sell" strategy: "Our view, in the most practical terms, was how to get a welfare bill. Well, you don't get it by abandoning Corman. But you don't get it by ramming it down Ullman's throat, either" (Linda E. Demkovich, "State and Local Officials Rescue Welfare Reform—Too Late," *National Journal* 10, no. 24, June 24, 1978, p. 1008).

As work on the plan proceeded at an intense pace, a wave of tax-cutting fever was engendered by the debate in California over Proposition 13; opinion polls indicated that those who supported tax reductions saw expenditures on welfare programs as a prime target for budget-cutting. With fiscal conservatism the credo of the day, White House officials initiated some furious buckpassing in an effort to clear the president from implications that he might bear some responsibility for the misleading and billowing PBJI cost estimates. A White House source who "leaked" a story to the *New York Times* did his best to portray Carter as a conscientious budget-balancer (albeit a bit naive one), who had been deliberately deceived by the "big spenders" in HEW and the White House Domestic Policy Staff. According to the May 15 op-ed piece:

> Why the original $2.8 billion figure? Mr. Carter's subordinates on the domestic policy staff and in the Department of Health, Education and Welfare wanted welfare reform. Mr. Carter said he wouldn't go for it unless the cost was held down. So they apparently misled Mr. Carter to get the program past him originally. Once he found out what had happened, according to a White House source, he did not feel he could admit the true dimensions of the error without seeming incompetent, so in the budget he raised the cost to only $8.8 billion [actually the difference between 1978 and 1982 dollars], or less than a third to a half of what it will turn out to be.
>
> The key "sinners" in this story, the source said, were two of the abler people in the Carter Administration, Joseph A. Califano, Jr. . . . and Bert Carp. . . . Suzanne Woolsey of the Office of Management and Budget knew what was going on but she is a kind and gentle soul with little taste for the bureaucratic hardball that blowing-the-whistle would have required.*[47]

Equipped with a president who finally understood that comprehensive welfare reform was très cher, and a Congress that realized that a welfare reform bill would have to be sent to the Senate Finance Committee by July for any chance of action, negotiators for the New Coalition and the administration made rapid progress. Following a May 24 meeting at which a rough outline of a proposal was presented to Ullman,

*For an account of OMB's ineffectual attempt to blow the whistle, see Chapter Nine. In a letter to the *New York Times*, Aaron pointed out, "Charles Peters [editor of the *Washington Monthly*] asserts that a small group of President Carter's advisors deliberately misled the President about the cost of welfare reform. That is false. The estimates were discussed in detail among all the Cabinet officers involved, with all the appropriate members of the President's staff and, finally, at some length with the President himself" (Henry Aaron, "Welfare Reform: Why Cost Estimates Increased," *New York Times*, May 24, 1978, p. A-22).

Corman, Califano, and Congressman Rangel (an important subcommittee member), it was agreed that a larger group of key participants would meet to discuss the plan on June 7.[48]

On June 6 California voters overwhelmingly endorsed Proposition 13. At the meeting the following day, at which Corman, Ullman, Califano, Eizenstat, Governor Michael Dukakis (representing the New Coalition), and Congressmen Carl Perkins (D–Ky.) and Augustus Hawkins (D–Calif.)* were present, agreement was reached to forge ahead on drafting a bill by June 19 (based on an outline of the proposal),† but Ullman agreed to support the proposal only if the cost could be kept below $10 billion in 1982.[49] As committee staff members and HEW planners began drafting a bill, they discovered that the cost would be about $14 billion. This was unacceptable to Ullman, but scaling down the plan to $10 billion would have required changes that were rejected by HEW planners‡ and by Corman, who was unenthusiastic even about the $14 billion plan. Faced with protracted negotiations, members of the New Coalition asked Speaker O'Neill whether a compromise was worth pursuing, given the stringent time limits the Senate would be working under and the histrionic budget-cutting of HEW then being carried out by Congress.[50] O'Neill asked Senate Majority Leader Robert Byrd on June 21 what course the Senate would pursue, and Byrd informed him that the Senate would probably not take up welfare reform even if the House passed a bill.[51] On June 22, O'Neill assembled the House Democratic whips to tell them that the welfare reform initiative was being dropped. O'Neill informed them, "There isn't any point in bringing up even a truncated version of the President's bill, which, in any case, would have rough going in the House's present budget-cutting mood."[52]

Several days after the administration and its congressional friends had given up on substantive welfare reform in the 95th Congress, an unlikely coalition to pass a "welfare reform" bill appeared in the Senate. Senator Long, the conservative chairman of the Senate Finance Committee, joined Senators Moynihan and Alan Cranston (D–Calif.) in proposing a

*Perkins was chairman of the Education and Labor Committee. Hawkins was chairman of that committee's Subcommittee on Employment Opportunities.

†The fundamental differences between the New Coalition bill and PBJI were that the New Coalition bill did not extend coverage to single individuals and childless couples, that it slashed the number of jobs the government would provide from 1.4 million to 650,000, and that it would not fold AFDC, SSI, and food stamps into a single cash payment.

‡According to sources familiar with the negotiations, Corman and HEW were worried that the $4 billion reduction would necessitate lowering the basic benefit, eliminate the provision of support to two-parent families, or prevent the cashing-out of food stamps for AFDC recipients.

"no frills" bill that would ensure some state fiscal relief by 1980 and expand the earned income tax credit,* but would not mandate any structural reform in the welfare system. Long had indicated his willingness to support these provisions when PBJI was first released in August 1977, and was opposed to reforming and consolidating the welfare system. Thus his support for cut-rate welfare reform hardly came as a surprise.

Liberal colleagues of Moynihan and Cranston were stunned, however, by their sponsorship of the bill. Moynihan, the Chairman of the Finance Subcommittee on Public Assistance, had been one of the primary architects of FAP and over the years had loudly championed the need for a guaranteed income, while Cranston, the majority whip, had lamented in September 1972 the impending demise of FAP.[53] Moynihan had reversed field in an especially abrupt manner. When PBJI was released in August 1977, the freshman senator described it as "the most important piece of social legislation since the New Deal. . . . [It] is a magnificent program and very well crafted."[54] Two months later, under pressure from liberal organizations and organized labor, Moynihan announced that the legislation was "grievously disappointing" and that the proposed benefits were "not high enough." Although he favored the basic principles of the proposal, Moynihan argued that, without liberal support, "we must entertain the grave possibility that welfare reform can never come about. We will have to rewrite it."[55] Nevertheless, in January, Moynihan contended PBJI was "a good program and does a superb job of balancing different kinds of interests and coming to some optimal results. . . . My problem is fiscal relief." He added, "I am optimistic and I am resolute . . . [that] we can get a bill through this year."[56] Despite such fluctuations, no one suspected Moynihan's 1978 "rewrite" of PBJI would ignore such principles as the extension of a minimum national benefit level, the mandating of AFDC-UF, the creation of a large public service jobs program, and the consolidation of existing welfare payments into a single cash payment.

Various speculations were sounded as to why the senators had retreated from their previous positions—Moynihan, for example, was alleged to be so frustrated by the inability to pass a comprehensive welfare reform plan that he was now willing to settle for a great deal less—but there was at least one obvious motivation behind the senators' strategy. California and New York were both suffering severe fiscal problems, some of which were accounted for by a dramatic growth of welfare expenditures. In addition, California voters had recently expressed overwhelming support for Proposition 13, and with New York City verg-

*The bill also would have created tax incentives for employers to hire welfare recipients.

ing on bankruptcy, Moynihan had an interest in heading off a similar tax revolt in his own state. When the bill was drafted, the monetary needs of New York and California were prominently reflected: as the American Public Welfare Association noted, "A close look at the proposed fiscal relief provision reveals that California and New York between them, are likely to receive somewhere in the neighborhood of 40% (or $900 million) of the $2.2 billion add-ons allocated in fiscal year 1980. The other 48 states would share the remaining 60%, or $1.3 billion."[57]

Administration officials were distraught over the bill and were soon at odds with Moynihan, who was incensed by an effort of "someone at the Council of Economic Advisers" to scuttle his bill by requesting the *New York Times* and *Wall Street Journal* to publish hostile editorials.[58] The administration contended that there was only one powerful lobby for welfare reform—state and local governments—and, if a bill were passed with some measure of fiscal relief, it would dim the interests of the state and local governments in structural reforms and eliminate the possibility of passing a welfare reform bill in the 96th Congress. Moynihan dismissed this objection as "nonsense" and argued that the administration was as likely to succeed in passing a bill in the 96th Congress as it had been in the 95th.[59]

The Carter administration was also concerned over the use of "block grants" for dispensing fiscal relief; the block grant concept, which was a favorite of Long's, allowed states more leeway in determining how they would spend funds, but it troubled many liberals, who felt that, in the wake of the tax revolt, dollars would be diverted from welfare. When Moynihan held hearings on the bill on September 12, administration spokesmen opposed the bill, as did state and local representatives (who wholeheartedly supported fiscal relief but were opposed to the block grant approach). A disgruntled Moynihan responded by accusing administration officials of "indifference" and having "dumped" welfare reform.[60]

Two days after the hearing, Senator Edward Kennedy (D–Mass.) hastily introduced his reform bill, the Welfare Reform and Fiscal Relief Act. Kennedy's $7.1 billion plan was similar to the New Coalition bill, which the Carter administration had dropped in June, and Kennedy acknowledged privately that he had no hope of passing the bill before the end of the session. Kennedy was concerned, however, that Senators Long and Moynihan would be able to push their bill through the Senate Finance Committee and wanted to be sure that there was a clear alternative to the "no frills" approach should it reach the Senate floor. As it turned out, the Moynihan-Cranston-Long bill, the State and Local Welfare Reform and Fiscal Relief Act, never got out of committee. Senators

Danforth and Ribicoff (sponsors of the Baker-Bellmon bill) opposed the bill and, with the end of the session and election day rapidly approaching and without support from the administration or the state and local lobby, Moynihan and his co-sponsors decided to drop their initiative.

Before the 95th Congress closed, only three provisions were passed that related to welfare reform. Everybody's favorite, the earned income tax credit, was modestly expanded, allowing welfare recipients who were working to receive up to one hundred dollars extra per year. The purchase requirement in the food stamps program was eliminated and more stringent eligibility requirements were created for recipients with higher incomes. After the debate over the legitimacy of the CETA offset had inconclusively drawn to a close, CETA was, in fact, renewed in October and better targetted on low-income workers (although the level of funding was reduced).

In November, as the session drew to a close without one of the five reform bills having been passed, Senator Moynihan got in some last licks at the Carter administration by dramatically highlighting controversial aspects of the Seattle-Denver income maintenance experiment (SIME/DIME). Since June 1976, officials of Stanford Research Institute (SRI, the organization responsible for conducting SIME/DIME) had periodically submitted memoranda or reports to HEW that revealed that unusually large and statistically significant marital dissolution rates had occurred in the SIME/DIME experiment. Aaron and Barth, however, did not learn of the results until after they were published in the *American Journal of Sociology* in May 1977.[61] The high dissolution rates were clearly problematic for advocates of a guaranteed income, and HEW made no great effort to bring them into the public debate. Their interest in reticence may have been strengthened by the lack of agreement between HEW and SRI on the explanation for the experimental results (although both offered rather perplexing and convoluted theories) and on the lack of a clear understanding of the implications of the high marital dissolution rates for future social policy.* On January 6, 1978, Moynihan's

---

*During the first three years of SIME/DIME, black families were 61 percent more likely to break up than those in the control group. Similar figures applied to intact white families (58 percent). The findings were complicated, however, by the fact that marital breakup was higher among people who were on plans with low benefits than those on high benefits. In addition, there were other incongruities such as: in the third year of the experiment, marital breakup among whites sharply decreased and was actually lower than in the control group; family breakup among Hispanics did not increase sizeably throughout the three years; high (statistically significant) marital dissolution rates were not found in the other three, smaller NIT experiments; and some generous aspects of the experiment were unlikely to be replicated in the "real" welfare system. Even without these inconsistent

subcommittee sent Califano a letter asking him to be prepared to comment on the marital instability findings.[62] On February 7, Califano and Aaron engaged in several short debates with Moynihan about the implications of the findings in the course of testimony before Moynihan's Public Assistance Subcommittee.[63] Ten days later, HEW sponsored a private conference on the marital instability data, at which six academicians were present, and, at which not much consensus was reached regarding the troublesome findings. Research Institute officials contended that the findings were significant, while HEW officials tended to dismiss them due to incongruities in the data or their inapplicability to "real life" situations. When Moynihan resumed hearings in April, John Bishop, a research associate at the Institute for Research on Poverty (who had brought the marital dissolution findings to the attention of the committee's staff a year earlier),[64] engaged Moynihan in a lengthy public discussion about the solidity and scope of the findings.[65]

In November, Moynihan announced he would hold hearings to discuss the marital instability results and accused HEW of concealing findings from the NIT experiments (the same charge which, eight years earlier, had been leveled at him by a member of the Senate Finance Committee).* As he told *Fortune* magazine: "We certainly haven't been given any great help from HEW. They would not come forward and talk about the findings until I raised questions about them. I fear they may have been hiding them."[66] Moynihan described the findings as being "as important as anything I have seen in my lifetime to the formation of making judgments about a large social problem"[67] and exclaimed, "But were we wrong about a guaranteed income! Seemingly it is calamitous. It increases family dissolution by some 70%, decreases work, etc. Such is now the state of the science, and it seems to me we are honor-bound to abide by it for the moment."[68] He subsequently lamented:

> In effect I was residing over a hearing that discredited fifteen years of social policies that I had been trying to press, but if one has any claim to being a social scientist, one must insist in a situation like that of bringing people forward and say, "Tell us

aspects, there still remained the issue of what should be done about the marital instability problem. As Tom Joe observed, "What will you do—starve people to make them stay together?" (Linda E. Demkovich, "Good News and Bad News for Welfare Reform," *National Journal*, Dec. 30, 1978, p. 2061).

*In 1970, when Moynihan was one of Nixon's senior White House aides, Senator John Williams accused him of misleading Nixon about work reduction in the NIT experiments in order to gain Nixon's support for FAP. See Daniel P. Moynihan, *The Politics of a Guaranteed Income: The Nixon Administration and the Family Assistance Plan* (New York: Vintage, 1973), pp. 509–512.

what you found out." If we found a "breakthrough" polio vaccine which seemed to increase the incidence of polio by 150 percent, you'd be pretty goddamned mad at HEW if they didn't tell anybody, but rather recommended nationwide innoculations.

In response to Moynihan's criticisms, HEW simply contended that the findings were ambiguous and that they had not altered the administration's support for a guaranteed income as long as it was accompanied by a jobs component. (HEW went so far, in fact, as to argue that PBJI was designed on the basis of the income maintenance experiments and that the inclusion of a large full-time jobs program resulted from lessons learned in the SIME/DIME experiment.)*[69] Noting that the results on marital instability had been a matter of public record for some time, Aaron suggested after testifying, "If the Seattle-Denver story had been written straight, there would have been no news."[70] Moynihan didn't buy that either and stated, "I don't know what our final judgment on the research with respect to public policy will be . . . [but] we must now be prepared to entertain the possibility that we were wrong."[71]

Moynihan's strained relationship with the administration, his overwhelming interest in fiscal relief, and HEW's attempt to bring congressional staff into the New Coalition bill-drafting process were all important outgrowths of the failure to pass PBJI, and would leave a lasting imprint on the Carter administration's attempt to reform the welfare system in 1979.

THE 1979 PLAN

Preliminary planning for the 1979 proposal began in October and November of 1978. As part of the budget process, HEW had to come up with estimates of how much their reform proposal would cost. In December, HEW requested that $7 billion of additional expenditures be devoted to welfare reform. Word was returned from Eizenstat and OMB staff that $6 billion was a more appropriate sum and, in January, the Domestic Policy Staff constructed a tentative proposal based on material developed by HEW. During February and early March, the working proposal was given private but wide circulation, and HEW considered how it could lower the cost of the plan to $5.5 billion, which Carter had set as his upper goal.

---

*The commitment to a large full-time public service employment program was put into PBJI by President Carter and DOL, over HEW objections. The results of SIME/DIME were not presented to the president, and when they were briefly presented to Califano, the work disincentive effects were portrayed as minor. See Chapter Four, pp. 69, 79–80.

The planning process out of which the proposal grew was in stark contrast to the one that generated PBJI. The administration, for example, consulted extensively with congressional staff in developing the 1979 plan, even up to the point of having important committee staff members over to the Executive Office Building to haggle over details with Stu Eizenstat, Bert Carp, Mike Barth, Arnie Packer, and others. The administration did not, on the other hand, set up a public consulting body with representatives of important institutions and interests to consider alternative welfare approaches, nor did it make an effort to draw the public into policymaking by creating a massive "outreach" effort sponsored through the HEW regional offices. The administration also decided almost immediately to opt for an incremental, inexpensive plan, along the lines of the New Coalition "consensus" proposal, which could be divided into two related bills—one for the jobs side and one for the cash side. Furthermore, the administration dropped the controversial offsets* and adopted the CBO estimate of the cost of the expanded EITC.

In organizing a more discrete consulting process, Califano put special emphasis on reaching an agreement between Corman and Ullman. As he explained:

> As the president himself became less and less influential vis-à-vis the issue, I was then faced with the problem of how to get a bill out with a lot of credibility. Well, it was more important that the bill come out of the state organizations, the state-city alliance, and the Hill, than from the president, because our "shooting out of the box" was not like Lyndon Johnson shooting out of the box. It was important for the president and his position in the liberal Democratic party to continue to be for welfare reform, but his influence on the Hill was sharply reduced by the time he sent up the bill in '79.
>
> I thought it was more important to have Corman and Ullman in agreement than it was to have any presidential splash in sending the bill up. I spent more time with Corman and Ullman in '79 than I spent with Carter or Eizenstat.

Consultation, in fact, went well with Corman and Ullman. Corman had given up on passing a comprehensive reform proposal, but wanted as much program consolidation as possible, including (especially) the cashing-out of food stamps. The cost of a total cash-out, however, was prohibitive, and HEW bought Corman's support for the plan by proposing a cash-out of food stamps for SSI recipients who were not living as part of a larger household. Corman, in turn, made it clear that he

---

*Some of the offsets, such as the wellhead tax, had failed to pass Congress. Others, such as HEW savings from Medicaid fraud, were simply dropped.

expected Carter's support for any changes his subcommittee would make, even if they added to the cost of the bill.[72] Ullman also lent his support to the effort as long as the cost was held down—not too difficult a task given the $5.5 to $6 billion limit.

The administration ran into more trouble with Senator Moynihan. Moynihan refused to support the tentative proposal because there was not enough fiscal relief in it for New York State. In addition, he argued that the modest increase in benefit levels the administration was considering would not accrue to welfare recipients in a high-benefit state like New York. In mid-March, Moynihan met with Carter in New York City, and according to one account of their meeting,

> [Moynihan] pound[ed] the table, [and] told Mr. Carter that he had to support increased aid to the high-benefit states because otherwise New York State had no hope of affording any kind of increase in grants to its welfare recipients. According to those who were there, Mr. Carter stared icily at Mr. Moynihan and said: "Pat, I hope you realize this is something where you and I are going to have to continue to disagree."[73]

The administration did largely stick to its guns, despite continued pressure from Moynihan. In late March, for example, Moynihan granted an interview to the *New York Times*, in which he labeled the tentative proposal as "derisory" towards New York's interests and said, "If the President is going to propose a bill which continues in that form, then I'm not going to be for the bill."[74] Moynihan subsequently explained:

> My wife and I had lunch with the president and Mrs. Carter before they were going to send up the second bill. I told the president "that first bill," and he interrupted me: "God, I worked on that first bill." "You obviously did," I said, "and that was a presidential bill. This second bill is just a civil servant's program and not worth committing too much of yourself to. It might pass, but it won't make any difference; it extends the AFDC-UF program to fourteen states in the South." He agreed, "Oh yeah, the first bill, boy, did I work on that." I went on to indicate that you could never interest me in a bill that would involve a massive transfer of wealth to the South; something large happened to welfare even between FAP and [PBJI], and that is that New York City went bankrupt. The days in which we would use our political influence to make the South take northern money are over, but I could never get that through to Joe Califano or the White House. It was very hard for anyone from southern Georgia to really believe New York City was bankrupt. The idea just didn't grip the president's mind. "I'm from Plains, Georgia, and you're telling me you're bankrupt on Park Avenue? Come on! . . ."

Moynihan's opposition was based, in part, on a disagreement over the cost estimates of the bill. Roughly $850 million of fiscal relief was in the $6.0 billion plan. Of the $1.6 billion allocated to improvements on the cash side, $1.1 billion was for raising benefit levels, primarily in the South, and roughly $525 million was put aside for fiscal relief. Another $325 million of fiscal aid was to be provided through the jobs program, which would take some people off the welfare rolls and put them into public service jobs. Moynihan was not convinced, however, that states would ever see any fiscal relief due to the jobs program, and fastened on the $525 million figure as inadequate. Citing the marital instability results of the negative income tax experiments, Moynihan frankly observed that a guaranteed income was "still a grand ideal, a noble ideal, but the time has come to think of ourselves."[75] Administration officials responded simply by pointing out that "most welfare recipients may live in the big-benefit states but more people living in poverty are in the low-benefit states. . . . At the minimum we need a program that helps those people."[76] Other, more severe critics charged that Moynihan had "sold out" to obtain Long's support (who was opposed to a guaranteed income but favored fiscal relief).

In early April, some changes were made in the federal matching rate formula (not simply in response to Moynihan) that slightly increased the amount of fiscal aid in the bill and the percentage available to New York State.* Apparently this was enough to satisfy Moynihan, for when the plan was announced in May, he grudgingly agreed to sponsor it in the Senate, although he labeled the plan a "tireless tinkering" and declared that, "by this act, the President abandons the goal of welfare reform, which is to change the system."[77] Also, during April, OMB hammered out an agreement with HEW over the cost estimates; a $5.7 billion plan was presented to and approved by President Carter.†

The proposals, known as the Work and Training Opportunities Act of 1979 and the Social Welfare Reform Amendments of 1979, essentially constituted a scaled-down version of the New Coalition proposal. The central features of the bills were: a minimum benefit of 65 percent of the poverty level would be established nationally; the AFDC-unemployed parent program would be mandated in those states that did not have one, but coverage would not be extended to childless couples or individuals; (3) the earned income tax credit would be expanded to give poor families with a working adult sixty-five dollars extra per year (on

---

*The amount of fiscal aid increased from $855 million (in January) to $937 million, $145 million, or roughly 15 percent, of which went to New York State.

†The size of the expanded EITC was cut down by $300 million to lower the figure to $5.7 billion.

the average); $937 million of fiscal relief would be granted to the states, totaling 16 percent of the additional expenditures in the welfare bill (11 percent of the new expenditures in PBJI were targetted for state fiscal relief); (5) 400,000 new CETA jobs would be funded and 220,000 other jobs would be created, either through retargeting CETA or encouraging private-sector job creation; and (6) changes from prospective to retrospective accounting and from irregular to monthly reporting would save $300 million, cut down errors and fraud, and presumably make the program more responsive to recipient needs. Other changes in AFDC included simplification of income and asset deductions, and a slightly more generous earned income disregard.

When the two proposals were unveiled on May 23, 1979, their reception was encouraging. Moynihan gave his reluctant approval, and Corman and Ullman, who had been at such odds over PBJI, agreed to sponsor the cash portion and move it expeditiously through Ways and Means. Ullman admitted, "It's not a perfect bill but it buys some long overdue reforms at a reasonable price, and that's a major breakthrough."[78] Corman termed the proposals "a very realistic starting point."[79] Senators Baker and Bellmon also expressed support for the plan.[80]

The cost estimates encountered no serious obstacles either. CBO's estimate of the cash portion was higher than the administration's, but only by about $1 billion. A preliminary estimate of the jobs side was also higher, but again, not by a tremendous amount ($1.6 billion). The Ways and Means Committee had relatively few problems with the cash portion of the bill and, after having made some minor changes, cleared it in mid-September. Soon after, the Agriculture and Rules Committees cleared the Ways and Means bill, and on November 7 the House passed the bill by a margin of 222 to 184, narrowly rejecting in the process a Republican-sponsored alternative* that would have set up a five-year, eight-state demonstration project of block grants to replace AFDC.[81]

Not since the House passage of FAP in 1972 had welfare reform appeared so imminent. The jobs portion of the administration's bill was expected to work its way through the House Education and Labor Committee as well as the House at the start of the 1980 session. The primary obstacle to the welfare reform bills, according to some participants, would come in the Senate, especially from Senator Long. As Califano explained in October 1979:

> The tragedy is the goddamn thing will never go through the
> Senate if we don't get it over there early enough. Long will

*Long sponsored such an alternative in the Senate (S. 1382).

never let the national minimum benefit through Senate Finance. The only way to get it through the Senate would be to put enough fiscal relief in there and a few items for Long. I still think you'd hang it up in conference on that issue. . . . You might then be able to add nationalizing on the floor.

The prospects for passing a reform bill were also complicated by the fact that senators with important roles in the welfare area—Ted Kennedy,[82] Howard Baker, and Robert Dole (R–Kan.)—were potential 1980 presidential candidates. (Dole, for example, who was the ranking Republican member of the Senate Finance Committee, strongly opposed the bill.) A senior White House official commented in this vein:

The primary obstacle to passing a bill is getting any serious work done in an election year. The key will be whether Henry Bellmon and Howard Baker and those Republicans will stick with it. They don't have to come back and speak for us but they have to be willing to fight Long's block grant approach. Frankly, if I could get the bill out of the Senate Finance Committee for as small a price as the national minimum it would be terrific. We could get that back later. The Southern states are every bit, probably more, concerned about mandating two-parent coverage than they are about the minimum. The real threat in the Senate Finance Committee doesn't have anything to do with the national minimum; it's going to be this block grant approach.

Finally, there was also a more indirect concern—the Senate's lack of interest. The incremental approach the administration adopted did not invoke the outrage that previous attempts at far-reaching reform did; but neither did it invoke much enthusiasm, especially at a time when tightening up on programs for the economically disadvantaged was politically attractive. As Moynihan observed, "The limited goals and modest hopes reflected in the small price tag suggest that few will be strongly in favor of it. . . . We must bear in mind that while a program can perish from an excess of ambition, so can it dissipate and vanish when there is so little to it that no one much cares."[83]

Moynihan's concern proved prescient. In the midst of international crises,* a battle with Senator Kennedy for the Democratic nomination, and charges from Republicans that he had "gone soft" on the nation's defense, Carter seemed to lose his appetite for welfare reform. He revised his original budget estimate in March 1980, slashing domestic programs to produce a balanced budget: the jobs demonstration proj-

*On November 4, 1979, three days before the cash bill passed the House, the Iranian embassy and sixty-six American hostages were seized. On December 24, the Soviet Union invaded Afghanistan.

ects,* for example, were among the first projects to go, and in a March 25, 1980, letter to Congressman Hawkins (chairman of the Labor Subcommittee on Employment Opportunities), Stu Eizenstat requested that funding for the administration's jobs bill be delayed for a year until 1982. This effectively killed the welfare jobs bill and, as Senator Moynihan observed, was "widely perceived in Washington as a decision by the administration to drop welfare from its agenda not only for this year but possibly for this decade."[84] A staff member for Hawkins' subcommittee added, "We would have been laughed out of Congress for taking a bill to the floor for fiscal '83."

While the jobs bill languished in the House, the cash bill—intended to be coordinated with it—never got off the ground in the Senate. As a Senate Finance Committee staffer explained:

> Finance was busy with health insurance early in 1980 and then, in July, the Senate Democratic leadership decided to push a tax cut plan to undercut the appeal of Reagan's proposals; that calendar jamming meant we didn't even have hearings on the cash bill in 1980. Fundamentally, of course, there was no chance of getting cash reforms through this Committee once they knew the jobs weren't coming with it. Welfare reform, I think, ultimately died a near-noiseless death.

REFLECTIONS ON CARTER'S WELFARE REFORM EFFORTS

Participants in the welfare debate voiced a variety of reasons why the Carter administration failed to reform the welfare system in 1977 and 1978. Perhaps the most sanguine assessment of the administration's actions was given by Bert Carp:

> In hindsight there must have been some way to do it better, but going up with CBO's cost figures would have gotten us less far than we got. Welfare had no chance of getting off the ground, if you could not forcefully make the point that the real additional cost is not very great and that's why we presented charts which clearly spelled out what offsets we were taking.

*According to preliminary reports from the projects, job creation for welfare recipients— along the lines of the administration's plan—was more successful than had been anticipated on the basis of previous job programs. Similar findings emerged from a job demonstration project run by the nonprofit Manpower Demonstration Research Corporation. (See Linda E. Demkovich, "If Given the Opportunity," *National Journal*, March 1, 1980, p. 367. For a fuller discussion, see Manpower Demonstration Research Corp., *Summary and Findings of the National Supported Work Demonstration* [Cambridge, Mass.: Ballinger, 1980] and "Statement of Neil J. Hurley," in U.S. Congress, House, Committee on Education and Labor, Subcommittee on Employment Opportunities, *Welfare Jobs Legislation*, 96th Cong., 2nd sess. [Washington, D.C.: U.S. Government Printing Office, 1980], pt. 2, pp. 196–199.)

Those decisions were made with people's eyes open. I must admit, I think Joe did fine; I think we all did fine. I have no criticisms of Joe; I have no criticisms of the process. I don't look back on this and wish we had done anything important very differently.

Events over which we did not have complete control after we sent the bill up had as much to do with the eventual outcome of events as what was done inside the administration. The composition of the special subcommittee had as much to do with the fact that the bill didn't pass the House as any single factor. If the subcommittee had cut back the bill, rather than liberalizing it, I think Ways and Means would have taken up the bill and reported it, even if they cut it back further . . . I don't believe any of this was done without forethought and intelligent calculation. When you lose, you're always a turkey.

Representative Corman, like Carp, minimized the role of the administration in accounting for PBJI's demise. Corman emphasized obstacles elsewhere, especially the recalcitrant opposition of Long and Ullman:

I didn't feel much a part of the designing [of PBJI]—the New Coalition process was handled better in terms of consultation—but Joe certainly did keep me informed about what was going on, and I liked what they came up with. Joe and I met perhaps every other week to discuss legislative strategy; we considered going, for example for an Ad Hoc Committee on Welfare Reform, but knew we couldn't get more than the Ad Hoc Subcommittee. And I think the president and Joe were about as effective lobbyists for the bill as you could find. Joe did a good job of getting the outside interest groups to agree on a bill [H.R. 10950] and in the New Coalition process. Admittedly, I had a big stake [in welfare reform], but the president never showed me he had lost his interest in the bill. He always assured me, and everything I asked him for, Stu [Eizenstat] did or he took care of. I still believe he's an honest, compassionate man who was anxious to go as far as we could in improving the system.

I don't think Proposition 13 stopped the bill or the subcommittee's liberalizations [to H.R. 9030]—we would have had to fundamentally abandon it to satisfy Long and Ullman. Ullman voted against FAP and felt that PBJI—which extended universal coverage—was somehow also a negative income tax to which he was violently opposed. He also was unhappy with the cost and the cash out of food stamps. Had we gotten something through the House it probably would have died in the Senate because of Long's opposition. If the two relevant committee chairmen had been as much for [PBJI] as they were against it, we would have legislated in 1977. . . . I don't think what it will take to get some fundamental reforms in the welfare system, considering the role of the Senate and the Senate Finance Committee. Of course, you have to remember that people in the fifties wondered how the hell you could get the civil rights legislation through [Senator] Eastland's committee. So things can happen.

Ben Heineman of HEW felt the welfare effort had in part been the victim of poor planning at the White House. As he explained:

An important, immediate reason welfare reform failed in the 95th Congress is that the White House did not have its sense of priorities very straight. The minute you put energy legislation, tax reform, and welfare into Ways and Means, only one of them is going to make it. A big decision was made by the president in 1978 to first go for tax reform, and Ways and Means spent four months knocking all the reform out of the program. I'm convinced that even in a Proposition 13 year, we could have had the time to work a "New Coalition-type" compromise through Ways and Means—but that would have required a Herculean and concentrated effort and we abandoned any hope in June because we knew there were ninety legislative days left, and all that was going to be on taxes and energy. We knew there was no way we could get an agreement through Ways and Means in time to get it through Senate Finance. Given the press of other legislative business, welfare reform never had a chance.

Although Califano acknowledged the difficulties that were raised by the legislative logjam created by the administration, he selected Proposition 13 as the most important factor that blocked passage of the bill. Reflecting on the cost controversy surrounding the plan, he argued:

That gets to be such a game. I don't think those cost offsets cost us the welfare program. I think that became politicized. . . . Proposition 13 was the most important thing that stopped the bill. . . . The plan fell on hard times. And the hard times it fell on were a conservative mood in the country, a tremendous desire to balance the budget, and the lack of any constituency for poor people. . . .

You know, from the viewpoint of what you can pass and the world we were living in, the president had a better sense of it than anybody else in government; he put his finger on a critical issue with the zero-cost [limit]. . . . When the special subcommittee made the program more expensive than we had made it, it was dead. . . . I think if we had to do it again, we should have come to some kind of agreement with the Congressional Budget Office going in. . . . [That] was just one of those things which slipped through the cracks.

Califano was uncertain whether his views on welfare reform had altered over the course of the two-year debate and professed considerable pessimism about the prospects for reform:

> I'm trying to think . . . through [how my views have changed]. I don't know. The substance, no. We're basically on the right track. The tactics, maybe. I'm not sure anymore whether you ought to go with the big plan or go inch by inch. The problems are so difficult.
>
> People talk about regionalization in the oil program. Regionalization in the social welfare programs is tremendous. New York and California get 50 percent or more of that fiscal relief but they only have four votes in the Senate. Also, poor people don't vote. They're not well organized and the typical welfare rights mother that beats and screams across the table (typical is unfair—but those organizational types) lose more votes than they get. . . . Endemic to dealing with an issue like welfare is that it has no constituency for it except "good people." . . .
>
> I don't know [how the political strategies may need to change]. You've got to form some kind of an alliance. There are some fundamental realities—you're never going to get a national minimum as long as Russell Long feels as strongly as he does; whether he can be swung around or not, I don't know.
>
> The problem got worse as the president got weaker because if you don't have a guy that will really go out there you just won't. . . . Johnson got those programs passed. The economic pie was constantly expanding, nobody had to pay for them. . . . We didn't have that [but] we also didn't have a president as strong as Johnson or as adept with dealing with Congress. In an appropriate balance of powers, if we ever return to it, we could get a much broader and simpler piece of welfare legislation passed, and you would handle a lot of these questions in the regulatory process.

Others who reviewed the failure to pass PBJI placed part of the blame on the planning process. Charlie Schultze commented, for example, that despite the administration's time-consuming and expensive effort to "consult" key parties in the welfare debate, some important aspects of consultation did not receive adequate attention:

There were two basic assumptions we never really questioned. First, there is a general tendency in the early stages of an administration to say, "Let's get a good plan, the right plan, together and then present it to the Hill." I've been tempted by that myself, but in a subject as messy as welfare it turns out not to be a sound approach. You have to bring the Hill in early (unless you were Lyndon Johnson, who was a master in dealing with Congress and had a massive majority). We should have brought people from the Hill more directly into the planning process, especially once the basic HEW-Labor dispute was resolved. There is an advantage to having been around people on the Hill who dealt with welfare; they all have their pet theories, but nevertheless they also have some appreciation that putting a welfare reform plan together is very difficult. Someone like Carter, who is very smart, but not rubbed up against this before, reaches the first stage of sophistication and realizes, "My God, we could do all this, we could have a cash program, a negative income tax with a low marginal tax rate," and so on. It's almost like he's discovering the wheel for the first time. As smart and perceptive as Carter was, as far as I could tell, he had very little background in the politics of welfare reform.

Schultze added:

On the other hand, it seems clear that we didn't give adequate thought to some of the basic choices facing us—such as comprehensive versus incremental reform. Nobody gave much thought to it because it was so clear that the president was going to take the disgraceful tax system and reform it. By God, he was going to get a new energy program, reform welfare, and so on. His inclination, and this comes out literally in the early meetings, was to suggest that we were writing on a clean blackboard; that is, how would you do it from scratch? I didn't question that adequately. I think we all took the view, "Here's a president who's got at least two or three major areas he's going to go at with a clean broom—give him the chance."

Perhaps the harshest critic of the process was Senator Moynihan:

What happened during the development of PBJI is that the economists took over. The entire process got caught up with economic models of how people behave and an absolute absorption in the equations and marginal tax rates of how one fools around with earnings. All of this avoided, to use D. H. Lawrence's phrase, the "dirty little secret," that the problem of welfare involves dependent women and children, not able-bodied males. One must remember that they set up an incredible policymaking apparatus which produced nothing. It was a complete failure—they never even got into the Committee on Ways and Means! The president told me that he spent hours and hours on this project; he was at his desk at five o'clock in the morning, and it was all for naught because of the bureaucrats. I mean you have to have a sense of humor—they had policy meetings in an HEW auditorium! These people were arrogant and did not know their business. I was not being consulted, but I assumed, at least, that HEW was not going to produce such a complicated plan that it was incomprehensible even to economists. These bureaucrats were *idiot savants*—a term the French use to describe a witless person who exhibits skill in some limited field. They could add up the number of freight cars that went by but couldn't tell you anything about the world.

Finally, the president never lobbied for this. What he put his time in—and maybe this is one of the stories of the Carter administration—was from five to nine in the morning going through those diagrams. But he never lobbied; he had no interest in it once he sent the bill up.

Some administration officials contended that the failure of PBJI might, in some sense, ultimately have improved the chances of passing a good reform bill. As Aaron explained:

The political events set in motion by President Carter's 1977 proposal . . . made it possible for elected officials of quite diverse political coloration to support significant changes in the welfare system. . . . The plans advanced by Senators Baker, Bellmon, Danforth, and Ribicoff, by Congressman Ullman, by the New Coalition, and by Senator Kennedy, all would have cost from one-third to a bit over one-half as much as the administration's proposal, or about seven to twelve billion dollars. . . . By presenting a comprehensive reform costing far more than Congress could contemplate, the administration inadvertently created an atmosphere in which modifications in welfare that were far from cheap seemed sufficiently modest to elicit the support of acknowledged conservatives as well as liberals. . . . Although I can't say we considered it at the time, I think that this is the best argument that one can make for having pushed for comprehensive overhaul of the system in 1977. Certainly no one familiar with the history of attempts to reform welfare thought that comprehensive reforms stood any chance whatsoever in 1977. If something had ended up passing in 1979, or

1980, it would have been possible to argue plausibly that its success was attributable to the fact that our initial position was sufficiently far-out. On the other hand, it is also possible to argue that a real opportunity was lost in 1977.

Several participants in the reform effort held the latter view. As one of Carter's advisers rather bluntly put it:

> Would you say it's a good thing we had FAP or else we wouldn't have had Better Jobs and Income? It's a good thing we failed on FAP or else we would never have had a president to introduce PBJI? Well, now that the president did, people are saying it's a good thing he introduced PBJI because now we can introduce something else. What kind of bullshit is that?!

Regardless of whether Carter's aborted attempts at reform ultimately increased the likelihood of welfare reform, some aspects of the welfare debate remained immutable. The preparation of the 1979 plan, for example, was essentially carried out by the same cast of characters who had designed PBJI and earlier welfare plans. Although Aaron left HEW in December 1978, to return to Brookings, he was replaced by Heineman, who hired John Palmer as a deputy to help oversee the development of a welfare plan. Palmer, who was also from Brookings, had headed the HEW office of Income Security Policy in 1973 and 1974, and had figured prominently in the design of the Income Supplement Plan. Barry Van Lare of the New Coalition joined HEW's Social Security division as associate commissioner of family assistance, and was replaced at the New Coalition by Scott Bunton, who had worked with the National Governors' Conference during PBJI. After the plan was announced, a "crisis of confidence" shook the Carter administration in July 1979, and Carter fired three cabinet officers, one of whom was Califano. He was replaced by Pat Harris of HUD, who had been involved in the planning of PBJI and who, like Califano, had a reputation for being an outspoken and ardent liberal. Packer and Jodie Allen remained at the Department of Labor; Barth and Todd were still at HEW; Stu Eizenstat and Bert Carp were solidly encamped at the White House; and Senators Long and Moynihan, Congressmen Ullman, Corman, Hawkins, Perkins, and Foley, all still held the chairmanships of their respective "key" committees. And finally, of course, there were still the poor people—according to government statistics, nearly 25 million people lived below the poverty level when Carter took office. In 1981, after four years of stymied debate, no one claimed the numbers had changed.

CHAPTER ELEVEN

Carter
as
Policymaker

AS CANDIDATE AND PRESIDENT-ELECT, JIMMY CARTER APPEARED TO know what he wanted regarding welfare reform. He had supported Richard Nixon's Family Assistance Plan and advocated "comprehensive," as opposed to "incremental," welfare reform. Moreover, he had indicated approximately what form he wanted welfare reform to take. He had spoken of three distinct categories of poor people—the unemployable poor, the employable but jobless poor, and the working poor—and he had outlined policy objectives for each group.

Unlike most presidents, moreover, he appeared to give good advance indications as to how he would function as a decision-maker.

> Exact procedure is derived to some degree from my scientific or engineering background—I like to study first all the efforts that have been made historically toward the same goal, to bring together advice or ideas from as wide or divergent points of view as possible, to assimilate them personally or with a small staff, to assess the quality of the points of view and identify the source of those proposals and, if I think the source is worthy, then to include that person or entity into a group I then call in to help me personally to discuss the matter in some depth. Then I make a general decision about what should be done involving time schedules, necessity for legislation, executive acts, publicity to be focused on the issue. Then I like to assign task forces to work on different aspects of the problem, and I like to be personally involved so that I can know the thought processes that go into the final decisions and also so that I can be a spokesman, without prompting, when I take my case to the people, the legislature or Congress.[1]

With respect to any issue on which he proposed to lead, his advisers could reasonably expect him to take charge personally, to immerse himself in the details and then act forcefully.

The beginnings of Carter's attempt to achieve welfare reform were auspicious. He began to create momentum almost immediately: by January 25, 1977, five days after his inauguration, he had committed his administration to producing a welfare reform plan by May 1, and his secretary of Health, Education, and Welfare, an experienced political adviser, had started to work on it.

It is difficult to read the account in the preceding chapters of how the Carter administration handled the welfare reform issue without feeling that something went awry, that all did not go as well as it might have or as it was intended to. The basis for this feeling is *not* that the Program for Better Jobs and Income (PBJI) later failed in Congress. Many veterans of welfare reform policymaking believe that no guaranteed income plan based on a negative income tax, such as PBJI, had a chance of being enacted and, furthermore, given the conservative mood in Congress and among the public at large, that no approach to welfare reform would have passed the 95th and 96th Congresses. Moreover, the administration had so overloaded the Senate Finance and the House Ways and Means Committees that it was unlikely that their chairmen would choose to take up a proposal that neither liked. A president can lose and still be judged to have been effective, however, and to have enhanced his administration's credibility in the process. Somehow, the story of the Carter administration and welfare reform fosters the opposite impression.

The issue of welfare reform had been thoroughly studied, and experts on the issue were at every hand. Another president's full-scale attempt to achieve welfare reform had been fully and ably documented, and participants in that attempt were ready to help the new president. Analysis, experience, and political wisdom seemed readily at hand. Yet a number of anomalies characterized the policymaking process:

• At no time did the president's advisers seem to be doing what Carter really wanted them to do. A proposal and an adviser Carter really liked—triple track and its sponsor, Tom Joe—played minor roles in the process; the "no additional cost" restriction was neither understood nor accepted by those developing the proposal; as the days grew short before the May 1 deadline, a high-level presidential adviser could not persuade two cabinet officers and their presidentially appointed subordinates to resolve their differences so that Carter could meet his commitment. There was something wrong with the way the president and his staff were communicating his desires to Califano and his associates, who were systematically kept at arms' length by the White House.

• Achieving comprehensive welfare reform was first and foremost a political problem—which even a casual reading of welfare reform history would have made clear. The basic issues that made Congress reluctant to adopt the kind of reform Carter appeared to favor were philosophical and value-laden more than they were analytic or technical. Yet little real political discussion affecting the policymaking process occurred at the top levels of the Carter administration. What debate there was—as opposed to formal briefings—was relentlessly technocratic and abstract and devoid of passion or purpose.

• Despite the technocratic and abstract orientation of the planning process and the president's attention to detail, the administration's proposal was vulnerable precisely on its technical flaws: the wrong cost estimates were used, and the jobs program, the only factor the president seemed to endorse personally, was embarrassingly vague and lacking in detail.

It is difficult to escape the impression that early high-level discussion of the issue among the president, his political associates, and advisers experienced in welfare reform could have brought the real issues to the surface quickly, that a month of staff work by the cadre of political and technical experts readily available to work on the issue would have given Carter an adequate basis for deciding on the approach he wanted to take, and that another month of staff work—bringing the process to March—would have produced the outlines of a legislative proposal at least as well thought out as the one that emerged on September 12. Additional time might then have been spent on what really mattered: devising a legislative strategy. Instead, despite a promising start, the process as a whole seemed feckless and fumbling, wasteful of the time and energies of the officials involved. The president appears to have lost control of it altogether.

Why was Carter ineffective as a policymaker with respect to an issue on which he might have been expected to be at his best? Two answers emerge from an examination of the case and from a comparison of Carter's performance on welfare reform with the other presidential performances summarized in Chapter One. First, and more narrowly, the president made several ill-advised management decisions concerning the process to be followed in developing the proposal and in the way he employed that process. Second, and more broadly, the president failed in his leadership responsibilities. The next sections of this chapter explore these propositions in greater detail.

THE POLICY DEVELOPMENT PROCESS

The process Carter created to develop his welfare reform proposal was relatively straightforward: he asked his secretary of Health, Education, and Welfare, Joseph A. Califano, Jr., to take the lead in developing a proposal by May 1, 1977. He directed his own staff to stay out of Califano's way. The first choice was clearly a casual one, yet it was no worse than most choices presidents make under such circumstances. Neither Roosevelt nor Eisenhower nor Johnson gave any more thought to the policy development process than Carter did. Neither did Nixon, who was fundamentally process-oriented. When confronting an issue he cared about, each president reacted more or less instinctively. The second choice was more deliberate and was related to Carter's determination to rely primarily on his cabinet officers, rather than White House staff, for policy advice. Other presidents used their executive office staffs to see to it that their wishes were being carried out. Carter gave his staff no role at all. Moreover, their belated, and welcome, involvement stemmed from a request from Califano and Marshall, not Carter.

It is doubtful that this process could have worked as Carter intended it to. Cabinet officers are simply not in a position to supervise their peers, and no one understood this better than Califano. Carter compounded the problem by appearing on occasion to have placed both Califano and Marshall in charge. Placed in an awkward position—caught between being *the* presidential adviser on welfare reform, a cabinet colleague of Marshall's, and leader of his own department—Califano, more politically astute than Carter and his inexperienced staff, became preoccupied with leading a disorganized and confused body of troops through a political minefield.

Carter's decision to have the welfare reform issue handled chiefly in the cabinet agencies, rather than superintended by his staff, had some potential advantages; the experts were in the agencies, and they would readily respond to the call. In this case, however, this proved more of a disadvantage. Centering debate in the cabinet agencies ensured that the bureaucrats who had been working on welfare reform for most of the decade and their language—the language of marginal tax rates, retrospective accounting, EITC kink points, and so forth—would dominate the discussion. With Califano and Marshall inundated with information on important but highly technical topics and passing it along to Carter in their chart shows (known within the government as "dog and pony shows"), Carter, given his penchant for detail, ended up muddling with matters that were peripheral to what should have been his real concerns. Observers of PBJI's later congressional difficulties have pointed out that giving the HEW bureaucracy the lead in reform had a similar effect on public consideration of PBJI. One commented:

Those at HEW who had to explain this proposal to potential allies were often faulted for not making things clear. Largely drawn from academic or research organizations, they not only failed to simplify complicated programs; they also seemed to insinuate at some meetings that if the proposal seemed unclear the fault lay with the listener, not with HEW.

The same kinds of problems were raised in dealing with the Congress. The Carter Administration has frequently been criticized for [its] handling of the Congress, and H.R. 9030 [PBJI] was seen as another instance of this weakness. Once again a major complaint was the failure to provide the kind of information needed to bolster support for the welfare proposal. "The style was all wrong," one congressional staff member noted: "Congressmen need to be given particular examples of how something affects their constituents, and all HEW talked about was norms and medians and national averages."[2]

The focus of the FAP debate had been quite different. Rather than being primarily a struggle between departmental officials over whose institutional preferences would prevail, the FAP process revolved around a struggle between two of Nixon's White House aides, Arthur Burns and Pat Moynihan, over what political philosophy would prevail. The issues Nixon was called on to decide were those that should have been decided by a president. The arguments waged during FAP over costs and who would be made worse off, for example, were minor compared to the attention these issues got during formulation of PBJI.[3] Nixon read long memos on Speenhamland, the eighteenth-century scheme of British poor relief.[4] Carter did not receive, nor apparently did he request, any memos on the history of previous reform attempts.

Nevertheless, debate clearly did not need to get bogged down as badly as it did simply because options were being developed in the cabinet agencies. Nor does that account for the ironic fact that the program was vulnerable on technical grounds, especially the cost estimates. Irving Janis, the Yale University psychologist, has pointed out that advisory groups can exert tremendous pressure on individuals to conform with decisions that, barring the existence of the group and the pressure for consensus, the members might have been led to examine more carefully. This phenomenon, "groupthink," has, in Janis' view, been the source of numerous public policy fiascos. It can occur when group members are insulated from the public and outside experts, share an illusion of invulnerability and a belief in the inherent morality of the group's purposes, and exhibit a strong desire to achieve concurrence. The "informal cabinet" exhibited all these characteristics except the last and most important—group cohesiveness.* In fact, the informal cabinet's meetings were marked by bitter struggles between HEW and DOL officials. But Janis does shed some light on the group dynamics that troubled PBJI:

> When a group has a low degree of cohesiveness, there are . . . sources of error in decision-making in addition to deliberate conformity out of fear of recrimination. One that is especially likely to plague a noncohesive group of politicians or administrators is a win-lose fighting stance, which inclines each participant to fight hard for his own point of view (or the point of view of his organization), without much regard for the real issues at stake. . . . The incompatible members of a shot-gun committee often indulge in painfully repetitive debates, frequently punctuated with invective, mutual ridicule, and maneuvers of one-upmanship in a continuous struggle for power that is not at all conducive to decisions of high quality. . . . Policymaking groups lacking amiability and esprit de corps, even though spared the unfavorable symptoms of groupthink, will sometimes show more symptoms of defective decision-making and produce worse fiascos than groups that are moderately or highly cohesive.[5]

Janis' description here is remarkably akin to the language that members of the informal cabinet used to describe their meetings. Several participants contended that Packer and Aaron, the chief spokesmen for the lead agencies, were "in an ego-struggle." Another observed that "there was a lot of one-upmanship in those meetings," and still another participant characterized discussions as "out-machoing" each other. The bland principles Carter enunciated in May caused such a depression among HEW staff that they all "went out and got drunk." HEW-DOL differences were so wide that the confrontations apparently took on a win-lose, "zero sum" quality. As DOL's Gary Reed explained, "It was always they presented one proposal, we presented another."

In short, the president created a process that denied him advice on those kinds of issues that he needed to confront in order to make sound

---

*The informal cabinet was composed of experts, most of whom felt quite strongly that liberal reforms of the welfare system were a pressing necessity. Their discussions were private and, through the Domestic Policy Staff's control of membership, exposure to dissenters was limited. The chief dissenters, OMB staff, were cut out of meetings and discredited because their director (Bert Lance) was not leading their charge and because the effectiveness of the agency in general was fading. As Califano commented, with some disgust, about OMB's last-minute memo on the cost estimates, "That's all they ever did on these programs."

policy decisions and that provided poor quality advice on those issues that were taken up.

CARTER AS POLICY PLANNER

In addition to defects in the policy development process, there were problems with the way Carter used that process. Carter's chief aims in the welfare reform effort seemed to have been threefold. He wanted an inexpensive plan, a comprehensive reform that emphasized the provision of jobs, and a plan produced rapidly so as to fulfill his campaign promises and get the issue moving in Congress. An inexpensive plan was not produced, deadlines were missed, and, though a jobs strategy was pursued, the proposal had the trappings of a negative income tax. Why did the president not get what he wanted?

Part of the blame can be laid on the planning process. But there is more to the story. Some inkling of why events backfired can be gained by examining Carter's use of the zero-cost limit as a planning device. From the outset, even at the transition meeting, it was clear that Carter was preoccupied with the budgetary cost of welfare reform. In his desire to keep the price tag on a major initiative as low as possible, he was no different from Roosevelt, Johnson, or Nixon. Nor is it surprising that he was reluctant to give the liberal Califano and his big-spending department a blank check. The president's objective was consistent with both his pledge to balance the budget and his commitment to zero-based budgeting: look for economies in the status quo before thinking about spending more money.

The problem with the zero-cost limit was not the concept but its use. A comprehensive reform of the welfare system that had a chance of passing Congress could not have been inexpensive, especially given Carter's own policy preferences. Had Carter decided to retreat from some of those preferences—had he, for example, decided not to extend coverage to childless couples and single individuals (a preference he finally did abandon in 1979), or not have as much program consolidation (for example, by leaving the food stamps program intact)—he might have made an inexpensive yet comprehensive reform plan a possibility. But he did not. Without spending significant additional funds, there is no way to create a "simpler national" program, "welfare rules that strengthen families," a "phased reduction of the states' share" of monies, and increased "manpower opportunities," unless one's "reform" was intended, unlike Carter's, to make the overwhelming mass of recipients worse off. Though Carter was not averse to making some of the better-paid recipients worse off, he knew that he would not get the needed votes with a penurious plan. As Califano wrote to Carter in May 1977, "The politics of welfare reform are treacherous under any circumstances, and they can be impossible at no higher initial cost, because it is likely that so many people who are now receiving benefits will be hurt." Stu Eizenstat, Carter's chief domestic policy adviser, put this point a bit more bluntly when he conceded, "It's virtually impossible to talk about a new design without spending more money. You've got to talk about something like $15 billion." Despite such reservations, "no one," as Frank Raines put it, "was willing to insist to the President that a reformed structure would cost extra money because they were afraid he would say, 'Forget it.'"

The zero-cost limit could have been useful to Carter only if it had been used to force his advisers to give him information in the form he wanted it so that he could see what he was buying with additional funds. But neither Carter nor his staff insisted that Califano follow through. As Gary Reed of DOL observed:

> The entire process was never really put into what you can buy with additional increments of money. . . . Because of the questionable offsets, Carter was not really seeing a zero-cost option but a more expensive one. In effect, he was looking at a five to ten billion dollar option although he never had a chance to decide in a rational way what he would like to buy with that extra money. Did he want more jobs? Higher guarantees? Lower tax rates? It was all muddled up in this process.

As Reed points out, the zero-cost limit could have been a useful tool for highlighting what goals the president wanted to pursue;[6] instead, it was employed in a manner that seemed to muddle rather than clarify the president's aims and contributed to Carter's failure to resolve HEW-DOL differences by his May 1 deadline. The quixotic quest for a cheap, yet comprehensive, reform ultimately led the administration to make the inevitable "more" look like less by adding indirect cost offsets to PBJI to lower its price tag and tended to mask the real choices involved in welfare reform.

Suppose Carter had succeeded in getting Califano to follow his order: "give me the perfect plan and I'll worry about the politics." What if Califano, Marshall, and Eizenstat had been warned not to add questionable offsets to the plan or raise the benefit levels for the SSI population so as to make the plan appear more politically attractive? What if Eizenstat had written Carter in late March telling him not only that the "worseoffness" estimates were not ready, but would not be ready by May 1? Had

Carter, for example, been confronted in May with a tentative plan that was so spartan that it made millions of recipients worse off while using up all funds for fiscal relief, he might well have taken a more realistic view of the fiscal implications of reform. And, if he decided to drop the initiative (as he threatened at the April 11 briefing), or adopt a more incremental option, that was rightfully his prerogative. The common complaint leveled against analysts, that "they ignore politics," doesn't seem to hold here. Had Carter's advisers been forced to show a little less "political savvy" and a bit more allegiance to what Carter wanted, they might well have helped themselves as well as the president.

Although Carter did preoccupy himself with fiscal constraints and technical matters, it would be unfair to argue that he did not confront any of the value tradeoffs raised by welfare reform. Certainly his decision to opt for the DOL guaranteed jobs program was one clear choice in this area, and seemed to reflect both Carter's values and his political instincts. Carter preferred, for example, that people get a job, not a check, and accordingly rebutted assertions by HEW economists that jobs could not be created for welfare recipients. As he commented at the April 11, 1977, briefing: "Sixty percent of the people who work full-time in Plains are high school dropouts. . . . If you give people a chance, they will work." Carter's experience with his farm hands gave him, in the view of his chief speechwriter, Jim Fallows, a profound sensitivity to and distrust of elitism. As Fallows explained, "No one could miss Carter's real message: unlike anyone else in the room, he was talking about people he had seen."[7]

Yet he failed to convert his strong feelings in such matters into political energy that would sustain the momentum of the welfare reform effort. At the time PBJI was announced, there essentially was no mechanism for delivering the jobs. It was not Carter's fault that internal DOL conflicts had blocked the department from designing a jobs program, but by leaving the sponsorship of PBJI in the departments and minimizing the White House role, Carter had in effect maintained his distance from his own proposal, a distance that continued after PBJI was released. As White House aide Frank Raines explained late in 1977, "[PBJI] is being dealt with as a normal legislative proposal—nothing more."[8] It would not have been out of character, moreover, for a president who promised personally to assess the quality of different points of view to have asked his advisers the kinds of questions that embarrassed the administration later when they came from Congress and spur them to a higher-quality planning effort.

Carter demonstrated the same reluctance to make hard choices and a similar inflexibility in his use of deadlines to discipline the policy development effort. As governor of Georgia, Carter had come to rely on deadlines to force action from sluggish subordinates, and he began to do the same as president. Though the May 1 deadline was a casual Califano proposal, Carter made the politically maladroit move of publicly committing his administration (and Califano) to it. No one was happy with it. Califano sought repeatedly to change it. Frank Moore, head of Carter's congressional liaison office, moaned at a March 29, 1977, White House staff meeting: "We're talking about ten or so major things, and eight of them have to go through Ways and Means."[9] When apprised by Secretary of the Treasury Michael Blumenthal in the April 26, 1977, briefing on reform that the timing of welfare legislation had a bearing on the tax legislation, Carter simply responded: "I have no preferences; my preference is to move ahead with everything at once."

Conceivably, Carter might have used deadlines to gain a better understanding of his own priorities, but he seemed to employ them instead simply to get out as many legislative proposals as he could. As it turned out, "moving ahead with everything" meant arriving with nothing, if by "everything" Carter can be understood to have meant well-thought-out, politically astute proposals. None of the president's major legislative proposals put forth during this period—the tax, energy, and hospital cost reforms—survived Congress in anything approaching their original form. And the welfare legislation never made it out of the House of Representatives, which even Nixon's ill-fated Family Assistance Plan passed twice.

Indeed, in retrospect, the use of a deadline as a management tool was irrelevant to the problem of obtaining an administration position on welfare reform. The chief obstacles to developing a well-conceived political strategy were only in small part matters that efficient use of time would overcome. Major political, philosophical, and strategic questions were at issue in welfare reform. Carter could conceivably have resolved them to his own and his advisers' satisfaction in a few carefully focused discussions. But such discussions were never held and the deadline was not met.

CARTER: A COMPARATIVE ASSESSMENT

The preceding discussion suggests that President Carter created a policy development process that placed—or forced—him into a direct managerial role, and that he then failed to perform effectively in that role. There is a larger sense, however, in which the president failed. We can clarify this point by comparing his performance as a policymaker on welfare reform with the performances of other presidents in handling major domestic policy issues. Common to those episodes of policymaking summarized in chapters one and two, are several aspects of the behavior of Presidents Franklin Roosevelt, Eisenhower, Johnson, and Nixon that exemplify the unique contributions presidents can make to the success of policy initiatives.

• Each of these presidents was able to communicate a clear sense of how the policy in question was related to the larger aspirations of his presidency. At the same time, none of them allowed himself to get bogged down in details that were irrelevant to those aspirations.

Roosevelt saw his industrial recovery proposal as essential to restoring the economy to health and, in the longer run, to establishing better relationships between business and government. Eisenhower viewed defense reorganization as essential to the maintenance of presidential and civilian control over what he was to call the "military-industrial complex." Both Johnson and Nixon saw the opportunity in the policy development process to establish grand visions of what they hoped to achieve: Johnson wanted nothing less than the eradication of poverty at its roots; Nixon sought to alter permanently the role of government in American society, which he regarded as destructive of work incentives and self-reliance. Their larger themes were a source of energy for the policy development process.

In contrast, Carter seemed to encourage his advisers to focus on discrete, technical issues, rather than inspiring them to a noble calling. Welfare reform was only one of the major domestic issues Carter chose to address early on in his term. Yet, except for momentary consideration of the timing of tax reform, PBJI seemed unrelated to other domestic initiatives pursued by the administration during 1977: comprehensive energy legislation, the economic stimulus package, social security financing, hospital cost control, and the elimination of the purchase requirement for food stamps (the latter having direct implications for welfare reform). Whereas Nixon's announcement of FAP coincided with proposed changes in federal-state relations (through revenue-sharing), PBJI was not tied to larger themes of purposes.[10] In the hundreds of pages of memoranda and in the records and recollections of discussions generated during the seven months of welfare reform debate within the administration, there is scarcely a word about how welfare reform was related to the problems of the cities, federal-state relationships, the economy, or equality of opportunity by race and sex. In the memoranda sent to Carter before the final July 28, 1977, meeting on PBJI, no one even mentioned the riots that had accompanied the New York City blackout two weeks earlier. Tom Joe, who had advised candidate Carter, wrote to Stuart Eizenstat shortly before the plan was released: "The planing effort pursued a design subject to little real debate on its ability to accomplish fundamental goals. Cursory debate about fragmented and disjointed issues (such as filing unit, accounting period, marginal tax rates, etc.) has dominated the time and energy of everyone concerned."

The opportunities were there. By the time of the final meeting on July 28, 1977, a number of important changes had occurred in the May proposal that raised serious questions about the proposal's effect on existing recipients and that made "reform" seem increasingly similar to the existing system. Also, Carter's advisers' search for money to fund the zero-cost plan had expanded to include several more billion dollars from the wellhead tax, extended unemployment insurance, Medicaid fraud, and an expanded EITC. Perhaps most important, the questions that had been regularly but timidly raised within the administration during April and May about the cost estimates were being unabashedly put forward by OMB staff. As they presciently wrote Carter before the meeting: "You may have a $16 billion budget problem on your hands. . . . In terms of budget planning, it would be preferable to make no more than modest commitments above a true "no cost" level at this time and then to proceed as funds become available from revenues or economies."

During the final briefing on July 28, not one of these issues was systematically evaluated. When OMB's problems with the cost estimate were raised, for example, they were blithely dismissed. But, remarkably enough, skirting the issue of whether PBJI cost nothing or $16 billion did not prevent Carter in the same meeting from examining in excruciating detail Califano's request for additional funds for marginal aspects of welfare reform. Carter, for example, asked HEW whether, if two "modified family-based filing units" (that is, parents, minor children, and related unmarried adults) lived in the same household, would permitting a so-called "embedded family" (the mother and child) to file as a separate unit be adequate recognition of the efficiency of living in a larger household. Carter apparently suggested that, if the eight-hundred-dollar "head of household" bonus was eliminated for the "embedded AFDC family," the distribution of cash benefits would be fairer. This meticulous examination of Califano's request for additional funds was followed by Carter's request to HEW to consider lowering the basic benefits in the plan to finance the extra costs. When HEW responded (not surprisingly, given their interest in raising benefits) that the basic benefit could not be lowered, Carter almost casually approved the $2.8 billion of funds above "zero cost." This was a classic case of missing the forest for the trees. Only Carter could have been the chief forester; instead, he was just another lumberjack. Somehow Carter became more concerned with the *appearance* of rigorously pursuing a cheap plan than the reality of doing so.

• With the possible exception of Roosevelt, each of these presidents made effective use of executive office associates and advisers to create and sustain clarity of purpose among subordinates.

Under Eisenhower, General Andrew Goodpaster and Bryce Harlow were able to supply the needed specificity to Eisenhower's directives to Secretary of Defense Neil McElroy to develop a defense reorganization plan. Johnson first relied on Budget Director Kermit Gordon and Council of Economic Advisers Chairman Walter Heller to oversee the staff work, then turned to Sargent Shriver, his choice to head the proposed Office of Economic Opportunity, to prepare the legislation. Nixon worked through a succession of advisers—Pat Moynihan, George Schultz, and John Ehrlichman—to create the proposal he wanted. Even under Roosevelt, the nerve center of the effort to create the National Industrial Recovery Act was the office of Budget Director Lewis Douglas, with whom Roosevelt met daily.

Carter seemed to employ no one in those kinds of roles. No one spoke for him; he used no intermediaries. He almost seemed to say: develop a proposal if you can; if you cannot, struggle and then come back to me. His chief policy advisers on this issue, Stuart Eizenstat and Jack Watson, appeared to know as little about what Carter wanted as Califano did. Moreover, in retrospect, the efforts of advisers who sought to break various impasses had seemingly anomalous results. Despite sustained effort, Schultze, the respected chairman of the Council of Economic Advisers and an experienced executive, was simply unable to arrange a compromise between senior DOL and HEW officials—Carter appointees all—who had developed no sense of what the president really wanted or that such a compromise would be in the president's interest. When Carp later hit upon the idea that would reconcile the interdepartmental conflict, then adroitly maneuvered its acceptance, neither the president nor his cabinet officers appeared to take much notice of its meaning or significance. A relatively junior White House aide had become the decision-maker on the crucial issue almost by default.

• Each of these presidents was effective in sustaining momentum and making things happen within his administration. Each kept in touch with developments either personally or through associates, and each made mid-course corrections when the process faltered.

Roosevelt employed several devices to drive the policy development process: competition among ambitious advisers with strong views, an inclination to tip his hand during meetings in order to achieve concrete progress, and a willingness to force the pace toward convergence by ordering his advisers to keep working until they could agree. In his orderly and relatively low-key way, Eisenhower maintained pressure on his subordinates and used public and private forums to indicate his intentions and sustain forward movement. His advisers sensed his personal interest, and they responded appropriately. Johnson swathed his advisers in his boundless energy, brought them to his ranch to work, and actively recruited them to his cause by the force of his personality. Nixon repeatedly sought advice, determined the pace, orchestrated the bureaucratic politics, and played advisers off against each other. In addition, each of these presidents seemed accessible in personal and informal settings. Each appeared flexible, and often resourceful, when confronting obstacles or changed circumstances. Roosevelt, for example, first marked time on industrial recovery, then parried a congressional thrust with a counter proposal, and, when that faltered, developed one of his own.

Carter, in contrast, was relatively passive and inflexible. Once he had decided on the process he wanted followed, he took little personal interest in following through and showed little resilience when his advisers ran into difficulties or sought his help. The substitution of principles for a plan on May 2, 1977, the compromise that broke the deadlock between the Department of Labor and the Department of Health, Education, and Welfare, and the decision on how much the program would "cost," all seemed to be products of his advisers' despairing attempts to get somewhere in spite of not quite knowing where they were going or why. Carter, for example, made a decision to opt for comprehensive welfare reform before he had consulted with those of his advisers, who were knowledgeable about welfare. He made this decision at the transition group meeting because, according to Bert Carp, "If Congress wasn't going to pass a comprehensive bill, that was their responsibility, but he had a responsibility to propose it. It was a campaign promise." Nixon, of course, had made similar promises, but he nonetheless kept incremental options open during the course of the FAP debate.

After the transition group meeting, Carter did not seem to hear his advisers' warnings that cheap comprehensive reform was politically impossible. At the April 11 briefing, Henry Aaron pointed out that it was politically very difficult to lower someone's benefits; Califano added that if the president was serious about reform being inexpensive he ought to consider a "Russell Long approach and do demonstration projects." Carter insisted, though, on inexpensive comprehensive reform, to which Califano grimly replied, "At zero-cost we are retaining so many inequities that we would be shot out of the water. I haven't expected these alternatives." Carter, however, was apparently so sure that Califano would bring in an unnecessarily generous program that he may have failed to hear his advisers' warning signals about the course of action he was pursuing. In light of the president's apparent abdication of a realistic leadership role, Carter's advisers had to make do. In the end the president accepted the result without much display of understanding or enthusiasm.

• Each president who confronted conflict was effective in recognizing and resolving it within his administration.

Both Roosevelt and Nixon confronted sharp divisions among their advisers. Each was able to defuse the potentially debilitating effects of these conflicts in three ways: by insisting that they make the maximum effort to compose their differences, by making necessary compromises, and by persuading all parties that their views had been heard and fully considered.

Roosevelt's main problem was with Secretary of Labor Frances Perkins and with her ally, Senator Robert Wagner. Though Roosevelt did not particularly want a sizeable public works program in his industrial recovery program, in the end he accepted one no doubt because politically valuable associates believed it to be important. Disagreements over the form of the industrial cooperation provision were ironed out while Roosevelt's advisers were "locked in a room" at his instruction.

Conflicts within the Nixon administration were potentially serious threats to the president's achievement of his aims. They were rooted in ideological differences within his own party, differences that were also reflected in Congress. Nixon's solution was severalfold. He allowed a full and uninhibited debate among his advisers. He encouraged dissenters to present alternative proposals, then heard them out. He used John Ehrlichman to mediate reconcilable differences. Finally, he took full control of the decision-making process and patiently and personally convinced his more conservative advisers that they were no longer arguing with the liberals at HEW; they were arguing with him. His final position summoned them all to the higher cause of governmental reform on behalf of which he believed they could all be united.

Though the discussion that took place at the briefings made him fully aware of the sharp division among his advisers, Carter never openly confronted it. In particular, he appeared to make no effort to assuage Joe Califano's keenly felt political and programmatic misgivings. As a result, Califano was hardly a bulwark against criticism of Carter's plan, especially on the issue of the jobs program. As Califano's comments in Chapter Ten indicate, the guaranteed job aspects of PBJI got lost during the congressional debate and Califano acknowledged that he remained skeptical about the possibilities of such a program. Even more central, however, to Carter's seeming inability to gain the full-hearted support of his advisers was his failure to pick up on the distinct aspects of their concerns and employ them to his advantage. Califano was approaching welfare reform almost entirely as a political issue, yet at the first briefing Carter told him to devise a plan that "ignored the politics." When Califano and Eizenstat insisted at the next briefing on discussing the congressional obstacles confronting comprehensive reform, Carter seemed content to rebut their assertions by relying on Pat Cadell's poll of the public's view of a negative income tax, rather than demonstrating concern about the legislature. In this, Carter's view seemed reminiscent of a famous conversation he had had with Speaker of the House Tip O'Neill. The first time the two met, O'Neill asked Carter how he intended to deal with Congress. "He told me," O'Neill recalled, "how he had handled the Georgia legislators, by going over their heads directly to the people. I said, 'Hey, wait a minute, you have 289 guys up there [the House Democrats] who know their districts pretty well. They ran against the [Ford] administration and they wouldn't hesitate to run against you.' He said, 'Oh, really?'"[11]

Carter clearly had a chance to enrich his approach to welfare reform by seeking out the political judgments of his cabinet members, especially since, coming at the beginning of his administration, they were eager to please him. This was revealed most graphically by the apparent conviction with which Carter's advisers thought they were devising an inexpensive reform plan. As Eizenstat wrote Carter about the zero-cost plan in July, "This plan is the most frugal possible. Your 'no-cost' directive has had an exceptionally good impact from a discipline standpoint." Similarly, Califano proudly remarked on national television the day after the plan was announced, "I do have confidence [in our estimate]. . . . No numbers in a subject this complicated can be perfect, but there have never been better numbers than there are now."

• None of these presidents allowed the policy development process to become divorced from political reality as they understood it. Each devised a political strategy for dealing with the Congress that was, in effect, an extension of the internal decision-making process, and each played a personal role in its execution.

Roosevelt's effort to promote industrial recovery was conceived in politics. Seeing a threat to his political leadership, Roosevelt seized the initiative, and, from then on, the effects of his actions on his legislative prospects were never very far from his mind. Though motivated by personal rather than political concerns, Eisenhower, too, was acutely conscious of congressional sensibilities, and he used his access to the congressional leadership and to the public at large to build momentum for his reorganization plan. Johnson was, by nature, a shrewd political leader. He demonstrated this most effectively in mounting his War on Poverty when he chose Phil Landrum to sponsor the Economic Opportunity Act in the House and when he mobilized media interest by his trip to Appalachia. In making his historic departure from his party's stand on public welfare, and in abandoning it in 1972, Nixon was actively conscious of FAP's political ramifications, especially within his own party. During the three years in between, he never lost control of the political strategy to achieve welfare reform.

In contrast, Carter did not display any sustained awareness of the political significance and ramifications of what he was seeking to do. Though he at first asked Califano to keep Congress informed, Carter later told him to "give me the perfect plan. I'll worry about the politics." But Carter did not seem to worry about the politics. It was not until two days before the date of the promised welfare reform announcement that he began calling congressional leaders for their thoughts on the "principles" of welfare reform. After the plan was presented to the president in late July, he went through another furious, last-minute effort to consult the congressional leadership. The fact that these last-minute consultations and Ullman's and Long's dissatisfaction with the program were well publicized also made it difficult for Ullman and Long to back away from opposing PBJI once it was released. More importantly, nowhere was the realization evidenced that the congressional consultation should play a vital role in the development of the plan. It was not that congressmen and their staff were not talked to; it was simply that their views were not successfully incorporated into the plan—a feeling that Long, Ullman, and Corman all expressed at one point or another during the process. Carter (and Califano), for example, simply ignored the judicious advice of Congressmen Ullman and Corman about sending up an omnibus bill to the Hill. And Carter seemed to devote almost no attention to devising a strategy for passing reform—which committees to go through, what compromises could readily be made, how reform would affect the schedule of other legislation, and so on.

It might be argued that Carter, lacking experience in Washington, was initially naive, but that he showed he had learned the lessons of congressional politics when advancing his incremental reform proposal in 1979, a proposal that was sufficiently attractive to pass the House. An alternative interpretation is that the 1979 proposal signalled Carter's ultimate loss of control of the·issue. White House staff, working with HEW and DOL, largely put together the proposal, which fell far short of the president's 1977 goals; the plan was not comprehensive, did not have the semblance of a job guarantee for family heads, and did not provide universal cash coverage. It was Eizenstat and Califano who announced the plan, and, as Califano recalled, "I actually spent more time with Corman and Ullman in 1979 than with Carter or Eizenstat."

How are we to account for Carter's performance on this issue? In part, of course, it is rooted in the personality and style of the man which, coupled with his inexperience (he was the first president since Wilson to lack Washington experience), made the ambitious and rambunctious Califano a management problem. In this case, however, further explanation may lie in the views the principals had of each other. Carter, for example, might well have regarded Joe Califano (the president was unavailable for comment) as the consummate Washington insider, the master bureaucratic and legislative tactician, who would supply the experience and the sensitivity to the nuances of the legislative process that Carter himself lacked. Carter might have thought that what Califano had done to translate Lyndon Johnson's vision of a Great Society into programmatic achievement he could do for Jimmy Carter's visions of good public policy. Califano, on the other hand, might well have seen Carter as "a politician like me," lacking Johnson's experience but sharing Johnson's—and Califano's—desire for proposals that Congress would pass. Thus, though apparently agreeing that the time was right for welfare reform, they might have meant different things: Carter, that the time was right for a technically sound overhaul of the system; Califano, that the time was right for getting Congress to move.

Such mutual misperceptions would help explain the inexperienced president's apparent failures of leadership. He expected more help, and a different kind of help, than he got from his principal adviser in this case. Califano for his part kept waiting for the political closure that was not to come. He failed to take seriously the guidance he did get because it was inconsistent with his political instincts. No amount of activity by the participants could overcome the confusion wrought by these mutual misperceptions.

A president who would lead his administration, the Congress, and the country must not fall victim to such misperceptions. He must figure out what he wants and be able to communicate his vision and a sense of urgency to others: his subordinates in the executive branch, legislators, and the public. He must, moreover, be able to sustain momentum and direct it by his continued interest and involvement in an issue, by the questions he asks and the way he reacts to what he sees and hears, by his instructions, signals, and cues. He must also check, of course, to see that his advisers are responsive to his interests.

Above all, the president must be an effective political leader, both inside and outside his administration. He must, that is, be able to antici-pate the sources and strength of opposition to his proposals and the potential gains and costs to him and his administration of attempting to overcome it, and thus employ a strategic sense to gauge how much to propose and how much to settle for. Carter seems to have done few of these things in designing his welfare reform proposal.

At the end of Carter's first year in office, White House aide Frank Raines has remarked about PBJI: "Carter was more involved in this than any other [domestic] issue."[12] Judging by the evidence in the preceding chapters, his time was not wisely spent.

APPENDIX 1

GLOSSARY OF WELFARE TERMINOLOGY

The income security system is composed of two types of programs: "income assistance" programs and "social insurance" programs. Social insurance programs provide benefits to persons who have contributed to a program's support (usually through earmarked taxes) and who have a distinguishing characteristic that qualifies them for support—that is, they are aged, disabled, or unemployed. Benefits are paid without regard to individual or family income. In contrast to social insurance benefits, income assistance benefits, or "welfare" as they are widely known, are conditioned on a test of need—they are income- or "means-tested." The Program for Better Jobs and Income would have altered some social insurance programs, almost all major welfare programs, and the manpower system (CETA, WIN, etc.). The expenditures on these programs as of 1977 (in billions of dollars) are as follows:*

Social Insurance Programs		Income Assistance or "Welfare" Programs	
Social Security	$71.0	Medicaid	$17.2
Medicare	21.0	AFDC	10.3
Unemployment Insurance	14.3	SSI	6.3
		Food Stamps	4.5
Disability Insurance	10.9	Veterans Pensions	3.1
Workmen's Compensation	6.7	Housing Assistance	3.0
Veteran's Compensation	5.7	Basic Educational Opportunity Grants	1.8
Railroad Retirement	3.6	Earned Income Tax Credit	1.3
Black Lung	1.0	General Assistance	1.3
TOTAL	$134.2	TOTAL	$48.8

*These figures are from HEW, "An Overview of the Income Security System," Paper no. 1, *Report on the 1977 Welfare Reform Study: The Consulting Group on Welfare Reform*, Supp. 1, vol 2 (Washington, D.C.: Office of the Assistant Secretary for Planning and Evaluation, May 1977).

A glossary of terms used to describe social insurance and welfare programs appears below:*

ACCOUNTABLE PERIOD: The time over which income is measured to determine eligibility and benefit payments.

ASSETS TEST: A complicated test that measures a recipient's wealth. Welfare recipients undergo income and assets tests.

BASIC BENEFIT LEVEL: The benefit received (annually) when the recipient has no income. Also sometimes called the guarantee.

BENEFIT REDUCTION RATE (marginal tax rate): The amount by which benefits are reduced when a recipient's countable income is increased by one dollar. For example, a 30 percent benefit reduction rate means that when a recipient's income increases by one dollar, benefits are reduced by thirty cents. Thus, the recipient will retain seventy cents out of an additional dollar of countable earned income.

BREAKEVEN LEVEL: In a welfare program, the level of income at which the recipient ceases to be eligible for benefits.

CATEGORICAL COVERAGE: Transfer programs in which eligibility is defined not only by income but by additional factors such as demographic characteristics (for example, age, number of parents present, disability).

COMPREHENSIVE CASH COVERAGE: A strategy that envisions the replacement or "cashing out" of in-kind or voucher programs with a roughly equivalent amount of cash benefits. Usually associated with the negative income tax.

CUMULATIVE TAX RATE: In cases where an individual receives benefits under two or more welfare programs, each of which is subject to a marginal tax rate, the cumulative tax rate is the combined effect of the two or more marginal tax rates. If a cumulative tax rate is 80 percent, each dollar of countable income earned will cause an eighty-cent reduction in benefits paid.

DISREGARD (set aside): Income that is not included in calculating countable income. In SSI, for example, the first twenty dollars per month of unearned income and the first sixty-five dollars of earned income per month are "disregarded" in determining countable income.

FILING UNIT: The person or group of persons who may (or must) apply to receive benefits. An extended filing unit might include all persons who live in a household (grandparents, etc.), rather than just a family-based unit.

*These terms are adapted from *ibid.*, pp. 224–226.

HORIZONTAL EQUITY: People in similar circumstances (for example, in similar need) should receive similar treatment.

IN-KIND BENEFITS: Transfer benefits that come directly in the form of a good or service (e.g., food stamps). Includes voucher payments whose use is restricted to the purchase of specific goods or services. Cash and in-kind benefits are the two forms in which income assistance is given.

MARGINAL TAX RATE: See BENEFIT REDUCTION RATE.

NOTCH: An extreme case of high benefit reduction that occurs when a very small increase in countable income causes a very large drop in benefits (for example, moving over the AFDC income ceiling and thereby losing all Medicaid benefits).

TARGET EFFICIENCY: The extent to which benefits go to those who "need" them; need is generally defined in terms of income. For example, the proportion of all benefits under a particular program that goes to families with incomes below the poverty line is one measure of target efficiency.

UNIVERSAL COVERAGE: Coverage based entirely on need and size of filing unit.

VERTICAL EQUITY: Those in relatively greater need should receive relatively larger benefits; those who earn more should have relatively larger disposable incomes.

WORK REQUIREMENT: A program requirement by which benefit eligibility is conditioned upon job search, job training, vocational rehabilitation, or other measures intended to return an individual to employment.

APPENDIX 2

THE CAST: IMPORTANT PARTICIPANTS*

THE DEPARTMENTS

HEW

JOSEPH CALIFANO, secretary
Ben Heineman, executive assistant
HENRY AARON, assistant secretary for planning and evaluation
Michael Barth, deputy assistant secretary for income security policy
John Todd, director, Income Security Policy staff
ISP staff
Dan Marcus, General Counsel's Office
James Cardwell, commissioner, Social Security

Department of Labor

RAY MARSHALL, secretary
ARNOLD PACKER, assistant secretary for policy evaluation and research
Alan Gustman, Packer's assistant
Gary Reed, director, Income Maintenance

Department of Treasury

MICHAEL BLUMENTHAL, secretary
Laurence Woodworth, assistant secretary for tax policy

HUD

PATRICIA R. HARRIS, secretary

The White House and the Executive

President JIMMY CARTER
Vice President Walter Mondale

Domestic Policy Staff

Jack Watson, presidential coordinator for intergovernmental affairs
JIM PARHAM, aide to Watson

STUART EIZENSTAT, director
BERT CARP, deputy director
Staff: Frank Raines, Bill Spring

Other White House personnel: Frank Moore, congressional liaison; Jody Powell, press secretary; James Fallows, chief speech writer

*Small capitals flag the chief actors during 1977.

Council of Economic Advisors

CHARLES SCHULTZE, chairman
Bill Nordhaus, member

Office of Management and Budget

BERT LANCE, director
Bo Cutter, executive director
SUE WOOLSEY, associate director for human resources

THE CONGRESS

Senate

RUSSELL LONG, chairman, Senate Finance Committee
PAT MOYNIHAN, chairman, Subcommittee on Public Assistance
Michael Stern, head of Senate Finance Committee staff

House

AL ULLMAN, chairman, Ways and Means Committee
JAMES CORMAN, chairman, Subcommittee on Public Assistance
THOMAS FOLEY, chairman, Agriculture Committee
CARL PERKINS, chairman, Education and Labor Committee
AUGUSTUS HAWKINS, chairman, Subcommittee on Employment Opportunities
Ken Bowler, chief staff person for Ways and Means (on welfare)

OUTSIDE PARTICIPANTS

Tom Joe, consultant
Jodie Allen, vice president of Mathematica, Inc.; later staff member, DOL
Bert Seidman, AFL-CIO, director, Department of Social Security

Friday consulting group

Henry Freedman, director, Center of Social Welfare Policy and Law
Nezzie Willis, welfare mother
Catherine Day-Jermany, manager of paralegal training, Washington Legal Services Corporation
Barry Van Lare, chief lobbyist for the New Coalition and director, Division of Human Resources, National Governors' Conference

APPENDIX 3

CHRONOLOGY: KEY DATES

1976

December 9	Welfare Reform Transition Group meets with Carter. Carter indicates desire for comprehensive reform.
December 26	Meeting of the cabinet on St. Simon's Island, Georgia. Califano tells Carter he can have welfare plan to him by May 1.

1977

January 25	Carter press conference. Carter announces that Califano will have a comprehensive plan to him by May 1.
January 26	Califano announces formation of consulting group.
February-March	HEW and DOL dispute merits of a negative income tax versus a guaranteed jobs approach.
March 25	First presidential briefing. Carter orders Califano to employ zero-cost planning for reform effort.
April 11	Second presidential briefing. Carter threatens to drop welfare effort unless cost can be held down.
April 26	Third presidential briefing. Carter leans toward DOL's guaranteed jobs approach.
April 28, 29	Charles Schultze fails to get Califano and Aaron of HEW and Marshall and Packer of DOL to resolve differences.
May 2	Carter announces principles for welfare reform.
May 13	White House staff negotiate HEW-DOL compromise.
May 23	Carter's advisers send him memos on compromise; Carter approves plan.
May 25	Califano announces "tentative" plan and state meetings.
June	Meetings with states on welfare reform.
July 28	Final presidential briefing on PBJI.
August 3, 4	Carter meets with Ullman and Long.

August 6	Carter announces PBJI in national telecast.
September 12	Representative Corman introduces PBJI (H.R. 9030).
September 19, 21	Califano and Marshall testify before House Welfare Reform Subcommittee. Corman requests CBO cost estimate.
November 29	Preliminary CBO cost estiamte sent to Corman.
December 1	Carter gives "pep talk" to members of Corman subcommittee.
December 4	Interview with James Reston. Carter appears to retreat from welfare reform.

1978

January 19	Carter omits welfare reform from state of the union address.
January 25	Two senior Carter aides indicate they see little hope of passing welfare reform in 1978.
February 8	Welfare Reform Subcommittee approves a liberalized version of H.R. 9030 (H.R. 10950) and narrowly rejects Representative Ullman's substitute.
February-March	House Ways and Means Committee overloaded with tax reform, energy bills; Ullman opposes H.R. 10950; bill stalls.
March 6	CBO appraises H.R. 10950 as costing $20 billion.
March 10	Carter meets with Corman, Ullman, Long, Moynihan, and Califano
March 23	Califano testifies before Senate Human Resources Committee. He indicates administration interest in an incremental compromise.
March-April	Negotiations stall.
May 16	Drafting of New Coalition bill begins.
June 6	Proposition 13 passes in California.
June 7	Ullman insists at meeting that costs of New Coalition bill be below $10 billion; Corman balks at changes.
June 21, 22	Senate Majority Leader Byrd and Speaker of the House O'Neill agree to drop welfare reform.
June 28	Senators Moynihan, Cranston, and Long announce support of "no frills" bill.
September 19	Administration spokesman and National Governors Conference oppose "no frills" bill.

November 17	Moynihan holds hearings on marital instability findings in negative income tax experiments.

1979

March-April	Moynihan unhappy with fiscal relief in 1979 proposal.
May 23	Califano and Eizenstat release incremental plan with separate cash and jobs component.
November 4	66 American hostages seized at U.S. embassy, Teheran.
November 7	Cash portion of 1979 plan passes House after clearing Ways and Means.
December 24	Soviet Union invades Afghanistan.

1980

March	Carter slashes domestic programs to balance budget.
March 25	Eizenstat notifies Representative Hawkins of year delay in funding for jobs portion of reform. 96th Congress ends without action on welfare reform.

HEW AND DOL PROPOSALS

HEW PROPOSAL: CONSOLIDATED CASH ASSISTANCE
(ZERO COST)
(IN $ BILLIONS)

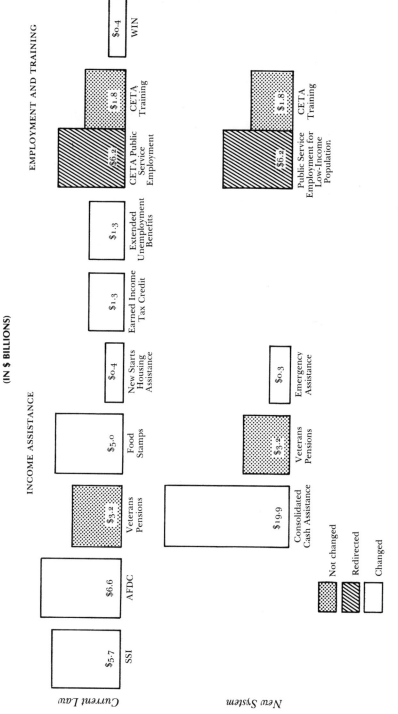

EMPLOYMENT AND TRAINING

INCOME ASSISTANCE

Current Law

SSI $5.7

AFDC $6.6

Veterans Pensions $3.2

Food Stamps $5.0

New Starts Housing Assistance $0.4

Earned Income Tax Credit $1.3

Extended Unemployment Benefits $1.3

CETA Public Service Employment $6.2

CETA Training $1.8

WIN $0.4

New System

Consolidated Cash Assistance $19.9

Veterans Pensions $3.2

Emergency Assistance $0.3

Public Service Employment for Low-Income Population $6.2

CETA Training $1.8

Not changed

Redirected

Changed

DOL PROPOSAL: CASH ASSISTANCE OR GUARANTEED JOBS
(ZERO COST)
(IN $ BILLIONS)

DOL PROPOSAL: ZERO COST TRADE-OFFS*

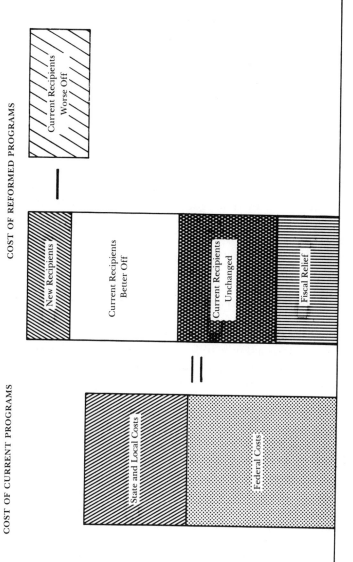

COST OF REFORMED PROGRAMS

Current Recipients
Worse Off

New Recipients

Current Recipients
Better Off

Current Recipients
Unchanged

Fiscal Relief

COST OF CURRENT PROGRAMS

State and Local Costs

Federal Costs

*Presented at the April 11 presidential briefing.

APPENDIX 5

OMB MEMORANDUM SUMMARIZING WELFARE OPTIONS
AS OF APRIL 9, 1977

SUBJECT   HEW Briefing for the President on Welfare Reform

At the last briefing the President requested the Department of Health, Education, and Welfare to present a zero new-cost welfare reform proposal, and also improvements which could be included with $1 billion increments of new resources. They have arrayed three plans: a consolidated cash assistance program, a multiple (three) track cash assistance program suggested by Tom Joe and the AFL/CIO, and a categorical cash assistance *or* guaranteed jobs program promoted by the Department of Labor.

The attached draft charts will be presented. They raise many questions because the program descriptions are not complete, the effects and incentives for people to move between tracks is not evident, and the rationales for different treatment of people in similar circumstances are not clear.

Central to each option in the presentation is an assumed $4,300 guarantee level for a family of four. It appears that this level (about 75% of the poverty level—$5,850) was set in light of the benefits currently received by many families. Any plan is quite sensitive to this level.

CONSOLIDATED CASH ASSISTANCE

The uniform Federal guarantee for a family of four under this proposal would be $4,300. All households would receive cash with benefits decreasing by $1 for every $2 of earned income, until earned income reached $8,600 at which point the welfare benefit would be zero. Unearned income (primarily transfer payments) would reduce benefits at a higher rate. To qualify for benefits, households with employable adults would have to register for work and some part-time jobs would be made available at the minimum wage.

In order to keep this option at zero new-cost, strong work incentives are not included, there are no explicit deductions from earned income for social security and Federal, State and local income taxes and work-related expenses. To strengthen work incentives, additional costs would be incurred. Additionally, a block grant to States for emergency assistance to assist families with a sudden loss of income, is suggested for this option. There is a danger that this would lead to a *de facto* reinstallation of the Aid to Families with Dependent Children program.

MULTIPLE TRACK CASH ASSISTANCE (TOM JOE AND AFL/CIO)

Track 1: Households with no employable adults (disabled, or with young children) would receive the basic guarantee (i.e., $4,300 for a family of four) with a benefit reduction dollar-for-dollar on all income.

Track 2: Working households with children would receive an earned income credit (10%–12% of earnings up to $4,000) and a benefit reduction at the same rate on the portion of earnings above $4,000.

Track 3: Poor households with an employable member but currently unemployed would receive special unemployment benefits if that person has never worked or after exhausting 26 or 39 weeks of regular unemployment insurance. These benefits would be at the guarantee level, with each dollar of earned income reducing benefits by 60¢ and unearned income reducing benefits dollar-for-dollar. Such income-tested unemployment benefits would require work registration, and include job training and public service employment components.

This proposal does not address the relationship between the regular unemployment benefits for the first 26 weeks and the subsequent income-tested special benefits. It assumes that the initial unemployment benefits are adequate for all families and no means-tested supplement is required—however, regular unemployment benefits may well be smaller than the Federal benefits the family would receive after 26 weeks—depending on the State, prior earnings, and family size of the unemployed. Also, as unemployment benefits are set by States who tax employers, *there would be an incentive for the States to reduce the unemployment benefits.* This could add substantially to Federal costs, if the Federal Government decided to supplement regular unemployment benefits up to the Federal guarantee level.

Many working families could easily increase (or only minimally decrease) their income by becoming unemployed, especially in those States with high unemployment benefits. They would thereby avoid social security taxes (about 6% of earnings) and work-related expenses (union dues, transportation, child care, etc.). *This is a strong work disincentive.*

CATEGORICAL CASH ASSISTANCE OR GUARANTEED JOBS—DEPARTMENT OF LABOR PROPOSAL

This proposal is also in the process of being developed.

It retains food stamps (with elimination of the purchase requirement), Supplemental Security Income (for the aged, blind and disabled), and limits Aid to Families with Dependent Children to single parent families with children under 12.

For working families in private employment with children, up to $4,000 of earnings would be supplemented by 5% for each person (up to 25%). Benefits would be reduced at a similar rate on income (apparently both earned and unearned income) beyond $4,000.

Guaranteed jobs (1.3 million) with an annual salary at the minimum wage ($5,200) would be available for the heads of families with children over age 12 for those with income below the poverty line. Employable, single persons and couples without children would not be eligible for any welfare benefit except food stamps, which is presently the case. The aged, blind and disabled would continue to receive Supplemental Security Income benefits. A limited number of jobs would be available for other household heads with younger children.

This system would make it unprofitable to seek and stay in low wage (mostly part-time or seasonal), private sector jobs—those under $5,200/ year. As the guaranteed jobs would be guaranteed for one year (unless other earnings raised family income above $10,000/year), the employed head of a two-parent family is inclined to quit low wage, private sector work, seek a guaranteed job, and then have the spouse go into private sector work— thus pyramiding income, and increasing the Federal liability to finance guaranteed jobs, and bidding up wage levels.

APPENDIX 6

PORTIONS OF SECRETARY MARSHALL'S APRIL 21 MEMORANDUM TO SECRETARY CALIFANO

Scale. With respect to program size, we have been able in the recent past to mount large-scale jobs programs. Peak enrollment in the PSE program was 375,000 in 1976. While this has been a counter-cyclical program targetted to the unemployed generally, still it has enrolled sizeable proportions from families with low income and from families receiving some form of public assistance. Forty percent of the PSE enrollees in recession year 1975 were from poor families and 25 percent were from families receiving some public assistance. (The enclosed table summarizes enrollment levels, enrollee characteristics, wages and costs of several jobs programs.)

As you know, we are now planning to more than double the PSE categories of CETA and to target the added projects exclusively to low income people. Reports on this planning from CETA prime sponsors are generally encouraging. The difficult job of developing meaningful projects and of identifying target low income groups is now well underway. In the city of Atlanta, for example, the prime sponsor now has requests from city agencies and community organizations to enroll 1,700 workers in new projects. This is a somewhat larger number than anticipated funding will cover. Atlanta's projects will include weatherization of low income housing, tutoring of young students, home care for the aged, etc.

Wages. The large-scale PSE programs have normally paid prevailing wages. However, our experience includes another large program category, "work experience," in which wages have been set at or very near the Federal minimum. Work experience programs enrolling several hundred thousand annually have been targeted mainly at two groups among the poor, youth and older workers. The latter group is part of Operation Mainstream, which attempts to conserve natural resources, rehabilitate housing, and improve public facilities and services in rural areas. The most complete study of this program indicates that enrollees were paid an hourly rate of $1.65 in 1969. The Federal cost per man/year was about $4,600 in 1969. These low wage work experience programs have been able to attract targeted workers, although most participants have not come from prime age groups.

295

Targetting. Work experience programs have been targetted entirely on the poor. About half of the recent enrollment has come from families receiving some form of public assistance. Two jobs programs stand out in our experience in terms of exclusive targetting on the current welfare population: the PSE component of the WIN program and a set of Welfare Demonstration Projects started during the 1971 recession. The WIN PSE program is comprised entirely of AFDC recipients. Last year about 40 percent did not complete high school. About one-third were minorities and slightly more than half were women.

The Welfare Demonstration Projects were intended to determine whether employable welfare recipients could be given jobs rather than cash assistance. Seven thousand AFDC recipients participated at 12 sites in 4 states. Participants were somewhat more employable than the overall AFDC population, but 44 percent were categorized as significantly dependent on welfare, having received benefits for two or more years. Fifty-four percent did not complete high school. Most participants were women (79%), blacks (85%), and the main breadwinners for their families (90%).

Meaningful Work. The Welfare Demonstration Projects, whose scale was large in the sites selected, served as a good test of our ability to develop real, not make-work, jobs for low skilled workers (mainly women in this case). Seventy percent worked in health, education and other social service agencies. Occupationally, almost one-half of the jobs were of a personal service type, such as child care worker and community service aide. Clerical jobs amounted to about one-third, and laboring jobs accounted for about one-fifth of the total.

About 95 percent of agency directors judged the jobs to be helpful to their agencies. Some 90 percent of supervisors rated participants about as productive as their regular employees. Virtually all of the participants found their jobs to be interesting and useful and not make-work. Job retention in the program averaged 15 months; only 20 percent quit because of their own or their supervisors' dissatisfaction.

DOL WORK SUPPORT EFFORTS

Program	Year Data Apply	Total New Enrollees	% Poor*	% Public Assistance†	Cost per Man/Year	Average Hourly Wage	Statutory Minimum Wage
PUBLIC SERVICE EMPLOYMENT							
CETA (I, II, VI)	1975	424,290	41	26	$7,800	$3.25‡	$2.10
WIN (PSE)	1976	10,219	100	100	$7,819	$2.81	$2.30
WORK EXPERIENCE							
Operation Mainstream	1969	41,000	96	n.a.	$4,631	$1.65	$1.60
CETA (youth)	1975	324,821	68	n.a.	$2,855	NA§	$2.10
CETA (summer youth)	1975	845,500	69	n.a.	NA	NA§	$2.10
WELFARE DEMONSTRATION PROJECT							
PEP	1972–74	7,250	100	100	NA	$2.94	$1.60–$2.00

*Technically, "economically disadvantaged," defined as members of families receiving cash welfare payments, or whose family income does not exceed the poverty level.

†Includes AFDC, food stamps, public housing, SSI, and others.

‡Based on federal share only and assumed 2,000 hours/year. State and local augmentation permitted, but amount not known.

§Predominantly minimum wage.

APPENDIX 7

DEPARTMENT OF HEALTH, EDUCATION, AND WELFARE
OFFICE OF THE SECRETARY
WASHINGTON, DC 20201

April 23, 1977

NOTE TO THE SECRETARY

RE: Comments on Memo from Secretary Ray Marshall—"Jobs for Welfare Reform"

The purpose of Secretary Marshall's memo is to convince you that recent experience with Public Service Employment suggests that it will be feasible for them to create a large number of suitable jobs in the appropriate time. This note puts Marshall's memo into some more neutral perspective.

The issue is accurately posed: does whatever success the Labor Department has had in its separate, relatively small programs suggest that job opportunities can be developed (1) in much larger numbers, (2) while paying the minimum wage, (3) which are suitable for low-skilled workers, and (4) which provide meaningful and productive work experience. The answer is highly uncertain. Doubts are raised by the following considerations, which are used in Marshall's memo.

1. *Scale.* The largest program with which we have had actual experience is less than one-third of what is proposed. Further, studies indicate that 40 to 90% of those employed (in counter-cyclical employment programs) simply replaced workers who would have been hired by the States and localities anyway. Even then, only 15% of those hired (not 25%) were from the public assistance rolls.

2. *Wages.* As their own table indicates, wages in the CETA Public Employment Programs, on the average, exceeded the minimum wage by 50%. Only the work experience programs paid wages near the minimum. These jobs were taken primarily by the very young and older

298

workers in rural areas. Surely the Neighborhood Youth Corps is not an adequate model and, at its peak, the largely rural Operation Mainstream program totaled less than 32,000 slots (many filled by persons over 45 years of age). We therefore have very little experience with paying minimum wages to prime-age workers.

3. *Targeting.* Once again we are talking about small numbers; 10,000 to 50,000 in the WIN-PSE program. The Welfare Demonstration Projects were expensive, only 57% of costs were for wages. In both instances, the great majority of participants had recent employment experience.

Secretary Marshall's memo has not changed the statement that *we have had very little experience in rapidly creating large numbers of minimum wage jobs for prime-age workers.*

One final caution. We should not be put in the pure nay-sayer position. We should support a re-targeting of CETA as fast as is possible. But we should point out that raising false expectations has costs, as does developing a job problem mess to parallel the welfare mess.

[signature: Mike]
Michael C. Barth

NOTES

CHAPTER ONE

1. Richard M. Nixon, *The Memoirs of Richard Nixon* (New York: Grosset and Dunlap, 1978), pp. 426–427.

2. Arthur M. Schlesinger, Jr., *The Coming of the New Deal* (Boston: Houghton Mifflin, 1959), pp. 535–536.

3. Donald R. Richberg, *My Hero* (New York: G. P. Putnam and Sons, 1954), p. 164.

4. Raymond Moley, *The First New Deal* (New York: Harcourt, Brace, and World, 1966), p. 90.

5. George Martin, *Madame Secretary: Frances Perkins* (Boston: Houghton Mifflin, 1976), pp. 265–266.

6. *Ibid.*, p. 265.

7. Richberg, *My Hero*, p. 265.

8. Martin, *Madame Secretary*, p. 268.

9. *Ibid.*, based on Martin's interview with Douglas. Richard E. Neustadt has suggested to the authors that the complaint is suspect. Clever in his political relationships, Roosevelt may have made many people feel this way, or those people may have used this claim as an excuse for having lost an argument.

10. Schlesinger, *The Coming of the New Deal*, p. 98.

11. James P. Warburg, *The Money Muddle* (New York: Alfred A. Knopf, 1934), p. 133.

12. James L. Sundquist, *Politics and Policy: The Eisenhower, Kennedy, and Johnson Years* (Washington, D.C.: Brookings Institution, 1968), p. 174.

13. *Ibid.*, p. 388.

14. Interview with Neil H. McElroy, Columbia University Oral History Project, p. 74.

15. Dwight D. Eisenhower, *Waging Peace, 1956–1961* (New York: Doubleday, 1965), p. 245.

16. *Ibid.*, p. 251.

17. Emmet J. Hughes, *The Ordeal of Power* (New York: Atheneum, 1975), p. 261.

18. Lyndon Baines Johnson, *The Vantage Point: Perspectives of the Presidency, 1963–1969* (New York: Holt, Rinehart and Winston, 1971), p. 71.

19. *Ibid.*

20. Sundquist, *Politics and Policy*, p. 145.

21. Johnson, *The Vantage Point*, p. 71.

22. *Ibid.*, p. 73.

23. Quoted by Elizabeth Goldschmidt in Merle Miller, *Lyndon: An Oral Biography* (New York: G. P. Putnam and Sons, 1980), p. 363.

CHAPTER TWO

1. For a detailed historical account of welfare system growth, see Laurence E. Lynn, Jr., "A Decade of Policy Developments in the Income Maintenance System," in Robert H. Haveman, ed., *A Decade of Federal Anti-Poverty Programs: Achievements, Failures, and Lessons* (New York: Academic Press, 1977), pp. 55–117.

2. Califano in Merle Miller, *Lyndon: An Oral Biography* (New York: G. P. Putnam and Sons, 1980), p. 363.

3. M. Kenneth Bowler, *The Nixon Guaranteed Income Proposal: Substance and Process in Policy Change* (Cambridge, Mass.: Ballinger, 1974), p. 40.

4. Daniel P. Moynihan, *The Politics of a Guaranteed Income: The Nixon Administration and the Family Assistance Plan* (New York: Vintage, 1973), p. 67.

5. Richard M. Nixon, *The Memoirs of Richard Nixon* (New York: Grosset and Dunlap, 1978), pp. 425–426.

6. Vincent J. Burke and Vee Burke, *Nixon's Good Deed: Welfare Reform* (New York: Columbia University Press, 1974), pp. 48–49. (The authors are henceforth referred to as the Burkes.)

7. Burkes, *Nixon's Good Deed*, p. 64.

8. *Ibid.*, p. 65.

9. *Ibid.*, p. 67.

10. *Ibid.*

11. *Ibid.*, pp. 68–69.

12. Nixon, *Memoirs*, p. 342.

13. *Ibid.*

14. Bowler, *The Nixon Guaranteed Income Proposal*, p. 50.

15. Burkes, *Nixon's Good Deed*, p. 79.

16. *Ibid.*, p. 84.

17. *Ibid.*

18. Bowler, *The Nixon Guaranteed Income Proposal*, p. 52.

19. Burkes, *Nixon's Good Deed*, p. 82. (Italics in original.)

20. *Ibid.* (Italics added.)

21. *Ibid.*, p. 87.

22. *Ibid.*, p. 90.

23. *Ibid.*, p. 101.

24. *Ibid.*, p. 103.

25. *Ibid.*, p. 104.

26. *Ibid.*, p. 106.

27. Bowler, *The Nixon Guaranteed Income Proposal*, p. 69.

28. Nixon, *Memoirs*, pp. 426–427.

29. Bowler, *The Nixon Guaranteed Income Proposal*, p. 152.

30. Moynihan, *The Politics of a Guaranteed Income*, p. 285.

31. Burkes, *Nixon's Good Deed*, pp. 155–156.

32. Moynihan, *The Politics of a Guaranteed Income*, p. 523.

33. *Ibid.*

34. Cited in *ibid.*, p. 531.

35. *Ibid.*

36. Cited in *ibid.*, p. 533.

37. *Ibid.* For a contrasting view, see Nick Kotz and Mary Lynn Kotz, *A Passion for Equality* (New York: W. W. Norton, 1977), pp. 269–271 and 276–277.

38. Bowler, *The Nixon Guaranteed Income Proposal*, pp. 134–147.

39. *Ibid.*, p. 134.

40. Cited in *ibid.*, p. 134.

41. Cited in *ibid.*, p. 138.

42. *Ibid.*

43. Abraham Ribicoff, "He Left at Half Time," *New Republic*, Feb. 17, 1973, p. 26.

44. Bowler, *The Nixon Guaranteed Income Proposal*, p. 139.

45. Ribicoff, "He Left at Half Time," p. 26.

46. *Ibid.*

47. Nixon, *Memoirs*, p. 428.

48. On the late 1972 "Mega" plan, see Laurence E. Lynn, Jr., and John M. Seidl, "Policymaking in HEW: The Story of the Mega-Proposal," *Policy Analysis* 1, no. 2 (Spring 1975): 232–273, 344–367. On the 1973–1974 ISP plan, see "Caspar Weinberger and Welfare Reform," in Laurence E. Lynn, Jr., *Designing Public Policy: A Casebook on the Role of Policy Analysis* (Santa Monica, Calif.: Goodyear, 1980), pp. 82–103.

49. J. Glen Beall, Jr., "Comprehensive Welfare Reform: Congressional Prospects," *Journal of the Institute for Socioeconomic Studies* 2, no. 1 (Spring 1977): 20, 27.

50. Cited in Bowler, *The Nixon Guaranteed Income Proposal*, p. 138.

51. American Enterprise Institute, *Welfare Reform: Why?* (Washington, D.C.: The Institute, 1976), p. 13.

52. Laurence E. Lynn, Jr., "A Decade of Policy Developments," p. 117.

53. *Ibid.*

54. Martin Anderson, *Welfare* (Stanford, Calif.: Hoover Press, Stanford University, 1979), p. 149.

CHAPTER THREE

1. "Choices for HEW Secretary, CIA Director and Energy Chief," *New York Times*, Dec. 2, 1976, p. A-11.

2. John K. Iglehart, "HEW's Califano Wants to Set the Great Society in Motion," *National Journal*, June 25, 1977, p. 990.

3. Leonard Hausman, "Cumulative Tax Transfer Programs: How They Tax the Poor," in U.S. Congress, Joint Economic Committee, Subcommittee on Fiscal Policy, *Studies in Public Welfare*, paper no. 14, April 15, 1974 (Washington, D.C.: U.S. Government Printing Office, 1974). The maximum marginal tax rate in the AFDC program was lowered from 100 to 67 percent in 1969, but this decrease was partially offset by an increase in the tax rate of other programs, especially food stamps.

4. Confirmation hearings of Joseph A. Califano, Jr., Senate Finance Committee, 95th Cong., 1st sess., Jan. 13, 1977, p. 4.

5. Al Ullman, letter to Joseph A. Califano, Jr., April 1, 1977.

6. National Governors' Conference, Committee on Human Resources, Welfare Reform Task Force, *National Welfare Reform: A Bicentennial Priority* (Washington, D.C.: The Conference, June 1976), p. 9. States and program administrators also supported consolidation of existing programs, expansion of work opportunities, and expansion of coverage on a universal basis to childless couples, unemployed fathers, and single individuals, as well as mandating a national minimum payment standard.

7. "Report on Welfare Reform," *Public Welfare* (special issue) 35, no. 2 (Spring 1977): 17–22.

8. Statement by the AFL-CIO Executive Council on Welfare Reform, Feb. 24, 1977, Bar Harbor, Fla. The AFL-CIO was opposed to comprehensive cash coverage. They felt that "proponents of such proposals . . . fail to recognize the multiple causes of poverty as well as the varied characteristics of those who were poor. . . . Experience has shown that efforts to achieve adequate financial support for the poor in a single program pit those persons who are receiving income from wages, or could if they were properly trained and there were enough jobs available, against those who must rely on the support payment" (background paper prepared for the AFL-CIO Executive Council, Feb. 24, 1977, p. 2).

9. Congressional Budget Office, *Welfare Reform: Issues, Objectives, and Approaches* (Washington, D.C.: U.S. Government Printing Office, July 1977), p. 24.

10. James R. Storey et al., *The Better Jobs and Income Plan* (Urban Institute Welfare Reform Policy Analysis Series, no. 1; Washington, D.C.: The Institute, Jan. 1978), p. 24.

11. Four experiments were commissioned by HEW to test the impact of an NIT on work effort. Three of the experiments were conducted in urban areas (New Jersey, Gary, and Seattle-Denver) and one in a rural area (rural Iowa and rural North Carolina). The New Jersey experiment was limited to two-parent families of the working poor, Gary dealt only with black families whose members included either one or two children, and the rural experiment focused on wage-earning and farming families in racially distinct areas in North Carolina and Iowa. Seattle-Denver, the most extensive experiment of the lot, covered one- and two-parent families from various ethnic backgrounds. Seattle-Denver covered 4,800 families who were eligible for payments over a period of three, five, or twenty years. The other three experiments covered 1,800 families (or fewer) and allowed families to be eligible for three years.

12. U.S. Department of Health, Education, and Welfare, *Summary Report: New Jersey Graduated Work Incentive Experiment* (Washington, D.C.: U.S. Government Printing Office, 1973), p. vi.

13. An alternative strategy that received little political support was the "social insurance" approach, generally associated with Alvin Schorr, a social worker and former deputy director for research at OEO. Schorr wished to increase income support by expanding social insurance programs, that is, programs such as

unemployment and disability insurance, where benefits were an earned right and not related to need, rather than by expanding "income-tested" welfare programs, such as AFDC and food stamps. Schorr felt that an improved social insurance system, the creation of a refundable tax credit, raising minimum wages, and setting up children allowances would generate adequate income support and be a less demeaning and more popular method of assisting recipients.

14. William Morrill, "Actors and Proposals in Income Security Policy—Response to Your Note of January 22," memorandum to HEW Secretary Matthews, April 1, 1976, p. 3.

15. Jimmy Carter, speech to the National Governors Conference, July 6, 1976, in *The Presidential Campaign, 1976*, vol. 1, pt. 1 (Washington, D.C.: U.S. Government Printing Office, 1978), pp. 284–285.

16. Jimmy Carter, "Urban Policy for the Remainder of the Twentieth Century," speech delivered in New York City, April 1, 1976, in *The Presidential Campaign, 1976*, vol. 1, pt. 1, p. 121.

17. Transcript of press conference from Plains, Ga., Aug. 16, 1976, in *The Presidential Campaign, 1976*, vol. 1, pt. 1, pp. 379–380.

18. "The Choices for Carter and Congress," *National Journal*, Jan. 8, 1977, p. 52.

19. *New York Times*, Jan. 12, 1977, p. A-19.

20. Nick Kotz, "The Politics of Welfare Reform," *New Republic*, May 14, 1977, pp. 16–21.

21. Jimmy Carter, marginal comments, Jan. 21, 1977, on undated issue paper concerning triple-track reform options.

22. Arnold H. Packer, "Categorical Public Employment Guarantees: A Proposed Solution to the Poverty Problem," in U.S. Congress, Joint Economic Committee, Subcommittee on Fiscal Policy, *Studies in Public Welfare*, paper no. 9, pt. 1, Aug. 20, 1973 (Washington, D.C.: U.S. Government Printing Office, 1973), pp. 68–127.

23. Arnold H. Packer, "Employment Guarantees Should Replace the Welfare System," *Challenge*, March-April 1974, pp. 22, 23.

24. Henry Aaron, draft of a memorandum to Joseph A. Califano, Jr., Jan. 21, 1977, p. 2.

25. HEW news release, Jan. 26, 1977, pp. 1, 3.

26. Kotz, "The Politics of Welfare Reform," p. 18.

27. Joseph A. Califano, Jr., draft of a memorandum to the president, undated, p. 1.

28. *Ibid.*, p. 1.

29. Interview, ISP staff members, June 30, 1978.

30. 42 *United States Code* §1314b.

31. Consulting Group on Welfare Reform, "Minutes, February 11, 1977, Meeting," in Department of Health, Education, and Welfare, *Report on the 1977 Welfare Reform Study: The Secretary's Report to the President*, Supp. 1, vol. 1 (Washington, D.C.: HEW, May 3, 1977), p. 20.

32. *Washington Post*, Feb. 12, 1977, p. A-12.

33. *Ibid.*

34. Linda E. Demkovich, "Carter Gets Some Outside Advice for His Welfare Reform Package," *National Journal,* April 30, 1977, p. 674.

CHAPTER FOUR

1. Henry Aaron, draft of a memorandum to Joseph A. Califano, Jr., Jan. 21, 1977, p. 1.

2. Nick Kotz, "The Politics of Welfare Reform," *New Republic,* May 14, 1977, p. 17.

3. Michael Barth, "Welfare Reform and Your Monday Meeting with the Secretary," memorandum to Henry Aaron, Jan. 28, 1977, p. 5.

4. Aaron, draft of memorandum to Califano, Jan. 21, 1977, p. 3.

5. Joseph A. Califano, Jr., "The Politics of Innovation and the Revolution in Government Management," speech before the Washington Chapter of Sigma Delta Chi, April 19, 1967, pp. 1, 6 (processed).

6. Franklin Raines, "Policy Advocacy: The Case of the Family Assistance Program," pt. A (case no. C94-77-162, Kennedy School of Government, Harvard University, Cambridge, Mass., 1977), p. 26.

7. Essentially, ISP staff had to integrate the transfer income model (TRIM), developed at the Urban Institute in 1974, with data on labor supply responses that had been gathered in the Seattle-Denver income maintenance experiment. TRIM could only simulate a cash or in-kind transfer program and could not simulate programs with major job creation and work requirement components. Besides incorporating labor supply adjustments (in response to alterations in benefit levels and wage rates), HEW was faced with the immensely complicated task of developing a methodology for predicting participation in public employment programs. Aaron estimated that such a task might take as long as three years to complete in a consulting firm or university.

8. Linda E. Demkovich, "Carter Gets Some Outside Advice for His Welfare Reform Package," *National Journal,* April 30, 1977, p. 673.

9. Joseph A. Califano, Jr., "Putting the Public into Public Policy Development," *Journal of the Institute for Socioeconomic Studies* 3, no. 2 (Summer 1978): 1, 3, 4.

10. Demkovich, "Carter Gets Some Outside Advice," p. 674.

11. Henry Freedman, Nezzie Willis, and Catherine Day-Jermany, "Memorandum on Welfare Reform" to Joseph A. Califano, Jr., April 20, 1977 (coauthored by Adele M. Blong, associate director of the Center on Social Welfare Policy and Law), in Department of Health, Education, and Welfare, *Report on the 1977 Welfare Reform Study,* Supp. 1, vol. 2 (Washington, D.C.: HEW, May 1977), p. 488.

12. Henry Aaron, "Ways and Means Contacts on Welfare Reform," memorandum to Joseph A. Califano, Jr., March 1, 1977, p. 1.

13. Henry Aaron, letter to David Whitman, May 10, 1979.

14. "New Coalition Staff Comments on the Reports of the Welfare Consulting Group," April 18, 1977, in *Report on the 1977 Welfare Reform Study,* Supp. 1, vol. 2, p. 482.

15. Kotz, "The Politics of Welfare Reform," p. 18.

16. Department of Health, Education, and Welfare, Income Security Policy Staff, "Briefing for the Secretary: The Work Issue—Incentives, Requirements, and Jobs," briefing paper, March 9, 1977, pp. 2–4.

17. *Ibid.*, p. 5.

18. *Ibid.*, p. 7.

19. *Ibid.*, pp. 7–8.

20. Arnold Packer, "Welfare Reform Briefings," memorandum to Ray Marshall, March 14, 1977, p. 1.

21. *Ibid.*, p. 2.

22. *Ibid.*

23. *Ibid.*, p. 3.

24. Joseph A. Califano, Jr., memorandum to the president, March 23, 1977, pp. 1, 2.

25. Stu Eizenstat, "Meeting with Secretary Califano," memorandum to the president, March 24, 1977, pp. 1, 2.

26. *Ibid.*, p. 2.

27. Jack Watson, "Meeting with Joe Califano," memorandum to the president, March 24, 1977, p. 1.

28. Kotz, "The Politics of Welfare Reform," p. 18.

29. *Ibid.*, pp. 19, 21.

CHAPTER FIVE

1. Jimmy Carter, "Planning a Budget from Zero," speech to the National Governors Conference, June 1974, in *The Presidential Campaign, 1976,* vol. 1, pt. 1 (Washington, D.C.: U.S. Government Printing Office, 1978), p. 18.

2. Nick Kotz, "The Politics of Welfare Reform," *New Republic,* May 14, 1977, p. 19.

3. See, for example, Joseph A. Califano, Jr., "Congress Has Been Bypassed in Analysis Technology," *Washington Post,* July 13, 1971, p. A-18.

4. Henry Aaron, "Welfare Reform Cost and Caseload Estimates," memorandum to Jim Moran, Senate Budget Committee, March 30, 1977, pp. 1, 2.

5. Consulting Group on Welfare Reform, "Minutes, April 1, 1977, Meeting," in Department of Health, Education, and Welfare, *Report on the 1977 Welfare Reform Study: The Secretary's Report to the President,* Supp. 1, vol. 1 (Washington, D.C.: HEW, May 1977), pp. 1, 2.

6. *Ibid.*

7. John E. Todd and David Lindeman, "'Official' Offsets," memorandum to ISP staff, April 5, 1977, p. 1.

8. William Barnes, "Redirecting CETA," HEW issue paper, April 26, 1977, p. 3.

9. Kotz, "The Politics of Welfare Reform," p. 19.

10. Stu Eizenstat and Frank Raines, "Meeting with Secretary Califano," memorandum to the president, April 8, 1977, p. 1.

11. Sue Woolsey, "Welfare Reform Meeting with the President," memorandum to Bert Lance, April 9, 1977, p. 1.

12. *Ibid.*, p. 2.

13. Consulting Group on Welfare Reform, "Minutes, April 8, 1977, Meeting," in HEW, *Report on the 1977 Welfare Reform Study,* Supp. 1, vol. 1, pp. 2–3.

14. *Ibid.*

15. Eizenstat and Raines, "Meeting with Secretary Califano," April 8, 1977, p. 2.

16. Jack Watson and Jim Parham, "Welfare Reform Meeting," memorandum to the president, April 9, 1977, p. 2.

17. Nicholas Lemann, "Carter's Paper Presidency," *Washington Post,* Sept. 3, 1978, p. C-5.

18. See Robert Shogan, *Promises to Keep* (New York: Cromwell, 1977), p. 240.

19. Joseph A. Califano, Jr., memorandum to the president on welfare reform principles, April 11, 1977, p. 2.

20. Ray Marshall, "Welfare Reform Design," memorandum to the president, April 13, 1977, p. 1.

21. *Ibid.*

22. Stu Eizenstat and Frank Raines, "Secretary Califano's Memo on Principles of Welfare Reform," memorandum to the president, April 13, 1977, p. 1.

23. *Ibid.*

24. Jack Watson and Jim Parham, "Welfare Reform," memorandum to the president, April 15, 1977, p. 1.

25. *Ibid.*

26. John E. Todd, "Status of 4/21 President's Briefing," memorandum to Henry Aaron (through Mike Barth), April 18, 1977, pp. 1, 3, and 4.

27. *Ibid.*

28. Kotz, "The Politics of Welfare Reform," p. 20.

29. *Ibid.*

30. *Ibid.*

31. Todd, "Status of 4/21 President's Briefing," pp. 1, 3, and 4.

32. Henry Aaron, note to Joseph A. Califano, Jr., April 18, 1977, p. 1.

33. *Ibid.*, pp. 1, 2.

34. *Ibid.*, p. 2.

35. Ray Marshall, "Jobs for Welfare Reform," memorandum to Joseph A. Califano, Jr., April 21, 1977, p. 1.

36. *Ibid.*

37. *Ibid.*, p. 2.

38. Kotz, "The Politics of Welfare Reform," p. 20.

39. *Ibid.*

40. Michael C. Barth, "Comments on Memo from Secretary Ray Marshall—'Jobs for Welfare Reform,'" note to Joseph A. Califano, Jr., April 23, 1977, p. 1.

41. *Ibid.*, p. 2.

CHAPTER SIX

1. Quoted in "Byrd Says Energy Bill to Stall Two Top Issues," *Detroit News,* April 24, 1977, p. 20, and "U.S. Senate to Delay Welfare Reform," *Los Angeles Times,* April 24, 1977, p. 6.

2. "Welfare Reform Plan Is Delayed," *San Francisco Chronicle*, April 26, 1977, p. 22.

3. "Moynihan Predicts No Welfare Reform until Fall," *New Orleans Times-Picayune*, April 26, 1977, p. 3.

4. Stu Eizenstat, Bert Carp, Bill Spring, and Frank Raines, "Perspective on Welfare Reform," memorandum to the president, April 26, 1977, p. 3.

5. Stu Eizenstat, "Welfare Reform," note to the president, April 26, 1977, p. 1.

6. Bert Lance, "Employment and Training Component of Welfare Reform," memorandum to the president, undated, p. 1.

7. *Ibid.*, pp. 2, 3.

8. Alan Gustman, "A Few Last Minute Points on Welfare Reform," memorandum to Ray Marshall, April 26, 1977, p. 1.

9. Income Security Policy Staff, various charts for April 26, 1977, briefing for President Carter.

10. Nick Kotz, "The Politics of Welfare Reform," *New Republic*, May 14, 1977, pp. 20–21.

11. *Ibid.*

12. *Ibid.*

13. Jack Watson, "Scheduling on Tax Reform and Welfare Reform," memorandum to the president, April 27, 1977, p. 1.

14. Charles Schultze, "Welfare Reform," memorandum to the president, April 29, 1977, p. 1.

15. *Ibid.*, pp. 1–3.

16. *Ibid.*, pp. 3–4.

17. *Ibid.*, p. 4.

18. Stu Eizenstat, Jack Watson, Bert Carp, and Jim Parham, "Welfare Reform Statement," memorandum to the president, April 29, 1977, p. 1.

19. Joseph A. Califano, Jr., "Welfare Reform," memorandum to the president, April 29, 1977, p. 2.

20. *Ibid.*, p. 5.

21. *Ibid.*, p. 3.

22. *Ibid.*, pp. 4, 5.

23. Eizenstat, Watson, Carp, and Parham, "Welfare Reform Statement," April 29, 1977, p. 1.

24. Ray Marshall, "Welfare Reform Proposals," memorandum to the president, April 29, 1977, pp. 1, 2.

25. Joseph A. Califano, Jr., cover memo on memorandum to the president, untitled, April 29, 1977, p. 1.

26. Califano, "Welfare Reform," April 29, 1977, p. 6.

27. Nick Kotz, "The Politics of Welfare Reform," pp. 20–21.

28. Jim Fallows, memorandum to the president, May 1, 1977, p. 2.

29. Office of the White House Press Secretary, "Statement by the President," May 2, 1977, p. 1.

30. *Ibid.*, pp. 1–2.

31. Editorial, *Washington Post*, May 3, 1977.

32. Linda E. Demkovich and Joel Haveman, "Welfare Reform: Does Carter Have the Key?" *Los Angeles Times*, May 18, 1977, sec. 5, p. 2.

CHAPTER SEVEN

1. Tom Wicker, column, *New York Times,* May 3, 1977, p. 41.
2. George F. Will, "The Welfare State: Reform Means Only Tinkering," *Los Angeles Times,* May 25, 1977, p. II-7.
3. "House Panel Tells Califano of Problems," *Detroit News,* May 5, 1977, p. E-8.
4. CBS Morning News, *Transcript,* May 3, 1977, pp. 6–7.
5. U.S. Congress, Senate Finance Committee, Subcommittee on Public Assistance, *President's Statement on Principles of Welfare Reform,* hearings, May 5, 1977 (Washington, D.C.: U.S. Government Printing Office, 1977), p. 42.
6. *Ibid.,* pp. 26–27.
7. *Ibid.,* p. 41.
8. *Ibid.*
9. *Ibid.,* p. 84.
10. *Ibid.,* pp. 60–63.
11. *Ibid.,* p. 64.
12. Ray Marshall, "A Welfare Reform Compromise," memorandum to Joseph A. Califano, Jr., May 13, 1977, p. 1.
13. *Ibid.,* p. 2.
14. Stu Eizenstat, "Progress on Welfare Reform Proposal," memorandum to the president, May 14, 1977, p. 1.
15. Tom Joe, "HEW-DOL Welfare Reform Agreement," memorandum to Stu Eizenstat, May 18, 1977, pp. 1, 2.
16. Jodie T. Allen, "Latest 'Compromise' Welfare Reform," memorandum to Henry Aaron and Arnold Packer, May 18, 1977, p. 3.
17. *Ibid.*
18. Arnold Packer, "Welfare Reform Agreement," memorandum to Henry Aaron, May 16, 1977, p. 1.
19. *Ibid.*
20. Joseph A. Califano, Jr., "Welfare Reform Proposal," memorandum to the president, May 19, 1977, p. 3.
21. Donald Hirsch, "Welfare Reform—Information," note to Pete Libassi, Richard Beattie, and Dan Marcus, May 17, 1977, p. 1.
22. Califano, "Welfare Reform Proposal," May 19, 1977, p. 13.
23. *Ibid.,* pp. 10, 11.
24. *Ibid.,* p. 8.
25. *Ibid.,* p. 14.
26. Jack Watson and Jim Parham, "Comments on the HEW/Labor Welfare Reform Proposals," memorandum to the president, May 23, 1977, p. 1.
27. Stu Eizenstat, Charlie Schultze, and Bert Lance, memorandum to the president, untitled, May 20, 1977, p. 1.
28. *Ibid.,* p. 2.
29. *Ibid.*
30. "Statement of Secretary Joseph A. Califano, Jr., on Welfare Reform," *HEW News,* May 25, 1977, p. 2.

31. "Carter Aides Cite Difficulties Posed by Welfare Goals," *Washington Post*, May 26, 1977, p. A-16.

32. "Califano Outlines Welfare Aid Linked to Job Requirement," *New York Times*, May 26, 1977, p. A-18.

33. "Carter System to Require Recipient to Work," *Chicago Tribune*, May 26, 1977, p. 1.

34. *Ibid.*

35. "President Stresses Welfare Limit Despite Warning," *New York Times*, May 27, 1977, p. A-11.

36. *Ibid.*

37. "Transcript of the Carter News Conference on Domestic and Foreign Matters," *New York Times*, May 27, 1977, p. A-10.

38. David E. Rosenbaum, "Carter Aides Predict a Savings of Billions in New Welfare Plan," *New York Times*, June 2, 1977, p. A-1.

39. Jim Parham, "Welfare Reform," memorandum to Henry Aaron and Arnold Packer, June 6, 1977, p. 1.

40. Califano, "Welfare Reform Proposal," May 19, 1977, tab C.

41. Henry Aaron, "Report on June 1 and 2 Meetings with State and Local Officials on Welfare Reform," memorandum to Joseph A. Califano, Jr., June 6, 1977, pp. 1, 2.

42. Michael Barth, "Second Report on Welfare Reform Meetings with State and Local Officials," memorandum, June 20, 1977, pp. 1, 2.

43. *Ibid.*, p. 2.

44. *Ibid.*, p. 4.

45. Jodie T. Allen, "New Coalition Meeting—June 6, 1977," memorandum to Allan [*sic*] Gustman, June 9, 1977, p. 1.

46. Jodie T. Allen, "New Coalition Meeting—Friday, June 10, 1977," memorandum to Allan [*sic*] Gustman, June 15, 1977, p. 1.

47. Jodie T. Allen, "New Coalition Meeting, Tuesday, June 28, 1977, Region 3," memorandum to Arnold Packer, June 30, 1977, p. 1.

48. *Ibid.*, p. 2.

49. Jodie T. Allen, "New Coalition Meeting, Tuesday, June 22, 1977, Region 2," memorandum to Alan Gustman, June 24, 1977, p. 1.

50. Michael Barth, note to Income Security Policy staff, July 11, 1977, p. 1.

CHAPTER EIGHT

1. "Minutes from June 3 Meeting of the DOL Welfare Reform Group," p. 2.

2. Ben W. Heineman, Jr., memorandum to Bert Carp, Frank Raines, and Jim Parham, June 29, 1977, sec. III, p. 14.

3. Arnold Packer and Ernest Green, "Options for Delivering Welfare Reform," memorandum to Ray Marshall, July 7, 1977, p. 1.

4. Henry Aaron, "Discussing Options and Procedures with Henry Aaron," *Public Welfare*, Summer 1977, pp. 12–19.

5. Arnold Packer, "Possible Way to Integrate Tax Reform and Welfare Reform," memorandum to Henry Aaron, July 1, 1977, pp. 1, 2.

6. Ben W. Heineman, Jr., "Jobs and Benefit Structure," memorandum to Henry Aaron and Mike Barth, July 7, 1977, p. 1.

7. Arnold Packer, "Welfare Reform Cash Benefit Structure," memorandum to Ray Marshall, July 15, 1977, p. 1.

8. Arnold Packer, "Alternative Benefit Structure," memorandum to White House staff, July 15, 1977, p. 6.

CHAPTER NINE

1. Bert Seidman, memorandum to Joseph A. Califano, Jr., June 2, 1977, p. 1.

2. Henry Freedman and Adele Blong, "President's Welfare Proposal Taking Form: HEW Schedules Meetings with States to Discuss Plan," June 14, 1977, Center for Social Welfare Policy and Law, New York, N.Y., pp. 1–2.

3. Center for Community Change et al., letter to the president, June 23, 1977, p. 2.

4. Jimmy Carter, "Subsidized Housing and Welfare Reform," memorandum to the secretaries of HEW and HUD and the chairman of the Council of Economic Advisers, undated (forwarded on July 7, 1977), p. 1.

5. OMB, Office of Housing, Veterans, and Labor, "Subsidized Housing and Welfare Reform," 2nd draft, July 7, 1977, pp. 4, 13.

6. Joel Haveman and Rochelle L. Stanfield, "Housing as Part of Welfare: An Agency Battles for Its Turf," *National Journal*, July 30, 1977, pp. 1190–1192.

7. *Ibid.*, p. 1191.

8. Austin Scott and David Broder, "Tug-of-War over Housing Subsidies," *Washington Post*, July 14, 1977, p. A-1.

9. *Ibid.*

10. *Washington Post*, July 27, 1977, p. A-1.

11. "The Honorable Joseph A. Califano, Jr., Secretary of HEW: Meeting with the Press on Welfare Reform," HEW Press Office, July 20, 1977, pp. 4, 6.

12. Joseph A. Califano, Jr., "The Welfare Reform Plan," memorandum to the president, July 25, 1977, p. 35.

13. Patricia Harris, "Housing Policy and Welfare Reform," memorandum to the president, July 26, 1977, pp. 1, 3.

14. Haveman and Stanfield, "Housing as Part of Welfare," pp. 1190–1192.

15. *Ibid.*, p. 4.

16. *Ibid.*

17. Stu Eizenstat, "Secretary Harris' Memo on Housing/Welfare," memorandum to the president, July 27, 1977, p. 1.

18. William D. Nordhaus, "Integration of Various Tax Credits in the Welfare Reform Proposal," memorandum to Henry Aaron, July 21, 1977, p. 1.

19. W. Michael Blumenthal, "HEW's Proposals for Changes in the Earned Income Tax Credit," memorandum to the president, July 28, 1977, p. 2.

20. Income Security Policy Staff, "Cost Worksheet," Aug. 4, 1977, p. 3.

21. Lance, "Welfare Reform," July 27, 1977, p. 1.

22. *Ibid.*, pp. 2, 6.

23. *Ibid.*, p. 3.

24. *Ibid.*, attachment A.

25. *Ibid.*, attachment B.

26. Califano, "The Welfare Reform Plan," July 25, 1977, pp. 1–2.

27. *Ibid.*, p. 3.

28. *Ibid.*, pp. 40–41.

29. Arnold Packer, "Welfare Reform," memorandum to Ray Marshall, July 25, 1977, pp. 1, 3.

30. Tom Joe, "HEW's Proposed Welfare Reform Plan," memorandum to Stu Eizenstat, July 27, 1977, pp. 2–5.

31. Jim Parham, "Welfare Reform," July 27, 1977, pp. 1–2.

32. Eizenstat et al., "Welfare Reform Memo," July 27, 1977, p. 11.

33. Joseph A. Califano, Jr., Ray Marshall, Charles Schultze, and Stu Eizenstat, "Welfare Reform Decision Memorandum," July 31, 1977, p. 9.

34. *Ibid.*, p. 6.

35. *Ibid.*, pp. 14, 20.

36. Stu Eizenstat, memorandum to the president, untitled, July 31, 1977, p. 1.

37. *Ibid.*, p. 2.

38. Joseph A. Califano, Jr., memorandum to the president, untitled, Aug. 1, 1977, p. 1.

39. *Ibid.*, p. 2.

40. *Ibid.*

41. Stu Eizenstat and Frank Raines, "Chairman Ullman's Suggestion on Revising the Welfare Reform Proposal," memorandum to the president, Aug. 2, 1977, p. 2.

42. David E. Rosenbaum, "Ullman Is Critical of Welfare Plan; Carter May Consider Delaying It," *New York Times*, Aug. 3, 1977, p. A-1.

43. Stu Eizenstat et al., "Working Women and Children under Welfare Plan," memorandum to the president, Aug. 3, 1977, p. 1.

44. *Ibid.*, p. 2.

45. *Ibid.*, p. 3.

46. *New York Times*, Aug. 4, 1977, p. A-6.

47. David E. Rosenbaum, "Carter Delays Plan on Welfare System," *New York Times*, Aug. 5, 1977, p. D-13.

CHAPTER TEN

1. Steven R. Weisman, "Carter Offers Welfare Revisions; Would Cut Costs in This Region," *New York Times*, May 24, 1979, pp. A-1 and A-18.

2. "President Carter's Proposal for Welfare Reform," HEW press office release, May 23, 1979, p. 56.

3. "Carter's Sweetening of His Welfare Plan Blunts Some Criticism," *St. Louis Post-Dispatch*, Aug. 7, 1977, p. 5-A.

4. Testimony of Joseph A. Califano, Jr., in U.S. Congress, House, Committees on Agriculture, Education and Labor, and Ways and Means, Welfare Reform

Subcommittee, *Joint Hearings on H.R. 9030, a Bill to Replace the Existing Federal Welfare Programs,* 95th Cong., 1st sess., pt. 1, Sept. 19–21, 1977, serial 95-47 (Washington, D.C.: U.S. Government Printing Office, 1977), p. 60.

5. The dates of the editorials are as follows: *Washington Post,* Aug. 7, 1977; *Memphis Commercial Appeal,* Aug. 10, 1977; *Los Angeles Times,* Aug. 10, 1977; *Kansas City Times,* Aug. 10, 1977; *New York Times,* Aug. 9, 1977; "Working to Reform Welfare," *Time,* Aug. 15, 1977, pp. 6–7; and *Louisville Courier-Journal,* Aug. 10, 1977.

6. *Washington Post,* Aug. 7, 1977, editorial page.

7. "Carter, Congress, and Welfare: A Long Road," *Congressional Quarterly,* Aug. 13, 1977, p. 1701.

8. *New York Times,* Aug. 7, 1977, p. 1.

9. "No. 3 GOP'er in House Backs Welfare Reform," *Birmingham Post-Herald,* Aug. 8, 1977, p. A-7.

10. "Carter, Congress, and Welfare: A Long Road," p. 1699.

11. *Washington Post,* Aug. 7, 1977, p. A-1.

12. Louis Harris, "Harris Survey: Welfare Reform Support Unprecedented," *Houston Post,* Sept. 15, 1977, p. 20.

13. Michael Barth, "Note to ISP Staff," Aug. 8, 1977, p. 1.

14. Arnold Packer, memorandum to Jodie Allen et al., untitled, Aug. 5, 1977, p. 1.

15. "Something Less than the Millennium," *Time,* Aug. 15, 1977, p. 7.

16. Joseph A. Califano, Jr., "Interview with Joseph Califano on 'Face the Nation,'" *CBS News Transcript,* Aug. 7, 1977, pp. 7, 8.

17. *Ibid.,* pp. 10–11.

18. Russell B. Long, "Statement of Senator Russell B. Long on Welfare Reform," press release, Aug. 15, 1977, p. 3.

19. "Califano Optimistic over Differences with Long," *Houston Post,* Aug. 18, 1977, p. 12.

20. House Committees on Agriculture, Education and Labor, and Ways and Means, Welfare Reform Subcommittee, *Joint Hearings on H.R. 9030,* pt. 1, p. 113.

21. Robert J. Fersh, *Program for Better Jobs and Income* (American Public Welfare Association, Staff analysis; Washington, D.C.: The Association, Nov. 10, 1977), pp. 4–5.

22. Gordon L. Weil, *The Welfare Debate of 1978* (White Plains, N.Y.: Institute for Socioeconomic Studies, 1978), p. 89.

23. Jimmy Carter, "Remarks of the President at Democratic National Committee Meeting," Office of the White House Press Secretary, Oct. 7, 1977, p. 3.

24. Income Security Policy staff, "Welfare Reform: A Short Political History," May 9, 1977, pp. 7–8.

25. Jeff Peterson, "Quick Politics of Welfare Reform," memorandum to Dick Warden, undated.

26. Henry Aaron, "Response to CBO Cost Estimate of H.R. 9030," memorandum to Joseph A. Califano, Jr., undated, pp. 4 and 6.

27. See pp. 5 and 6 of the HEW cost estimates on H.R. 9030 provided to the Special Subcommittee on Welfare Reform (when H.R. 10950 was reported out

to the full committee). The final CBO cost estimate of H.R. 9030 was $19.14 billion; without the contested offsets and disputed EITC cost the HEW final estimate was $19.36 billion.

28. Linda E. Demkovich, "The Numbers Are the Issue in the Debate over Welfare Reform," *National Journal*, April 22, 1978, p. 636.

29. Quoted in Sandra Fleishman, "Carter's Welfare Package Doesn't Satisfy Sarasin," *Waterbury Republican* (Conn.), Dec. 2, 1977, p. 33.

30. *New York Times*, Dec. 5, 1977, p. 42.

31. Mary Russell and David Broder, "Carter Aides See Delay in Passing Welfare Revision," *Washington Post*, Jan. 25, 1978, p. A-1.

32. David Broder and Spencer Rich, "Carter Still Sees Hope for Passing Welfare Revision," *Washington Post*, Jan. 26, 1978, p. A-1.

33. *Ibid.*

34. *Ibid.*

35. "Worst Obstacles Yet to Come for Welfare Program," *New Orleans Times-Picayune*, Dec. 19, 1977, p. 8.

36. See Austin Scott and Spencer Rich, "Carter's Welfare Proposals Face Sharp Challenges in the House," *Washington Post*, Nov. 27, 1977, p. A-7, and David E. Rosenbaum, "Outlook Is Gloomy on Welfare Changes," *New York Times*, Dec. 11, 1977, p. A-1.

37. Weil, *The Welfare Debate of 1978*, pp. 99, 100.

38. Martin Donsky, "Compromise Talks Open in Effort to Salvage Some Welfare Reform," *Congressional Quarterly*, April 29, 1978, p. 1064.

39. U.S. Congress, Senate, Committee on Human Resources, *Better Jobs and Income Act, 1978*, hearings, 95th Cong., 2nd sess., March 22–23, 1978 (Washington, D.C.: U.S. Government Printing Office, 1978), pp. 236, 270.

40. Weil, *The Welfare Debate of 1978*, p. 102.

41. Linda E. Demkovich, "State and Local Officials Rescue Welfare Reform—Too Late," *National Journal*, June 24, 1978, p. 1007.

42. See the testimony of Charles Rangel in U.S. Congress, Senate Finance Committee, Subcommittee on Public Assistance, *Welfare Reform Proposals*, hearings, 95th Cong., 2nd sess., May 4, 1978 (Washington, D.C.: U.S. Government Printing Office, 1978), pt. 5, p. 1229.

43. Jim Luther, "Welfare," Associated Press release, May 4, 1978.

44. Senate Finance Committee, Subcommittee on Public Assistance, *Welfare Reform Proposals*, May 4, 1978, pt. 5, p. 1230.

45. Luther, "Welfare."

46. Demkovich, "State and Local Officials Rescue Welfare Reform—Too Late," p. 1008.

47. Charles Peters, "More Dollars and More Dollars and, etc.," *New York Times*, May 15, 1978, op-ed page.

48. Demkovich, "State and Local Officials Rescue Welfare Reform—Too Late," p. 1008.

49. *Ibid.*

50. Spencer Rich, "Major Welfare Revision Is Dead for This Congress," *Washington Post*, June 23, 1978, p. A-2. On the HEW budget cuts see David

Whitman, "Fraud, Abuse, and Waste at HEW" (case C94-80-837, Kennedy School of Government, Harvard University, Cambridge, Mass., 1980), and David Blum, "Jarvis Fever," *New Republic,* June 24, 1978, pp. 14–16.

51. Demkovich, "State and Local Officials Rescue Welfare Reform—Too Late," p. 1007.

52. Rich, "Major Welfare Revision Is Dead for This Congress."

53. During the fight over FAP, Cranston had supported amendments that would eliminate restrictions on the federal share of welfare expenditures. His support for increased fiscal relief, however, did not preclude strong support for welfare reform. See Senator Cranston's statement in the *Congressional Record,* Sept. 15, 1972, pp. 30941–30942.

54. "Carter, Congress, and Welfare: A Long Road," p. 1701.

55. Spencer Rich, "Moynihan Unhappy at Welfare Plans," *Washington Post,* Oct. 1, 1977, p. A-8.

56. "Moynihan on Welfare—From FAP to the Carter Plan," *National Journal,* Jan. 28, 1978, pp. 147, 148.

57. American Public Welfare Association, *Welfare Reform and the Ninety-Fifth Congress* (Washington, D.C.: The Association, Dec. 1978), pp. 80–81.

58. Edward C. Burks, "Moynihan Charges White House Is Trying to Destroy Welfare Bill," *New York Times,* July 12, 1978, p. A-14.

59. *Ibid.*

60. Linda E. Demkovich, "A Preview of Coming Attractions," *National Journal,* Sept. 23, 1978, p. 1519.

61. In separate letters to David Whitman, Aaron and Barth both stated that they did not learn of the marital dissolution results before the summer of 1977.

62. Senate Finance Committee, Subcommittee on Public Assistance, *Welfare Reform Proposals,* Feb. 7, 1978, pt. 1, p. 23.

63. *Ibid.,* pp. 23–28, 53–55, 59–64, 135–136.

64. *Ibid.,* April 25, 1978, pt. 3, p. 831.

65. *Ibid.,* pp. 814–852.

66. "Some Negative Evidence about the Negative Income Tax," *Fortune,* Dec. 4, 1978, p. 146.

67. Linda E. Demkovich, "Good News and Bad News for Welfare Reform," *National Journal,* Dec. 30, 1978, p. 2063.

68. Martin Anderson, "Welfare Reform on 'the Same Old Rocks,'" *New York Times,* Nov. 27, 1978, op-ed page.

69. See, for example, Henry Aaron's statement in U.S. Congress, Senate, Committee on Finance, Subcommittee on Public Assistance, *Welfare Research and Experimentation,* hearings, 95th Cong., 2nd sess., Nov. 17, 1978 (Washington, D.C.: U.S. Government Printing Office, 1978), pp. 279–280.

70. Demkovich, "Good News and Bad News for Welfare Reform," p. 2063.

71. "Moynihan Says Recent Studies Raise Doubts about 'Negative Income Tax' Proposal," *New York Times,* Nov. 16, 1978, p. A-23.

72. Linda E. Demkovich, "Another Chance for Welfare Reform," *National Journal,* March 10, 1979, p. 404.

73. Steven R. Weisman, "Clash between Carter and Moynihan Slows Welfare Reform Plan," *New York Times*, April 1, 1979, pp. A-1, A-36.

74. *Ibid.*, p. A-36.

75. *Ibid.*

76. *Ibid.*

77. Weisman, "Carter Offers Welfare Revisions; Would Cut Costs in This Region," pp. A-1, A-18.

78. *Ibid.*, p. A-18.

79. *Ibid.*

80. See Andrew Cherlin, "Welfare Reform, Take Two," *New Republic*, June 30, 1979, p. 11.

81. A number of other alternative reform bills were sponsored in the House and Senate although none drew much support. An alternative, for example, introduced by Senator Javits and Congressman Rangel (S. 965, H.R. 4122) "provided somewhat more fiscal relief and benefit increases" than the administration's bill (Harrison H. Donnelly, "Scaled-Down Carter Welfare Plan Announced," *Congressional Quarterly*, May 26, 1979, p. 1013). On the jobs side, Congressmen Perkins and Hawkins, in addition to sponsoring the Carter bills, sponsored an expensive alternative (H.R. 4465) that would have made PSE jobs available on an entitlement basis to welfare recipients (including singles and childless couples). The jobs would have been available under an existing title of CETA.

82. See "Welfare: President Proposes New Legislation to Overhaul Nation's Welfare System," *Bureau of National Affairs Daily Report for Executives*, May 23, 1979, p. G-11. Senator Kennedy supported the legislation (*ibid.*).

83. Daniel P. Moynihan, address before the 1979 Legislative Conference of the National Association of Counties, Washington, D.C., March 13, 1979, p. 8.

84. Daniel P. Moynihan, address before the 1980 Conference of the National Urban League, New York, Aug. 5, 1980, p. 11.

CHAPTER ELEVEN

1. Neal R. Peirce, "The View from the Top of the Carter Campaign," *National Journal*, July 17, 1976, pp. 993–994.

2. Harvey D. Shapiro, "Welfare Reform Revisited: President Jimmy Carter's Program for Better Jobs and Income," in Lester M. Salamon, ed., *Welfare: The Elusive Consensus* (New York: Praeger Special Studies, 1978), p. 215.

3. Daniel P. Moynihan, *The Politics of a Guaranteed Income: The Nixon Administration and the Family Assistance Plan* (New York: Vintage, 1973), p. 190.

4. Vincent J. Burke and Vee Burke, *Nixon's Good Deed: Welfare Reform* (New York: Columbia University Press, 1974), pp. 70–71; Moynihan, *The Politics of a Guaranteed Income*, pp. 179–181.

5. Irving Janis, *Victims of Groupthink* (Boston: Houghton Mifflin, 1972), p. 200.

6. Nicholas Lemann made a similar point about Carter's use of the zero-cost tool: "[Carter] is admirably concerned with reducing the size and cost of govern-

ment. . . . The least believable of Carter's campaign promises—that he'll balance the budget—may be the one he most deeply wants to come true. Hence his injunction [to reform welfare at zero-cost] to Califano.

"What he didn't do, however, was ask Califano and Marshall what all the federal income supplements—Social Security, unemployment, welfare, food stamps, veterans' benefits, pensions and so on—cost and what they did. The president's mind does not comfortably embrace the idea of arguing out welfare program by program—inciting the kind of competitive presentation of views that would stimulate him to figure out where duplication exists, where money is being paid to people who don't need it or need less than they're getting. . . . He makes quantitative judgments where he should be making qualitative ones" (Nicholas Lemann, "Carter's Paper Presidency," *Washington Post*, Sunday Magazine sec., Sept. 3, 1978).

7. See James Fallows' essay on Carter, "The Passionless Presidency," *Atlantic Monthly*, May 1979, p. 45.

8. Shapiro, "Welfare Reform Revisited," p. 214.

9. Robert Shogan, *Promises to Keep* (New York: Cromwell, 1977), p. 197.

10. This seemed to be a general problem for Carter. As James Fallows contended: "Carter believes fifty things, but no one thing. He holds explicit, thorough positions on every issue under the sun, but he has no large view of the relations between them, no line indicating which goals (reducing unemployment? human rights?) will take precedence over which (inflation control? a SALT treaty?) when the goals conflict" (Fallows, "The Passionless Presidency," p. 42).

11. Cited in Bruce Mazlish and Edwin Diamond, *Jimmy Carter* (New York: Simon and Shuster, 1979), p. 235.

12. Shapiro, "Welfare Reform Revisited," p. 177.

BIBLIOGRAPHY

INTERVIEWS

Unless otherwise indicated in the text, verbal quotes come from interviews conducted at the following times:

Aaron, Henry.   November 1978 and April 1979.
Allen, Jodie T.   November 1978.
Barth, Michael.   June 1978 and November 1978.
Bowler, Kenneth.   November 1978.
Bunton, Scott.   October 1979.
Califano, Joseph A., Jr.   October 1979.
Cardwell, James B.   November 1978.
Carp, Bertram.   October 1979.
Champion, Hale.   October 1979.
Congressional Budget Office: William Hoagland, John Korbell, Dave Mundell, Robert Reischauer.   November 1978.
Corman, James C.   October 1980.
Freedman, Henry.   March 1979.
Gufstafson, Tom.   December 1978.
Harris, Robert.   January 1979.
Heineman, Benjamin, Jr.   November 1978.
Income Security Policy Staff: William Barnes, Dave Lindeman, Charles Seagrave, Mark Worthington.   June 1978.
Joe, Thomas.   November 1978.
Kleinberg, David.   June 1978.
Lerman, Robert.   December 1978.
Marcus, Daniel.   November 1978.
Marshall, Raymond.   November 1980.
Michel, Richard.   October 1979.
Moynihan, Daniel.   November 1980.
Nordhaus, William.   October 1979.
Packer, Arnold.   November 1978 and May 1979.
Parham, James.   December 1978.
Raines, Franklin.   November 1978.
Reed, Gary.   June 1978 and November 1978.
Schultze, Charles.   November 1980.
Smith, Wray.   November 1978.
Spring, William.   December 1978.
Springer, William.   December 1978.
Stern, Michael.   February 1979.
Todd, John.   June 1978, December 1978, and May 1979.
Van Lare, Barry.   November 1978.

White, Barry.   December 1978.
Wolf, Douglas.   October 1979.
Woolsey, Suzanne.   November 1978.

BACKGROUND MATERIAL TO CARTER'S WELFARE EFFORTS

Aaron, Henry.   "Financing Welfare Reform and Income Distribution."   Paper presented at a Conference at UCLA, Sept. 29, 1972.   Printed in Institute of Industrial Relations, UCLA.   *Welfare: A National Policy,* pp. 55–64.   Los Angeles: The Institute, 1973.

———.   *Shelter and Subsidies: Who Benefits from Federal Housing Policies?* Washington, D.C.: Brookings Institution, 1972.

———.   *Why Is Welfare So Hard to Reform?*   Washington, D.C.: Brookings Institution, 1973.

———.   "Cautionary Notes on the Experiment."   In Joseph A. Pechman and P. Michael Timpane, eds.   *Work Incentives and Income Guarantees: The New Jersey Negative Income Tax Experiment,* pp. 88–114.   Washington, D.C.: Brookings Institution, 1975.

———.   *Politics and the Professors.*   Washington, D.C.: Brookings Institution, 1977.

Allen, Jodie T.   *A Funny Thing Happened on the Way to the Welfare Reform.* Urban Institute Paper.   Washington, D.C.: The Institute, 1972.

———.   *Perspectives on Income Maintenance: Where Do We Go from Here and How Far?*   Urban Institute Paper.   Washington, D.C.: The Institute, April 1972.

———.   "Vincent J. Burke and Vee Burke, Nixon's Good Deed: Welfare Reform."   *Policy Analysis* 2, no. 4 (Fall 1976): 697–702.

American Enterprise Institute.   *Welfare Reform: Why?*   Round table with Wilbur J. Cohen, Barber B. Conable, Jr., Paul W. MacAvoy, and Abraham A. Ribicoff, May 20, 1976.   Washington, D.C.: The Institute, 1976.

Anderson, Martin.   *Welfare.*   Stanford, Calif.: Hoover Press, Stanford University, 1979.

Barth, Michael C., George J. Carcagno, and John L. Palmer.   *Toward an Effective Income Support System: Problems, Prospects, and Choices.*   Madison, Wisc.: Institute for Research on Poverty, University of Wisconsin, 1974.

Boland, Barbara.   "Participation in the Aid to Families with Dependent Children Program."   In U.S. Congress, Joint Economic Committee, Subcommittee on Fiscal Policy.   *Studies in Public Welfare,* 93rd Cong., 1st sess., Paper no. 12, pt. 1, Nov. 4, 1973.   Washington, D.C.: U.S. Government Printing Office, 1973.

Bowler, M. Kenneth.   *The Nixon Guaranteed Income Proposal: Substance and Process in Policy Change.*   Cambridge, Mass.: Ballinger, 1974.

Browning, Edgar K.   *Redistribution and the Welfare System.*   American Enterprise Institute, Evaluative Study no. 22.   Washington, D.C.: The Institute, July 1975.

Burke, Vincent J., and Vee Burke.   *Nixon's Good Deed: Welfare Reform.*   New York: Columbia University Press, 1974.

Califano, Joseph A., Jr. "The Politics of Innovation and the Revolution in Government Management." Speech before the Washington Chapter of Sigma Delta Chi, April 19, 1967. Washington, D.C.: Office of the White House Press Secretary, 1967.

———. "Congress Has Been Bypassed in Analysis Technology." *Washington Post,* July 13, 1971, p. A-18.

Campbell, Colin D., ed. *Income Redistribution.* Washington, D.C.: American Enterprise Institute, 1977.

Carter, Jimmy. "Urban Policy for the Remainder of the Twentieth Century." Speech delivered in New York City, April 1, 1976. In *The Presidential Campaign, 1976,* vol. 1, pt. 1, pp. 119–125. Washington, D.C.: U.S. Government Printing Office, 1978.

———. "Transcript of Carter Press Conference," Plains, Ga., Aug. 16, 1976. In *The Presidential Campaign, 1976,* vol. 1, pt. 1, pp. 378–383. Washington, D.C.: U.S. Government Printing Office, 1978.

———. "The Family Is the Cornerstone of American Life." Speech delivered to National Conference of Catholic Charities, Oct. 4, 1976. In *A Government as Good as Its People,* pp. 206–212. New York: Simon and Schuster, 1977.

———. "Welfare Reform: Position Paper." In *The Presidential Campaign, 1976,* vol. 1, pt. 1, pp. 607–608. Washington, D.C.: U.S. Government Printing Office, 1978.

Committee for Economic Development. *Welfare Reform and Its Financing.* New York: The Committee, July 1976.

DeWitt, Karen E. "Welfare Report: Administrative Task Force Develops Plans to Overhaul the Welfare System." *National Journal,* Sept. 8, 1973, pp. 1315–1320.

Duke University. *The 1977 Welfare Policy Project.* Durham, N.C.: Institute of Policy Sciences and Public Affairs of Duke University, with the Ford Foundation, 1977. Includes Edward Hamilton and Francine R. Rabinovitz, "Whose Ox Would Be Healed? The Financial Effects of Federalization of Welfare"; Natalie Jaffee, "Attitudes toward Public Welfare Programs and Recipients: A Review of Public Opinion Surveys, 1935–1976"; Abe Lavine, "Administration of Public Welfare in the Case of AFDC"; Sar A. Levitan, "Work and Welfare in the 1920's"; David W. Lyon, "The Dynamics of Welfare Dependency: A Survey"; Herman Miller and Roger Heirrot, "Microsimulation"; William Lee Miller, "Welfare and Values in America"; Lester M. Salamon, "Toward Income Opportunity: Current Thinking on Welfare Reform."

Eccles, Mary. "Sensitive Issues: Welfare, Social Security." *Congressional Quarterly,* Sept. 11, 1976, pp. 2467–2469.

Goodwin, Leonard. *Do the Poor Want to Work?* Washington, D.C.: Brookings Institution, 1972.

Hannan, Michael T., Nancy Tuma, and Lyle P. Groeneveld. *The Impact of Income Maintenance on the Making and Breaking of Marital Unions: Interim Report.* Center for the Study of Welfare Policy, Stanford Research Institute, Research Memorandum no. 28. Stanford, Calif.: The Center, June 1976.

———. *First Dissolutions and Marriages: Impacts in 24 Months of the Seattle and*

Denver Income Maintenance Experiments.   Center for the Study of Welfare Policy, Stanford Research Institute, Research Memorandum no. 35.   Stanford, Calif.: The Center, Aug. 1976.

Harris, Robert.   "Policy Analysis and Policy Development."   *Social Service Review,* Sept. 1973, pp. 360–372.

Hausman, Leonard.   "The Politics of a Guaranteed Income: The Nixon Administration and the Family Assistance Plan—A Review Article."   *Journal of Human Resources* 8 (Fall 1973): 411–421.

Hoffman, Wayne, and Ted Marmor.   "The Politics of Public Assistance Reform: An Essay Review."   *Social Service Review,* March 1976, pp. 11–22.

Holsendolph, Ernest.   "HEW Preparing a Welfare Plan."   *New York Times,* Oct. 27, 1974, p. A-1.

Joe, Tom.   "A Review of the Politics of a Guaranteed Income."   *Social Work,* May 1973, pp. 3, 4, 112–116.

Knott, Jack, and Aaron Wildavsky.   "Jimmy Carter's Theory of Governing."   *Wilson Quarterly,* Winter 1977, pp. 49–67.

Kotz, Nick, and Mary Lynn Kotz.   *A Passion for Equality.*   New York: W. W. Norton, 1977.

Levy, Frank.   "Observations of a Participant."   *Policy Analysis* 1, no. 2 (Spring 1975): 445–450.

———.   "How Big Is the American Underclass."   Graduate School of Public Policy, University of California–Berkeley, Working Paper no. 39.   Berkeley, Calif.: The Graduate School, Nov. 1975.

Lyday, James M.   "An Advocate's Process Outline for Policy Analysis: The Case of Welfare Reform."   *Urban Affairs Quarterly,* June 1972, pp. 385–402.

Lyndon B. Johnson School of Public Affairs, University of Texas at Austin.   *Welfare Reform Policy Research Project,* no. 28, vol. 2.   Austin: The School, 1978.

Lynn, Laurence E., Jr.   "A Decade of Policy Developments in the Income Maintenance System."   In Robert H. Haveman, ed.   *A Decade of Federal Anti-Poverty Programs: Achievements, Failures, and Lessons,* pp. 341–374.   New York: Academic Press, 1977.

———.   "Caspar Weinberger and Welfare Reform."   *Designing Public Policy: A Casebook on the Role of Policy Analysis,* pp. 82–103.   Santa Monica, Calif.: Goodyear, 1980.

Lynn, Laurence E., Jr., and John M. Seidl.   "Policy Analysis at HEW: The Story of the Mega-Proposal."   *Policy Analysis* 1, no. 2 (Spring 1975): 232–273.

"Mega: Income and Employment Policy."   *Policy Analysis* 1, no. 2 (Spring 1975): 344–367.

Moynihan, Daniel P.   *The Politics of a Guaranteed Income: The Nixon Administration and the Family Assistance Plan.*   New York: Vintage, 1973.

Nathan, Richard P.   "Workfare/Welfare."   *New Republic,* Feb. 24, 1973, pp. 19–21.

———.   "Food Stamps and Welfare Reform."   *Policy Analysis* 2, no. 1 (Winter 1976): 61–70.

———.   "Comprehensive Reform vs. Incrementalism: An Exchange of Views between Richard P. Nathan and John L. Palmer." *Journal of the Institute for Socioeconomic Studies* 2, no. 2 (Spring 1977): 1–9.

National Association of Counties. *Welfare Reform: A Plan for Change.* Washington, D.C.: The Association, June 1976.

National Governors' Conference. *National Welfare Reform: A Bicentennial Priority.* Report of the Welfare Reform Task Force, Committee on Human Resources. Washington, D.C.: The Conference, June 1976.

National Urban League. *Income Maintenance: The National Urban League Position.* Washington, D.C.: The League, July 1975.

Packer, Arnold H. "Categorical Public Employment Guarantees: A Proposed Solution to the Poverty Problem." In U.S. Congress, Joint Economic Committee, Subcommittee on Fiscal Policy. *Studies in Public Welfare*, 93rd Cong., 1st sess., Paper no. 9, pt. 1, Aug. 20, 1973, pp. 68–127. Washington, D.C.: U.S. Government Printing Office, 1973.

————. "Employment Guarantees Should Replace the Welfare System." *Challenge*, March-April 1974, pp. 21–27.

Piven, Frances Fox, and Richard A. Cloward. *Regulating the Poor: The Function of Public Welfare.* New York: Pantheon, 1971.

Plotnik, Robert D., and Felicity Skidmore. *Progress against Poverty: A Review of the 1964–1974 Decade.* New York: Academic Press, 1975.

President's Commission on Income Maintenance Programs. *Poverty amid Plenty: The American Paradox.* Report of the Commission. Washington, D.C.: U.S. Government Printing Office, 1969.

Raines, Franklin. "Policy Advocacy: The Case of the Family Assistance Program," pts. A and B. Case nos. C14-77-162 and 163. Kennedy School of Government, Harvard University, Cambridge, Mass., 1977.

Ribicoff, Abraham. "He Left at Half Time." *New Republic*, Feb. 17, 1973, pp. 24–26.

Salamon, Lester M. *Welfare: The Elusive Consensus.* New York: Praeger Special Studies, 1978.

Schorr, Alvin L. *Jubilee for Our Times: A Practical Program for Income Equality.* New York: Columbia University Press, 1977.

Steiner, Gilbert Y. *The State of Welfare.* Washington, D.C.: Brookings Institution, 1971.

————. "Reform Follows Reality: The Growth of Welfare." *Public Interest* 34 (Winter 1974): 47–65.

Storey, James R. "Systems Analysis and Welfare Reform: A Case Study of the Family Assistance Plan." *Policy Sciences* 4 (March 1973): 1–11.

U.S. Congress, Joint Economic Committee, Subcommittee on Fiscal Policy. "Public Income Transfer Programs: The Incidence of Multiple Benefits and the Issues Raised by Their Receipt." *Studies in Public Welfare*, 93rd Cong., 1st sess., Paper no. 1, April 10, 1972. Washington, D.C.: U.S. Government Printing Office, 1972.

————. "Handbook of Public Income Transfer Programs." *Studies in Public Welfare*, 93rd Cong., 1st sess., Paper no. 2, Oct. 16, 1972. Washington, D.C.: U.S. Government Printing Office, 1972.

————. "The Effectiveness of Manpower Training Programs: A Review of Research on the Impact on the Poor." *Studies in Public Welfare*, 93rd Cong., 1st sess., Paper no. 3, Nov. 20, 1972. Washington, D.C.: U.S. Government Printing Office, 1972.

————. "Income Transfer Programs: How They Tax the Poor." *Studies in Public Welfare*, 93rd Cong., 1st sess., Paper no. 4, Dec. 22, 1972. Washington, D.C.: U.S. Government Printing Office, 1972.

————. "Issues in Welfare Administration," pts. 1–3. *Studies in Public Welfare*, 93rd Cong., 1st sess., Paper no. 5, Dec. 31, 1972–March 12, 1973. Washington, D.C.: U.S. Government Printing Office, 1973.

————. "How Public Benefits Are Distributed in Low-Income Areas." *Studies in Public Welfare*, 93rd Cong., 1st sess., Paper no. 6, March 26, 1973. Washington, D.C.: U.S. Government Printing Office, 1973.

————. "Issues in the Coordination of Public Welfare Programs." *Studies in Public Welfare*, 93rd Cong., 1st sess., Paper no. 7, July 2, 1973. Washington, D.C.: U.S. Government Printing Office, 1973.

————. "Income-Tested Social Benefits in New York: Adequacy, Incentives, and Equity." *Studies in Public Welfare*, 93rd Cong., 1st sess., Paper no. 8, July 8, 1973. Washington, D.C.: U.S. Government Printing Office, 1973.

————. "Concepts in Welfare Program Design." *Studies in Public Welfare*, 93rd Cong., 1st sess., Paper no. 9, Aug. 20, 1973. Washington, D.C.: U.S. Government Printing Office, 1973.

————. "The New Supplemental Security Income Program: Impact on Current Benefits and Unresolved Issues." *Studies in Public Welfare*, 93rd Cong., 1st sess., Paper no. 10, Oct. 7, 1973. Washington, D.C.: U.S. Government Printing Office, 1973.

————. "The Labor Market Impacts of the Private Retirement System." *Studies in Public Welfare*, 93rd Cong., 1st sess., Paper no. 11, Oct. 30, 1973. Washington, D.C.: U.S. Government Printing Office, 1973.

————. "The Family, Poverty, and Welfare Programs," pts. 1 and 2. *Studies in Public Welfare*, 93rd Cong., 1st sess., Paper no. 12, Nov. 4, 1973, and Dec. 3, 1973. Washington, D.C.: U.S. Government Printing Office, 1973.

————. "How Income Supplements Can Affect Work Behavior." *Studies in Public Welfare*, 93rd Cong., 1st sess., Paper no. 13, Feb. 18, 1974. Washington, D.C.: U.S. Government Printing Office, 1974.

————. "Public Welfare and Work Incentives: Theory and Practice." *Studies in Public Welfare*, 93rd Cong., 1st sess., Paper no. 14, April 15, 1974. Washington, D.C.: U.S. Government Printing Office, 1974.

U.S. Department of Health, Education, and Welfare. *Summary Report: New Jersey Graduated Work Incentive Experiment*. Washington, D.C.: U.S. Government Printing Office, Dec. 1973.

————. *Income Supplement Program: 1974 HEW Welfare Replacement Proposal*. Technical Analysis Paper no. 11. Washington, D.C.: Office of Income Security Policy, Office of the Assistant Secretary for Planning and Evaluation, Oct. 1976.

Weinberger, Caspar W. "The Reform of Welfare: A National Necessity." *Journal of the Institute for Socioeconomic Studies* 1, no. 1 (Summer 1976): 1–27.

Williams, Walter. *The Struggle for a Negative Income Tax: A Case Study 1965–1970.* Institute of Governmental Research, University of Washington, Public Policy Monograph no. 1.   Seattle: The Institute, 1972.

Worthington, Mark D., and Laurence E. Lynn, Jr.   "Incremental Welfare Reform: A Strategy Whose Time Has Passed." *Public Policy* 25 (Winter 1977): 49–80.

ARTICLES, BOOKS, PAMPHLETS, AND STATEMENTS ON
WELFARE REFORM DURING THE CARTER YEARS

Aaron, Henry, "Discussing Options and Procedures with Henry Aaron." *Public Welfare*, Summer 1977, pp. 12–19.

———.   "Reforming Welfare." *New York Times*, Dec. 12, 1977, p. 35.

———.   "Sightings for the Future in Welfare Reform."   In 104th National Conference on Social Welfare. *The Social Welfare Forum, 1977*, pp. 188–202.   New York: Columbia University Press, 1978.

———.   "Welfare Reform: Why Cost Estimates Increased." *New York Times*, May 24, 1978, p. A-22.

———.   "The Welfare System: A Planner's Dilemmas."   Address before the National Eligibility Workers Association, Third Annual Convention, Raleigh, N.C., Sept. 28, 1978.

———.   "Welfare Reform: What Kind and When?"   Mimeo.   Washington, D.C.: Brookings Institution, Jan. 1979.

———.   *On Social Welfare*, pp. 45–86.   Cambridge, Mass.: Abt Books, 1980.

AFL-CIO, Executive Council on Welfare Reform.   Statement, Feb. 24, 1977.

———.   Statement, Aug. 29, 1977.

———.   Statement, Feb. 24, 1978.

AFL-CIO, Public Employment Department.   "The Welfare Issue: What's at Stake for Public Service Employees?"   July 11, 1977.   Reprinted in U.S. Senate, Finance Committee. *Welfare Reform Proposals*, 95th Cong., 2nd sess., pt. 3, pp. 701–735.   Washington, D.C.: U.S. Government Printing Office, 1978.

Allen, Jodie T.   "Let's Not Talk about Welfare Reform." *Washington Post*, Jan. 10, 1977, p. A-25.

———.   "Women's Roles and Welfare Reform: An Exchange of Views." *Challenge*, Jan./Feb. 1978, pp. 49–50.

American Public Welfare Association. *Welfare Reform and the Ninety-Fifth Congress.*   Washington, D.C.: The Association, Dec. 1978.

Anderson, Martin.   "Welfare Reform on 'the Same Old Rocks.'" *New York Times*, Nov. 27, 1978, op-ed page.

Andrews, Mark.   "84% Want to Scrap Current Welfare System: Poll." *New York Daily News*, Aug. 15, 1977.

Bacon, Donald.   "Another Go at the Welfare Mess: Will It Work?"   *U.S. News and World Report,* Aug. 8, 1977, pp. 45–48.

"Baker and Bellmon Push Guaranteed Income Plan."   *Human Events,* April 1, 1978, p. 1.

Barth, Michael C.   "Welfare Policy: Near and Longer Term."   *Journal of the Institute for Socioeconomic Studies* 5, no. 3 (Autumn 1980): 38–49.

Beall, J. Glen, Jr.   "Comprehensive Welfare Reform: Congressional Prospects."   *Journal of the Institute for Socioeconomic Studies* 2, no. 1 (Spring 1977): 20–27.

Bethell, Tom.   "Treating Poverty."   *Harper's,* Feb. 1980, pp. 16–24.

Blum, David.   "Jarvis Fever."   *New Republic,* June 24, 1978, pp. 14–16.

Broder, David.   "Carter Set Stage on Welfare."   *Charlotte Observer,* Aug. 10, 1977, p. 19-A.

Broder, David, and Spencer Rich.   "Carter Still Sees Hope for Passing Welfare Revision."   *Washington Post,* Jan. 26, 1978, p. A-1.

Broder, David, and Mary Russell.   "Carter Aides See Delay in Passing Welfare Revision."   *Washington Post,* Jan. 25, 1978, p. A-1.

Brooke, Edward W.   "The Objectives of Welfare Reform."   In 104th National Conference on Social Welfare. *The Social Welfare Forum, 1977,* pp. 203–212.   New York: Columbia University Press, 1978.

Burke, Vee.   "Welfare Reform Issue Brief."   U.S. Library of Congress, Legislative Research Service, Education and Public Welfare Division, no. IB77069, Oct. 3, 1979.

"Byrd Says Energy Bill to Stall Two Top Issues."   *Detroit News,* April 24, 1977, p. 20.

Califano, Joseph A., Jr.   "Statement of Joseph A. Califano, Jr., Secretary of Health, Education, and Welfare."   *HEW News,* Jan. 26, 1977.

———.   "Remarks by Secretary Joseph A. Califano, Jr., before the Washington Press Club Luncheon."   HEW Press Office, April 27, 1977.

———.   "Interview with Joseph Califano."   *CBS Morning News,* May 3, 1977, pp. 6–9.

———.   "Statement of Joseph A. Califano, Jr., on Welfare Reform."   *HEW News,* May 25, 1977.

———.   "The Honorable Joseph A. Califano, Jr., Secretary of HEW: Meeting with the Press on Welfare Reform."   Pro-Typists, Inc., HEW Press Office, July 20, 1977.

———.   "Interview with Joseph Califano."   *CBS News—Face the Nation,* Aug. 7, 1977, pp. 1–15.

———.   "Statement by the Secretary of Health, Education, and Welfare."   *Public Welfare,* Summer 1977, p. 12.

———.   "Putting the Public into Public Policy Development."   *Journal of the Institute for Socioeconomic Studies* 3, no. 2 (Summer 1978): 1–8.

"Califano Optimistic over Differences with Long."   *Houston Post,* Aug. 18, 1977, p. 12.

Carleson, Robert B.   "The Reagan Welfare Reforms."   *Journal of the Institute for Socioeconomic Studies* 5, no. 2 (Summer 1980): 1–13.

"Carter, Congress and Welfare: A Long Road." *Congressional Quarterly*, Aug. 13, 1977, pp. 1699–1703.

"Carter's in a Bind on Jobs Portion of His Welfare Program." *Detroit News*, Aug. 31, 1977, p. B-5.

"Carter's Sweetening of His Welfare Plan Blunts Some Criticism." *St. Louis Post-Dispatch*, Aug. 7, 1977, p. 5-A.

Charlton, Linda. "Joseph Anthony Califano, Jr." *New York Times*, Dec. 24, 1976, p. A-11.

"The Choices for Carter and Congress." *National Journal*, Jan. 8, 1977, pp. 52–55.

Cloward, Richard A., and Frances Fox Piven. "The Welfare Vaudevillian." *The Nation*, Sept. 22, 1979, pp. 236–239.

Copeland, Warren R. "Welfare Reform and Social Change." *Christian Century*, May 31, 1978, pp. 580–581.

Corman, James. "An Interview with James Corman." *Bureau of National Affairs Daily Report for Executives*, Dec. 22, 1978, pp. J-5–J-7.

Cowan, Edward. "Republicans Contend Energy Levies Are Designed as General Tax Raise." *New York Times*, April 26, 1977, p. A-20.

Currie, Elliot. "A Piece of Complicated Gimmickry." *The Nation*, Sept. 17, 1977, pp. 230–233.

Danziger, Sheldon, Irwin Garfinkel, and Robert H. Haveman. "Poverty, Welfare, and Earnings: A New Approach." *Challenge*, Sept./Oct. 1979, pp. 28–34.

Demkovich, Linda E. "Carter Gets Some Outside Advice for His Welfare Reform Package." *National Journal*, April 30, 1977, pp. 673–675.

———. "Welfare Reform: Can Carter Succeed Where Nixon Failed?" *National Journal*, Aug. 27, 1977, pp. 1328–1334.

———. "Corman of California: The House's Man on Welfare." *National Journal*, Oct. 1, 1977, pp. 1523–1525.

———. "Carter's Welfare Reform Package Is Being Re-formed on the Hill." *National Journal*, Dec. 17, 1977, pp. 1958–1961.

———. "The Numbers are the Issue in the Debate over Welfare Reform." *National Journal*, April 22, 1978, pp. 633–637.

———. "State and Local Officials Rescue Welfare Reform—Too Late." *National Journal*, June 24, 1978, pp. 1007–1009.

———. "Leaving the Dead Cat at the Door." *National Journal*, July 15, 1978, p. 1137.

———. "A Preview of Coming Attractions." *National Journal*, Sept. 23, 1978, p. 1519.

———. "Good News and Bad News for Welfare Reform." *National Journal*, Dec. 30, 1978, pp. 2061–2063.

———. "Another Chance for Welfare Reform." *National Journal*, March 10, 1979, p. 404.

———. "It May Be a Race against the Clock for Welfare Reform Package in 1980." *National Journal*, Jan. 26, 1980, pp. 150–152.

————. "If Given the Opportunity." *National Journal,* March 1, 1980, p. 367.

————. "How Reagan Would Turn the Welfare System Back to the States." *National Journal,* Oct. 25, 1980, p. 1809.

Demkovich, Linda E., and Joel Haveman. "Welfare Reform: Does Carter Have the Key?" *Los Angeles Times,* May 18, 1977, sec. 5, p. 2.

Donnelly, Harrison H. "Scaled-Down Carter Welfare Plan Announced." *Congressional Quarterly,* May 26, 1979, pp. 1013–1014.

Donsky, Martin. "Compromise Talks Open in Effort to Salvage Some Welfare Reform." *Congressional Quarterly,* April 29, 1978, pp. 1064–1068.

Doolittle, Frederick, Frank Levy, and Michael Wiseman. "The Mirage of Welfare Reform." *Public Interest* 47 (Spring 1977): 62–87.

Drew, Elizabeth. "In Search of a Definition." *New Yorker,* Aug. 27, 1979, pp. 45–73.

Dumpson, James R. "Social Welfare." In *The State of Black America, 1978,* pp. 112–120. Washington, D.C.: National Urban League, 1978.

Evans, B. Stanton. "At Home" column. *National Review Bulletin,* Nov. 18, 1977, p. B-174.

"Experiment Finds Cash Grants Tend to Split Welfare Families." *New York Times,* May 21, 1978, p. 50.

Fallows, James. "The Passionless Presidency, Part I." *Atlantic Monthly,* May 1979, pp. 33–48.

————. "The Passionless Presidency, Part II." *Atlantic Monthly,* June 1979, pp. 75–81.

Friedman, Barry, and Leonard Hausman. "Welfare in Retreat: A Dilemma for the Federal System." *Public Policy* 25, no. 1 (Winter 1977): 25–48.

"Future Planner or Past President." *New York Times,* May 1, 1977, p. A-16.

Gallup, George. "Public Wants Cheaters Off Welfare Rolls." *Houston Post,* June 26, 1977, p. 3-B.

Garfinkel, Irwin. "What's Wrong with Welfare." *Social Work* 23 (May 1978): 185–191.

Gest, Kathryn Waters. "Welfare Reform: Carter Studying Options." *Congressional Quarterly,* April 30, 1977, p. 796.

————. "Welfare Reform: Congress Is Skeptical." *Congressional Quarterly,* Sept. 24, 1977, pp. 2011–2013.

Gilder, George. "The Coming Welfare Crisis." *Policy Review* 11 (Winter 1980): 25–36.

Gordon, Nancy M. "Women's Roles and Welfare Reform: An Exchange of Views." *Challenge,* Jan./Feb. 1978, pp. 47–48, 50.

Hannan, Michael T., Nancy Brandon Tuma, and Lyle P. Groeneveld. "Income and Marital Events: Evidence from the Income Maintenance Experiments." *American Journal of Sociology* 82 (May 1977): 1186–1211.

Harris, Louis. "Welfare Reform Support Unprecedented." *Houston Post,* Sept. 15, 1977, p. 2-D.

Haveman, Joel, and Rochelle L. Stanfield. "Housing as Part of Welfare: An Agency Battles for Its Turf." *National Journal,* July 30, 1977, pp. 1190–1192.

"House Panel Approves Welfare Reform Plan." *New York Times*, Feb. 9, 1978, p. A-13.

"House Panel Tells Califano of Problems." *Detroit News*, May 5, 1977, p. E-8.

Iglehart, John K. "HEW's Califano Wants to Set the Great Society in Motion." *National Journal*, June 25, 1977, pp. 990–993.

"Is Real Welfare Reform an Impossible Dream?" *Nation's Business*, Jan. 1979, pp. 34–39.

Jackson, Jesse. "Welfare Reform Needs a Big Stride." *Detroit News*, Aug. 30, 1977, p. 7-B.

Joe, Barbara E. "Reagan's Welfare Fraud." *Washington Monthly*, Oct. 1980, pp. 34–36.

Joe, Tom. "Triple Track: A Strategy of Income Security and Employment Opportunities for Low Income Americans." Mimeo. Washington, D.C.: Lewin and Associates, April 25, 1977.

Jordan, Vernon E., Jr. "To the Urban League's Jordan, the Plan Is 'Barely Acceptable.'" *Los Angeles Times*, Aug. 14, 1977, sec. 4, p. 3.

Kaplan, Seth. "HEW vs. HUD." *New Republic*, Aug. 6 and 13, 1977, pp. 15–16.

Kilpatrick, James J. "Welfare: Hang on to Mess We Have." *New Orleans Times-Picayune*, Oct. 12, 1977, p. 20.

Korbell, John J., and G. William Hoagland. *Welfare Reform: Issues, Objectives, and Approaches.* U.S. Congress, Congressional Budget Office, Background Paper, July 1977. Washington, D.C.: U.S. Government Printing Office, 1977.

Kotz, Nick. "The Politics of Welfare Reform." *New Republic*, May 14, 1977, pp. 16–21.

Lekachman, Robert. "Welfare Reform: A Critique." *Social Policy*, Jan./Feb. 1978, center insert.

Leman, Christopher. *The Collapse of Welfare Reform: Political Institutions, Policy, and the Poor in Canada and the United States.* Cambridge, Mass.: MIT Press, 1980.

Lemann, Nicholas. "Carter's Paper Presidency." *Washington Post*, Sept. 3, 1978, pp. C-1 and C-5.

Lenkowsky, Leslie. "The Gaps in Carter's Welfare Plan." *Wall Street Journal*, July 7, 1977, p. 12.

———. "Welfare Reform and the Liberals." *Commentary*, March 1979, pp. 56–61.

Lerman, Robert I. *Welfare Reform Alternatives: Employment Subsidy Proposals versus the Negative Income Tax.* Institute for Research on Poverty, University of Wisconsin, Madison, Special Report no. 12. Madison, Wisc.: The Institute, Aug. 1977.

Levy, Frank. "What Ronald Reagan Can Teach the United States about Welfare Reform." In Walter Burnham and Martha Weinberg, eds. *American Politics and Public Policy*, pp. 336–363. Cambridge, Mass.: MIT Press, 1978.

Levy, Frank, and James R. Storey. "The Chances for Welfare Reform." *Washington Post*, June 3, 1978, op-ed page.

Long, Russell B.   "Statement of Senator Russell B. on Welfare Reform."   Press release, Aug. 15, 1977.

Marshall, Ray.   "The New Administration's Program for the Poor."   In 104th National Conference on Social Welfare.   *The Social Welfare Forum, 1977*, pp. 215–220.   New York: Columbia University Press, 1978.

————.   "Targeting Jobs for the Poor."   *Washington Post*, April 2, 1980, op-ed page.

McGrory, Mary.   "Welfare Reform: Is There Real Hope?"   *Los Angeles Times*, Sept. 16, 1977, sec. 2, p. 7.

McPherson, Myra.   "Hidden Conflict in Welfare Planning."   *Washington Post*, Aug. 2, 1977, p. A-2.

Miller, Arthur H.   "Will Public Attitudes Defeat Welfare Reform?"   *Public Welfare*, Summer 1978, pp. 48–54.

Mitchell, Grayson.   "$4,300 Minimum Income for Family of Four Studied."   *Los Angeles Times*, April 22, 1977, p. 6.

————.   "Corman Would Deny Welfare to Those Who Refuse to Work."   *Los Angeles Times*, Nov. 1, 1977, sec. 1, p. 5.

Moynihan, Daniel P.   "Moynihan on Welfare: From FAP to the Carter Plan."   *National Journal*, Jan. 28, 1978, pp. 146–148.

————.   "The Rocky Road to Welfare Reform."   *Journal of the Institute for Socioeconomic Studies* 3, no. 2 (Spring 1978): 1–10.

————.   "Interview with Daniel Moynihan: Some Negative Evidence about the Negative Income Tax."   *Fortune*, Dec. 4, 1978, pp. 145–147.

————.   Address before the 1979 Legislative Conference of the National Association of Counties, Washington, D.C., March 13, 1979.

————.   Address before the 1980 Conference of the National Urban League, New York, Aug. 5, 1980.

"Moynihan Says Recent Studies Raise Doubts about 'Negative Income Tax' Proposal."   *New York Times*, Nov. 16, 1978, p. A-2.

Nathan, Richard P., Robert F. Cook, Janet M. Galchick, and V. Lane Rawlins.   *Monitoring the Public Service Employment Program: The Second Round*.   National Commission on Manpower Policy, Special Report no. 32.   Washington, D.C.: The Commission, March 1979.

National Governors' Conference.   *National Welfare Reform: A Program for Change*.   National Governors Conference Task Force Report.   Washington, D.C.: The Conference, Feb. 1977.

National Urban League, Research Department.   "Toward a Viable Economic Maintenance System for All Groups: Guiding Principles."   Prepared for the HEW–Black Welfare Reform Task Force, April 7, 1977.

————.   *The Myth of Income Cushions for Blacks*.   Washington, D.C.: The League, 1980.

"No. 3 GOP'er in House Backs Welfare Reform."   *Birmingham Post-Herald*, Aug. 8, 1977, p. A-7.

Oh, John C. H.   "The Presidency and Public Welfare Policy."   *Presidential Studies Quarterly* 8, no. 4 (Fall 1978): 377–390.

Packer, Arnold.   "Women's Roles and Welfare Reform: An Exchange of Views."   *Challenge*, Jan./Feb. 1978, pp. 45–47.

————. "The Administration's Approach: The Premise of the Better Jobs and Income Proposal." In State of Washington, Department of Social and Health Services. *Proceedings of the 1978 Conference on the Seattle and Denver Income Maintenance Experiments,* pp. 29–36. Seattle: The Department, Oct. 1979.

Palmer, John, ed. *Creating Jobs.* Washington, D.C.: Brookings Institution, 1978.

Peters, Charles. "More Dollars and More Dollars and, etc." *New York Times,* May 15, 1978, op-ed page.

Public Welfare 5, no. 2 (Spring 1977) special issue, esp. 17–22.

Quinn, Jane Bryant. "Somewhere Along the Way, Welfare Program Switched." *Wichita Eagle,* Aug. 16, 1977, p. 12-A.

Rein, Martin, and Lee Rainwater. "How Large Is the Welfare Class?" *Challenge,* Sept./Oct. 1977, pp. 20–23.

Rence, Cynthia, and Michael Wiseman. "The California Welfare Reform Act and Participation in AFDC." *Journal of Human Resources* 13, no. 1 (Winter 1978): 37–59.

Rich, Spencer. "Moynihan Unhappy at Welfare Plans." *Washington Post,* Oct. 1, 1977, p. A-8.

————. "Minimum Salary of $10,500 Backed for Some Welfare Public Service Jobs." *Washington Post,* Feb. 7, 1978, p. A-3.

————. "Major Welfare Revision Is Dead for This Congress." *Washington Post,* June 23, 1978, p. A-2.

————. "'Nab-a-Dad' Program: Hostage to Welfare Bills." *Washington Post,* July 28, 1979, p. A-4.

————. "House Approves a Version of Carter Welfare Plan." *Washington Post,* Nov. 8, 1979, p. A-2.

————. "Welfare Benefits Greatly Eroded by Long Inflation." *Washington Post,* July 7, 1980, p. A-1.

Roberts, Steven V. "Modest Welfare Reforms Given a Chance This Time." *New York Times,* Nov. 4, 1979, p. E-3.

Rosenbaum, David E. "Califano Outlines Welfare Aid Linked to Job Requirement." *New York Times,* May 26, 1977, p. A-1.

————. "President Stresses Welfare Limit Despite Warning." *New York Times,* May 27, 1977, p. A-11.

————. "Carter Aides Predict a Savings of Billions in New Welfare Plan." *New York Times,* June 2, 1977, p. A-1.

————. "Much More than Dollars Figure in Welfare Costs." *New York Times,* June 26, 1977, p. E-3.

————. "Ullman Is Critical of Welfare Plan; Carter May Consider Delaying It." *New York Times,* Aug. 3, 1977, p. A-1.

————. "Senators Fighting Carter on Welfare." *New York Times,* Oct. 3, 1977, p. A-1.

————. "Outlook Is Gloomy on Welfare Changes." *New York Times,* Dec. 11, 1977, p. A-1.

————. "House Passes a Bill Mandating Minimum for Welfare Checks." *New York Times,* Nov. 8, 1979, p. A-1.

Schaffly, Phyllis. "Carter's Welfare Plan Is Costly." *New Orleans Times-Picayune*, Oct. 3, 1977, sec. 5, p. 14.

Schramm, Martin. "Califano's Version of Firing Disputed." *Washington Post*, July 21, 1979, p. A-1.

Scott, Austin. "Carter Aides Cite Difficulties Posed by Welfare Goals." *Washington Post*, May 26, 1977, p. A-1.

Scott, Austin, and David Broder. "Tug-of-War over Housing Subsidies." *Washington Post*, July 14, 1977, A-1.

Scott, Austin, and Spencer Rich. "Carter's Welfare Proposals Face Sharp Challenges in the House." *Washington Post*, Nov. 27, 1977, p. A-7.

Shogan, Robert. *Promises to Keep.* New York: Cromwell, 1977.

Singer, James W. "The Welfare Package: 1.4 Million Jobs, 1.4 Million Questions." *National Journal,* Nov. 12, 1977, pp. 1764–1768.

———. "The Unassuming Man at Labor Has Had a Big Year." *National Journal*, March 18, 1978, pp. 416–420.

"Six Welfare Issues." *Christian Science Monitor*, March 9, 1977, editorial page.

"Sometimes the Concept Works." *National Journal*, July 16, 1977, p. 1106.

Sundquist, James L. "Jimmy Carter as Public Administrator: An Appraisal at Mid-Term." *Public Administration Review*, Jan./Feb. 1979, pp. 3–11.

Todd, John, and Henry Aaron. "The Use of Income Maintenance Experiment Findings in Public Policy, 1977–1978." In *Proceedings of the Industrial Relations Research Association, 1978*, pp. 46–56. Madison, Wisc.: University of Wisconsin, 1978.

"Transcript of the Carter News Conference on Domestic and Foreign Matters." *New York Times*, May 27, 1977, p. A-10.

"U.S. Senate to Delay Welfare Reform." *Los Angeles Times*, April 24, 1977, p. 6.

Washington, State of, Department of Social and Health Services. *Proceedings of the 1978 Conference on the Seattle and Denver Income Maintenance Experiments.* Seattle, Wash.: The Department, Oct. 1979.

Weil, Gordon L. *The Welfare Debate of 1978.* White Plains, N.Y.: Institute for Socioeconomic Studies, 1978.

Weinberger, Caspar. "Carter's Political Chips Undercut Welfare Plan." *San Diego Union*, Sept. 25, 1977, p. C-1.

Weisman, Steven R. "Clash between Carter and Moynihan Slows Welfare Reform Plan." *New York Times*, April 1, 1979, p. A-1.

———. "Carter Offers Welfare Revisions; Would Cut Costs in This Region." *New York Times*, May 24, 1979, p. A-1.

"Welfare: A Surprising Test." *Newsweek*, Nov. 27, 1978, pp. 33–34.

"Welfare Plan a 'Tax Relief for Millions.'" *St. Louis Post-Dispatch*, Aug. 8, 1977, p. 1.

"Welfare: President Proposes New Legislation to Overhaul Nation's Welfare System." *Bureau of National Affairs Daily Report for Executives*, May 23, 1979, pp. G-9–G-11.

"Welfare Reform: A Look at the Reagan Record." *National Journal*, July 19, 1980, p. 1179.

"The Welfare Reform Amendments Act." *Congressional Digest*, Jan. 1980, entire issue.

"Welfare Reform Plan Is Delayed."   *San Francisco Chronicle*, April 26, 1977, p. 2.

"What Price Welfare."   *Houston Post*, Dec. 13, 1977, p. 2-D, editorial.

Whitman, David.   "The Class Conflict behind the Miami Riot."   *USA Today*, Nov. 1980, pp. 23–25.

Woolsey, Suzanne.   "Relating Budget and Human Concerns with Suzanne Woolsey."   *Public Welfare*, Summer 1977, pp. 19–23.

Wooten, James.   "Doubts on Success of Carter's Welfare Reform Package Are Increasing."   *New York Times*, Aug. 2, 1977, p. A-14.

"Working to Reform Welfare."   *Time*, Aug. 15, 1977, pp. 6–8.

"Worst Obstacles Yet to Come for Welfare Program."   *New Orleans Times-Picayune*, Dec. 19, 1977, p. 8.

MATERIALS FROM THE PUBLIC RECORD

U.S. CONGRESS: HEARINGS

House Committees on Agriculture, Education and Labor, and Ways and Means, Welfare Reform Subcommittee.   *Joint Hearings on H.R. 9030, a Bill to Replace the Existing Federal Welfare Programs.*   95th Cong., 1st sess., 1977: Sept. 19–21 (pt. 1); Sept. 29–30 and Oct. 11–12 (pt. 2); Oct. 14 and 31 and Nov. 1 (pt. 3); Nov. 2–4 (pt. 4); New York, N.Y., Nov. 9–10 (pt. 5); Salem, Ore., Nov. 9 and Oakland, Calif., Nov. 14 (pt. 6); Minneapolis, Minn., Nov. 16, and West Memphis, Ark., Nov. 17 (pt. 7); Los Angeles, Calif., Nov. 17–18 (pt. 8); Miami, Fla., Nov. 22, Harrisburg, Pa., Nov. 22, and Hawaiian Islands, Nov. 21–23 (pt. 9).   Washington, D.C.: U.S. Government Printing Office, 1977.

House Budget Committee, Task Force on Distributive Impacts of Budget and Economic Policies.   *President Carter's Welfare Reform Proposals*, 95th Cong., 1st sess., Oct. 13, 14, and 21, 1977.   Washington, D.C.: U.S. Government Printing Office, 1977.

House Budget Committee, Task Force on State and Local Government.   *Fiscal Impact of Welfare Programs on States and Localities*, 95th Cong., 1st sess., Oct. 27, 1977.   Washington, D.C.: U.S. Government Printing Office, 1977.

House Education and Labor Committee, Subcommittee on Employment Opportunities.   *Welfare Jobs Legislation*, 96th Cong., 1st sess., Oct. 25, 1979.   Washington, D.C.: U.S. Government Printing Office, 1979.

————.   *Welfare Reform Legislation*, 96th Cong., 1st sess., June 15, 18, 20, 22, 26, 1980.   Washington, D.C.: U.S. Government Printing Office, 1980.

House Ways and Means Committee, Subcommittee on Public Assistance and Unemployment Compensation.   *Special HEW Report on Welfare Reform*, 95th Cong., 1st sess., May 4, 1977.   Washington, D.C.: U.S. Government Printing Office, 1977.

————.   *Welfare Reform Legislation*, 96th Cong., 1st sess., June 15, 18, 20, 22, 26, and 27, 1979.   Washington, D.C.: U.S. Government Printing Office, 1979.

Senate Finance Committee, Subcommittee on Public Assistance.   *Public Assistance Amendments of 1977*, 95th Cong., 1st sess., July 12, 18, 19, and 20, 1977.   Washington, D.C.: U.S. Government Printing Office, 1977.

————.   *Welfare Reform Proposals*, 95th Cong., 2nd sess., 1978: Feb. 7 and 9 (pt.

1); April 17–18 (pt. 2); April 25–26 (pt. 3); May 1–2 (pt. 4); May 4 (pt.
5). Washington, D.C.: U.S. Government Printing Office, 1978.

———. *Welfare Block Grant Fiscal Relief Proposal*, 95th Cong., 2nd sess., Sept. 12,
1978. Washington, D.C.: U.S. Government Printing Office, 1978.

———. *Welfare Research and Experimentation*, 95th Cong., 2nd sess., Nov. 15–17,
1978. Washington, D.C.: U.S. Government Printing Office, 1978.

———. *How to Think about Welfare Reform for the 1980's*, 96th Cong., 2nd sess.,
Feb. 6 and 7, 1980. Washington, D.C.: U.S. Government Printing Office,
1980.

Senate Committee on Human Resources. *Better Jobs and Income Act, 1978*, 95th
Cong., 2nd sess., March 22–23, 1978. Washington, D.C.: U.S. Government
Printing Office, 1978.

PRESIDENT CARTER'S STATEMENTS ON WELFARE REFORM

"Remarks and a Question-and-Answer Session with Department Employees at
the Department of Health, Education, and Welfare," Feb. 16, 1977. In *Public
Papers of the Presidents of the United States: Jimmy Carter, 1977*, vol. 1, pp. 158–
174. Washington, D.C.: U.S. Government Printing Office, 1977.

"Remarks of the President, Joseph A. Califano, Secretary of HEW, and Dr. F.
Ray Marshall, Secretary of Labor: Question and Answer Session," May 2,
1977. Washington, D.C.: Office of the White House Press Secretary, 1977.

"Statement by the President," May 2, 1977. Washington, D.C.: Office of the
White House Press Secretary, 1977.

"Question and Answer Session with a Group of Editors, Publishers, and Broad-
casters," May 21, 1977. In *Public Papers of the Presidents of the United States:
Jimmy Carter, 1977*, vol. 1, pp. 951–952. Washington, D.C.: U.S. Government
Printing Office, 1977.

"Press Conference," May 27, 1977. Washington, D.C.: Office of the White
House Press Secretary, 1977.

"Interview with the National Black Network," July 22, 1977. In *Public Papers of
the President of the United States: Jimmy Carter, 1977*, vol. 2, pp. 1344–
1345. Washington, D.C.: U.S. Government Printing Office, 1977.

"Remarks of the President to National Urban League Convention," July 25,
1977. Washington, D.C.: Office of the White House Press Secretary, 1977.

"Press Conference No. 12," July 28, 1977. Washington, D.C.: Office of the
White House Press Secretary, 1977.

"Message to Congress," Aug. 6, 1977. Washington, D.C.: Office of the White
House Press Secretary, 1977.

"Press Conference No. 13," Aug. 6, 1977. Washington, D.C.: Office of the
White House Press Secretary, 1977.

"Remarks of the President at Democratic National Committee Meeting," Oct. 7,
1977. Washington, D.C.: Office of the White House Press Secretary, 1977.

"Remarks in a Panel Discussion at a Public Policy Forum Sponsored by the
Community Services Administration," Oct. 21, 1977. In *Public Papers of the
Presidents of the United States: Jimmy Carter, 1977*, vol. 2, pp. 1843–
1845. Washington, D.C.: U.S. Government Printing Office, 1977.

"Remarks before the National Conference on Fraud, Abuse and Error, and Memorandum from the President for the Secretaries of HEW, Agriculture, Labor, HUD and the Directors of OMB and the Community Services Administration," Dec. 13, 1978. In *Public Papers of the Presidents of the United States: Jimmy Carter, 1978*, vol. 2, pp. 2228–2233. Washington, D.C.: U.S. Government Printing Office, 1978.

"Message to the Congress," May 23, 1979. Washington, D.C.: Office of the White House Press Secretary, 1979.

U.S. DEPARTMENT OF HEALTH, EDUCATION, AND WELFARE: PRESS RELEASES ON CARTER'S WELFARE REFORM PROPOSALS

"Statement by Joseph A. Califano, Jr., Secretary of Health, Education and Welfare." *HEW News*, Jan. 26, 1977.

"Remarks by Secretary Joseph A. Califano, Jr., before the Washington Press Club Luncheon," April 27, 1977. Washington, D.C.: HEW Press Office, 1977.

Report on the 1977 Welfare Study: The Secretary's Report to the President. Supp. 1, vols. 1 and 2: *The Consulting Group on Welfare Reform*; Supp. 2, vols. 1 and 2: *National Outreach Efforts: Reports from the Regions*; Supp. 3, vols. 1–4: *Public Hearing, March 10, 1977*. Washington, D.C.: Office of the Assistant Secretary for Planning and Evaluation, HEW, May 3, 1977.

"Statement of Secretary Joseph A. Califano, Jr., on Welfare Reform." *HEW News*, May 25, 1977.

"The Honorable Joseph A. Califano, Jr., Secretary of HEW: Meeting with the Press on Welfare Reform." Pro-typists, Inc., HEW Press Office, July 20, 1977.

"Welfare Reform." *HEW News*, Aug. 6, 1977, rev. Aug. 18, with errata sheet added on Aug. 29, 1977.

"Better Jobs and Income Act, H.R. 9030: A Summary and Sectional Explanation," Sept. 13, 1977. Washington, D.C.: Office of the Secretary, 1977.

"Staff Papers on the Better Jobs and Income Act, H.R. 9030," Oct. 3, 1977. Office of the Secretary, Washington, D.C., 1977.

"President Carter's Proposal for Welfare Reform: Work and Training Opportunities Act of 1979 and the Social Welfare Reform Amendments of 1979," May 23, 1979. Washington, D.C.: HEW Press Office, 1979.

ANALYSES OF THE ECONOMIC AND ADMINISTRATIVE IMPACT OF CARTER'S WELFARE REFORM PROPOSALS

American Enterprise Institute. *The Administration's 1979 Welfare Reform Proposal*. Legislative Analysis no. 7. Washington, D.C.: The Institute, Sept. 1979.

American Federation of State, County, and Municipal Employees, Department of Public Policy Analysis. *The Carter Welfare Plan: A Critical Analysis*. Washingtgon, D.C.: The Department, Sept. 1977.

American Public Welfare Association, National Council of State Public Welfare Administrators. "Technical Paper on H.R. 9030." In House Committees on Agriculture, Education and Labor, and Ways and Means, Welfare Reform Subcommittee. *Joint Hearings on H.R. 9030, a Bill to Replace the Existing Federal Welfare Programs*, 95th Cong., 1st sess., pt. 3, Nov. 1, 1977, pp. 1893–1918. Washington, D.C.: U.S. Government Printing Office, 1977.

Anderson, Martin. "Why Carter's Welfare Reform Plan Failed." *Policy Review* 5 (Summer 1978): 37–39. A fuller version is in Anderson. *Welfare*, pp. 169–209. Stanford, Calif.: Hoover Press, Stanford University, 1979.

Bawden, Lee D. "A Comparison of the Existing System and the Proposed System with Respect to the Adequacy of Benefit Levels," Oct. 14, 1977. In House Budget Committee, Task Force on Distributive Impacts of Budget and Economic Policies. *President Carter's Welfare Proposals*, hearings, 95th Cong., 1st sess., pp. 70–78. Washington, D.C.: U.S. Government Printing Office, 1977.

Bell, Carolyn Shaw. "The Carter Bill—Is It Welfare Reform?" *Journal of the Institute for Socioeconomic Studies* 3, no. 2 (Summer 1978): 9–19.

Blong, Adele, and Timothy Casey. "Administration's Welfare Reform Plan." New York, N.Y.: Center on Social Welfare Policy and Law, Sept. 2, 1977.

California, State of, Health and Welfare Agency. *Better Jobs and Income Act: H.R. 9030.* Health and Welfare Agency Staff Analysis. Sacramento, Calif.: The Agency, Oct. 31, 1977.

Danziger, Sheldon, Robert Haveman, Eugene Smolensky, and Karl Tauber. *The Urban Impacts of the Program for Better Jobs and Income.* Institute for Research on Poverty, University of Wisconsin, Discussion Paper no. 538-79. Madison, Wisc.: The Institute, Jan. 1979.

Fersh, Robert J. *Program for Better Jobs and Income.* American Public Welfare Association Staff Analysis. Washington, D.C.: The Association, Nov. 10, 1977.

Halpern, Janice D., and Sharon J. Spaight. *Welfare Reform: An Analysis of the Financial Impact on the Northeast Region of Welfare Reform Proposals.* Federal Reserve Bank, Boston Research Department, Special Study. Boston: The Bank, July 1978.

Hoffman, Wayne Lee. *Work Incentives and Implicit Tax Rates in the Carter Welfare Reform Plan.* Urban Institute Welfare Reform Policy Analysis Series no. 2. Washington, D.C.: The Institute, Dec. 1977.

————. *The Earned Income Tax Credit: Welfare Reform or Tax Relief.* Urban Institute Welfare Reform Policy Analysis Series no. 5. Washington, D.C.: The Institute, Sept. 1978.

Keith, John P., and Joseph M. Thomas. "The Impact of the Carter Welfare Reform Proposal on the New York Region: A Preliminary Assessment." *Journal of the Institute for Socioeconomic Studies* 2, no. 4 (Autumn 1977): 65–76.

Levy, Frank. *The Harried Staffer's Guide to Current Welfare Reform Proposals.* Urban Institute Welfare Reform Policy Analysis Series no. 4. Washington, D.C.: The Institute, Aug. 1978.

Lyndon B. Johnson School of Public Affairs. University of Texas at Austin. *Welfare Reform Policy Research Project*, no. 28, vols. 1 and 3. Austin: The School, 1978.

Miles, Rufus E., Jr. *The Carter Welfare Reform Plan: An Administrative Critique.* National Academy of Public Administration, Occasional Paper. Washington, D.C.: The Academy, Jan. 1978.

Massachusetts, State of, Office of Lieutenant Governor Thomas P. O'Neill III. "Impact of Welfare Reform on Massachusetts." Memorandum to members of the congressional delegation, Boston, Mass., Nov. 28, 1977.

Minnesota, State of, Department of Public Welfare. Memorandum from Edward Dirkswagen to members of the congressional delegation on Carter's welfare proposal, Oct. 11, 1977. Reprinted in House Budget Committee, Task Force on Distributive Impacts of Budget and Economic Policies. *President Carter's Welfare Reform Proposals,* hearings, 95th Cong. 1st sess., Oct. 13, 14, and 21, 1977, pp. 107–117. Washington, D.C.: U.S. Government Printing Office, 1977.

Northeast-Midwest Institute. *The Regional Distribution of Public Service Jobs.* (Principal author, Charlotte Short.) Washington, D.C.: The Institute, Feb. 6, 1978.

Northeast-Midwest Institute and CONEG Policy Research Center. *Welfare Reform in 1978: A Regional Analysis of Various Options.* Washington, D.C.: The Institute and Center, 1978.

Northwood, L. K. "Some Critical Questions in the Political Economy of Social Welfare: The Carter 'Welfare Reform' Proposals." *Journal of Sociology and Social Welfare* 5, no. 4 (July 1978): 538–567.

Shapiro, Harvey D. "Welfare Reform Revisited: President Jimmy Carter's Program for Better Jobs and Income." In Lester M. Salamon. *Welfare: The Elusive Consensus,* pp. 174–218. New York: Praeger Special Studies, 1978.

Storey, James R., Robert Harris, Frank Levy, Alan Fechter, and Richard Michael. *The Better Jobs and Income Plan.* Urban Institute Welfare Reform Policy Analysis Series no. 1. Washington, D.C: The Institute, Jan. 1978.

Sulvetta, Margaret B. *The Impact of Welfare Reform on Benefits for the Poor.* Urban Institute Policy Analysis Series no. 3. Washington, D.C.: The Institute, April 1978.

U.S. Congress, Congressional Budget Office. "Statement of Robert D. Reischauer." In House Budget Committee, Task Force on Distributive Impacts of Budget and Economic Policies. *President Carter's Welfare Reform Proposals,* hearings, 95th Cong., 1st sess., Oct. 13, 14, and 21, 1977, pp. 31–65. Washington, D.C.: U.S. Government Printing Office, 1977.

———. "Statement of Robert D. Reischauer." In House Budget Committee, Task Force on State and Local Government. *Fiscal Impact of Welfare Programs on States and Localities,* hearings, 95th Cong., 1st sess., Oct. 27, 1977, pp. 2–20. Washington, D.C.: U.S. Government Printing Office, 1977.

———. Alice Rivlin, Director, to Representative James C. Corman. Letter on preliminary cost estimate for H.R. 9030. Washington, D.C., Nov. 29, 1977.

———. Alice Rivlin, Director, to Representative James C. Corman. Letter on revised cost estimates for H.R. 9030. Washington, D.C., Jan. 25, 1978.

———. Alice Rivlin, Director, to Representative James C. Corman. Letter on cost estimates for H.R. 10950, with revised estimate on H.R. 9030. Washington, D.C., March 6, 1978.

————. *The Administration's Welfare Reform Proposal: An Analysis of the Program for Better Jobs and Income.* (Principal authors, John Korbell and G. William Hoagland.) Budget Issue Paper for Fiscal Year 1979. Washington, D.C.: U.S. Government Printing Office, April 1978.

————. Alice Rivlin, Director, to Senator Daniel P. Moynihan. Letter on costs of 1979 Social Welfare Reform Amendments. Washington, D.C., Oct. 16, 1979.

————. Alice Rivlin, Director, to Representative Augustus Hawkins. Letter on preliminary cost estimate of 1979 Work and Training Opportunities Act. Washington, D.C., Oct. 31, 1979.

————. *An Analysis of the Administration's Social Welfare Reform Amendments of 1979.* Human Resources and Community Development Division, Staff Draft Analysis. Washington, D.C.: U.S. Government Printing Office, Oct. 1979.

U.S. Congress, General Accounting Office. "Review of the Better Jobs and Income Bill," May 23, 1978. 95th Cong., 2nd sess. Washington, D.C.: U.S. General Accounting Office, 1978.

U.S. Congress, Joint Economic Committee. *Work, Welfare, and the Program for Better Jobs and Income,* 95th Cong., 1st. sess., Oct. 14, 1977. (Prepared by Barry L. Friedman and Leonard J. Hausman.) Washington, D.C.: U.S. Government Printing Office, 1977.

————. *The Program for Better Jobs and Income: A Guide and a Critique,* 95th Cong., 1st sess., Oct. 17, 1977. (Prepared by Sheldon Danziger, Robert Haveman, and Eugene Smolensky.) Washington, D.C.: U.S. Government Printing Office, 1977.

————. *The Program for Better Jobs and Income: An Analysis of Costs and Distributional Effects,* 95th Cong., 2nd sess., Feb. 3, 1978. (Prepared by Robert Haveman and Eugene Smolensky.) Washington, D.C.: U.S. Government Printing Office, 1978.

U.S. Congress, Senate Finance Committee. "Questions Submitted by Members of the Committee to Secretaries Califano and Marshall." In Senate Finance Committee, Subcommittee on Public Assistance. *Welfare Reform Proposals,* hearings, pt. 2, app. A and C, pp. 205–255, 273–348, 349–388. Washington, D.C.: U.S. Government Printing Office, 1978.

U.S. Department of Health, Education, and Welfare. "State Supplements: Estimating Fiscal Relief and Hold Harmless." Mimeo. Washington, D.C.: Income Security Policy Staff, Aug. 15, 1977.

————. "Welfare Reform." *HEW News,* Aug. 6, rev. Aug. 18, 1977.

————. "Testimony of Joseph A. Califano, Jr.," Sept. 19 and 21, 1977. In House Committees on Agriculture, Education and Labor, and Ways and Means, Welfare Reform Subcommittee. *Joint Hearings on H.R. 9030, a Bill to Replace the Existing Federal Welfare Programs,* 95th Cong., 1st sess., pt. 1, pp. 8–125, 229–244, 472–640. Washington, D.C.: U.S. Government Printing Office, 1977.

————. "Testimony of Henry Aaron," Oct. 13, 1977. In House Budget Committee, Task Force on Distributive Impacts of Budget and Economic Policies. *President Carter's Welfare Proposals,* hearings, 95th Cong., 1st sess., pp. 2–30. Washington, D.C.: U.S. Government Printing Office, 1977.

————. "Testimony of Henry Aaron," Oct. 27, 1977.   In House Budget Committee, Task Force on State and Local Government.   *Fiscal Impact of Welfare Programs on States and Localities*, hearings, 95th Cong., 1st sess., pp. 47–95.   Washington, D.C.: U.S. Government Printing Office, 1977.

————. "Cost Sheets for Decisions of the Subcommittee on Welfare."   Mimeo. Washington, D.C.: Office of the Secretary, Jan. 24, 1978.

————. "State Fact Sheets Covering the Better Jobs and Income Program." Mimeo.   Washington, D.C.: Income Security Policy Office, Feb. 23, 1978.

————. "Cost and Caseload Estimates for H.R. 10950," sec. 1.   (Prepared for the House Welfare Reform Subcommittee.)   Washington, D.C.: Income Security Policy Staff, 1978.

————. Betson, David, David Greenberg, and Richard Kasten.   *A Simulation of the Program for Better Jobs and Income.*   Technical Analysis Paper no. 17.   Washington, D.C.: Office of Income Security Policy, Office of the Assistant Secretary for Planning and Evaluation, Jan. 1979.

————. "President Carter's Proposal for Welfare Reform: Work and Training Opportunities Act of 1979 and the Social Welfare Reform Amendments of 1979."   Washington, D.C.: HEW Press Office, May 23, 1979.

U.S. Department of Labor.   "Testimony of Ray Marshall, Secretary of Labor," Sept. 19 and 21, 1977.   In House Committees on Agriculture, Education and Labor, and Ways and Means, Welfare Reform Subcommittee.   *Joint Hearings on H.R. 9030, a Bill to Replace the Existing Federal Welfare Programs*, 95th Cong., 1st sess., pt. 1, pp. 245–279, 413–471.   Washington, D.C.: U.S. Government Printing Office, 1977.

————. "Testimony of Ray Marshall," March 22, 1978.   In U.S. Congress, Senate Committee on Human Resources.   *Better Jobs and Income Act, 1978*, hearings, 95th Cong., 2nd sess., pp. 168–215.   Washington, D.C.: U.S. Government Printing Office, 1978.

————. "Subsidized Public Service Jobs and Training: Second Edition."   In U.S. Congress, Senate Finance Committee.   *Welfare Reform Proposals*, hearings, 95th Cong., 2nd sess., pt. 1, pp. 143–158.   Washington, D.C.: U.S. Government Printing Office, 1978.

————. "Testimony of Jodie Allen," Feb. 13, 1980.   In U.S. Congress, House Education and Labor Committee, Subcommittee on Employment Opportunities.   *Welfare Jobs Legislation*, hearings, 96th Cong., 2nd sess., pp. 30–61, 87–135.   Washington, D.C.: U.S. Government Printing Office, 1980.

Virginia, State of, Department of Welfare.   "Analysis of the Better Jobs and Income Act."   In U.S. Congress, House Committees on Agriculture, Education and Labor, and Ways and Means, Welfare Reform Subcommittee.   *Joint Hearings On H.R. 9030, a Bill to Replace the Existing Federal Welfare Programs*, 95th Cong., 1st sess., pt. 4, Nov. 2–4, 1977, pp. 2945–2978.   Washington, D.C.: U.S. Government Printing Office, 1977.

Wiseman, Michael.   *A Welfare Surprise: Carter in the Reagan Camp?*   Welfare and Employment Studies Project, Institute of Business and Economic Research, University of California–Berkeley, Working Paper no. 79-2.   Berkeley, Calif.: The Institute, Sept. 1979.

INDEX

Aaron, Henry, 47, 47n, 72, 81n, 110, 139, 147, 180, 181, 193, 197, 203, 220, 235, 260–261, 267; and briefing Califano, 58–62, 73–75, 78; and Califano, 77; and Carter welfare reform principles, 136; and consulting group, 53–56, 69; during development of plan, 112, 113n, 116, 118; on EITC, 190, 191; and internal HEW group, 174, 175; and marital dissolution studies, 248; in presidential briefings, 83, 88, 104, 120, 122, 123; and state supplements, 183, 186; and zero cost, 91–94

Accountable period, 130–131, 167, 169, 177, 178, 287

Administrative issues during Carter welfare reform, 121, 128, 170, 171, 173; costs, 79, 80, 121, 178, 179; feasibility, 130; set-up, 86, 87, 159, 165, 174, 177, 179, 206; simplification, 26, 106, 108, 122, 129, 137, 154, 169, 209, 212, 221

AFDC (Aid to Families with Dependent Children), 94, 101, 106, 157, 186, 211, 219; and AFDC-UF, 40, 44, 94, 241; background to reform of, 18, 27, 29, 32, 37–40, 86, 88, 157; consolidation of, 111, 129, 133; Long's opposition to, 123, 222; offset, 95, 98; state governments and, 164–170

AFL-CIO. *See* Labor, organized

AFSCME (American Federation of State and County Municipal Employees), 91, 194, 231

Aged. *See* SSI

Agnew, Spiro T., 20, 24, 27

Agriculture, Department of, 53

Aid to Dependent Children, 36

Aid to Families with Dependent Children. *See* AFDC

Allen, Jodie, 71, 153–154, 167n, 169–171, 180–184, 190, 193, 261

American Conservative Union, 235

American Journal of Sociology, 247

American Public Welfare Association, 39, 194, 234, 246

Americans for Democratic Action, 194

American Society of Newspaper Editors, 11

Anderson, John, 230

Anderson, Martin, 19, 21, 21n, 33

Assets test, 121–122, 132, 164, 176, 177, 178. *See also* Means test

Average tax rate, 148, 148n, 149

Bafalis, Skip, 233

Baker, Howard, 141, 240, 253, 254. *See also* Job Opportunities and Family Security Act

Baker-Bellmon bill. *See* Job Opportunities and Family Security Act

Barth, Michael, 48, 48n, 49, 55, 58–61, 64, 69, 73, 75, 77–79n, 83, 85, 88, 92–97, 100, 108, 110, 111, 114–116, 120, 122, 137–138, 145, 146, 151, 168–169, 171, 174, 180, 183, 193, 220, 230, 237, 242, 261

Baruch, Bernard, 7

Beall, J. Glen, Jr., 33

Beame, Abe, 102, 103

Bellmon, Henry, 240, 253. *See also* Job Opportunities and Family Security Act

Benefit levels, 32, 40, 86, 96, 96n, 99, 112, 121; disparity between states, 17, 18, 38, 40, 185–186, 217; uniform minimum (basic), 18, 64, 102–103, 106, 111, 113n, 130, 147, 216, 218, 241, 245, 258, 287; uniform minimum and the states, 165–166, 178, 180, 184

Benefit reduction rate, 41, 42, 61, 88, 109, 144, 147–149, 151, 153, 154, 287; average (average tax rate), 148, 148n, 149; cumulative, 165, 180, 183; and expanded EITC, 187–191, 202, 218; and state supplementation, 165–166, 182, 184–185

Bennett, Wallace F., 26, 28, 29

Benton, Scott, 261

Bishop, John, 248

Black, Hugo, 7